Reparation, Restitution, and the Politics of Memory
Réparation, restitution et les politiques de la mémoire

Beyond Universalism
Partager l'universel

Studies on the Contemporary
Études sur le contemporain

Edited by / Édité par
Markus Messling

Editorial Board
Souleymane Bachir Diagne (Columbia University, NY)
Tammy Lai-Ming Ho (Hong Kong Baptist University)
Christopher M. Hutton (University of Hong Kong)
Ananya Jahanara Kabir (King's College London)
Mohamed Kerrou (Université de Tunis El-Manar)
Soumaya Mestiri (Université de Tunis)
Olivier Remaud (EHESS Paris)
Sergio Ugalde Quintana (El Colegio de México)

Volume 3

Reparation, Restitution, and the Politics of Memory

Réparation, restitution et les politiques de la mémoire

Perspectives from Literary, Historical, and Cultural Studies

Perspectives littéraires, historiques et culturelles

Edited by
Mario Laarmann, Clément Ndé Fongang, Carla Seemann, and Laura Vordermayer

DE GRUYTER

This project has received funding from the European Research Council (ERC) under the European Union's Horizon 2020 Research and Innovation programme – Grant Agreement Number 819931

European Research Council
Established by the European Commission

ISBN 978-3-11-162782-3
e-ISBN (PDF) 978-3-11-079951-4
e-ISBN (EPUB) 978-3-11-079953-8
ISSN 2700-1156
DOI https://doi.org/10.1515/9783110799514

This work is licensed under the Creative Commons Attribution-NonCommercial-NoDerivatives 4.0 International License. For details go to https://creativecommons.org/licenses/by-nc-nd/4.0/.

Creative Commons license terms for re-use do not apply to any content (such as graphs, figures, photos, excerpts, etc.) not original to the Open Access publication and further permission may be required from the rights holder. The obligation to research and clear permission lies solely with the party re-using the material.

Library of Congress Control Number: 2022951548

Bibliographic information published by the Deutsche Nationalbibliothek
The Deutsche Nationalbibliothek lists this publication in the Deutsche Nationalbibliografie; detailed bibliographic data are available on the internet at http://dnb.dnb.de.

© 2024 the author(s), editing © 2024 Mario Laarmann, Clément Ndé Fongang, Carla Seemann, and Laura Vordermayer, published by Walter de Gruyter GmbH, Berlin/Boston
This volume is text- and page-identical with the hardback published in 2023.
This book is published open access at www.degruyter.com.

Cover image: based on an original idea by Hannes Brischke
Typesetting: Integra Software Services Pvt. Ltd.

www.degruyter.com

Acknowledgements / Remerciements

Reparation, Restitution, and the Politics of Memory was conceived subsequent to an international summer school we organized in Italy in 2021.[1] The volume owes much of its insights and critical thought to the excellent teaching of Olivier Remaud, Aurélia Kalisky, Patricia Oster-Stierle, Markus Messling, Christiane Solte-Gresser, Jonas Tinius, and Angelica Pesarini, many of whom have also contributed a chapter to this publication. The same can be said of the numerous participants, whose competence and dedication made the summer school a place of profound knowledge and radical criticism, some of whom have equally contributed to this volume (Clément Ndé Fongang, Hannah Grimmer, Sahra Rausch, Lucia della Fontana, Fabiola Obame, and Ibrahima Sene). Our thanks goes out to Igiaba Scego, for her crucial intervention in the course of the conference and her support of our idea of translating the short story "L'icona" into French, and to Helena Janeczek and Maike Albath for an inspiring artist talk.

At the same time, the book deliberately exceeds the framework of the summer school, including further important perspectives from a range of scholars, activists, and writers, active both within and beyond university contexts. We thank hn. lyonga for his powerful texts, but also his encouragement and his critical thoughts on the conception of this volume; Kader Attia for his generous support in all stages of this project; Ibou Diop and Alexandre Gefen for the readiness to contribute their thoughts and knowledge. We also thank barazani.berlin and the various associations and NGOs united as Decolonize Berlin for the crucial advocacy work some of them have been doing for decades now, and the numerous discussions that have also informed this volume. It responds to a global contemporary debate, whose innumerable actors, both individual and collective, have shaped our thoughts and whose commitment to material and epistemological decolonization needs to be acknowledged here.

But first and foremost, we want to express our immense gratitude to Markus Messling and Christiane Solte-Gresser, without whom neither the summer school nor this book would have been possible in this way. Taking both schemes on board for his ERC project *Minor Universality*, Markus Messling facilitated the necessary institutional, financial, and conceptual structure. Christiane Solte-Gresser assisted us throughout the project by providing financial, organizational, and

---

1 https://www.uni-saarland.de/einrichtung/ceus/ceus-veranstaltungen/exzellenzlabor-europa/exzellenzlabor-europa-2021.html (2 October 2022).

Open Access. © 2023 the author(s), published by De Gruyter. This work is licensed under the Creative Commons Attribution-NonCommercial-NoDerivatives 4.0 International License.
https://doi.org/10.1515/9783110799514-202

intellectual support. Both of them continuously challenged our reflections on reparation, and their joint keynote address from 2021 is equally part of this volume. We also thank Freddy Ndi and Tetyana Vorobyova for their tireless help in editing the texts assembled here, and our colleagues at Saarland University who provide the context for our ideas and thoughts to develop.

Mario Laarmann, Clément Ndé Fongang,
Carla Seemann, Laura Vordermayer

Contents / Table des matières

Acknowledgements / Remerciements —— V

Mario Laarmann, Clément Ndé Fongang, Carla Seemann, Laura Vordermayer
Reparation, Restitution, and the Politics of Memory. A Methodological and Historical Introduction —— 1

Part I: **Restitution and Reparation**
Première partie : **La restitution et la réparation**

Igiaba Scego
L'icône —— 23

Markus Messling & Christiane Solte-Gresser
Qu'est-ce qu'une pratique culturelle de réparation ? La stèle d'Axoum et « L'icona » d'Igiaba Scego —— 33

Part II: **Museums, Art, and Entangled Histories**
Deuxième partie : **Le musée, les arts, et les histoires entrelacées**

Kader Attia
Les Entrelacs de l'Objet | The Object's Interlacing —— 65

Jonas Tinius & Angelica Pesarini
(Ir)reparability Begins in the Body: Towards a Museum of Disrepair —— 91

Clément Ndé Fongang
Repairing Cultural and Museum Cooperation between Cameroon and Europe —— 109

Patricia Oster
Les statues considérées comme des protagonistes des histoires européennes d'interdépendance et de désunion —— 135

Part III: **Commemorative Politics and the Public Sphere**
Troisième partie : **Les politiques de la mémoire et le domaine public**

Hannah Katalin Grimmer
To Represent the Non-Representable. A Mnemonic Restitution of the Body in Claudia Fontes' *La Reconstrucción del Retrato de Pablo Míguez* —— 155

Sahra Rausch
Repairing the 'Suffering of the Others'? The OvaHerero and Nama Genocide between Recognition and Misrecognition —— 177

Part IV: **Reparation through Literature**
Quatrième partie : **La réparation par la littérature**

hn. Iyonga
and **I mean /** *and* **I am saying** —— 199
Half-Hymns, Prayers, and Fortifications —— 202

Ibou Diop
Qui répare qui ? Comment et pourquoi ? Une éthique et esthétique de la relation —— 207

Alexandre Gefen
La réparation au prisme des débats sur l'universel —— 217

Ibrahima Sene
Forms and Obstacles of Reparation in Bernhard Jaumann's *Der lange Schatten* —— 225

Part V: **Reparation and Ecology**
Cinquième partie : **La réparation et l'écologie**

Olivier Remaud
Trouble against Trouble —— 245

Lucia della Fontana
Conte de fées et réparation écologique : *La lucina* d'Antonio Moresco —— 255

Fabiola Obame
De l'imagination environnementale à la restauration des liens écouméniques —— 271

Contributors / Contributeurs —— 289

Index —— 293

Mario Laarmann, Clément Ndé Fongang, Carla Seemann, Laura Vordermayer

Reparation, Restitution, and the Politics of Memory. A Methodological and Historical Introduction

> *What is it like to be living without burning anything?*
> Camille de Toledo

> *The way in which we can address the irreparable is to still have in us what Barack Obama famously called the 'audacity of hope.'*
> Souleymane Bachir Diagne

Paintings of a rainforest gradually swallowing up the stations of the cross in a Catholic park turned refugee camp on Pulau Galang, Indonesia.[1] A pile of wooden shoes that have once served subaltern Indian brick workers to endure their inhuman working conditions, the flipside of the promise of modern development.[2] Rhizomatic mindmaps tracing the creolization of the German language.[3] The threat that runs through the different artworks at the 2022 Berlin Biennale for Contemporary Art clearly carries the signature of this year's curator: Kader Attia, whose artistic and theoretical work is preoccupied with the notion and the practice of *repair*.[4] Be it his interest in the mutilated soldiers of World War I, often referred to as *gueules cassées* (Fig. 3, page 13), his fragmented globes held together by innumerable stitches (Fig. 1, page 4), or his broken mirrors, which trouble the self-image of the onlooker through cracks and metal brackets (Fig. 2, page 10) – repair is not a superficial or purely aesthetic category in Attia's work, but a radical one that analyzes and engages the premises of the world as we know it. What the 2022 Berlin Biennale and Kader Attia's own artistic work reveal is the violence that runs through Western Modernity; the social contract and world-system, as Immanuel

---

[1] Tammy Nguyen, *Jesus is taken down from the Cross* (2022) and 13 other paintings in a series created for the Berlin Biennale 2022.
[2] Birender Yadav, *Walking on the Roof of Hell* (2016), exhibited at the Berlin Biennale 2022.
[3] Moses März, *Kreolisierung der deutschen Sprache* (2021–22) and other artworks in the series *Karten zur Kreolisierung der Welt*, commissioned for the Berlin Biennale 2022.
[4] Research that led to the publication of this article was supported by a PhD studentship of the project "Minor Universality. Narrative World Productions After Western Universalism," which received funding from the European Research Council (ERC) under the European Union's Horizon 2020 research and innovation programme (Grant agreement No. 819931).

Open Access. © 2023 the author(s), published by De Gruyter. This work is licensed under the Creative Commons Attribution-NonCommercial-NoDerivatives 4.0 International License.
https://doi.org/10.1515/9783110799514-001

Wallerstein (1974) would call it, which has arguably combined democracy with capitalism, colonialism, racism and anti-semitism, and other forms of segregation and exploitation in a schizophrenic way since its inception.[5] As Attia writes in his curatorial statement:

> In fact, the present world is the way it is because it carries all of the wounds accumulated throughout the history of Western modernity. Unrepaired, they continue to haunt our societies. This world of wounds is based on the extraordinary crimes committed by modernity – from slavery to colonialism, with racism an ideological lever to establish the certainty of its supremacy over subjugated peoples, the West founded modern capitalism upon the brutalization of others. But while racist crimes and genocides have been normalized to justify the extraction of wealth from the Gobal South, the West has acted in just as genocidal a manner by constructing hatred against segments of its own populations, like that inflicted upon European Jewry throughout history, resulting in the singular crime of the Holocaust (Attia 2022, 22–24).

The Berlin Biennale's interest in Attia's notion of repair is neither an exception nor a coincidence, but rather, we would argue, a consequence of contemporary political and cultural debates. In the fields of cultural studies, memory studies, post-/decolonial studies, museology and anthropology, but also foreign politics, the concepts of reparation and restitution can be said to have gained renewed momentum over the past roughly two decades, and it is their urgency and transformative potential which have inspired this very volume. It aims to examine different discourses and practices of reparation, bringing together perspectives from cultural studies, memory studies, post- or decolonial studies, and literary studies. Throughout the book, contributions from these disciplines are complemented by literary and poetic texts as well as chapters drawing on philosophy, art, and literary studies in order to explore the multiple facets of reparation. We will introduce these various contributions on the following pages, as we attempt to provide an overview of the thematic complex at hand.

The notion of repair is clearly linked to the multiple claims for financial reparations in recent years, but it equally informs demands to restitute looted

---

[5] This connection has been made multiple times. One might think of Aimé Césaire's critique of colonialism as the flip side of humanism in his *Discours sur le colonialisme* (1955), Hannah Arendt's identification of European imperialism with Antisemitism and racial thinking in *The Origins of Totalitarianism* (1951), or just simply go back to the texts of influential republicanists such as Ernest Renan who would state quite frankly that a "nation which does not colonize is irrevocably doomed to socialism, to the war between rich and poor" (2011 [1872], 95), thus legitimizing both capitalism as such, and colonialism as one of its tools. For a more recent intervention one might also think of Ariella Azoulay's (2021) provocative postulation that "modernity is an imperial crime." Unless indicated otherwise, all translations into English are our own.

artworks, cultural objects, spiritual entities, and even human remains[6] as well as the various politics of memory at work today – be it the French president Emmanuel Macron's public repentance for colonial crimes,[7] the heated debates in Germany on the multidirectionality of history and the singularity of the Holocaust,[8] or the negotiation of Germany's self-image in the wake of the recent reconstruction of the Prussian city palace in the center of Berlin.[9] Highlighting the last two decades seems plausible as the year 2001 brought renewed attention to long-standing claims for financial reparations for slavery and colonialism, and this attention has grown ever since. In France, May 21, 2001, marks the passage of the Loi Taubira, which officially recognizes slavery and the slave trade as a crime against humanity. While this recognition has come a long way and implies important changes to French school curricula and commemorative culture, claims for financial reparation had been removed from the original text before presenting it to the *Assemblée nationale* (Tin 2013, 40–42). In contrast, the 3rd UNESCO World Conference against Racism, held in Durban in early September of the same year, brought the topic to global attention. Retrospectively, the conference is mainly remembered

---

[6] For the German context, this renewed interest in the topic of restitution and provenance research is expressed, for example, in the establishment of the Department for "Cultural Goods and Collections from Colonial Contexts" at the German Lost Art Foundation in 2019. For an overview of their work see Larissa Foerster (2021).

[7] One of the strategies in Macron's foreign policy is the commissioning of reports investigating France's liability for crimes committed in its (former) colonies, such as the genocide in Rwanda, the Algerian War of Independence, or the looting of cultural objects as part of colonial endeavors. While this strategy is clearly one of reparation and has long influenced other European countries's foreign policies, critics see it as a geopolitical tool of a "Colonisation 2.0" (Tampa 2022).

[8] The current debate, also known as *Historikerstreit 2.0*, began in the spring of 2020, when the Cameroonian philosopher Achille Mbembe, one of the best-known theorists of postcolonialism, was disinvited from the Ruhrtriennale. Mbembe, who in his writings reflects on the interconnectedness of the Holocaust and colonialism as two sides of the history of modernity, was accused of thereby doubting the singularity of the Holocaust. While critics of Mbembe thus defended the inviolability of German memory politics centered around the Shoah, his supporters argue that his reasoning is "an extension of German memory culture that also holds the potential for a multidirectional revision of remembrance beyond residual Eurocentrism" (Rothberg 2020). For an overview of the debate see also Urban (2022).

[9] In 2002, the German parliament decided to rebuild the Prussian baroque city palace whose remains had been removed by the GDR leadership after WWII and replaced by the Palace of the Republic in the 1970s. Upon demolition of the latter in 2008, the so-called "Humboldt Forum" was erected and has opened gradually since 2020, holding various ethnographical collections on display at the time of writing. The building was sharply criticized from the beginning, as a "symbol of colonial power and genocide" (Dege 2021) as well as an expression of a conservative backlash and a negation of East German history (see, for example, Müller 2020).

for its clashes over Israel's role in the middle east, but it also saw the firm advocacy of a number of African countries and African-American NGOs for reparations. While these claims did not amount to much action at the time, they successfully reintroduced the topic to the global agenda, setting the ground for the founding of the *Mouvement International pour les Réparations* in Martinique in 2001 or the 2003 demands of reparation voiced by the Haitian president Jean-Bertrand Aristide, to name but two examples.

Fig. 1: Kader Attia, *Chaos + Repair = Universe*, 2014. Sculpture. Mirror fragments, metal wires. Exhibition view "Sacrifice and Harmony," MMK Museum für Moderne Kunst, Frankfurt/Main, 2016. Courtesy of the artist and Galleria Continua. Photo: Axel Schneider.

On a larger scale, this intensification of the discussion on reparations and repair in recent years seems to speak to the historical moment in which we still find ourselves today. As the anthropologist David Scott argues, the end of the Cold War in 1989 has brought a gradual return to questions of material injustices and a critical attention to the history and constitution of our social systems as such. Calls for financial reparation seem to be one important factor in this post-postcolonial era, or *postcolonial present*, as Scott (1999) calls it, and part and parcel of the larger process to repair what Attia calls the "world of wounds." The great number of major events and publications since the Durban conference point to this observation, be it the 2013 establishment of the pan-Caribbean CARICOM Reparations Commission, the reparations paid by the UK to victims of their colonial rule in Kenya (also in 2013), the publication of Ta-Nehisi Coates' influential *The Case for Reparations* in 2014, or the much criticized *Aussöhnungsabkommen*, a reconciliatory treaty conceived by Germany and the Namibian government in 2021. The latter is addressed in Sahra Rausch's chapter (Part III of this volume), which elaborates on the different power-political interests at play in the official recognition of the crimes committed by Germany's colonial army against the OvaHerero and Nama between 1904–1908. As she argues in her discourse analysis of German newspaper articles and political statements, the Federal government officially recognized the committed colonial crimes as genocide as late as 2015 while at the same time denying concrete political or legal consequences as well as material claims put forward by the OvaHerero and Nama groups. The (post)colonial relationship between Namibia and Germany is equally relevant for Ibrahima Sene's analysis of Bernhard Jaumann's *Der lange Schatten* (2015) in Part IV: He argues that the novel generates a dialogue between different groups and actors involved, represented by individual characters in the narrative. In so doing, according to Sene, *Der lange Schatten* examines the conditions and the possibilities of reconciliation.

As Louis-Georges Tin has shown in his historical survey *Esclavage et réparations* (2013, 45), debates over reparations always need to be understood with reference to the context in which they arise, such as the historical moment, the actors involved, as well as the political interests and power relations at play. In the immediate aftermath of emancipation, for instance, it was hardly ever the formerly enslaved people who received reparations. Instead, the British, French, Dutch, and others compensated the plantation owners for the loss of their alleged 'property,' the US revoked its promise of '40 acres and a mule' after the end of the American Civil War, and Haiti was forced to pay reparations first to France, then to the United States, until 1947.[10] For contemporary scholarship, at least two consequences arise from these observations: the need to analyze and contextualize historical and contemporary cases and discussions of reparations, and the urgency to determine the ethical, economical, philosophical, but also geo-strategical interests at play, on the side of both scholars and activists, but also other actors such as politicians and museums.

1 Material Reparations to Redress the Nazi Past

But what exactly do we mean when we talk about reparations? Historically, the practice of the defeated party paying indemnity after losing a war goes back to

---

[10] A detailed account of these cases can be found in Tin (2013) or Araujo (2017), to name but two examples.

antiquity; it reflected the balance of power between the victor and the vanquished and was used primarily to cover war expenses, whereas the damages suffered in the civilian sector received little attention. This understanding of a *ius victoriae*, according to which the winning party was automatically entitled to claim indemnity, changed in the 20th century. In the peace negotiations after World War I, compensation was considered a debt to be paid by the party which had initiated the war and was thus held responsible for the damage caused. In the treaty of Versailles, indemnities became 'reparations' that were to be determined by a Reparation Commission – the question of compensation was now linked to the question of guilt. The categories of the damages which were to be compensated for are defined and listed in the treaty; they include damages inflicted on civilians "as a result of cruelty, violence or maltreatment" (as quoted in Günnewig 2019, 102).

After World War II, as decided upon in the Potsdam Agreement, Germany paid reparations to the Allies primarily in the form of contributions in kind, namely by the dismantling of industrial plants in the occupied zones and the delivery of goods. This practice came to an end with the increasing tensions of the Cold War: Demands for reparations were postponed and finally dropped in the treaty for the reunification of Germany, concluded in lieu of a peace treaty (Neiman 2019, 312). While the German government thereby considers the question of reparations to be concluded, Greek and Polish demands remain to this day.[11] Payment to Jewish refugees was settled by the Reparations Agreement between Israel and the Federal Republic of Germany (*Luxemburger Abkommen*). The Federal Republic entered into agreement with the state of Israel and the Jewish Claims Conference on September 10, 1952, and accepted to pay a compensation of 3 billion German marks to Israel or to deliver it in the form of goods within 12 years. The payments were intended to support Jewish refugees who had acquired Israeli citizenship through immigration. In addition, 450 million German marks were paid to the Jewish Claims Conference, which were to be used for the settlement of Jewish refugees outside Israel (Hockerts 2001, 178–179).

As the historian Susan Neiman argues, for the Federal government at the time "it was crucial to avoid the word reparations" (2019, 312) in the context of the agreement. Not only did the term have negative connotations after the treaty of Versailles, but German politicians also wanted to circumvent a legal precedent. Instead, chancellor

---

[11] Recently, Poland demanded war reparations from Germany in the amount of 1.3 trillion euros (see Oltermannn 2022). According to Krzysztof Wojciechowski (quoted in Paczkowski 2022*)*, administrative director of the Collegium Polonicum, Poland's ruling conservative Law and Justice (PiS) party is at least partially instrumentalizing the issue to distract attention from political failures and economic problems prior to the 2023 elections.

Konrad Adenauer used the German term *Wiedergutmachung* ("to make things good again") in his speech to the German Bundestag on September 27, 1951, which later led to the 1952 agreement. Unlike the concept of reparation, which was codified in international law, *Wiedergutmachung* did not have any legal dimensions and thus underlined that the payments were made voluntarily. From the Jewish perspective, the term was rejected then as it is today. As the current representative of the Jewish Claims Conference, Rüdiger Mahlo, puts it:

> The systematic disenfranchisement and persecution, the suffering, the barbaric destruction of Jewish life in Europe, the murder of entire families, the theft of property, the lives of murdered parents, grandparents, children cannot be repaired, cannot be "made good" (Mahlo, as quoted in Smolenski 2022).

Wiedergutmachung in this literal sense also implies the desire to undo the past, to pay off 'debts' without dealing with one's guilt and responsibilities. The political scientist Samuel Salzborn transfers this diagnosis to the German way of dealing with their National Socialist past more generally, speaking of the repression of the Shoah in German commemorative culture in a psychoanalytical sense (Salzborn 2020). He thus admonishes us to critically question the way we deal with our histories and that despite different attempts to approach the question of reparation legally and materially, history can never be 'undone.'

In the same context, material reparations have also posed various problems from the beginning. Although the German government has so far made payments of 80 billion euros to Jewish victims, by no means all of them have received compensation. Of 4.5 million applications for compensation payments submitted to date, one in four fails due to German bureaucracy: Often, Nazi persecution cannot be proven as files have been lost in the archives.[12] Other exclusions from compensation resulted from the 1953 Federal Compensation Act (*Bundesentschädigungsgesetz*), which legally defined compensations for individual victims of Nazi persecution. Compensations were paid to individuals who had lived within the borders of the Reich in 1937 and had been persecuted by the regime for political, racist, or religious reasons, or to the surviving relatives of Nazi victims. Besides the fact that financial compensation was intended only for German victims of Nazi persecution (Herbert 1989, 273–302), it also implied other problematic exclusions. As historians have shown, "the law excluded a number of victim groups in principle, in particular homosexuals, victims of forced sterilization under the 'Law for the Prevention of Hereditarily Diseased

---

12 This was reported by the radio station Deutschlandfunk on the occasion of the 70th anniversary of the *Luxemburger Abkommen* on September 15, 2022 (Thoms 2022).

Offspring' [*Erbgesundheitsgesetz*], 'asocials,' as well as deserters or persons convicted of 'undermining military force' [*Wehrkraftzersetzung*]" (Hockerts 2013). Moreover, the Sinti and Roma, whose persecution under National Socialism was still interpreted as a legitimate 'security measure' even in legal commentaries on the Federal Compensation Act of 1954/55, were a particularly discriminated group (Sparing 2014). In most cases, they were not classified as persecuted and were denied the payment of indemnities.[13] As the German example shows, the idea to practice *Wiedergutmachung* produced an idea of who was 'worth' being compensated and who was not and reveals significant limitations of a legal approach to the problem of reparation. The example shows that material compensation for injustice suffered is necessarily only *one*, on its own usually insufficient, side to processes of reparation.

2 Material and Symbolic Reparation

On a more theoretical level, the philosopher and novelist Kwame Appiah takes an etymological approach as his point of departure when theorizing the notion of "reparation." The Latin term "reparare" means to "restore" or "renew." Two slightly differing notions of reparation emerge from this, defining reparation either as the act of restoring, of giving back what has been wrongfully taken, or – since the past oftentimes cannot be undone – as the act of putting the victim in a state they would be in if they had not suffered the injustices done to them. Both definitions seem to face a number of obstacles as soon as one tries to apply them in practice, as Appiah (2004, 26–28) points out.

What seems clear is that the loss of human lives, the violence and the atrocities experienced by the victims of crimes against humanity cannot reasonably be measured in economic terms. What has been done is irreversible, and what has been lost is irretrievable. From a strictly economic point of view, even the material damage caused by colonial systems is difficult to put a number on, and where attempts to quantify it have been made, they show the enormous economic and structural injustices colonialism has induced. They reveal an apparent impossibility of repayment that would compensate for the loss suffered by colonized societies, arguably to this day: In 2017, Utsa Patnaik from Jawaharla Nehru University in New Delhi estimated the value of the resources the British Empire drew from India from 1765 to 1938 at 9,184.41 billion pound sterling – ten times the United Kingdom's entire annual GDP in 2015 (Patnaik 2017, 311). The essentially unaffordable sum led

---

[13] For a more detailed examination of the jurisdiction and (denied) compensation of the Sinti and Roma in the 1950s and 1960s see Stengel (2004).

the Indian diplomat and politician Shashi Tharoor to plead first and foremost for *symbolic* reparation: In his speech at the Oxford Union in 2015, he proposes that Britain should pay a symbolic amount of one pound per year during a period of 200 years – not as a compensation, but rather as a gesture of atonement. "The ability to acknowledge a wrong that has been done, to simply say sorry," Tharoor argues, "will go a far, far, far longer way than some percentage of GDP in the form of aid" (Tharoor 2015, 14:42–14:47).

Reparation, therefore, must be thought of as a multifaceted concept in which we can distinguish at least two dimensions: a material and a symbolic one. Upon further reflection, it becomes evident that both dimensions are inextricably intertwined; while their relation to one another is of a dynamic nature, changing according to historical contexts and social and political conditions, neither of them can be omitted from our understanding of reparation. As Souleymane Bachir Diagne has recently put it, more is at stake than material questions in isolation:

> We are talking here about the most radical loss possible [. . .], which is the loss of humanity itself. [. . .] It must be said that such a loss, the very loss of humanity, is by definition irreparable. [. . .] So, the concept of reparation – and this is the paradoxical nature of it – is about the irreparable; is about what is, in essence, beyond repair (Diagne 2020, 1:37–2:57).

A number of insights can be drawn from these observations on the loss of humanity and the idea of symbolic reparation. First, as Kader Attia shows, attempts at reparation cannot be understood as a return to an original, unbroken state, but rather as a process that implies an "awareness of the wound" (Attia 2018, 14) that was inflicted. 'To repair' in his approach means not to remove injuries, but to keep them visible, if need be, and integrate them in our understanding of history and the present. Second, the act of reparation points to the fact that humanity has not simply been destroyed on the side of the so called 'victim.' As Aimé Césaire (1955, 21) points out in his *Discours sur le colonialisme*, the perpetrator has simultaneously destroyed their own humanity. And third, to follow Diagne's train of thought, in order to – not repair, but at least address – this irreparable relationship, a common effort for the future is necessary. "The way in which we can address the irreparable," Diagne says, "is to still have in us what Barack Obama famously called the 'audacity of hope'" (Diagne 2020, 5:11–5:23). In Diagne's reflections it becomes also clear, then, that repair is a communal practice, the collective working for a more equitable future.

If material reparations, in the sense of a simple compensation, are often insufficient, the notion of 'reparation' can nevertheless not be a purely idealistic one either. Symbolic gestures without material consideration of the economic disadvantages that have been inflicted and – in many cases – passed on to living descendants, fall short of addressing the structural injustices the crime engendered.

Fig. 2: Kader Attia, *Repaired Broken Mirror*, 2013. Sculpture. Mirror, metal wire. Exhibition view "Repairing the Invisible," SMAK, Ghent, 2017. Courtesy of the artist and Galerie Nagel Draxler. Photo: Dirk Pauwels.

Justice, in the words of the American philosopher Nancy Fraser (2004, 380), requires not only recognition, but also redistribution and representation; *symbolic* reparation is not the equivalent of *immaterial*. On the other hand, material reparations without a symbolic side to them can easily turn into an attempt at ridding oneself of a moral responsibility, too. This is what Achille Mbembe has in mind when he argues that restitutions of African looted art are insufficient without an apology or some other form of symbolic reparation. "So that the restitution of African objects is not the occasion for Europe to buy itself a good conscience at a cheap price, the debate must be recentred around the historical, philosophical, anthropological and political stakes of the act of restitution," Mbembe writes (2019, 70), clearly positing the claim for restitutions within the framework of both material and symbolic reparation.

3 Reparation and Restitution

To place the discussion of the restitution of looted cultural artifacts during colonial times within the framework of reparation, as Mbembe suggests, shows the relevance of the debate beyond individual cases of injustice. What is at stake is –

on the side of western countries – the recognition of a colonial history and structural colonial legacies, which would be a prerequisite for processes of reparation. It is to this end that Felwine Sarr and Bénédicte Savoy, in their 2018 report on the necessity and possibility of restitutions to Emmanuel Macron, have introduced the notion of an 'ethics of relation' which should be developed for and through processes of restitution, and of reparation in a broader perspective.

The struggles for restitution illustrate the importance of a more critical and self-reflective approach to the issues in question, revealing the different interests at play in processes of reparation. As Bénédicte Savoy (2021) has recently shown, the debate on restitutions had already been rather prominent between roughly 1965 and 1985. Interestingly, her archival research shows that in most cases, foreign offices were in favor of restitutions, hoping to better their political relations to formerly colonized countries, while an alliance of museum directors successfully managed to stifle the discourse (Savoy 2021, 198). Recent discussions on the politics of the so-called Humboldt Forum in Berlin on the one hand, and unapologetic German geopolitics on the other seem to continue this dynamic, as the alliance Barazani.berlin argues.[14] With this backdrop, in Part II of this book Clément Ndé Fongang reflects on how to recreate conditions for a new relationship based on reciprocity and mutual respect between the Global South and the Global North. Through a historical and postcolonial approach, he questions the legal and institutional mechanisms of cultural cooperation between Cameroon and European countries as well as the conditions of negotiation for the restitution of colonial treasures to African communities of origin. Decolonization and restitution appear here as important steps towards the reinvention of global relations.

Simultaneously, on the side of the formerly colonized countries and societies, arguments for restitution highlight yet another important factor. Besides the idea of post-colonial healing and relation-building, which risks, not infrequently, being instrumentalized for western geopolitical goals, restitutions can also foster forms of self-reparation. As Ariella Azoulay (2019) points out, when it comes to cultural artifacts and practices, what has oftentimes been lost for good is the cultural context and original meaning of these objects, the knowledge about their creation processes, their functions, their formal and semantic relation to other objects as well as their impact. Therefore, what she proposes is the mining, the reinvention of a 'potential history,' a form of decolonization that does not necessarily depend on a (former) perpetrator's willingness to re-establish an ethics of relation or to heal a common understanding of humanity. In the transcription of Kader Attia's film *Les Entrelacs de l'Objet | The Object's Interlacing*, featured in Part II of

---

14 See "Box 3" on the website of Barazani.berlin: https://barazani.berlin/box_3.

this volume, these ideas are developed further through a polyphony of voices influential in the contemporary discussion, such as Awa Cheikh Diouf, Bénédicte Savoy, Malik NDiaye, and others. The interweaving of their perspectives creates a dialogue that reveals the complexity of the topic of restitution, advocating at once for the possibility to revive cultural practices and epistemologies through the "resocialization" (Sarr and Savoy 2018, 56–59) of restituted objects (or subjects), and the necessity to keep in mind the mutable and productive nature of cultural practices and products.

Like Attia, Patricia Oster places the interconnectedness of objects at the center of her contribution in Part II, focusing on objects that originate from the European context and have been moved and displaced within it. She examines European statues in public space as protagonists of cultural transfer processes and thus as representatives of interwoven national histories. In examining a statue by the Swiss artist Urs Fischer, the bronze statue of Henri IV on Pont Neuf in Paris, and the Quadriga on Berlin's Brandenburg Gate she analyzes how different symbolic levels of meaning overlap in statues as "silent witnesses" of a political history. The article is based on her intervention at the international summer school "Restitution, reparations, *Reparation* – Towards a New Global Society?" (9–13 September, 2021) at Villa Vigoni, German-Italian Centre for European Dialogue, and has been translated by Monique Rival.

Finally, Jonas Tinius and Angelica Pesarini start out with a reflection on the same Villa Vigoni in their chapter. As the authors point out, the research center is not only a historical, but also a symbolic site of reflection on reparation in a multi-national European context. Building on the anthropology of art, museums and curatorial theories, as well as Attia's notion of repair, they conceive a "museum of disrepair" and propose ideas for future museology.

4 Memory Cultures and Reparation

The perspectives and discourses on reparation and restitution outlined so far have not been produced in a vacuum. Shaped not only by the obstacles and the criticism they have been facing, but also through the rivalry that might arise between different interest groups, struggles for memory and compensation are oftentimes connected to conflict and dispute. Understanding history and different commemorative cultures in this broader, interrelated perspective is the central idea of Michael Rothberg's famous concept of multidirectional memory: Rothberg challenges the idea that memory – and different memory cultures – need to be competitive, or as he puts it, "a zero-sum struggle over scarce resources" (2009, 3).

Often declared unique, the Holocaust, he argues, has also "enabled the articulation of other histories of victimization" (Rothberg 2009, 6) instead of preventing them. In the post-war period, the emergence of a public memory of the Holocaust was deeply intertwined and in dialogue with the process of decolonization, a minoritarian tradition Rothberg tries to reintroduce into the discourse.

Rothberg's plea for a dialogical exchange and an interconnection of different commemorative cultures without equating them also contains a political and, consequently, ethical momentum: "When the productive, intercultural dynamic of multidirectional memory is explicitly claimed," he posits, "it has the potential to create new forms of solidarity and new visions of justice" (Rothberg 2009, 5). His hope is that, through the experience of a shared relation to the past, new forms of empathy and solidarity might arise in the future. Hannah Grimmer (Part III) emphasizes the role art can play in this confrontation with a shared and entangled past. Analyzing the sculptural artwork *La Reconstrucción del Retrato de Pablo Míguez* by Argentinian artists Claudia Fontes, she explores how the victims of various Latin American civil-military dictatorships, killed and made invisible both physically and socially, can be represented through visual art and thus, literally and symbolically, be restituted a face and a body. In the works she analyzes, art features as an important means for the materialization of history and memory, makes it possible to represent the unpresentable, and can thus create a mnemonic place for individual and collective memories across the continent.

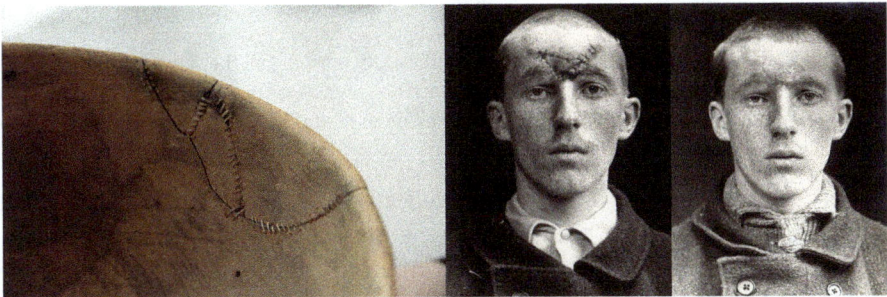

Fig. 3: Kader Attia, *Open Your Eyes*, 2010. Double slide projection. 80 slides each (detail). Courtesy of the artist. Collection MoMA New York, Collection Frac Pays de la Loire, Collection Moderna Museet Stockholm, private collection, and Galleria Continua. Photo: Martin Monestier, Musée du Service de Santé des Armées, Paris.

5 Reparation through Art and Literature

Beyond these reflections on visual art, the present volume also features a number of articles dealing with literature and poetry in relation to processes of reparation and restitution. What role can literature – and art more generally – play when it comes to processes of reparation? This is the underlying question, addressed with regard to a diverse range of texts and artworks. Can literature and poetry still be considered "miraculous weapons" against colonial oppression, as Aimé Césaire argued in 1946?

What seems clear is that the postcolonial school's postulation of agency through literature, criticized by Robert Young as mere methodological *textualism* or "textual idealism" (Young 2016 [2001], 398) in a study that marks his post-postcolonial, material turn, requires more scrutiny. Instead of arguing for agency *within* literature, we would argue that tools for agency might be developed *through* literature and art. This is what Kader Attia has in mind when he reflects on the usefulness of adding yet another exhibition to the "seemingly endless profusion of sprawling, monumental exhibitions" that mirror "the material excess of this global overproduction" (Attia 2022, 22). What he calls the *agency of art* is not to be found in simple politics of representation, but in art's capacity to deconstruct our understanding of the world "so that it may repair and evolve, generating new forms to interpret the present" (Attia 2022, 40). It is important to note that the artist is of course to a greater or lesser extent subject to the epistemologies of this present themselves. In his *Écrire en pays dominé* (1997), Patrick Chamoiseau considers this issue in a self-reflexive tone:

> How to write when your imagination, from the early morning all the way to your dreams, is nourished by images, thoughts, values that are not your own? How to write when what you *are* languishes out of reach from the forces determining your life? How to write when under domination (Chamoiseau 1997, 17)?

Alongside his newspaper articles, essay collections, and political manifestos, Chamoiseau unapologetically posits his fictional work as a means of political intervention: His strategy as a writer is to scrutinize the dominant epistemologies he traces back to "colonial modernity" (Chamoiseau 1997, 17) in order to infuse them with traditional Martiniquan knowledge in his literary texts, referring to himself – and artists more generally – as "warriors of the imagination" (Chamoiseau 1997, 303).

In this idealistic sense, literature and literary studies could be seen as tools for decolonization and reparation in the impact they have on our understanding of the world – as a point of departure for all material change. They are central to a "logic of reparation," as Rodolphe Solbiac would have it, which "pursues social transformation" (Solbiac 2018, 62) in its ability to describe the "world of wounds," its genesis and its reality, and to make it tangible for the reader. This is also the case for Berlin based writer hn. lyonga, his poem *"and I mean / and I am saying"* and accompanying essay "Half-Hymns, Prayers, and Fortifications" (Part IV). Necessarily subjective and situated in its view on the world, his writing denounces the violence emanating from German society for a Cameroonian subject in a personal and a structural sense. In so doing, it gains universal relevance in its ability to hold a mirror up to society at large and to demand an end to all forms of inferiorization, marginalization, and inequity.

If hn. lyonga denounces colonial legacies in the present, Ibou Diop reminds us that the decolonial potential of literature equally addresses the past and the future (Part IV). He traces the colonial epistemologies that have led to contemporary global inequality and structural racism – a situation he calls "coloniality" – and shows, through the example of Chinua Achebe, Assia Djebar, and others, how literature can be a source of reflection and inspiration for non-colonial ways of thinking and being.

All these observations are equally true for the work of Rome-based author Igiaba Scego, who addresses reparation and restitution as central topics in her short story "L'icona" (2018), here translated as "L'icône" by Laurent Vallance (Part I). The fictional story recounts the encounter of former Italian soldier Mario del Monte with Ethiopian emperor Haile Selassie, in the course of which del Monte returns to the king an icon stolen during the war in Ethiopia. As Markus Messling and Christiane Solte-Gresser point out in their contribution (Part I), the text addresses the topic of reparation with particular literary devices. They situate Scego's narrative in a broader context of definitional approaches to and discourses of the concept of reparation and argue that, in contrast to historiography, the literary text can employ specific aesthetic and narrative techniques (such as non-linear narration, focalization and narrative perspectives) to establish connections across time and geographical distance and bring into contact different experiences of history. In so doing, the literary text can be described as a micro-history – an individual experience disclosing its ties with historical processes on a larger scale.

Finally, in Part IV Alexandre Gefen suggests that the notion of repair can be relevant for the analysis of contemporary literature more generally and is not limited to reflections on coloniality: In line with critics such as Wolfgang Asholt (2013), Laurent Demanze (2019), or Markus Messling (2019) he argues that literature has observably returned to the question of reality in the course of the last three decades. In his chapter he questions the longstanding postulation of universal world literature, arguing that true universality can nevertheless be found in the concrete literary representations of the embodied vulnerabilities his work is dedicated to. These vulnerabilities even exceed the anthropocentric framework, as we should be well aware today and as he has shown repeatedly (Gefen 2021a; Gefen 2021b, 139–143): If we are talking about reparation, with relation to literature or not, climate change and the destruction of nature seem of paramount importance.

6 Reparation and Ecology

The violent drawbacks of Western modernity are not limited to forms of intra-human exploitation but have equally caused the destruction of nature, only taken seriously now in the face of the undeniable global climate crisis. Natural resources are a universal necessity and as such require care and foresight, but their destruction most often hits already vulnerable and exploited communities. Fabiola Obame's article shows that the subjects and issues of postcolonial critique on the one hand and ecocriticism on the other are inextricably intertwined (Part V). Shattering the presumed certainties which form the basis for our understanding of the world, the ecological crisis can be considered a crisis for the values of our societies. In this context, Obame proposes that literature has the potential to convey a new ecological awareness by creating an environmental imagination: Drawing on aesthetic and narrative devices, literary texts can give a voice to non-human entities and reveal to what extent humanity and the ecosystem are dependent on one another. In her analysis, Obame focuses on Nadine Gordimer's *The Conservationist* (1974) as well as Kate Grenville's *The Secret River* (2005) and Bessora's *Petroleum* (2004), arguing that these novels demonstrate the consequences of colonization for the people who continue to suffer from it but also for the planet, and reflect on different ways to repair relations between human communities as well as between humanity and nature.

Lucia della Fontana's analysis of Antonio Moresco's *La lucina* aims in a similar direction (Part V). She argues that the fairy tale as a genre possesses a specific imaginative potential that allows a multiplication of perspectives and thereby explores innovative modes of coexistence. In this sense, it possesses the capacity to disregard the requirement of mimetic representation for (realist) literature and to deconstruct our perception of the world, developing new ways of cohabitation.

These reflections on a reparative potential of imagination are also pursued in Olivier Remaud's essays "On n'achève pas un glacier qui sauve un peuple" (2021) and "Trouble contre trouble: le glacier et l'être humain" (2021), translated into English for this volume by Jack Cox under the collective title "Trouble against Trouble" (Part V). Drawing on scientists and experts in the field, Remaud points out that icebergs play an important part in securing the equilibrium of marine ecosystems as they secure the stability of the water cycle, which all living beings depend on. Threatened by global warming, the collapse of the glaciers would be tantamount to a global catastrophe. In the face of these developments, Remaud makes a strong case for a change in perspective: Instead of maintaining the reductive view of nature as a resource to be exploited, we should start taking seriously the various indigenous epistemologies that understand nature as animate and thus repair our relation to the multitude of animate and inanimate non-human actors.

7 Conclusion

Taking up the different threats developed in this introduction, we believe that in a truly transformative reflection on alternative and more equitable ways to conceive and inhabit the world, questions of ecology and of social justice should not contradict each other. Instead, they connect in the critique of our modern epistemologies and social systems that David Scott deems so necessary in our postcolonial present. Consequently, the central question the volume *Reparation, Restitution, and the Politics of Memory* asks and provides tentative answers for is this: How can we find a new and more equitable way to inhabit the world? It is in this sense that Camille de Toledo, in an eco-futurist play entitled *Witnesses of the Future*, asks the audience: "What is it like to be living without burning anything?" (de Toledo 2022). An intellectual provocation rather than a mere accusation, we are being asked to invent new ways of living that satisfy intersectional demands and are, at least in part, not yet readily at hand. In his essay *Habiter le monde* (2017), Felwine Sarr goes to the heart of this issue. His reflections on relationality explicitly include the relationship between humanity and nature, both animate and inanimate:

> Building a *human society*, and more largely, building a *society of the living* is the challenge of our age. Constructing a society which recognizes all of its members by extending the spectrum of those who belong to the community to foreigners, to animal and plant species, to lost ancestors, to Mother Earth, to those who are not yet there. This widened understanding of society demands rethinking our image of similarity, but also questions of alterity and belonging. It calls for an expansion of the political and, as a consequence, pushes us to rethink our way of inhabiting this world (Sarr 2017, 16).

Sarr's position might sound very philosophical in this passage, maybe utopian. Him being one of the actors at the crossroads between decolonization, ecology, restitution, and art, we nevertheless believe in the transformative potential his position envisions: The radical rethinking of our relation to each other and the world more largely, through all means possible, and the dedication to transform this reflection into action is the challenge of our time, and the only means through which we can address the (by definition irreparable) wounds of our shared modernity.

References

Appiah, Kwame Anthony. "Comprendre les réparations. Une réflexion préliminaire." *Cahiers d'études africaines* 173–174 (2004): 25–40. https://doi.org/10.4000/etudesafricaines.4518.
Araujo, Ana Lucia. *Reparations for Slavery and the Slave Trade. A Transnational and Comparative History*. London: Bloomsbury Academic, 2017.
Asholt, Wolfgang. "Un renouveau du 'réalisme' dans la littérature contemporaine?" *Lendemains – Études comparées sur la France* 38.150/151 (2013): 22–35.
Attia, Kader. "La réparation c'est la conscience de la blessure." In *Décolonisons les arts!* Eds. Leïla Cukierman, Gerty Dambury, and Françoise Vergès. Paris: L'Arche Éditeur, 2018. 11–14.
———. "Introduction." *Still Present!* Ed. Berlin Biennale für zeitgenössische Kunst. Berlin: Kunst-Werke Berlin, 2022. 20–41.
Azoulay, Ariella Aïsha. *Potential History. Unlearning Imperialism*. London: Verso, 2019.
———. *Modernity is an Imperial Crime* (23 April 2021). https://www.youtube.com/watch?v=zYZIoRVKLv4 (4 March 2022).
Césaire, Aimé. *Les armes miraculeuses*. Paris: Gallimard, 1946.
———. *Discours sur le colonialisme. Suivi du Discours sur la Négritude*. Paris: Présence Africaine, 1955 [2004].
Chamoiseau, Patrick. *Écrire en pays dominé*. Paris: Gallimard, 1997.
de Toledo, Camille. *Witnesses of the Future*. Unpublished performance staged as part of the exhibition The Pregnant Oyster – Doubts on Universalism at HKW Berlin (30 June–3 July, 2022) https://www.hkw.de/en/programm/projekte/veranstaltung/p_211571.php (21 September 2022).
Dege, Stefan. "Berlin's controversial Humboldt Forum opens." *Deutsche Welle* (20 July 2021). https://www.dw.com/en/berlins-controversial-humboldt-forum-opens-its-doors/a-58332615 (16 September 2022).
Demanze, Laurent. *Un nouvel âge de l'enquête: Portraits de l'écrivain contemporain en enquêteur*. Paris: Éditions Corti, 2019.
Diagne, Souleymane Bachir. *What is Reparation?* Rhinozeros asks . . . Souleymane Bachir Diagne (2020). https://www.rhinozeros-projekt.de/zeitschrift/das-projekt (13 September 2022).
Foerster, Larissa. "The Tide is Turning: Dynamics in the Postcolonial Provenance and Restitution Debate in Germany." *Europas Umgang mit Sammlungsgut aus kolonialen Kontexten*. Ed. Stiftung Genshagen, 2021. 32–38.
Fraser, Nancy, Hanne Marlene Dahl, Pauline Stoltz, and Rasmus Willig. "Recognition, Redistribution and Representation in Capitalist Global Society: An Interview with Nancy Fraser." *Acta Sociologica* 47.4. (2004): 374–382.
Gefen, Alexandre. *Réparer le monde: La littérature française face au XXIe siècle*. Paris: Édition Corti, 2017.
———. *L'Idée de la littérature. De l'art pour l'art aux écritures d'intervention*. Paris: Corti, 2021b.
———. "De l'écologie à l'écocritique." *Esprit* (2021a). https://esprit.presse.fr/article/alexandre-gefen/de-l-ecologie-a-l-ecocritique-43241 (21 September 2022).
Günnewig, Elisabeth. *Schadensersatz wegen der Verletzung des Gewaltverbotes als Element eines ius post bellum*. Baden-Baden: Nomos, 2019.
Herbert, Ulrich. "Nicht entschädigungsfähig? Die Wiedergutmachungsansprüche der Ausländer." In *Wiedergutmachung in der Bundesrepublik Deutschland*. Eds. Ludolf Herbst and Constantin Goschler. München: Oldenbourg, 1989. 273–302.

Hockerts, Hans Günter. "Wiedergutmachung in Deutschland. Eine historische Bilanz 1945–2000." *Vierteljahrshefte für Zeitgeschichte* 49.2 (2001): 167–214.

———. "Wiedergutmachung in Deutschland 1945–1990. Ein Überblick." *Bundeszentrale für politische Bildung* (7 June 2013). https://www.bpb.de/shop/zeitschriften/apuz/162883/wiedergutmachung-in-deutschland-1945-1990-ein-ueberblick/ (16 September 2022).

Mbembe, Achille. *Of African Objects in Western Museums*. Transl. Steven Corcoran. Münster: Rhema, 2019. 57–81.

Messling, Markus. *Universalität nach dem Universalismus: Über frankophone Literaturen der Gegenwart*. Berlin: Matthes & Seitz, 2019.

Müller, Yves. "Ein Volksschloss sicher nicht." *taz* (1 August 2020). https://taz.de/Debatte-um-das-Berliner-Stadtschloss/!5707717/ (16 September 2022).

Neiman, Susan. *Learning From the Germans: Race and the Memory of Evil*. New York: Farrar, Straus and Giroux, 2019.

Oltermann, Philip. "Germany Rejects Poland's Claim it Owes €1.3tn in War Reparations." *The Guardian* (2 September 2022). https://www.theguardian.com/world/2022/sep/02/germany-rejects-polands-claim-it-owes-13tn-in-war-reparations (16 September 2022).

Paczkowski, Jakub. "'Das ist eindeutig Stimmungsmache vor der Wahl'", Interview with Krzysztof Wojciechowski. *rbb* (3 September 2022). https://www.rbb24.de/studiofrankfurt/beitraege/2022/09/polen-deutschland-reparationen-pis-wahlkampf-interview.html (21 September 2022).

Patnaik, Utsa. "Revisiting the 'Drain,' or Transfer from India to Britain in the Context of Global Diffusion of Capitalism." In *Agrarian and Other Histories: Essays for Binay Bhushan Chaudhuri*. Eds. Shubhra Chakrabarti and Utsa Patnaik. New Delhi: Tulika Books, 2017. 277–318.

Renan, Ernest. *La réforme intellectuelle et morale*. Paris: Perrin, 2011 [1872].

Rothberg, Michael. *Multidirectional Memory. Remembering the Holocaust in the Age of Decolonization*. Stanford: Stanford University Press, 2009.

———. "Comparing Comparisons. From the 'Historikerstreit' to the Mbembe Affair." *Geschichte der Gegenwart* (23 September 2020). https://geschichtedergegenwart.ch/comparing-comparisons-from-the-historikerstreit-to-the-mbembe-affair/ (16 September 2022).

Salzborn, Samuel. *Kollektive Unschuld. Die Abwehr der Shoah im deutschen Erinnern*. Berlin, Leipzig: Hentrich & Hentrich, 2020.

Sarr, Felwine. *Habiter le monde. Essai de politique relationnelle*. Montréal, Québec: Mémoire d'encrier, 2017.

Sarr, Felwine and Bénédicte Savoy. *Restituer le patrimoine africain*. Paris: Philippe Rey & Seuil, 2018.

Savoy, Bénédicte. *Afrikas Kampf um seine Kunst. Geschichte einer postkolonialen Niederlage*. München: C.H. Beck, 2021.

Scott, David. *Refashioning Futures. Criticism after Postcoloniality*, Princeton: Princeton University Press, 1999.

Smolenski, Sonja. "Entschädigungszahlungen für NS-Opfer. Kampf um die Würde." *taz* (9 September 2022). https://taz.de/Entschaedigungszahlungen-fuer-NS-Opfer/!5874999/ (16 September 2022).

Solbiac, Rodolphe. "L'artiste, le savant et le politique dans la Caraïbe anglophone diasporique: de l'écriture réparatrice à l'action pour une transformation sociale réparatrice." *Études caribéennes* (2018). https://doi.org/10.4000/etudescaribeennes.11698.

Sparing, Frank. "NS-Verfolgung von 'Zigeunern' und 'Wiedergutmachung' nach 1945." *Bundeszentrale für politische Bildung* (18 March 2014). https://www.bpb.de/themen/europa/sinti-und-roma-in-europa/180869/ns-verfolgung-von-zigeunern-und-wiedergutmachung-nach-1945/ (16 September 2022).

Stengel, Katharina. *Tradierte Feindbilder. Die Entschädigung der Sinti und Roma in den fünfziger und sechziger Jahren*. Frankfurt am Main: Fritz-Bauer-Institut, 2004.

Tampa, Vava. "Françafrique is Back: Macron's visit to Cameroon Signals Colonisation 2.0." *The Guardian* (26 July 2022). https://www.theguardian.com/global-development/2022/jul/26/francafrique-is-back-macrons-visit-to-cameroon-signals-colonisation-20 (20 September 2022).

Tharoor, Shashi. *Britain Does Owe Reparations*. OxfordUnion (14 July 2015). https://www.youtube.com/watch?v=f7CW7S0zxv4 (22 September 2022).

Thoms, Katharina. "70 Jahre deutsch-israelisches "Wiedergutmachungs"-Abkommen." *Deutschlandfunk* (15 September 2022). https://share.deutschlandradio.de/dlf-audiothek-audio-teilen.html?audio_id=dira_DLF_5b709a2e (16 September 2022).

Tin, Louis-Georges. *Esclavage et réparations. Comment faire face aux crimes de l'histoire. . .* Paris: Stock, 2013.

Urban, Susanne. "The Shoah, Postcolonialism, and Historikerstreit 2.0. Germany's Past in Its Present." *Israel Journal of Foreign Affairs* 16.1 (2022): 83–97. https://doi.org/10.1080/23739770.2022.2065798.

Wallerstein, Immanuel. *The Modern World-System*. New York, San Diego, London: Academic Press, 1974.

Young, Robert. *Postcolonialism: An Historical Introduction*. Chichester, UK: John Wiley & Sons, 2016 [2001].

Part I: **Restitution and Reparation**

Première partie : **La restitution et la réparation**

Igiaba Scego
L'icône

Contexte: « L'icona » a été publiée en 2018 dans *Vite allo specchio. Dieci nuovi protagonisti della scena letteraria italiana / Spiegelungen. Zehn neue literarische Stimmen aus Italien*, un recueil bilingue de dix nouvelles écrites par de jeunes auteurs italiens publié par la maison d'édition nonsolo de Fribourg-en-Brisgau (fondée en 2017 et lauréate du Premio nazionale per la traduzione 2020 pour la traduction et la diffusion de la littérature italienne actuelle, décerné par le Ministère des biens et activités culturels et du tourisme de la République italienne). La nouvelle d'Igiaba Scego y a été traduite sous le titre « Die Ikone » par Ruth Mader-Koltay. La traduction en français pour ce volume a été réalisée par Laurent Vallance.

La passerelle était instable. Ou alors, il avait tout simplement du mal à garder l'équilibre sur les flots. « Ne vous en faites pas, Majesté », lui dit un homme de sa suite, un italien d'une quarantaine d'années, à la moustache fine et au sourire moqueur, « je vous garantis que personne ne tombera à l'eau, surtout pas vous. » Le truc consistait à mettre un pied devant l'autre, sans se presser, sans s'affoler. Un pied devant l'autre, comme les soldats qui marchent dans le désert, comme les mannequins qui défilent sur le podium. « Vous ne devez pas vous immobiliser, Majesté, avancez toujours, je vous en prie », reprit l'homme, qui portait des lunettes avec une épaisse monture en écaille de tortue et une cravate à pois. « C'est beaucoup plus simple que vous ne l'imaginez, avancez sans vous arrêter. » Sur cette passerelle, Haïlé Sélassié se sentait comme un enfant – fragile, pour la première fois depuis longtemps. Cette ville était si étrange, cette Venise gorgée d'eau où il avait échoué. « Et si jamais elle nous engloutissait ? », pensait-il. Mais en dépit de la peur insensée qui l'avait saisi, il avançait, un pas, deux pas, trois pas. Un pas après l'autre. Lentement. En faisant bien attention où il posait les pieds.

Autour de lui, Venise explosait d'azur. Submergée par sa mer intérieure et par le désarroi des touristes mal préparés. Beaucoup étaient chaussés de bottes en caoutchouc achetées en toute hâte pour affronter l'*acqua alta*. Ceux qui n'avaient pas réussi à trouver des bottes adaptées avaient enveloppé leurs pieds dans des sacs en plastique pour éviter au moins la désagréable sensation des chaussettes mouillées par la lagune. « Il faut bien vous couvrir les pieds », lui avait dit l'homme à la cravate à pois, « sinon, vous savez, vous risquez la pneumo-

Traduction : Laurent Vallance

nie. » C'était un fonctionnaire du ministère des affaires étrangères. Il lui avait été recommandé par Aldo Moro en personne, qui avait ajouté la remarque classique : « C'est le meilleur élément dont nous disposons à la Farnesina. » De fait, c'était le meilleur. Et comment ! Vraiment d'une grande efficacité. Le moindre désir de Haïlé Sélassié et de sa cour bigarrée était exaucé en quelques minutes. Si seulement il n'avait pas eu une telle voix. Il croassait comme un corbeau. Et en dépit des éloges d'Aldo Moro, l'empereur l'avait d'emblée trouvé insupportable. Il le supportait tout juste, par devoir.

Haïlé Sélassié n'arrivait pas à s'ôter de la tête que cet homme avec sa cravate à pois avait revêtu autrefois la chemise noire et qu'il avait suivi Mussolini en Ethiopie, dans son Ethiopie. Qu'il avait violé, décapité, tué, émasculé des Ethiopiens en entonnant à tue-tête des refrains du genre *Se il Negus non risponde e all'armi fa l'appello, noi gli farem gustar l'antico manganello* ! [Si le Négus ne répond pas et passe plutôt à l'attaque, nous allons lui faire goûter de la bonne vieille matraque !]

Et voilà maintenant que l'histoire contraignait ce fonctionnaire à le servir et à lui faire la révérence. Par chance, le monde avait changé. « Mais si l'occasion s'en présentait », pensait l'empereur, « ce type me tuerait. » Qui sait si la bonne vieille matraque ne lui trottait pas encore dans la tête.

Plus d'une fois, durant ces quelques jours, il essaya d'observer ses mains. Il voulait vérifier personnellement si elles n'étaient pas encore tachées de sang. Pas la moindre trace. Le temps avait effacé toute preuve.

Ce matin-là, pourtant, des pensées plus gaies occupaient l'esprit du vieil empereur. Haïlé Sélassié n'avait d'yeux que pour Venise. Il était distrait, presque abasourdi par cette ville suspendue sur l'eau. Il dit juste à sa cour bigarrée qu'il avait grande envie de marcher. Le fonctionnaire de la Farnesina avait bien essayé de l'en dissuader, en croassant quelque difficulté météorologique. « Je ne crains pas l'eau », avait répondu l'empereur d'un ton décidé. Et il avait refusé le taxi que l'Etat italien avait mis à sa disposition.

« Je ne peux pas repartir sans avoir vu la place Saint-Marc ». Bon gré mal gré, le fonctionnaire dont on l'avait flanqué avait dû organiser cette promenade difficile sur la lagune.

Place Saint-Marc...

Cette place, c'était le rêve secret de l'empereur, le rêve de l'enfant qu'il avait été et qu'il avait trop tôt cessé d'être.

En ce jour de novembre 1970, la place Saint-Marc, avec son campanile, ses coupoles en forme de profiteroles et ses pigeons grassement nourris, allait être enfin à lui. Et les géants, les deux Maures qui sonnaient les heures, allaient entériner de manière inattendue la victoire de l'empereur sur le destin qui dévore tout.

À Venise, ce matin-là, Haïlé Sélassié, à l'état civil Tafari Makonnen, Negus Neghesti, Puissance de la Trinité, ultime empereur d'Ethiopie, était heureux.

Il ne savait pas encore, toutefois, qu'il serait le dernier à exercer cette fonction. Il était trop tôt pour affronter l'avenir. Il le découvrirait quatre ans plus tard, en 1974, lorsqu'une soldatesque en chaleur le jetterait en prison et l'étoufferait avec un coussin avant de l'ensevelir en hâte, suprême affront, sans autre cérémonie, sans même une prière.

Mais ce jour-là était encore lointain. Pour lui, en ce mois de novembre 1970, il n'y avait que la joie de voir la place Saint-Marc, comme il en rêvait depuis qu'il était enfant.

Il faut préciser que tout ce voyage en Italie, au fond non prévu par l'empereur, avait été des plus étonnants, sa genèse en particulier.

Aucune visite aux envahisseurs qui avaient humilié l'Ethiopie dans les années 1930 ne figurait à l'agenda de Haïlé Sélassié. Pour les Ethiopiens, l'Italie était le pays qu'ils avaient vaincu à Adoua au 19ème siècle, une glorieuse victoire de l'Afrique contre une puissance impérialiste. Et le pays d'où était venu ensuite Mussolini, qui avait recouru à tous les moyens pour occuper la terre sacrée d'Ethiopie, même aux plus sournois, comme l'ypérite, les massacres, l'humiliation des corps, les camps de concentration. L'Italie avait fait pleuvoir les massacres sur la tête des Ethiopiens, et, à la fin de la guerre, elle ne leur avait pas restitué son butin, la belle stèle d'Axoum : en 1970, elle était toujours là où Mussolini l'avait fait installer, au cœur de la Rome impériale, place de Porta Capena, à quelques mètres du ministère des Colonies, alors en construction et devenu après la guerre le palais de la FAO, l'organisation des Nations Unies pour l'alimentation et l'agriculture.

L'Italie les avait fait souffrir.

L'Italie avait été une ennemie.

Mais il fallait tourner la page. L'empereur le savait. La guerre était finie. Victoire ! Dès les années 40, Haïlé Sélassié s'était montré grand seigneur. Il n'avait pas procédé à des purges contre les Italiens restés dans le pays. Il avait simplement réclamé que la stèle volée revienne à Axoum, à son emplacement d'origine, et que les criminels de guerre qui s'étaient rendus coupables de crimes horribles en Ethiopie soient jugés par un tribunal international. Malheureusement, ses demandes légitimes n'avaient pas été exaucées par les alliés.

L'Histoire, on le sait, se montre parfois mauvaise fille.

Haïlé Sélassié s'était rendu compte, alors, qu'il était seul face à un monde qui ne voulait rien tant qu'occulter le passé.

C'est pourquoi, lorsqu'Aldo Moro était venu le voir depuis la Somalie, il avait reçu le ministre italien en grande pompe. C'était l'occasion rêvée pour réécrire un scénario qu'il n'avait jamais apprécié – une occasion unique de rétablir la justice, qui avait été refusée à son pays.

Moro avait un beau visage.

L'empereur l'avait vu en photo dans le dossier que lui avaient préparé ses services secrets. Beau front, avait-il tout de suite pensé. Belle bouche. Cet Italien-là m'inspire confiance.

Le dossier n'omettait rien de la vie de Moro, pas même l'établissement où le futur ministre avait passé son bac, le lycée classique *Archita* à Tarente, où le politicien démocrate-chrétien avait appris à être un *Mensch*, un être humain. « Belle école », disait le dossier, « qui produira à l'avenir d'autres hommes dignes de ce nom. »

On mentionnait aussi ses ennemis. Moro n'en manquait pas – dont certains au-dessus de tout soupçon.

Haïlé Sélassié ne pouvait pas imaginer qu'un jour, cet Italien au front large et au regard franc serait enlevé et tué par un groupe armé, comme un agneau sacrificiel.

Il n'imaginait pas qu'ils allaient partager le même destin, une mort violente. Leur assassinat était écrit dans les étoiles – comme leur résurrection.

En juillet 1970, lors de ce dîner d'Etat à Addis Abeba, l'enjeu, toutefois, était bien différent. C'était la vie. Aldo Moro et Haïlé Sélassié, l'Italien et l'Ethiopien, l'un à côté de l'autre. Les deux dirigeants étaient vivants, actifs, souriants. Ils parlaient du présent. Ils vivaient leur présent.

Dans la touffeur de l'été éthiopien, Aldo Moro avait été surpris par les honneurs et l'accueil chaleureux que lui avaient réservés le pays africain et cet empereur charismatique, si petit par la taille. Il devait lui rendre la pareille. Il fallait qu'il invite Haïlé Sélassié en Italie avec tous les honneurs, pour mettre enfin un terme au contentieux de la stèle d'Axoum. Soit en la restituant, soit à la rigueur en versant à ce peuple une indemnité financière ou bien en lui offrant des hôpitaux, des écoles, quelque chose. Il fallait enterrer cette histoire qui empoisonnait les relations entre l'Ethiopie et l'Italie pour recommencer sur des bases nouvelles. Il fallait au moins essayer. Même si, il faut bien le dire, certains Italiens voyaient encore l'Afrique comme une grande colonie où vendre des armes et faire la pluie et le beau temps.

C'est ainsi que, quelques mois après la visite d'Aldo Moro, l'empereur se trouvait à Venise, en équilibre sur une passerelle, par un jour pluvieux de novembre 1970.

C'est Aldo Moro qui avait tenu mordicus à ce qu'il vienne, et qui avait œuvré pour l'inviter en Italie.

Le voyage avait commencé plus au sud, dans la capitale, quelques jours plus tôt. Pleuvait-il ou y avait-il du soleil le jour de son arrivée à Rome ? L'empereur ne s'en souvenait plus. Il avait atterri à l'aéroport de Ciampino – ça, il se le rappelait. De grands discours. Des flots de rhétorique.

Le grand empereur écoutait attentivement l'interprète, qui traduisait rapidement, y compris les soupirs.

Le président Saragat lui avait serré la main. Et Sandro Pertini, son successeur quelques années plus tard à la présidence de la République, lui avait murmuré une phrase que l'interprète avait traduite ainsi : « Majesté, j'ai été un partisan moi aussi. Nous avons combattu le même ennemi, cette même saloperie de fascisme ».

L'empereur avait souri. Souriant de même, Pertini avait ajouté : « A Ventotene, où j'ai été expédié en relégation, l'un de mes meilleurs amis venait de la Corne de l'Afrique ».

Haïlé Sélassié s'était dit alors que l'Histoire était bien surprenante. Comme les choses dans la vie sont embrouillées, finalement.

L'empereur et Sandro Pertini, un socialiste qui ne mâchait ses mots devant personne, avaient combattu le même ennemi. L'un en Italie, l'autre en Ethiopie. C'étaient deux frères qui s'ignoraient.

Après l'arrivée et l'accueil protocolaire à l'aéroport, le programme prévoyait un défilé en voiture. Tout avait été étudié dans les moindres détails. Escorté par des cuirassiers – comme le voulait le cérémonial –, le cortège devait conduire l'empereur au Quirinal, mais non sans avoir au préalable fait un détour chez le maire de la capitale, qui l'attendait avec des fanfares devant le Colisée.

Même s'il ne connaissait pas la ville, Haïlé Sélassié comprit tout de suite que quelque chose clochait dans l'itinéraire. Le parcours lui sembla d'emblée très entortillé. La voiture prenait trop de déviations, remontait des rues secondaires et le chauffeur, qu'il pouvait apercevoir à travers la vitre de séparation, suait et soupirait d'un air épuisé. Les soupçons qu'il avait conçus dès le départ furent confirmés le lendemain dans les journaux, que son interprète personnel lui traduisit fidèlement. Voici, par exemple, ce qu'écrivait Maurizio Montefoschi dans *Il Messaggero* du 7 novembre, sous le titre « *Roma applaude Haile Selassie* » :

La grande expérience des Romains en matière de déviation de la circulation a été mise au service du cérémonial, qui n'obéissait pas tant cette fois à des motifs protocolaires qu'à la délicatesse et au tact : grâce à une interdiction de tourner à gauche, aussi courtoise qu'impérative, on a évité à l'empereur d'Ethiopie l'émotion de passer à quelques mètres de l'obélisque d'Axoum, transplanté place de Porta Capena.

Les autorités italiennes avaient élaboré un itinéraire tortueux et escarpé pour ne pas qu'il se retrouve nez-à-nez avec sa stèle.

L'empereur ne s'offusqua pas outre mesure de cette péripétie. C'était un homme du monde. Il savait bien comment fonctionnait la diplomatie. Cette stèle, finalement, était l'objet du litige. Et il ne voulait pas se contenter de la voir. Cette stèle, sa stèle, Haïlé Sélassié, Négus Neghesti, Puissance de la Trinité, empereur d'Ethiopie, avait bien l'intention de la rapporter chez lui.[1]

Il souriait en écoutant l'interprète lui traduire toute la revue de presse. Un rire sarcastique, mêlé d'admiration. Les Italiens ne voulaient pas risquer le moindre incident. Au fond, cette attention à son égard était une marque d'estime. Elle ne lui déplut pas.

Le monde marchait vraiment sur la tête. Et c'est bien pourquoi les affaires de l'Etat requéraient une attention redoublée.

Pour lui, le grand Africain, Rome avait décidé d'emblée de revêtir ses plus beaux atours.

Sur les forums impériaux, là même où Mussolini avait célébré en 1937 l'annexion de l'Ethiopie à l'empire italien avec ses troupes en grand apparat, rue Haïlé Sélassié justement, grâce à Aldo Moro, il tenait sa revanche. La revanche de l'Ethiopie sur l'Histoire.

Rome était en fête. Toutes les rues étaient pavoisées de tapisseries grandioses du 17ème siècle aux couleurs vives, et débordaient de vie. C'était une étendue infinie de brocards et de soie, de jaunes et de bleus. Les Romains s'étaient pomponnés et ils étaient venus nombreux, de tous âges et de toute orientation politique, acclamer bruyamment l'empereur. Ils faisaient de grands gestes du bras pour le saluer. Certains d'entre eux avaient été « membres des *balilla* dans leur jeunesse et avaient chanté autrefois *Faccetta nera* », notait Montefoschi dans son article du *Messaggero*.[2] Beaucoup avaient la larme à l'œil. Ils étaient émus par cette grande présence si petite parmi eux. Haïlé Sélassié, le Négus, dont on parlait tant dans les

---

[1] Pourtant prévue par le traité de paix de 1947, la restitution n'a eu lieu qu'en avril 2005 et c'est seulement à l'été 2008, 34 ans après la mort de l'empereur, que l'obélisque de granite (du 3ème ou 4ème s. de notre ère, d'une hauteur de 23,4 m pour un poids de 152 t) a été réinstallé sur le site d'Axoum (classé par l'UNESCO au patrimoine mondial de l'humanité en 1980), aux frais de la République italienne.

[2] *Il Messaggero* est le principal quotidien de Rome. Dans cette nouvelle sont mentionnées deux chansons de l'ère coloniale italienne, *Stornelli neri* (*Ritournelles noires*, 1935, texte d'Armando Gill, musique de Nino Casiroli), dont est citée plus haut l'avant-dernière strophe, et *Faccetta nera* (1935 également, texte de Giuseppe Micheli, musique de Mario Ruccione), sans doute la plus célèbre de toutes, lancée par Carlo Buti (1902–1963). D'abord censurée par Mussolini, qui n'appréciait ni les traces de dialecte romain, ni surtout les hommages appuyés à « *Faccetta nera, bell'abissina* » (Frimousse noire, ô belle abyssinienne), elle a dû être remaniée, mais a connu un tel succès que le régime fasciste a fini par l'accepter. Igiaba Scego en a dénoncé le sexisme et le racisme dans un article de 2015 pour l'hebdomadaire *Internazionale*, intitulé « *La vera storia di Faccetta nera* » (www.internazionale.it/opinione/igiaba-scego/2015/08/06/faccetta-nera-razzismo, accès 04.11.2022). Voir aussi le site https://impararenconlastoria.blogspot.com/p/il-fascismo-e-le-sue-canzoni-una.html (accès 04.11.2022).

livres (y compris dans les manuels scolaires), était là devant eux, en chair et en os. Quel événement extraordinaire ! Quelle joie !

Cette joie, Mario del Monte la partageait aussi – un homme d'une cinquantaine d'années, né à Bevagna, qui avait grandi à Pérouse et s'était installé à Rome après la guerre, où il avait fondé une famille.

De caractère jovial, Mario del Monte avait de nombreux amis. Il allait faire sa partie de cartes le jeudi, dîner chez ses beaux-parents le vendredi et voir des films – sa passion – dès qu'il le pouvait. Sa femme en plaisantait : « Mario, tu me préfères Audrey Hepburn ». Ce n'était pas tout à fait faux. Il aimait tout ce qui était enregistré sur celluloïde : les coups de gueule de John Wayne, l'ironie de Paul Newman, la sensualité d'Ava Gardner et le blues de la fragile Marylin. Mais Audrey était la meilleure. Un papillon qui te donnait l'impression, quand il apparaissait à l'écran, de n'exister que pour toi.

Audrey...

Avant la guerre, et il était encore presque un enfant lorsqu'il était parti faire la campagne d'Afrique, le cinéma était un passe-temps parmi d'autres. Mais, après la guerre, c'était devenu autre chose, la seule bouée à laquelle s'agripper pour ne pas se noyer, pour ne pas mourir. Le cinéma, c'était le rêve, l'évasion, le divertissement. Pour être heureux, Mario del Monte n'avait besoin que d'une salle obscure, d'une belle histoire et de sa femme pour lui tenir la main dans la pénombre éclairée par l'écran. Ombrienne comme lui, Teresa savait qu'il était au fond un homme brisé. Quelque chose avait mal tourné dans cette guerre infâme où Mussolini les avait entraînés. Mais elle ne lui posait pas de question. Avec le temps, elle avait appris à glisser sur le passé de son mari. Il faut dire aussi que la vie avec leurs trois enfants et l'aînée à marier, cette « rebelle cabocharde », était déjà assez compliquée comme ça, et l'accaparait entièrement.

Teresa n'était pas au milieu de la foule en liesse. Elle était restée à la maison pour cuisiner, ou pour repasser des chemises, qui sait.

Mario, lui, était bien là, via dei Fori imperiali – tout tremblant.

Il avait quelque chose à remettre à l'empereur, un objet enveloppé dans un papier couleur brique. Il essaya bien, mais il lui fut impossible de s'approcher.

Il demanda alors quelques jours de congé. C'était un modeste fonctionnaire des Postes. « Après tout », dit-il à ses supérieurs, « je n'ai pas pris de vacances cette année ». Il ne confia rien à sa femme de son plan insensé. De cette obsession de rencontrer l'empereur d'Ethiopie. Il prétendit qu'il allait voir son frère à Turin. Mario savait que Haïlé Sélassié devait visiter les usines Fiat. C'était écrit dans tous les journaux. Ce qu'ils ne disaient pas, c'est que Me Agnelli avait requis un service d'ordre imposant. Mario fit encore une fois chou blanc. On ne l'avait pas laissé entrer. Il avait même été arrêté : sa barbe touffue et son regard glacial n'étaient pas faits pour rassurer les forces de l'ordre. Il avait tenté de nouveau sa chance à la gare centrale de Milan, mais il avait raté l'empereur d'un cheveu. On lui avait indiqué un mauvais quai. Et le temps de s'apercevoir de son erreur, il était trop tard : le train était déjà parti. Il restait à Mario une dernière chance, Venise. Il ne pouvait pas le manquer encore. Il se sentait calme. Il le tenait, désormais.

À Saint-Marc, il le laissa admirer la place couverte d'eau, de sa position étrange, en équilibre sur la passerelle. C'est seulement à l'arrêt du *vaporetto* (que l'empereur avait tenu à prendre comme les Vénitiens) qu'il lui cria à bonne distance, en amharique : « Majesté, je vous en prie, laissez-moi m'approcher ».

Quelle ne fut pas la surprise de Haïlé Sélassié d'entendre sa langue, parlée par cet Italien un peu chauve à la barbe fournie. Qui était-ce ? Il avait l'accent des habitants d'Addis. Vu son âge, il avait dû participer à l'occupation italienne de son pays. L'empereur fut tenté de lui tourner le dos. De l'ignorer. Mais il ordonna à sa cour de le laisser avancer.

Une fois devant lui, Mario fit ce qu'il rêvait de faire depuis longtemps : il se prosterna à ses pieds. Puis il commença à bredouiller des bouts de phrase confus dans un amharique de moins en moins assuré. « Que voulez-vous exactement ? », le pressa l'empereur avec une certaine impatience. Il était curieux et mourait d'envie de découvrir ce qui se cachait dans ce paquet couleur brique que l'Italien tenait soigneusement.

« Je voulais », dit Mario del Monte la voix brisée par un étrange sifflement, « Majesté, je voulais vous rendre quelque chose ».

Et Mario put lui raconter alors son départ comme volontaire en 1936 pour faire la guerre en Ethiopie. « Je ne connaissais rien de votre pays », dit-il comme pour se justifier. « Je croyais que je devais libérer des esclaves qui étaient entre vos griffes, Monsieur l'empereur. C'est ce qu'écrivaient les journaux. Personne ne devrait vivre en esclave. »[3]

Il se revit jeune engagé en Ethiopie, comme dans un film, avec une bande-son douloureuse qui résonnait derrière lui : une tête brûlée qui rêvait d'aventure et de belles femmes. Comme beaucoup, il était descendu à Massaoua et en quelques jours avait rejoint son régiment, stationné à la frontière.

Il faisait chaud en Afrique orientale, trop chaud dans cette Afrique de merde. Telle avait été sa première pensée. Et la deuxième, « Qu'est-ce que je fais ici ? ». Mario était un gars intelligent ; il comprit rapidement que la propagande dont il

---

[3] La propagande fasciste insistait beaucoup sur ce point qui lui servait à justifier la campagne d'Ethiopie. C'est pourquoi l'un des premiers actes du gouverneur de l'Erythrée, le général italien Emilio De Bono (1866–1944), est un édit, promulgué à Adoua le 14 novembre 1935, qui abolit officiellement l'esclavage au Tigré (*bando De Bono*).

avait été abreuvé en Italie avait menti. « Mais c'est au nord d'Adoua que je me suis rendu compte que j'étais un envahisseur. »

À ce moment-là, Mario se mordit la langue, qui se mit à saigner. Il aurait pu continuer son récit. Mais il ne le fit pas. Il n'arrivait pas à dire à l'empereur que ses compagnons d'armes avaient violé une fillette tandis que les *ascari*[4] faisaient le guet. Et qu'il n'avait pas réussi à l'empêcher. Dire l'image de l'enfant mourante, crucifiée aux corps moqueurs de ses bourreaux, qui lui avaient même demandé de prendre une photo. La fillette était morte devant son objectif, et ils l'avaient abandonnée là, en proie aux hyènes. Puis ils avaient incendié sa case. A quelques pas du crime, il avait ensuite trouvé une sainte, peinte sur une planchette en bois. Une sainte ancienne avec une auréole bleu foncé. Une sainte en deuil pour la mort de Jésus, mais heureuse de sa résurrection. Cheveux blonds et peau noire. Hélas ! comme elle ressemblait à la fillette qu'ils avaient tuée.

Il ne souffla mot à l'empereur de ce jour maudit. Il lui tendit simplement l'objet, qui n'était autre que l'icône trouvée dans la vallée du Tembien.

« Je veux vous demander pardon au nom de tous les Italiens », dit Mario del Monte.

« Cette icône vous appartient, Majesté. Je l'ai prise dans votre pays et conservée durant toutes ces années – dans la douleur. Et maintenant je vous la restitue, ainsi qu'à votre peuple. Car vous seul, Majesté, en êtes le légitime propriétaire. »

Et avant que Haïlé Sélassié n'ait pu formuler une réponse, Mario del Monte se serra encore davantage aux pieds de ce grand empereur, et se mit à pleurer.

---

4 Les *ascari* étaient les indigènes, d'abord érythréens et arabes, puis recrutés dans l'ensemble de l'Afrique orientale italienne (AOI), enrôlés comme soldats réguliers dans les troupes coloniales de l'armée italienne (l'équivalent donc des harkis dans l'armée française). Historiquement, ils sont les successeurs des bachi-bouzouks, mercenaires de l'Armée Hassan (levée en Erythrée par l'aventurier albanais Sangiak Hassan), rachetés par l'Italie en 1885 et rebaptisés *ascari* (« soldats ») en 1889.

Markus Messling & Christiane Solte-Gresser

Qu'est-ce qu'une pratique culturelle de réparation ? La stèle d'Axoum et « L'icona » d'Igiaba Scego

Résumé : Nous vivons des temps de transition qui sont marqués par l'urgence de réparation : comment « réparer » l'humanité après les grandes machines coloniales et totalitaires de déshumanisation ? La question se pose d'autant plus que la persistance des destructions hante le présent. Ainsi faut-il partir de l'irréparable qui semble être à la base de toute démarche possible quant à la construction d'un avenir. Le cas concret qu'analyse cet article est celui de la stèle d'Axoum, enlevée en Éthiopie par les forces fascistes italiennes en 1937. Elle fait partie du combat longtemps ignoré des nations africaines pour la restitution de biens culturels. Si le retour de la stèle est fondamental pour la société éthiopienne, il évoque des questions d'identité et de mémoire complexes : comment la société italienne travaille-t-elle le vide que la stèle restituée a laissé à la place de Porta Capena à Rome ? Quid du refoulé historique ? Comment la communauté éthiopienne en Italie vit-elle le débat autour de la restitution ? Le texte littéraire « L'icona » d'Igiaba Scego (2018) raconte le cas de la stèle d'Axoum en liant le niveau historico-politique et psychologique. Il aborde le thème des crimes historiques contre l'humanité et des tentatives de réparation par les moyens d'un savoir (politique, juridique, économique et social) mis en narration. Comment produit-il, par ses moyens esthétiques, par son jeu d'échelles, une expérience de violence et de culpabilité, de responsabilité et de réconciliation ? L'enquête littéraire démontre comment une identification individuelle et un objet transféré peuvent aller à contresens de la grande Histoire et des politiques gouvernementales. La mise en scène narrative ouvre vers la vérité intérieure, vécue de l'histoire. Ainsi en est-il dans la sphère du cas individuel, du social en micro, que des pratiques culturelles de réparation développent leur signification véritable[1].

---

[1] L'écriture de ce texte a été possible, pour Markus Messling, dans le cadre du projet « Minor Universality. Narrative World Productions After Western Universalism », financé par le Conseil Européen de la Recherche (ERC, « Horizon 2020 », n° 819931), pour Christiane Solte-Gresser dans le cadre de l'école doctorale « Cultures européennes du rêve » (GRK 2021), financée par la DFG (Deutsche Forschungsgemeinschaft ; Fondation allemande pour la recherche).

Mots-clés : post-colonialisme ; pratiques culturelles de réparation ; subjectivité ; vérité/expérience historique ; micro-histoire ; narration/narratologie ; poétique du savoir ; Igiaba Scego; stèle d'Axoum

L'ère des réparations

En août 2021, encore un pays s'écroule. Après vingt ans d'occupation en Afghanistan, la mission militaire de l'alliance occidentale échoue. La peine et la peur des citoyens afghans sont transmises en direct sur les écrans de notre monde globalisé. Le 17 août 2021, le président allemand Steinmeier donne une conférence de presse qui contient ces mots inouïs :

> Nous vivons ces jours-ci une tragédie humaine pour laquelle nous avons une responsabilité commune, ainsi qu'une césure politique qui nous bouleverse et qui changera le monde. Les images de la désespérance à l'aéroport de Kaboul sont honteuses pour l'Occident politique[2].

Si les échecs d'une politique militaire de l'alliance occidentale se multiplient depuis la première intervention dans le Golfe Persique – et puis dans les Balkans et encore en Iraq, au Soudan et dans la Corne de l'Afrique, en Lybie, en Syrie, puis au Mali –, l'échec de ce que Steinmeier appelle « l'Occident politique » a rarement, peut-être jamais dans une capitale occidentale, été prononcé avec une telle franchise. En 1989, quelques stratèges politiques rêvaient encore de la victoire finale de l'universalisme occidental, mais ce même universalisme s'écroule devant les yeux du monde et se démantèle clairement dans ce qu'il a toujours – au moins *aussi* – été : une défense de ses propres intérêts[3].

Le cas de l'Afghanistan démontre en même temps le dilemme qui accompagne notre époque de transition : les contre-politiques sont trop souvent des essentialismes culturels qui opposent à une essentialisation occidentale une présupposée « propre culture », soit elle religieuse, ethnique ou nationale. Si les contre-essentialismes ont eu une légitimité et une fonction dans la décolonisation qu'il ne faut pas bannir de notre conscience historique (Scott 1999, 224), ils ont, en grand, perdu la force émancipatoire. Ce qui apparaît de plus en plus urgent, c'est une réorientation de la critique culturelle et politique telle que la propose David Scott :

---

2 Frank-Walter Steinmeier : « "Wir erleben in diesen Tagen eine menschliche Tragödie, für die wir Mitverantwortung tragen, und eine politische Zäsur, die uns erschüttert und die Welt verändern wird", sagte Steinmeier. "Die Bilder der Verzweiflung am Flughafen Kabul sind beschämend für den politischen Westen" » (Steinmeier dans Hasenkamp 2021).
3 Cf. Wallerstein (2006, 1–29), Diagne (2014a, 15–21). Pour une approche historique, voir Hofmann et Messling (2021).

> They [his essays; M.M.] are seeking to gain a purchase on a global moment of considerable instability and uncertainty. It is a moment when hitherto established and authoritative conceptual paradigms and political projects (those defined in relation to Marxism and cultural nationalism, for instance, or various admixtures of nationalism and socialism, and so on) seem no longer adequate to the tasks of the present, and when, at the same time, new paradigms and projects have yet to assert themselves fully in the place of the old. These essays inhabit, in other words, a sort of Gramscian interregnum, a transitional moment that I shall characterize as "after postcoloniality" (Scott 1999, 10).

Cette constatation courageuse et clairvoyante, faite déjà en 1999 par David Scott dans son livre *Refashioning Futures. Criticism After Postcoloniality*, n'a rien perdu de son actualité. Scott ne conçoit pas cet « après » comme un jugement de la pensée postcoloniale, et il ne s'agit pas, pour lui, de rompre avec l'effort critique de démanteler des structures de pouvoir[4]. Ce qu'il maintient, c'est que la situation politique a changé depuis 1989, de sorte qu'il faut replacer les acquis du postcolonial dans les conditions du contemporain qu'on habite. Venant lui-même d'une politique de la théorie, Scott cherche à établir une nouvelle théorie du politique[5] : « I believe that the present invites us to take up the more difficult task of thinking fundamentally against the normalization of the epistemological and institutional forms of our political modernity » (Scott 1999, 20). Scott renvoie donc explicitement au projet de la « modernité » dont les enjeux seraient à réorienter. Ce fait nous semble évoquer deux implications fondamentales que nous développons en suivant d'autres traces :

Premièrement, le projet de la modernité était formulé dans le passé, sous quelque forme idéologique que ce soit (libéralisme, socialisme, communisme, etc.), en termes universalistes. Ceci nous incite à repenser ce que pourrait être l'humanité au-delà des terminologies universalistes héritées. On assiste clairement aux limites de l'universalisme occidental dans sa forme idéologique – qui aujourd'hui s'effondre. Parallèlement et pour diverses raisons, on voit aussi que les contre-discours dits « culturalistes » n'aboutissent pas à produire une vision plus convaincante par rapport à la question posée par Scott, concernant les concepts et les infrastructures politiques d'un vivre-ensemble juste. La question de ce qui nous lie reste donc fondamentale pour parler de standards et de droits. Mais comment repenser un tel universel après l'universalisme occidental[6] ? Ceci ne peut certainement pas être conçu comme une universalisation d'un centre ou des centres. Il s'agit plutôt de partir de la différence et de construire l'universel dans la multilatéralité.

---

4 Cf. Scott (1999, 221–224).
5 Il propose de passer « from a politics of theory to a theory of politics » (Scott 1999, 19).
6 Pour une enquête narratologique portant sur cette question, voir Messling (2023a).

Souleymane Bachir Diagne parle d'un « universel latéral de traduction » qu'il oppose à un « universel de surplomb » (Diagne et Amselle 2018, 75–76)[7], car il s'agit, selon lui, de produire cet universel dans la négociation, par la création d'un tiers commun, universel qui ne devient intelligible que dans la mise en relation des deux perspectives divergentes. Cette idée de partir de l'horizontal, il faut bien évidemment la penser en termes d'asymétries si l'on considère l'histoire coloniale et les inégalités qui en résultent. Parler d'universel veut donc dire parler de l'histoire de son refus[8].

Ces réflexions renvoient au deuxième constat qui découle de l'acte de repenser la modernité et qui nous semble pertinent dans ce contexte, à savoir que le futur ne peut être saisi que dans des processus réparatifs. Contrairement au progressisme de la modernité universaliste, qui vivait dans une projection permanente vers « l'avant », la question du futur se présente aujourd'hui, 30 ans après Scott, comme un défi qui sollicite des efforts réflexifs et une capacité à atténuer l'impact destructeur des idéaux de la modernité même. Dans ce sens, Ulrich Beck et Edgar Grande ont parlé d'une « seconde modernité » qui serait caractérisée par une « modernisation réflexive » (*reflexive modernization*) (Beck et Grande 2010, 409–443), c'est-à-dire par le fait que nous avons dû nous rendre compte que les prémisses de la modernité comportent en elles des facteurs et même des fondements – comme par exemple la nation, ou la différenciation de la connaissance – qui risquent de détruire les acquis sociaux de cette même modernité. Cette conclusion nous force à intégrer ce savoir dans toute conception du futur. Cela paraît évident par rapport à l'écologie (avec tout ce qui va avec : croissance et exploitation des ressources, le nucléaire, le climat etc.). Mais Dipesh Chakrabarty a montré, dans son célèbre article « The climate of history », que de la conscience de l'anthropocène naît une conscience de l'histoire mondiale qui refuse de considérer les pertes des particularités comme pertes possibles à subsumer dans le progrès ; ainsi désigne-t-il la conscience historique du contemporain comme « histoire universelle négative » (Chakrabarty 2009, 197–222).

Pour rebondir sur la proposition de Scott de comprendre notre contemporain comme un « après » dans lequel il faut réviser les conditions politiques de notre modernité, on pourrait donc dire que nous vivons des temps de transition qui sont marqués par la nécessité de réparation.

---

7 Voir aussi Diagne (2014b, 243–256).
8 C'est Frantz Fanon qui avait déjà mis à nu ce fait sans pitié dans *Les damnés de la terre* (2000 [1961]), préface de Jean-Paul Sartre, présentation de Alice Cherki et postface de Mohammed Harbi. Voir surtout Fanon (2000, 44–49).

Ce que réparer veut dire

Le terme de « réparation » pourrait suggérer qu'on puisse réparer des relations humaines comme l'on répare une voiture. Si déjà, le bon sens nous dit que cela ne peut jamais se faire, ceci devient évident quand on réalise que l'usage du terme développé ici se réfère à l'idéal de l'humanité. Des actes qui détruisent profondément la communauté des vivants sont pour cela appelés des « crimes contre l'humanité » ; c'est l'humanité elle-même qui s'effondre. Les temps qui sont les nôtres et qui se voient dans la nécessité de réparer la communauté humaine après les grandes machines coloniales et totalitaires de déshumanisation, montrent que nous avons affaire à des processus historiques qui sont irréparables. La persistance des destructions hante le présent. C'est donc de l'irréparable qu'il faut partir[9].

Si nous avons affaire à des effets d'irréparable, quel rôle peut alors jouer l'aspect matériel de la compensation ? Ou bien, pour le dire franchement : que coûte une vie anéantie par le travail lourd dans les plantations ou éradiquée par un génocide ? Même si les assurances-vie peuvent maintenir l'illusion que la valeur d'une vie détruite peut être quantifiée – car tout a son prix dans le capitalisme –, les destructions de l'humanité ne sont pas réparables : on ne peut pas réparer un génocide en payant une somme, de surcroît si elle dépasse tous les calculs (Kaleck 2021, 129–135). Les Allemands devraient bien le savoir. Mais les Européens, généralement, le savent par leurs expériences historiques : les réparations françaises après 1871, et les réparations allemandes après 1918, n'ont rien pu réparer en termes humains. Elles ont plutôt augmenté la haine et ont fait partie des causes menant, à chaque fois, à la prochaine guerre.

Quand on parle donc de réparation, il s'agit tout d'abord de réfléchir sur des processus qui enlèvent une asymétrie produite par l'expropriation ou la destruction, et ravivent la dignité de ces communautés qui ont été abaissées[10]. Il s'agit de processus de responsabilité prise et de reconnaissance entre égaux. C'est là pourtant que le matériel entre en jeu : pour pouvoir parler d'égalité, il faut corriger des asymétries produites et des désavantages qui en résultent. La compensation matérielle est donc souvent une base, une nécessité, pour pouvoir entrer dans un processus de réparation. Parfois, cela accompagne un processus de réparation déjà mis en route. Toutefois, la réparation matérielle ne pourra jamais être réalisée de manière satisfaisante. Ainsi Shashi Tharoor, membre du parlement

---
9 Voir la définition qu'a donnée Souleymane Bachir Diagne du terme de « réparation » : « Rhinozeros asks. . . Souleymane Bachir Diagne : What is reparation? », vidéo avec Diagne (Messling et al. 2021).
10 C'est dans ce sens que Kader Attia définit son projet artistique de réparation depuis longtemps. Voir Attia (2019, 11–14).

fédéral de l'Inde et ancien Secrétaire général adjoint de l'Organisation des Nations Unies, a soulevé dans son discours célèbre devant l'Oxford Union, que le coût du régime colonial britannique en Inde serait tellement élevé qu'il ne pourrait jamais être remboursé : si la partie du produit mondial brut qui revenait à l'Inde en 1700 tournait autour de 30 %, à la veille de l'indépendance, elle n'était plus que de 5 % (Tharoor 2021, 68–73). Devant l'exposition de tels faits – certainement plus complexes encore en termes de pertes humaines –, leur ampleur devient claire. Tharoor revendique que la Grande Bretagne devrait déposer, chaque année, un *pound* auprès du peuple indien pour rappeler ce fait immense, et reconnaître sa propre responsabilité. Ce serait un acte symbolique.

Bien entendu, Tharoor ne veut pas dire que les responsables ne devraient pas du tout payer. Les colonialismes européens ou l'esclavage sont aussi à considérer en termes financiers – c'est notamment un débat important aux États-Unis[11]. Mais ce qui est primordial dans la proposition de Tharoor, c'est l'acte réparatif qui non seulement met à nu la faute, mais en fait également un rituel de pénitence dans lequel les signes d'hégémonie sont inversés. L'exemple démontre que penser en termes de réparations historiques veut dire réfléchir à comment établir un équilibre difficile mais nécessaire entre la restitution matérielle et des pratiques symboliques de réparation. Cette balance ne vise pas à une réparation dans le sens d'une compensation totale. Avec Souleymane Bachir Diagne, il faut comprendre l'acte de réparation comme un geste qui puisse permettre un vivre-ensemble dans l'avenir. Diagne a proposé, en suivant la philosophie politique de Nelson Mandela, de penser ce processus à partir du concept social d'*ubuntu* (Diagne 2016, 11–19). Il s'agit ici de l'idée de définir l'humanité dans la réciprocité, sur laquelle se basait la mise en place de la Commission Vérité et Réconciliation sud-africaine qui a eu un impact fondamental sur le débat postcolonial des réparations[12]. Si la réparation se base donc sur la compensation matérielle, le long et véritable travail réparatif reste à faire au moyen de pratiques politiques, sociales et culturelles. Dans ce sens, les discussions autour de la restitution de biens culturels apparaissent comme une mise à l'épreuve, car « compenser consiste ici en une démarche visant à réparer la relation » (Sarr et Savoy 2018, 69).

---

[11] Voir le texte canonique de Coats (2014).
[12] Cf. Cassin, Cayla et Salazar (2004). Voir surtout dans ce volume le texte de Jacques Derrida (2004, 111–156), qui est non seulement en quelque sorte son héritage (son dernier texte), mais en soi une lecture réparative qui met l'idée hégélienne de réconciliation de l'histoire, en vue de son concept déplorable d'Afrique, à l'épreuve de l'*ubuntu* de Mandela et du court réel de l'histoire (sud-)africaine.

Problème de restitution : le cas d'Axoum

C'est suite au *Rapport sur la restitution du patrimoine culturel africain : Vers une nouvelle éthique relationnelle,* rédigé en 2018 par Felwine Sarr et Bénédicte Savoy missionnés par le président Emmanuel Macron, qui a relancé en grand le débat sur la restitution des biens culturels transportés dans les musées européens pendant le colonialisme. Dans son livre récent, *Le long combat de l'Afrique pour son art. Histoire d'une défaite postcoloniale* (2023), Bénédicte Savoy démontre que ce débat n'est pourtant pas nouveau, et qu'il ne revient pas, à nous contemporains, d'en être les premiers témoins, puisqu'il avait déjà été mené quarante ans plus tôt dans une situation postcoloniale au sens strict, après la libération des nations africaines. Ce sombre fait jette la lumière sur un premier échec de ce même débat ainsi que sur l'absurdité qui consiste dans l'usage de certains arguments, repris de nouveau dans les débats contemporains, qui servent à défendre la position intenable du refus de restitution[13].

Le cas dont nous allons parler ici est le cas de la stèle d'Axoum, enlevée en Éthiopie par les forces fascistes italiennes en 1937, qui, d'un côté, fait partie de l'histoire décrite par Bénédicte Savoy, et de l'autre côté, fait d'une certaine manière exception. Il fait partie, d'un côté, du combat longtemps ignoré des nations africaines pour la restitution de biens culturels si l'on considère le fait que la restitution de la stèle de granit, convenue à la Conférence de la Paix de Paris dès 1946/47 avec tous les autres bien culturels éthiopiens, tardera jusqu'à 2005 à être effectuée. Frappé par la foudre et détraqué en 2002, l'obélisque ne sera érigé à Axoum, au Tigré, qu'en 2008 (fig. 1). De l'autre côté, l'accord sur le retour de la stèle ayant été convenu directement après la Deuxième Guerre mondiale, il a précédé les développements faisant suite à la décolonisation des nations africaines par la résolution 3187 de l'ONU, rédigée à la conférence de Kinshasa en 1973 – le rapport étroit entre le vol et les crimes fascistes italiens en Éthiopie ainsi que l'intégralité de l'Empire éthiopien comme acteur étatique étant certainement les raisons primordiales.

Malgré les intérêts politiques de la République d'Italie de réinstaurer les liens avec l'Éthiopie, dont témoignent les visites d'Aldo Moro à Addis-Abeba et de Haïlé Sélassié à Rome en 1970, Igiaba Scego décrit dans *Roma negata. Percorsi postcoloniali nella città* ce temps intermédiaire avant la restitution comme un temps de l'oubli :

---

[13] Voir surtout Savoy (2023, 219–224).

Fig. 1 : Ré-installation de l'obélisque à Axoum, 2008. Photo: wikimedia commons. https://commons.wikimedia.org/wiki/File:Aksum-107557.jpg.

> Surtout, l'histoire n'a jamais été décolonisée en Italie. Le colonialisme a été englouti dans cet oubli, et les points de référence symboliques du fascisme ont été abandonnés à la dégradation comme s'ils étaient des radeaux fantomatiques dans un fleuve du non-dit (Bianchi et Scego 2020 [2014], 87)[14].

Si le monument était « dénué de toute signification » (Bianchi et Scego 2020 [2014], 90) pour les Italiens, au point que, même après son démontage en 2003 à la Porta Capena (fig. 2), il fut simplement envoyé dans un entrepôt, ceci ne fut jamais le cas pour les Éthiopiens qui ne cessèrent d'insister sur sa restitution (Bianchi et Scego 2020 [2014], 91).

Lorsque l'obélisque fut finalement rendu, le travail de réparation n'était donc pas accompli, mais lancé, et ceci à tous les niveaux :

(1) Tout d'abord, le retour de la stèle concernait la sphère des États. Pour l'Éthiopie, il s'agissait prioritairement de s'affirmer comme État souverain et de rétablir l'intégrité après l'humiliation coloniale. Le transfert technique compliqué de la stèle a par ailleurs été documenté par l'artiste Theo Eshetu comme un processus réparatif dans sa vidéo *The return of the Axum Obelisk* (2009)[15] qui se base, aussi, sur la

---

14 Trad. M.M.
15 https://daata.art/art/the-return-of-the-axum-obelisk (17 septembre 2022).

Fig. 2 : La stèle d'Axoum en démontage à la Porta Capena, 2003. Photo: wikimedia commons. https://commons.wikimedia.org/wiki/File:OBELISCOAXUM4281003A.jpg.

tradition de peinture éthiopienne[16]. Quand la stèle est rétablie à Axoum par une cérémonie gouvernementale en 2008 (fig. 3), elle devient, après des décennies de guerres et déstabilisations intérieures, « un instrument de renouveau national, d'unité et de sens civique » (Bekerie 2005, 87). Ceci évoque la question de l'identité politique et culturelle de la société éthiopienne, mais aussi la problématique des fonctionnalisations de la mémoire pour la construction des versions spécifiques de cette identité (Santi 2014, 220–222). Ceci va de même, bien sûr, pour la société italienne qui se voit confrontée au vide de l'emplacement où se trouvait ladite stèle. La discussion publique tourna surtout autour de la question de savoir s'il fallait placer à la Porta Capena un autre obélisque ou s'il y en avait déjà assez à Rome (Bianchi

---

16 Voir l'analyse de Lagatz (2021, 364–367).

Fig. 3 : La statue après sa restitution au Tigré, 2008. Photo: wikimedia commons. https://commons.wikimedia.org/wiki/File:ET_Axum_asv2018-01_img37_Stelae_Park.jpg.

et Scego 2020 [2014], 95–98). On y instaure finalement un mémorial consistant en deux colonnes antiques symbolisant les deux tours du World Trade Center de New York pour commémorer le 11 septembre 2001 (fig. 4).

Se référant à cet événement interprété comme attaque contre les symboles de l'Occident politique, le monument incarne l'idée que l'événement est le nouveau point de repère universel de la compréhension de l'histoire occidentale. Cette politique mémorielle « globale » ne touche évidemment pas à l'histoire italienne, elle ne l'intègre pas en complexifiant l'histoire glorifiée de la modernité occidentale. Sans rappeler les crimes qui résultent de l'impérialisme italien, l'affirmation monumentale de l'universalisme ne renvoie que plus fortement à ses abîmes. En conclusion du débat italien autour du mémorial, Igiaba Scego

Fig. 4 : Twin Towers Memorial, Piazzale di Porta Capena, 2020. Photo: Courtesy of David Lown. https://www.walksinrome.com/blog/the-twin-towers-memorial-rome.

écrit en 2014 :« Personne ne percevait ce vide sur la place comme un vide de mémoire » (Bianchi et Scego 2020 [2014], 97–98)[17].

(2) La restitution de biens culturels comme celui de la stèle d'Axoum modifie, de plus, le statut de l'objet même. Si celui-ci, par sa présence ou absence, est un acteur qui produit de nouvelles possibilités d'agir pour les sociétés (Appadurai 1986), il est aussi un reflet de ce que les sociétés désirent représenter à travers lui. Pour le régime fasciste de Mussolini, il symbolisait l'Empire colonial, la nouvelle

---

17 Trad. M.M.

grandeur de Rome. Pour la nation éthiopienne, datant de presque 2000 ans, il symbolise la continuité de l'histoire. L'anthropologue Eloi Fiquet s'est demandé si l'histoire fasciste n'était pas inscrite dans la stèle volée dans le sens où elle représente un objet d'obsession nationale qui hanta aussi l'Éthiopie là où la continuité nationale était artificielle et d'autant plus revendiquée (Santi 2014, 222–223). Sur un plan plus systématique, ce type de questions pose le problème de savoir si les biens culturels comme la stèle d'Axoum sont à concevoir comme un héritage national où un héritage de l'humanité. Cela implique aussi la question de savoir s'il faut penser leur usage en termes de transnationalisme ou de muséalisation nationale. Si ce binarisme semble rendre les choses assez simples, il est clair que ce genre de questions ne peut pas être posé sans considérer en même temps le fait du vol, et qu'il ne servait que trop souvent comme argument pour l'appropriation européenne. La transnationalisation ne peut-elle pas se faire uniquement dans le processus de réparation qui est, d'abord, un processus de nationalisation ? Mais pour quelle idée de nation ? Ce qui est un fait, c'est que la stèle d'Axoum est devenue patrimoine culturel de l'humanité certifié par l'UNESCO au moment de sa restitution en Éthiopie.

(3) Enfin, il y a une dimension de la restitution qui touche aux individus. Celle-ci peut être de nature multiple, politique comme émotionnelle, elle va au-delà des frontières nationales et elle a un aspect transgénérationnel. En ce sens, l'effet du « dire-vrai[18] » de l'histoire et de la reconnaissance de fautes ouvre des possibilités moins pour les victimes historiques – qui sont souvent mortes – que pour leurs enfants ou, plus généralement, pour le contexte contemporain entier, qui est marqué par la survivance d'effets psychologiques des injustices et violences subies (Solte-Gresser 2021, 11–30, 235–278, 405–441). Ainsi, la restitution de biens culturels permet-elle un repositionnement des sujets dans les sociétés concernées, l'objet faisant partie de la réorganisation biographique et identitaire de multiples personnes : on peut désormais s'identifier (ou non) avec l'acte réparatif, ce qui a un impact politique sur les différents acteurs et sur leur possibilité d'agir et de s'articuler. On verra, à travers l'analyse du texte « L'icona[19] » d'Igiaba Scego, comment une identification individuelle et un objet transféré peuvent aller à contresens de la grande Histoire, ainsi que des politiques gouvernementales. C'est dans la sphère du cas individuel, du social en micro, que des pratiques culturelles de réparation développent leur signification véritable.

---

18 On se réfère ici à l'importance que Michel Foucault a attribuée à la *parrêsia*, au fait du « franc-parler », du « dire-vrai » pour la constitution et résilience d'une subjectivité ; cf. Foucault (2009, 3–31).
19 Publié en 2018, et traduit en français pour le volume présent.

Les actes de réparation et l'importance du micro

Ce qui rend la théorie de la micro-histoire si intéressante pour les problèmes abordés ici, c'est que l'étude de cas, si fine soit-elle, ne s'accompagne pas de l'abandon d'un horizon universel. Au contraire, les enquêtes micro-historiques ne perdent jamais de vue le général : c'est par rapport à lui qu'elles cherchent à positionner de manière nouvelle un objet particulier et les connaissances qui y sont liées[20]. À la place d'un débat purement méthodologique, Giovanni Levi promeut une mise en perspective qui rendrait plus de justice à la complexité de la vie qu'une appropriation systémique qui devrait toujours se fonder sur un pré-modelage du monde (Levi 2000, 55). Ainsi, les tentatives pour articuler du particulier au général expriment-elles une conscience du présent qui ne peut plus présupposer l'universalité de manière simplement déductive, mais doit, au contraire, la fabriquer.

Ce n'est donc pas un hasard si les représentants de la micro-histoire se sont intéressés aux techniques narratives essentielles pour équilibrer cas particulier et perspective générale sous la forme d'un « jeu d'échelles » (Revel 1996). D'un point de vue herméneutique, c'est la forme de l'enquête qui permet d'articuler une situation concrète à une hypothèse générale et de lui conférer ainsi une plausibilité. Dans son célèbre essai sur la lecture indiciaire, Carlo Ginzburg a montré que l'enquête correspondait au régime de connaissance de la modernité elle-même (Ginzburg 2010 [1979], 139–180). Au présent, on peut constater des différences significatives par rapport au contexte initial : si, au XIXe siècle, l'enquêteur cherche à comprendre la pathologie de la société en partant du petit afin de reconstruire une totalité normative, c'est la fragilité et la défectuosité du contexte d'ensemble que l'enquête de notre ère réparatrice prend pour point de départ :

> [L'enquête] souligne les lignes de fracture, met en évidence que les fragments de réel ne se fondent pas dans une totalité retrouvée : elle dit la part de discontinuité, souligne les angles morts et les taches aveugles, prend acte de l'hétérogénéité des représentations, sans suture possible (Demanze 2019, 21).

Les bris de mémoire qui sont liés à des matériaux, documents et photographies, restent flous et leur statut est instable. Ils suivent des causalités – associations et expériences vécues – ni tout à fait transparentes ni entièrement logiques. Mais c'est précisément cela qui contribue à la perception d'ensemble, qui saisit une vérité de l'existence, et non une vérité de faits objective. Dans son livre *Un nouvel*

---

20 Voir la préface et l'avant-propos de Ginzburg (2019 [1976]).

âge de l'enquête, Laurent Demanze attribue au « paradigme inquisitorial » (Kalifa 2010, 4) contemporain une force formative : « Le réel, c'est précisément ce à quoi il faut *donner forme* dans un travail obstiné d'investigation critique et d'hypothèse figurative, pour tenter de saisir cela même qui échappe » (Demanze 2019, 20). Ce réel peut bien différer de la grande Histoire, celle avec grand H ; la littérature peut l'interpréter autrement, la déférer, la subvertir. Alexandre Gefen a développé l'idée que la littérature contemporaine entend réinventer le réel pour égaliser les asymétries, sauver, prendre soin de l'autre – tout court : pour réparer le monde (Gefen 2017).

En guise de structures silencieuses, la micro-histoire s'est intéressée aux hommes et aux femmes du passé en tant qu'acteurs porteurs de visions du monde et de stratégies spécifiques (Schlumbohm 1999, 20). Une telle approche comporte évidemment une dimension éthique, qu'il convient de prendre en compte dans un contexte marqué par « la conscience de la blessure » coloniale que Kader Attia a décrite de manière sensible et puissante à partir de sa propre biographie (Attia 2019). C'est ce potentiel éthique, esthétique et narratif de la littérature pour saisir les bris de mémoire, la part subjective de la réalité, et les expériences vécues, que notre analyse du récit « L'icona » d'Igiaba Scego vise à démontrer.

Écrire la réparation

Le récit « L'icona » d'Igiaba Scego[21] commence par une incertitude personnelle lors d'une visite officielle : le dernier empereur d'Éthiopie se tient sur une passerelle chancelante à Venise, craignant de tomber dans l'eau et essayant de garder son équilibre. Le déplacement à travers un espace historique, dans lequel le colonialisme et la Seconde Guerre mondiale ont laissé des traces profondes, est le thème central de ce texte hautement symbolique. Ce dernier raconte les itinéraires protocolaires, les trébuchements individuels, les détours destinés à empêcher de voir l'injustice historique, la marche soldatesque et inébranlable, les

---

21 Voir Scego (2018, 75–84). Ce texte occupe une position particulière dans l'œuvre littéraire d'Igiaba Scego dans la mesure où il ne traite pas, ou très peu, des questions de migration, de fuite, d'identité linguistique et culturelle, de problèmes familiaux et générationnels ou de modèles de rôle spécifiques au genre. Cependant, l'histoire coloniale de l'Italie, qui constitue le centre thématique de « L'icona », traverse toute l'écriture de l'autrice. Voir également Ali (2020, 157–166, notamment 158). Pour autant que nous sachions, le récit « L'icona » est jusqu'à présent passé presque inaperçu auprès des chercheurs. Pour une exception cf. la préface de Martha Kleinhans citée par la suite.

pauses inattendues et les tentatives toujours nouvelles de contrecarrer le cours de l'histoire[22].

Sur le plan rhétorique et narratif, l'autrice entremêle ici deux formes d'histoire en faisant passer un personnage authentique par des lieux particulièrement significatifs sur le plan historique jusqu'à lui faire croiser la route d'un homme « inférieur » avec lequel il partage un lien sans le savoir[23]. L'écriture de l'Histoire et l'écriture du vécu personnel, l'expérience historique collective et le traumatisme individuel causé par l'histoire sont ici étroitement liés. Le texte suit un triple principe d'enchevêtrement[24] : l'historiographie officielle avec ses données et ses faits est entrelacée avec l'expérience subjective d'un inconnu, lui-même exposé à la marche du temps. À la fois, l'espace et le temps sont court-circuités de manière programmatique, l'Italie et l'Éthiopie, le présent et le passé se croisent, jusqu'à ce que, dans la scène finale, tous les fils convergent en un seul point.

Réparation et poétique du savoir

« L'icona » aborde le thème de la réparation et plus précisément la question de la restitution de biens culturels. Le texte est d'ailleurs très explicite quant au lexique de la réparation ; il est question de « ricambiare », « risolvere », « restituire », « dare un risarcimento in denaro » et « chiedere scusa » (Scego 2018, 79, 83)[25]. Et de même que le texte joue sur la coïncidence hasardeuse entre la grande et la petite histoire, sur la rencontre entre des personnages attestés et des sujets individuels impliqués dans

---

22 Sur le lien significatif entre la marche, la guérison et le récit en tant que pratiques éthiques dans les textes d'Igiaba Scego, voir Benedicty-Kokken (2017, 114–115).
23 À cet égard, les approches philosophiques de l'histoire par Carlo Ginzburg et Giovanni Levi semblent être mises en œuvre ici de manière narrative et fictive : le récit de Scego porte sur une « microstoria » au sens propre comme figuré.
24 La construction narrative est plus complexe que ce qui est décrit ici. En effet, aux nombreux croisements s'ajoutent des stratégies de parallélisation, non seulement en ce qui concerne la constellation des personnages, mais aussi en ce qui concerne les destins politiques comparables des représentants d'État des deux nations autrefois hostiles (le ministre des Affaires étrangères Aldo Moro et l'empereur d'Éthiopie), tout comme l'expérience simultanée de cette visite d'État par deux personnages « mineurs », symbolisant l'ancien appareil de pouvoir fasciste. Un fonctionnaire et un ancien soldat sont tous deux impliqués dans ce passé violent, mais tirent des conclusions opposées de cet imbroglio.
25 Voir également d'autres passages dans lesquels le texte parle un langage clair concernant la question des réparations : « rimettere in campo la giustizia che era stata negata al suo paese », « che la stele depredata tornasse ad Axum », « che i criminali di guerra che si erano macchiati di colpe orrende in Etiopia fossero giudicati da un tribunale internazionale » (Scego 2018, 78).

l'histoire, il relie également l'œuvre d'art historiquement, politiquement et culturellement significative, la stèle volée d'Axoum, à un petit objet d'art sacré du quotidien, une icône volée par un soldat de l'armée fasciste pendant la « campagne d'Éthiopie[26] ». En traitant simultanément le pillage et la restitution des deux biens culturels, le récit met en scène le problème de la réparation sur plusieurs niveaux : un niveau historico-politique, un niveau culturel et un niveau individuel-psychologique. Cette démarche est originale d'un point de vue de la poétique du savoir.

Dans « L'icona », le thème des crimes historiques contre l'humanité et des tentatives de réparation est abordé en tant qu'un savoir narré dans la littérature[27] : la réparation est évoquée comme un problème politique, juridique, économique et social, par exemple dans les pensées, les souvenirs et les projets d'avenir de l'empereur (Scego 2018, 80–81, 87). Ce motif apparaît ainsi comme l'objet de négociations complexes au niveau politique et comme le sujet de discours qui sont intégrés dans le récit de fiction comme des débats factuels.

La deuxième catégorie de la poétique du savoir, à savoir la manière dont les discours sociaux de réparation sont toujours façonnés par des procédures esthétiques ou par certaines stratégies linguistiques et narratives, joue également un rôle important dans le récit de Scego. La narratrice cite un article de journal du *Messaggero* de 1970, qui relate, dans un langage plutôt poétique, les déviations que l'empereur est contraint de suivre à travers Rome dans le but de lui cacher l'obélisque volé d'Axoum. Cet article est lui-même conçu comme un court récit littéraire. Il souligne notamment l'aspect émotionnel lié à la visite d'État, utilise des métaphores (« l'obelisco trapiantato ») (Scego 2018, 80) à l'aide d'une syntaxe ponctuée d'intensifications et de reports, avec laquelle, non seulement l'empereur, mais également la phrase finale elle-même semble prendre des détours stylistiques jusqu'à finalement arriver à la mention du lieu historiquement significatif où trône la stèle volée[28].

---

26 Le récit entremêle de manière complexe faits historiques et fiction. Dans son essai *Roma negata* de 2014, Scego raconte l'histoire de Giovanni Battista De Monte, un officier de l'armée fasciste, qui avait trouvé une icône chrétienne en Éthiopie, l'a fait restaurer et l'a emportée en Italie après son retour en 1947, avant de la restituer au Negus lors de sa visite d'État ; voir Scego (2014, 70–98). Pour une reconstruction des dimensions factuelle et fictionnelle du récit cf. aussi Kleinhans (2020, 22–25).

27 En faisant la distinction entre un « savoir narré dans la littérature », des « procédures littéraires de transfert dans des textes de savoir » et le « savoir littéraire », nous suivons l'approche de Borgards, Neumeyer, Pethes et Wübben (2013). Lire aussi Klausnitzer (2008) et Ette (2004, 2005, 2010).

28 Par ailleurs, une autre citation du *Messaggero* faisant référence au passé des protagonistes nomme leur position politique par une référence à la pratique culturelle du chant, à savoir à une chanson qui représente métonymiquement le fascisme ainsi que la violence raciste et sexiste : « i balilla cresciuti, che un tempo avevano cantato facetta nera » (Scego 2018, 81). Igiaba Scego présente le contexte

La troisième catégorie est cependant la plus déterminante pour notre propos : comment le récit parvient-il à générer un savoir spécifiquement littéraire sur la réparation et la restitution[29] ? Le texte produit-il un savoir expérientiel sur la violence, la culpabilité, la responsabilité et la réconciliation qui est mis en scène avec des moyens véritablement esthétiques ? Nous étudions ces questions en examinant de plus près les méthodes narratives déjà mentionnées dans l'introduction : les constructions chronotopiques ainsi que les perspectives narratives et expérientielles qui y sont associées, les stratégies intertextuelles et intermédiales, la relation entre les objets narrés, le langage et l'expérience du corps, ainsi qu'une dimension autoréflexive par laquelle le texte lui-même expose le rôle des pratiques culturelles de réparation qu'il raconte.

Procédés littéraires de la réparation

Construction du chronotope

La traversée de l'espace géographique et urbano-architectural[30] (Venise, Addis-Abeba, Massawa, Rome, Adoua et la vallée du Tembien sont mentionnés) se combine de manière complexe à la structure temporelle du récit. Le texte entremêle le présent d'énonciation (la visite d'État de l'empereur d'Éthiopie en Italie en novembre 1970), le passé (la bataille historique de 1896, la guerre d'Éthiopie menée par Mussolini en 1935/36, la visite d'État du ministre des Affaires étrangères Aldo Moro en Éthiopie durant l'été 1970) et le futur (l'assassinat prochain d'Aldo Moro, ainsi que le coup d'État militaire futur en Éthiopie qui mènera à l'abdication et à la mort de l'empereur en 1974)[31]. L'acte de réparation proprement dit se trouve à

---

historique et culturel ainsi qu'une analyse profonde de ce chant fasciste et sexiste dans son texte « The True Story of "Facetta Nera" » (2015).

29 Sur les stratégies esthétiques du transfert de connaissances littéraires, voir plus en détail Solte-Gresser (2023).

30 Susanne Kleinert analyse les constructions narratives de l'espace d'Igiaba Scego sur fond de re-cartographie postcoloniale (*re-mapping*), une procédure qui se prête également à la lecture de ce récit ; voir Kleinert (2013, 203). Sur le lien entre l'espace urbain, le corps et l'émotion dans le récit de Scego, voir aussi Bernini (2014, 477–494).

31 Le texte entrelace dans un ordre anachronique les multiples strates de souvenirs des personnages individuels avec leur expérience actuelle. Il existe de nombreuses prolepses et analepses narratives (internes et externes) qui relient les différentes époques et les événements politiques aux lieux historiques correspondants. Concernant cette stratégie d'écrire l'Histoire, voir aussi *Roma negata. Percorsi postcoloniali nella città* de Scego (2014). Cet essai déjà cité traite et critique les différents discours de mémoire qui se croisent sur la Piazza Capena de Rome où se trouvait

la fin du texte et consiste en une restitution à l'empereur d'une icône volée en Éthiopie. Cet acte ne peut donc pas être raconté sans rappeler les différentes ramifications de son contexte historique, culturel et géographique. Ce qui est décisif ici, c'est que ces dimensions ne se retrouvent pas dans le récit dans un ordre linéaire, ni correct d'un point de vue historiographique. Elles apparaissent plutôt dans le texte de la manière dont les sujets concernés les vivent. Qu'il s'agisse du représentant officiel de l'histoire ou du suiveur inconnu, ces dimensions surgissent de manière erratique, fragmentée et radicalement personnalisée : les personnages sont impliqués émotionnellement et de manière corporelle dans l'histoire militaire voire s'y identifient de manière traumatique.

Ces perceptions subjectives sont dues au fait que le texte, en plus des nombreuses analepses et prolepses, présente des alternances de focalisation. Non seulement le récit fait souvent des allers-retours entre les espaces et les temps, mais ces sauts sont toujours liés aux perceptions de certains personnages. Les nombreuses dates et faits mentionnés ne sont donc pas reproduits tels quels, mais de la manière dont les sujets historiques individuels s'en souviennent, voire les évoquent[32]. C'est particulièrement le cas pour Mario del Monte, un des deux protagonistes du texte : un ancien soldat italien traumatisé qui a participé à la campagne d'Abyssinie. Et ce n'est certainement pas une coïncidence si le traumatisme de Mario del Monte, qui est le véritable centre du texte, est décrit du point de vue restreint de sa femme : « La moglie, Teresa [. . .] sapeva che Mario era rotto dentro. Qualcosa era andato storto in quella guerra infame in cui li aveva trascinati Mussolini. Ma non chiedeva » (Scego 2018, 82)[33]. Le motif du regard détourné et de la volonté de ne pas (sa)voir traverse tout le récit. L'épouse n'est pas

---

jusqu'à 2005 la stèle d'Axoum : la présence de la mémoire des attaques du 11 septembre 2001 et la négation, respectivement le reniement, de la violence colonialiste et fasciste italienne durant la Seconde Guerre mondiale. Contrairement au récit « L'icona », dans ce texte Scego traite le sujet de la restitution de la stèle d'Axoum de manière factuelle et scientifique : elle se réfère aux faits historiques, cite des articles de journaux et présente ses sources dans des notes en bas de page.

32 Même les articles de journaux cités textuellement apparaissent de manière subjective dans le texte, à savoir dans la traduction par un interprète de l'empereur.

33 La constellation des personnages peut être considérée comme inhabituelle dans l'œuvre narrative de Scego. Alors que, par ailleurs, les personnages féminins sont presque toujours au centre de l'action, qu'ils ne correspondent que légèrement aux attributions traditionnelles des genres ou qu'ils les reflètent de manière critique, il s'agit d'une histoire dont l'intrigue est portée exclusivement par des hommes. La fonction du seul personnage féminin se limite au rôle (presque ironique) d'épouse et de mère, qui ne veut rien savoir de l'histoire et s'occupe plutôt des trois enfants, travaille à la cuisine et repasse les chemises (Scego 2018, 82). Cependant, le centre (vide) du texte est le viol et le meurtre de la jeune Éthiopienne, qui elle-même n'entre dans le récit que comme un objet silencieux. La dénonciation de la violence sexuelle, à son tour, peut sans aucun doute être considérée comme l'un des thèmes centraux de l'œuvre de Scego. Voir également Kirchmair (2017, 256).

la seule à fermer les yeux sur les violences commises ; même au niveau de la visite officielle, il s'agit d'éviter que les traces de la violence politique et de l'injustice historique ne soient vues librement (« occultare il passato » ; « evita[re] [...] di passare [...] all'obelisco ») (Scego 2018, 78, 80).

La structure de l'intrigue du récit se déroule donc selon différentes attitudes à l'égard de l'Histoire ; notamment sur la base des oppositions entre voir et ne pas voir, entre écrire l'histoire et vivre l'histoire, ainsi qu'entre suivre l'idéologie politique et y résister, postures qui seront examinées plus en détail ultérieurement[34]. Le potentiel littéraire de ce récit de réparation consiste donc d'abord à utiliser des moyens esthétiques pour dépeindre « ce que l'on ressent en étant à la merci des faits historiques[35] ». Le texte rend ces expériences compréhensibles en tant que fiction littéraire grâce aux procédures narratives d'immersion, de recentrage (Ryan 1991, 21–23), d'empathie et d'orientation des perspectives.

Intertextualité et intermédialité de la réparation

Il est frappant de constater à quel point le récit aborde les questions de réparation en utilisant différents types de textes et de médias. Ils sont tous étroitement liés à la thématique de l'injustice à réparer. Dans l'ensemble, on peut distinguer ici deux types de médias différents issus des discours sur les réparations, que Scego oppose de manière programmatique : les « textes » (au sens large) documentaires visant à l'objectivité sont opposés aux moyens fictionnels et esthétiques de traiter la violence coloniale. Cependant, ils déploient tous leur signification au niveau symbolique, à savoir en tant qu'objets et textes issus des pratiques culturelles de la mémoire.

En plus des médias documentaires déjà mentionnés, un dossier politique ainsi que les plans des villes de Rome et de Venise, sur lesquels on peut lire les traces de la guerre et du colonialisme, jouent un rôle crucial dans le récit. Lors de la visite d'État, les murs sont décorés de tapisseries historiques du XVIIe siècle. S'y ajoutent des discours politiques, des négociations diplomatiques, des procès-

---

34 Scego « forces historiography to open up to postcolonial thinking », comme le dit Roberto Derobertis à propos du roman *Rhoda* (Derobertis 2011, 265).
35 Nous adoptons ici l'approche de Hayden White, qui voit le potentiel des textes littéraires pour la compréhension de l'histoire, entre autres, dans leur perspective expérientielle subjective des faits historiques. Il attribue aux textes autobiographiques la capacité de représenter « what it felt like to have had to endure such "facts" » (White 2004, 123).

verbaux et des allocutions publiques, qui reflètent le discours officiel sur les réparations de la part des pouvoirs étatiques en présence. Enfin, le viol est capturé dans une photographie de guerre, comme un document de démonstration inhumaine de pouvoir[36]. Del Monte attribue lui-même son endoctrinement idéologique à la propagande fasciste que l'on peut lire dans des articles de journaux. Et l'on parle sans cesse de textes historiographiques, comme ceux des livres d'école et d'histoire, dans lesquels une nouvelle page doit être tournée, qui doit être reprise et réécrite.

En revanche, il existe une tout autre façon de comprendre le monde, celle vécue et représentée par Mario del Monte, l'ancien soldat de la « campagne d'Éthiopie ». Cette approche de la réalité s'oppose aux faits objectifs, historiquement authentifiés et publiquement acceptés. Del Monte les confronte à l'illusion : à un monde du possible, de l'improbable et du rêve. Cinéaste passionné, del Monte s'échappe de la réalité et pénètre dans des mondes fictifs par le biais du cinéma. Ainsi, l'accent est d'abord mis sur le potentiel d'évasion que présentent l'art et la culture[37]. Grâce au 7e art, del Monte échappe à la rigidité émotionnelle; les films deviennent une bouée de sauvetage, le cinéma sert littéralement de moyen de survie (« la sola ancora alla quale aggrapparsi per non affogare e morire ») (Scego 2018, 81). Mais en plus, c'est précisément l'immersion dans l'aventure et la fiction qui fera de del Monte un « héros » à la fin du récit. Il puise dans ce récit d'aventure le courage de s'opposer au cours de l'histoire et, contre toute attente, d'obtenir une rencontre personnelle avec l'empereur.

Cependant, del Monte n'est pas seulement animé par le pouvoir de la fiction. C'est aussi parce qu'il utilise l'art d'une manière particulière, « esthétique » dirait-on, c'est-à-dire d'une manière qui l'affecte physiquement et émotionnellement, qu'il est capable d'exploiter son potentiel réparateur. Ainsi, il sait que l'icône qu'il trouve près du crime représente une sainte dont la représentation suit des conventions esthétiques. Toutefois, il perçoit également la représentation comme un être vivant qui ressent la douleur et la joie (« addolorata [. . .], ma felice ») (Scego 2018, 83). Grâce à cette perception s'établit un lien émotionnel direct avec sa propre situation : il remarque une similitude entre la sainte et la jeune fille assassinée ; et c'est ce transfert dans le médium de l'art qui enclenche l'acte réparateur. Del Monte

---

[36] Ce passage mériterait une interprétation plus profonde dans le contexte des travaux de Susan Sontag sur la photographie de guerre ; cf. Sontag (2003). Emma Bond voit également un lien entre le regard masculin, la violence sexuelle, le colonialisme/racisme et la photographie dans l'œuvre de Scego, mais sans aborder « L'icona » ; cf. Bond (2018, 306–309).
[37] Quantitativement parlant, les descriptions des visites de del Monte au cinéma, avec leurs mentions de certains acteurs et actrices et des sentiments qu'ils suscitent chez le spectateur, occupent un espace exceptionnellement important dans ce récit pourtant très court (Scego 2018, 81).

rapporte l'œuvre d'art, effectuant ainsi une restitution au sens littéral du terme. Puisque l'image représente symboliquement les atrocités commises et la disparition d'une vie humaine, il tente une triple action par ce geste réparatoire : il essaye simultanément d'affronter la violence irréparable, d'assumer sa co-responsabilité et de soigner sa psyché traumatisée.

Langage, corps et objets de la réparation

Le récit montre clairement que le problème de la réparation est avant tout politique, que ce soit sur le plan du collectif-historique ou sur le plan de l'individuel-thérapeutique. Toutefois, il y est traité de façon symbolique. La destruction de vies humaines, l'humiliation, la dégradation et l'instrumentalisation de l'Autre constituent le sombre abîme qui se cache derrière l'obélisque d'Axoum et l'icône de la vallée du Tembien. Le cœur même du dommage ne saurait être réparé. L'injustice peut, au mieux, être reconnue dans le traitement de l'irréparable (Diagne 2021) qui s'effectue à travers un langage détourné, celui de la métonymie et du symbolique. En effet, d'une part, la stèle d'Axoum figure le symbole d'une culture détruite par l'impérialisme, et d'autre part l'icône, parce qu'elle ressemble à la jeune fille assassinée, devient l'objet dans lequel les horreurs du colonialisme – comme le viol, la destruction ou le pillage – sont transférées. Cet aspect de reconnaissance symbolique de l'irréparable, qui doit toujours accompagner l'acte de restitution, se reflète aussi explicitement dans le récit d'Igiaba Scego : alors que, dans le contexte de la stèle d'Axoum, les crimes contre l'humanité sont évoqués par une série de substantifs, c'est-à-dire qu'ils sont abstraits et résumés (l'empereur pense aux « gas iprite, le stragi, l'umiliazione dei corpi, i campi di concentramento ») (Scego 2018, 78), l'histoire de l'icône oblige à une prise de considération, à s'engager par une lecture empathique et identificatoire aux événements passés : sont ainsi racontés le viol d'une petite fille bien concrète, les circonstances de sa mort sans oublier certains détails comme les rires moqueurs des tortionnaires, métaphorisés en hyènes (Scego 2018, 83).

Quel langage est utilisé pour parler de l'irréparable ? De même que l'histoire se voit traitée à travers deux formes opposées – la narratrice distingue l'historiographie officielle de l'exploration esthétique ou fictionnelle du monde – le texte explore également une dichotomie du langage. L'historiographie apparaît à l'empereur, de même qu'à Mario del Monte comme un monde de documents stériles et de phrases creuses (« E lì grandi discorsi. Tanta retorica ») (Scego 2018, 79), qui efface tout ce qui est humain et vivant. Haïlé Sélassié s'approprie l'histoire d'une manière différente : par le corps, les sens et un langage que l'on peut attribuer à l'art plutôt qu'à la raison et à la connaissance scientifique[38]. Mario del Monte fait également l'expérience de la réalité avec le corps et les sens, voire à travers l'esthétique. Au lieu du fameux Négus des livres et des leçons d'école[39], il découvre maintenant Haïlé Sélassié « in carne e ossa » (Scego 2018, 81). Il tremble, ressent de la joie et imagine les événements à venir, à savoir l'interruption du protocole et la restitution de l'icône, comme un film de cinéma. Et ce n'est pas seulement le personnage, mais le récit lui-même qui bascule sur le mode du roman d'aventure peu avant sa fin. Les vaines tentatives de rencontrer l'empereur sont rendues avec de nombreux détails qui accroissent la tension dramatique : il est question d'événements spectaculaires (une arrestation), de coïncidences imprévisibles (la mauvaise voie ferrée), d'une rencontre ratée à un cheveu près et de la toute dernière chance de mettre ce « piano folle » (Scego 2018, 82) en œuvre.

Il est donc logique que l'Histoire soit anthropomorphisée dans le discours de la pensée des deux personnages principaux. Elle apparaît comme un être vivant dont les protagonistes sont à la merci[40]. Grâce à ce procédé rhétorique, le récit montre comment les personnages retrouvent une partie de leur autonomie (leur *agency*) au fil des événements. D'objets de l'Histoire, de victimes des circonstances historiques[41], ils deviennent – au moins temporairement – des sujets agissants qui enterrent l'ancienne Histoire (« seppellire quella storia » (Scego 2018, 79), la co-écrivent ou ancrent/encrent leur propre histoire. « L'icona » réalise ces différents points par ses propres moyens narratifs et rhétoriques.

---

[38] Haïlé Sélassié perçoit le fonctionnaire qui l'aide à traverser la passerelle branlante avant tout à travers son corps, sa voix désagréable et croassante ; et sa participation présumée à la campagne d'Éthiopie n'est pas nommée en tant que telle, mais évoquée à travers la chemise noire des soldats, leurs mains tachées de sang et le refrain d'une chanson fasciste. La relation de l'empereur avec le ministre italien des Affaires étrangères Aldo Moro est également expliquée exclusivement par la perception de son corps : « [b]ella fronte [. . .] [b]ella bocca », « mi dà fiducia questo italiano », « fronte ampia », « espressione franca » (Scego 2018, 78–79).
[39] « il negus tanto raccontato dai libri (quello di scuola incluso) » (Scego 2018, 81). Dans le texte, le protagoniste apparaît continuellement avec toutes ses majestueuses désignations supplémentaires et ses titres officiels (par exemple, Scego 2018, 77).
[40] D'abord, on est « costretto dalla storia », l'histoire est décrite comme « bastarda », « disattese » et « molesta » (Scego 2018, 76, 78–79), elle prend les participants par surprise et renverse l'ordre (Scego 2018, 80), avant qu'il ne s'agisse finalement d'agir hors de l'« agenda » (Scego 2018, 77), de tourner une nouvelle page du livre de l'histoire, de renverser le scénario et le rôle que les personnages sont censés y jouer (Scego 2018, 78).
[41] L'empereur est dépeint comme le représentant d'une nation vaincue, freinée par l'Italie dans ses démarches de réparation. Del Monte, à son tour, doit se rendre compte qu'il a été manipulé par les fascistes et qu'il s'est laissé prendre à leur propagande avant d'être contraint de participer aux atrocités.

Or, le langage joue un rôle décisif non seulement en termes stylistiques et rhétoriques, mais aussi en ce qui concerne le contenu thématique du récit. Le fait que del Monte réussisse à établir le contact avec l'empereur et à l'amener à faire une pause est dû au fait qu'il rejette sa propre langue pour se rapprocher de celle de l'autre. L'italien interpelle l'éthiopien en amharique, utilisant même le dialecte d'Addis-Abeba, et gagne ainsi l'attention d'Haïlé Sélassié. Ce moment est décisif, car c'est là que del Monte inverse la perspective : il se met à la place de l'autre, abandonne la langue des coupables et reconnaît la langue des victimes comme la seule possible pour créer ainsi un espace d'interaction (Trabant 2009, 309–328).

Bien sûr, ce n'est pas une coïncidence si la nouvelle effectue un mouvement de rotation pour revenir à son point de départ : à la fin du texte, nous nous retrouvons de nouveau sur la passerelle oscillante de Venise, avec le danger de la marée, pouvant causer à tout moment un accident[42]. Et non seulement sur le plan spatial, mais aussi sur le plan psychologique, deux personnages s'affrontent ici dans un moment de faiblesse et d'instabilité. Il est intéressant de noter que ce processus de dissolution (du rigide et du strict) est associé à l'art et à l'onirisme pour les personnages des deux cultures : l'empereur se sent transporté dans son enfance ou comme dans un rêve sur la place Saint-Marc inondée ; del Monte se voit comme un personnage de long-métrage, la rencontre avec l'empereur ressemble à un miracle (Scego 2018, 81), et un rêve se réalise finalement pour lui aussi (Scego 2018, 83).

La forme sous laquelle del Monte présente finalement sa préoccupation existentielle est aussi éloignée que possible de la rhétorique diplomatique officielle et du langage désincarné, dénué d'émotion des livres d'Histoire. Au lieu de rapporter les atrocités, il se mord la langue jusqu'au sang. À ce stade, la voix narrative hétérodiégétique restitue ce que le personnage ne peut pas dire, et elle le fait – le discours littéraire le permet – sur le mode du non-dit voire de la prétérition[43] : « Non riusciva a dire all'imperatore di quando [. . .], [d]i come . . . » (Scego 2018, 83). Le traumatisme ne peut pas être raconté par la personne concernée comme une histoire rationnellement compréhensible. Del Monte, comme il est dit à plusieurs reprises, « [non] [a]rriv[a] al punto » (Scego 2018, 83), il n'aborde son acte et sa culpabilité que de manière détournée et à travers de vaines tentatives ; il bafouille, parle d'une voix déformée par la douleur, ne produit que des fragments de mots individuels et finit par interrompre brutalement son récit. Au-delà du plaidoyer d'excuses, que del Monte formule finalement au nom de tout

---

42 Sur le lien entre l'espace urbain, le corps humain et l'objet, voir Le Gouez (2008, 465–474).
43 Il s'agit donc d'une prétérition sur le niveau rhétorique.

son peuple (« tutti gli italiani ») (Scego 2018, 83), c'est surtout par son langage corporel que ce dernier fait comprendre à son homologue la nécessité de réparation.

Le texte se termine par un geste d'humilité ; l'empereur et l'ancien soldat ne sont plus à hauteur d'yeux, mais ce dernier se prosterne en pleurant à ses pieds. Au moment où la voix se brise, c'est l'objet d'art, l'icône, qui acquiert le pouvoir décisif d'agir : chargé d'une puissance d'action (*agency*) (Latour 2007 ; Brown 2003), l'objet change de mains et continue de raconter l'histoire là où la capacité humaine à la raconter échoue. Ces deux personnages deviennent ainsi simultanément des personnalités individuelles et des représentants de leurs pays respectifs[44]. Alors que la restitution de la stèle n'est que l'objet de négociations politiques relevant de questions du droit international et n'est donc pas réalisée dans la trame narrative[45], la restitution du bien culturel a lieu à un niveau personnel. L'icône est remise par un individu à un autre au moment où les deux participants sortent des rôles qui leur sont attribués. Ils abandonnent les schémas traditionnels de perception dualiste, voire simpliste de l'ami et de l'ennemi[46] ; ils admettent leur faiblesse et s'exposent au cours de l'Histoire en tant qu'êtres humains individuels « in carne e ossa » (Scego 2018, 81). L'individu réalise donc le geste d'humilité que l'État a manqué. On doit comprendre cet acte comme la compensation d'une faille politique.

Réparation et autoréflexivité

Les lacunes de l'historiographie, les éléments supprimés des livres d'histoire ou soumis à une désinformation politico-idéologique dans les médias publics, sont racontés ici avec des moyens poétiques et des procédures propres à la littérature. Non seulement la restitution de l'icône et de la stèle, mais aussi le récit de cette histoire en partie factuelle, en partie fictive, sur la tentative de restitution constitue donc une pratique culturelle de réparation. Par le concept d'une « pratique littéraire » de la réparation, nous faisons référence à l'ouvrage d'Alexandre Gefen, *Réparer le monde*, qui voit le potentiel le plus important de la littérature

---

[44] Del Monte parle pour « tutti gli italiani », le Négus représente « [i]l suo popolo » (Scego 2018, 83).

[45] Cependant, le fait que la stèle soit effectivement restituée en 2002, laissant un vide sur la Piazza Capena à Rome, est le sujet du roman de Scego, *La mia casa è dove sono*. Ici, la narratrice remplit le vide créé dans la ville avec des personnages de sa propre histoire familiale et pense à ériger un mémorial aux victimes du colonialisme. Cf. Scego (2010, 71–91).

[46] Ainsi « erano fratelli » (Scego 2018, 80), « [c]ombattevamo lo stesso nemico, lo stesso fottutissimo fascismo » et « "uno dei miei migliori amici era del Corno d'Africa". Haile Sellasie pensò in quel momento quanto la storia fosse sorprendente. Quanto tutto nella vita fosse alle fine ingarbugliato » (Scego 2018, 79–80).

contemporaine (notamment française) dans les possibilités réparatrices et thérapeutiques qu'elle peut offrir (Gefen 2017). Gefen exprime un changement de paradigme fondamental pour la littérature du XXIe siècle[47] ; il s'agit « d'exiger que la littérature et la lecture réparent, rénovent, ressoudent, comblent les failles des communautés contemporaines, de retisser l'histoire collective et personnelle ». Le potentiel de la littérature consiste selon lui à « mettre des mots sur le perdu ou l'indicible, chercher à cerner et à intervenir sur les blessures du monde » (Gefen 2017, 11).

Par des déplacements et des synthèses symboliques, « L'icona » aborde l'expérience subjective de l'impérialisme, de la guerre et de ses conséquences traumatiques. Lorsque la honte, la culpabilité et le traumatisme empêchent la parole et que les victimes n'ont pas ou plus de voix propre, une instance narrative littéraire doit se lever pour la prendre ou la leur rendre. C'est exactement ce que fait Igiaba Scego à l'aide de son récit. Cependant, la voix narrative littéraire ne traite pas les lacunes de l'Histoire en les comblant ou en les voilant. Au contraire, comme le souligne également Alexandre Gefen, elle fait de ces lacunes et de ces silences un sujet de discussion sur le plan symbolique en les explorant sur un plan narratif par le biais de l'empathie, de la transmission des affects et de la démarche vers l'Autre, vers ce qui dépasse son propre horizon et apparaît comme étranger (Gefen 2017, 13, 24).

Dans une interview, l'autrice elle-même exprime le potentiel transformateur et réparateur de la littérature – la narration de l'oublié, de l'exclu et du refoulé – comme suit :

> The system turns us into numbers. These numbers need to be transformed into stories, faces, relationships, eyes that gaze back at you, and this transformation is only possible through literature [. . .] because of the ways that literature can transform [. . .] those forgotten stories – I'm thinking of colonialism – into something material that you can grasp: a person, a story, a love story, a disappointment, a desperation (Ali 2020, 159).

Avec son histoire, Scego intervient elle-même dans le cours de l'histoire : les réparations obstinées et chancelantes autour de l'obélisque d'Axoum sont dynamisées littérairement par l'invention d'un personnage qui cherche à réparer et qui est disposé à le faire, et transposant ainsi le public et le collectif en individuel et subjectif.

---

[47] « Cette littérature affirme que la langue et le récit sont des puissances réparatrices tout en se déclinant aussi dans des traditions esthétiques fort diverses », formule Gefen (2017, 13) dans le prolongement des approches théoriques littéraires de Paul Ricœur et Roland Barthes. Il reprend ainsi le concept clé du *tiqqun olam* issu de la tradition mystique du judaïsme (« une doctrine de la responsabilisation et de la réparation du monde », Gefen 2017, 17), qu'il exploite pour son analyse de la littérature contemporaine.

Le récit démontre de manière impressionnante à quel point ces deux niveaux sont également politiques.

La réaction de l'empereur face à la restitution de l'icône est tue par le texte. Le récit ne permet donc pas de savoir si la réparation peut un jour réussir sur le plan économique, juridique ou politique. Mais en tant que pratique symbolique et culturelle de réparation, le texte pose la question de ses conditions, teste des pistes d'action et de comportement, incite à la responsabilité personnelle, réfléchit sur l'incapacité des mots et met en scène la lutte des acteurs pour trouver un geste approprié face aux crimes contre l'humanité.

« Il y a de nombreuses formes d'écriture » écrit W.G. Sebald, « mais c'est seulement dans la littérature que l'on a affaire, au-delà de l'enregistrement des faits et au-delà de la science, à une tentative de restitution » (Sebald 2009, 238). C'est donc comme cela que se place la mission de la narration par rapport à l'écriture de l'histoire : elle seule est en mesure de saisir la part de réalité qui ne se manifeste que lentement, en tant qu'événement intérieur de l'histoire, dans le récit[48]. Pour qu'il existe, il faut d'abord donner à cet événement une forme, car il se développe uniquement dans l'épanouissement d'une subjectivité, même s'il n'en est pas moins réel.

Références

Ali, Ashna. « Activist by Default. An Interview with Igiaba Scego ». *The Minnesota Review* 94 (2020) : 157–166.

Appadurai, Arjun. *The Social Life of Things. Commodities in Cultural Perspective.* Cambridge : Cambridge University Press, 1986.

Attia, Kader. « La réparation, c'est la conscience de la blessure ». *Décolonisons les Arts !*. Éd. Leïla Cukierman, Gerty Dambury et Françoise Vergès. Paris : L'Arche, 2019, 11–14.

Beck, Ulrich et Edgar Grande. « Varieties of Second Modernity: the Cosmopolitan Turn in Social and Political Theory and Research ». *The British Journal of Sociology* 61.3 (2010) : 409–443.

Bekerie, Avele. « The Rise of the Aksum Obelisk is the Rise of Ethiopian History ». *Horn of Africa* 23 (2005) : 85–101.

Benedicty-Kokken, Alessandra. « Une Méditerranée polyvalente, ou le trope du nomadisme dans l'œuvre littéraire d'Igiaba Scego et d'Abdourahman A. Waberi ». *RELIEF : Revue électronique de littérature française* 11.2 (2017) : 103–122.

Bernini, Stefania. « Tra Mogadiscio e Roma: Le mappe emotive di Igiaba Scego ». *Forum Italicum* 48.3 (2014) : 477–494.

Bianchi, Rino et Igiaba Scego. *Roma negata. Percorsi postcoloniali nella città.* Rome : Ediesse, 2020 [2014].

---

48 Cf. Messling (2023b).

Bond, Emma. « Photography: Memorial Intertexts in New Writing by Maaza Mengiste, Nadifa Mohamed, and Igiaba Scego ». *The Horn of Africa and Italy*. Éd. Simone Brioni et Shimelis Bonsa Gulema. Oxford : Peter Lang, 2018, 295–318.

Borgards, Roland, Harald Neumeyer, Nicolas Pethes et Yvonne Wübben. Éds. *Literatur und Wissen. Ein interdisziplinäres Handbuch*. Stuttgart : Metzler, 2013.

Brown, Bill. *A Sense of Things. The Object Matter of American Literature*. Chicago : University of Chicago Press, 2003.

Cassin, Barbara, Olivier Cayla et Philippe-Joseph Salazar. Éds. *Vérité, Réconciliation, Réparation*. Paris : Le Seuil/Le genre humain, 2004.

Chakrabarty, Dipesh. « The Climate of History: Four Theses ». *Critical Inquiry* 35.2 (2009) : 197–222.

Coats, Ta-Nihisi. « The Case for Reparations ». *The Atlantic* (2014). https://www.theatlantic.com/magazine/archive/2014/06/the-case-for-reparations/361631/ (30 août 2021).

Demanze, Laurent. *Un nouvel âge de l'enquête. Portraits de l'écrivain contemporain en enquêteur*. Paris : Corti, 2019.

Derobertis, Roberto. « "Holding all the Pieces together". Colonial Legacies and Postcolonial Futures in the Writings of Igiaba Scego and Cristina Ali Farah ». *Experiences of Freedom in Postcolonial Literatures and Cultures*. Éd. Annalisa Oboe et Shaul Bassi. New York : Routledge, 2011, 265–274.

Derrida, Jacques. « Versöhnung, ubuntu, pardon : quel genre ? ». *Vérité, Réconciliation, Réparation*. Éd. Barbara Cassin, Olivier Cayla et Philippe-Joseph Salazar. Paris : Le Seuil/Le genre humain, 2004, 111–156.

Diagne, Souleymane Bachir. « Penser l'universel avec Étienne Balibar ». *Raison publique* 19.2 (2014a) : 15–21.

_____. « L'universel latéral comme traduction ». *Les Pluriels de Barbara Cassin ou le partage des équivoques*. Éd. Michèle Gendreau-Massaloux et Xavier North. Lormont : Le Bord de L'Eau, 2014b, 243–256.

_____. « Faire humanité ensemble et ensemble habiter la terre ». *Présence Africaine* 1.193 (2016) : 11–19.

Diagne, Souleymane Bachir et Jean-Loup Amselle. *En quête d'Afrique(s) : universalisme et pensée décoloniale*. Paris : Albin Michel, 2018.

Ette, Ottmar. *ÜberLebenswissen. Die Aufgabe der Philologie*. Berlin : Kadmos, 2004.

_____. *ZwischenWeltenSchreiben. Literaturen ohne festen Wohnsitz (ÜberLebenswissen II)*. Berlin : Kadmos, 2005.

_____. *ZusammenLebenswissen. List, Last und Lust literarischer Konvivenz im globalen Maßstab. (ÜberLebenswissen III)*. Berlin : Kadmos, 2010.

Fanon, Frantz. *Les damnés de la terre*. Paris : La Découverte, 2000 [1961].

Foucault, Michel. *Le courage de la vérité. Le Gouvernement de soi et des autres II*. Cours au Collège de France (1983–1984). Paris : Gallimard/Le Seuil (Hautes Études), 2009.

Gefen, Alexandre. *Réparer le monde. La littérature française face au XXIe siècle*. Paris : Corti, 2017.

Ginzburg, Carlo. « Traces. Racines d'un paradigme indiciaire ». *Mythes, emblèmes, traces. Morphologie et histoire*. Éd. Carlo Ginzburg. Trad. Monique Aymart et al. Lagrasse : Verdier, 2010 [1979], 139–180.

_____. *Le fromage et les vers. L'univers d'un meunier du XVIe siècle*. Trad. Monique Aymard. Paris : Flammarion, 2019 [1976].

Hasenkamp, Milena. « Steinmeier sieht Mitverantwortung Deutschlands für „Tragödie" in Afghanistan ». *DER SPIEGEL Online*, 17 août 2021. https://www.spiegel.de/politik/deutschland/frank-walter-steinmeier-siehtmitverantwortung-fuer-tragoedie-in-afghanistan-bei-deutschland-a-c5f0101f-66b5-4c49-a86f-352f7db2902c (2 février 2023).

Hofmann, Franck et Markus Messling. Éds. *The Epoch of Universalism / L'époque de l'universalisme (1769–1989)*. Berlin, Boston : De Gruyter, 2021.

Kaleck, Wolfgang. « Reparationen für koloniale Völkermorde? ». *Rhinozeros. Europa im Übergang* 1 (2021) : 129–135.

Kalifa, Dominique. « Enquête et "culture de l'enquête" au XIXe siècle ». *Romantisme* 149.3 (2010) : 3–23.

Kirchmair, Maria. *Postkoloniale Literatur in Italien. Raum und Bewegung in Erzählungen des Widerständigen*. Bielefeld : transcript Verlag, 2017.

Klausnitzer, Ralf. *Literatur und Wissen. Zugänge – Modelle – Analysen*. Berlin, New York : De Gruyter, 2008.

Kleinert, Susanne. « Transkulturalität, Erzählperspektive und oraler Erzählstil in Igiaba Scego's *Oltre Babilonia* und *La mia casa è dovo sono* ». *Transkulturelle italophone Literatur : Letteratura italofona transculturale*. Éd. Martha Kleinhans et Richard Schwaderer. Wurtzbourg : Königshausen & Neumann, 2013, 201–218.

Kleinhans, Martha. « Vorwort ». *Dismatria und weitere Texte*. Éd. Igiaba Scego. Trad. Ruth Mader-Koltey. Fribourg-en-Brisgau : nonsolo, 2020, 5–31.

Lagatz, Merten. « Wiedersehensfreude in Axum ». *Beute. Ein Bildatlas zu Kunstraub und Kulturerbe*. Éd. Merten Lagatz, Bénédicte Savoy et Philippa Sissis. Berlin : Matthes & Seitz, 2021, 364–367.

Latour, Bruno. *Eine neue Soziologie für eine neue Gesellschaft. Einführung in die Akteur-Netzwerk-Theorie*. Francfort-sur-le-Main : Suhrkamp, 2007.

Le Gouez, Brigitte. « Recompositions identitaires chez Igiaba Scego, "écrivaine migrante" : Entre la mémoire somalienne et l'invention quotidienne de la Rome d'aujourd'hui ». *Culture et mémoire : Représentations contemporaines de la mémoire dans les espaces mémoriels, les arts du visuel, la littérature et le théâtre*. Éd. Carola Hähnel-Mesnard, Marie Liénard-Yeterian et Cristina Marinas. Palaiseau : Les Éditions de l'École Polytechnique, 2008, 465–474.

Levi, Giovanni. « The Origins of the Modern State and the Microhistorical Perspective ». *Mikrogeschichte, Makrogeschichte. Komplementär oder inkommensurabel ?* Éd. Jürgen Schlumbohm. Goettingen : Wallstein, 2000, 53–82.

Messling, Markus et al. « Rhinozeros asks. . . Souleymane Bachir Diagne: "What is reparation?" ». *Rhinozeros. Europa im Übergang*, vidéo, 2021. https://www.rhinozeros-projekt.de/zeitschrift/das-projekt (27 août 2021).

———. *L'universel après l'universalisme. Des littératures francophones du contemporain*. Trad. Olivier Mannoni. Préface de Souleymane Bachir Diagne. Paris : Presses Universitaires de France, 2023a [2019].

———. « *Thésée* ou *Les Berlin* de Camille de Tolédo. Subjectivité et vérité historique ». *Camille de Toledo*. Éd. Christine Marcandier. Paris : Éditions Classiques Garnier, 2023b (sous presse).

Revel, Jacques. *Jeux d'échelles. La micro-analyse à l'expérience*. Paris : Gallimard/Le Seuil, 1996.

Ryan, Marie-Laure. *Possible Worlds, Artificial Intelligence, and Narrative Theory*. Bloomington et Londres : Indiana University Press, 1991.

Santi, Massimiliano. *La stele di Axum: da bottino di guerra a patrimonio dell'umanità. Una storia italiana*. Milan : Mimesis, 2014.

Sarr, Felwine et Bénédicte Savoy. *Restituer le patrimoine africain*. Paris : Philippe Rey/Le Seuil, 2018.

Savoy, Bénédicte. *Le long combat de l'Afrique pour son art. Histoire d'une défaite postcoloniale*. Paris : Le Seuil, 2023 [2021].

Scego, Igiaba. *La mia casa è dove sono*. Milan : R.C.S. Libri, 2010.

———. « The True Story of "Facetta Nera" ». *Words without Borders. The Online Magazine for International Literature*, 2016 [2015]. https://www.wordswithoutborders.org/article/april-2016-women-write-war-the-true-story-faccetta-negra-igiaba-scego (23 mai 2021).

———. « L'icona ». *Vite allo specchio. Dieci nuovi protagonisti della scena letteraria italiana*. Éd. Simona Giorgi et al. Fribourg-en-Brisgau : nonsolo, 2018, 75–84.
Schlumbohm, Jürgen. « Mikrogeschichte – Makrogeschichte: Zur Eröffnung einer Debatte ». *Mikrogeschichte, Makrogeschichte. Komplementär oder inkommensurabel ?* Éd. Jürgen Schlumbohm. Goettingen : Wallstein, 2000, 7–32.
Scott, David. *Refashioning Futures. Criticism after Postcoloniality*. Princeton : Princeton University Press, 1999.
Sebald, W.G. « Une tentative de restitution ». *Campo Santo*. Trad. Patrick Charbonneau. Arles : Actes Sud, 2009.
Solte-Gresser, Christiane. *Shoah-Träume. Vergleichende Studien zum Traum als Erzählverfahren*. Paderborn : Fink, 2021.
———. « Materialität von Schrift und Weltwissen ». *Grundwissen der Literaturwissenschaft: Weltliteratur*. Éd. Vittoria Borsò et Schamma Schahadat. Berlin : De Gruyter, 2023 (sous presse).
Sontag, Susan. *Regarding the Pain of Others*. New York : Farrar, Straus & Giroux, 2003.
Tharoor, Shashi. « Können Reparationszahlungen die Schulden der Geschichte jemals begleichen ? ». *Rhinozeros. Europa im Übergang* 1 (2021) : 68–73.
Trabant, Jürgen. « Gebellte Sprache. Über das Deutsche ». *Berlin-Brandenburgische Akademie der Wissenschaften: Berichte und Abhandlungen* 13 (2009) : 309–328.
Wallerstein, Immanuel. *European Universalism: The Rhetoric of Power*. New York : New Press, 2006.
White, Hayden. « Figural Realism in Witness Literature ». *Parallax* 10 (2004) : 113–124.

Part II: **Museums, Art, and Entangled Histories**

Deuxième partie : **Le musée, les arts, et les histoires entrelacées**

Fig. 1: Kader Attia, *Les Entrelacs de l'Objet* (*The Object's Interlacing*), 2020. Installation contenant un vidéo (78 min.) et 17 objets (copies d'artefacts africains en bois ou en nylon, imprimées en 3D), faisant partie de l'exposition *Fragments of Repair/Kader Attia*, BAK, basis voor actuele kunst, Utrecht, 2021.
Photo: Tom Janssen.

Kader Attia
Les Entrelacs de l'Objet | The Object's Interlacing

Contexte: Le présent chapitre est un extrait transcrit du film *Les Entrelacs de l'Objet | The Object's Interlacing*, réalisé par Kader Attia en 2020 et diffusé notamment dans son exposition *Fragments of Repair* à Utrecht (2021, basis voor actuele kunst) et à Zürich (2020, Kunsthaus Zürich). Le film se base sur de multiples interviews avec des acteurs majeurs dans les débats actuels autour de la restitution d'objets culturels spoliés pendant le colonialisme et l'impérialisme européen – et du processus de réparation lié à ce débat. Il s'agit ainsi d'un croisement de réflexions d'activistes, intellectuels, artistes et commissaires d'exposition qui touche également au cœur de l'œuvre de Kader Attia lui-même, artiste et intellectuel franco-algérien dont les nombreux travaux scientifiques et artistiques traitent de la réparation des violences de notre modernité. Le texte qui suit est une sélection, un collage enchevêtré de textes organisés sur des thématiques majeures et non exclusives. La première section lance le débat sur le contexte d'acquisition des objets d'art africains dans les musées européens et permet à la seconde et troisième de rebondir sur les transformations à la suite de leurs déplacements. Alors que la quatrième section questionne leurs fonctions (artistiques, sociales, politiques, psychologiques) passées, présentes et futures, la cinquième réfléchit sur des questions épistémologiques et géopolitiques liées aux soi-disant objets d'art ou objets culturels. La sixième section démasque les raisons de l'échec d'une première tentative de restitutions dans les années 1980. Finalement, les deux dernières sections reviennent à des questions sous-jacentes mais principales dans ce débat, rappelant l'irréparabilité fondamentale de crimes contre l'humanité et l'importance de refuser toute idée de pureté culturelle. Ceci dit, la répartition des prises de parole en ces sections est certainement contestable, indiquée seulement par des impressions visuelles du film, et les différentes interventions sont présentées comme des aphorismes pour souligner leur caractère en même temps indépendant et dialogique – des entrelacs de contextes et de perspectives, similaires aux entrelacs des « objets » eux-mêmes.

Mots-clés : restitution ; réparation ; irréparabilité ; objets mutants ; resocialisation

Fig. 2: Sylvain Sankale. Kader Attia, *Les Entrelacs de l'Objet* | *The Object's Interlacing* (2020, 00:02:28).

Sylvain SANKALE : Quand on est confronté à une histoire comme la mienne qui peut croiser par endroits la grande histoire et la petite histoire. Quand cette histoire se déroule dans le champ de la colonisation avec toutes les dérives, les abus et les excès que l'on peut imaginer avec évidemment, non seulement l'histoire coloniale mais avant cela l'histoire de l'esclavage etc. etc. On doit être prêt à trouver de tout . . . !

Serge GUÉZO : Je suis descendant de la lignée du fils aîné du roi Guézo: c'est-à-dire qu'on peut m'identifier dans la lignée royale. Il y a Khéglabé Guézo. La particule équivaut au « de », à partir de laquelle on sait l'ordre de chacun.

SANKALE : Cela me pose des difficultés si par exemple je voulais, comme j'en ai l'ambition, écrire une espèce de saga familiale, à travers les siècles. Je me demande que faire de ces gens qui étaient objectivement des salopards (pour parler vulgairement) ? Est-ce que j'élude leur existence ou est-ce que j'assume ? Ceci ne veut pas dire apprécier, aimer, ou rien du tout ! Mais c'est dire une réalité historique qui est importante, parce qu'elle permet de montrer aussi la contradiction des personnages.

GUÉZO : Au Bénin, on considère qu'on a été défait par une guerre coloniale. Il y a eu deux officiers français, dont l'un va particulièrement rentrer dans l'histoire parce qu'il est métis : c'est le colonel Dodds. Son père est alsacien et sa mère sénégalaise de Saint Louis. Sa famille existe toujours, au Sénégal, et ce colonel, qui va être décoré, et qui connaîtra la gloire pour avoir mis fin à la guerre du Dahomey, a cette connaissance parce qu'étant africain, il a la sensibilité et la possibilité de pouvoir, sur le plan stratégique, contribuer à des trahisons.

SANKALE : Il est métis du Sénégal, né au Sénégal, de deux parents métisses du Sénégal ! Donc si tu veux il n'était pas là par hasard . . .

GUÉZO : Sur le plan de la connaissance de leur environnement, les Dahoméens connaissent mieux leur territoire. Cela va de soi. Le roi de Béhanzin prend la décision et ordonne au collège des prêtres et aux adeptes de la divinité Ogoun de le déplacer du centre – c'est à dire de la capitale du royaume Abomey vers la côte à Glékhoué (c'est à dire « le jardin des rois » ; c'est comme cela qu'on appelle Ouidah). Il décide de déplacer le dieu Ogoun, parce que c'est le dieu du tonnerre et de la guerre. En termes de symbolisme et de confiance, pour les soldats et les femmes amazones (les Agoledjié), c'est très important. Il faut rappeler que l'élite de l'armée était composée d'une armée de femmes et d'une armée d'hommes. Pour le terrestre et pour la victoire finale, il fallait que le dieu Ogoun joue son rôle métaphysique, psychique et mental. Ça va être un pouvoir ! Dodds sachant tout cela, c'était pour lui aussi un challenge de vaincre le dieu Ogoun! Il va aussi l'utiliser comme moyen de propagande, en disant : « Il y va de notre sort de vaincre : nous ne vaincrons pas seulement Abomey ou le roi Béhanzin, mais nous vaincrons également le dieu Ogoun ». Donc les missionnaires étaient également très intéressés par cette bataille qui s'annonçait. Et on rentre à ce moment-là dans la perception de deux mondes complètement différents : la notion de temporalité et d'a-temporalité, et la notion chrétienne ou manichéenne du bien et du mal. Et ceci va profondément changer nos comportements... En prenant un officier africain, du fait qu'il soit métissé, c'est une manière de dire que la meilleure des armes est le colonel Dodds. Et en décidant cela, ils pensent fragiliser l'armée dahoméenne.

SANKALE : Si on l'a choisi pour faire cette campagne, c'est parce qu'il était métis. On a dit qu'il n'y avait qu'un africain qui pouvait comprendre ce qui se passait... Tu vois ce que je veux dire... et c'est toute l'ambiguïté du métissage, où, finalement, il était africain tout en étant général français... Tu vois un petit peu la confrontation.

GUÉZO : La trahison ne vient pas de loin et ce sont les gens qui sont le plus proches de vous, qui vous connaissent le mieux, qui vont vous trahir et c'est la raison pour laquelle cela fait plus de mal. Pour la France, pour l'armée, pour le corps expéditionnaire de Nantes etc. ce dieu mérite tout le respect qui se doit, c'est-à-dire on ne l'a même pas exposé au Quai Branly mais au Louvre, pour montrer que ce n'est pas seulement un objet artistique, mais que cela a une valeur de propagande et de domination des âmes et consciences de civilisations passées ou perdues, puisque la colonisation va nous penser, nommer, déterminer, aliéner, pour finir par dire qu'on n'a pas d'histoire !

Les Entrelacs de l'Objet | The Object's Interlacing — 69

Fig. 3: Souleymane Bachir Diagne. Kader Attia, *Les Entrelacs de l'Objet | The Object's Interlacing* (2020, 00:12:16).

Felwine SARR : La rencontre de beaucoup de peuples d'Afrique avec ces monothéismes sémitiques a été l'occasion, dans certains cas, d'une volonté d'effacer, d'éliminer les productions culturelles et spirituelles que l'on considérait comme impies, que l'on considérait comme sauvages.

> SANKALE : C'est toute l'ambiguïté aussi des religieux... Les religieux catholiques disaient : « Bon, eh bien, puisque vous avez abandonné vos fétiches, amenez-les-nous ». Et donc les gens les ont amenés, puisqu'ils s'étaient convertis.

Souleymane Bachir DIAGNE : Au fond les objets qui sont devenus des objets d'arts africains, qui sont devenus des objets d'art, étaient censés participer à la cosmologie locale : Ils entraient dans cette cosmologie, ils avaient une signification religieuse, sociale et culturelle, qui consistait pour ces objets à vivre dans le cadre de la cosmologie locale. Les transformer en objets de musée, c'est déjà une première mutation... Les avoir aussi transportés, pour une majorité d'entre eux, hors d'Afrique et dans les musées européens et américains a été une autre mutation. Et puis aujourd'hui le fait d'envisager ce que signifient des musées en Afrique est aussi une autre forme de mutation. Ces objets sont donc des objets mutants, dans le sens où d'abord ils voyagent de territoires en territoires, mais aussi d'une signification donnée à une nouvelle signification...

> Bénédicte SAVOY : Ce n'est pas anodin de prendre à des cultures, quelles qu'elles soient, de prendre massivement des patrimoines culturels, des objets culturels, c'est-à-dire des objets qui servent de transmetteurs de génération en génération, pour continuer à produire de la culture, de la littérature etc.

DIAGNE : Et il y a une autre mutation qui est extérieure, mais qui aujourd'hui fait partie intégrante de ces objets, c'est pour ceux d'entre eux qui ont été pris en Afrique, en général dans des conditions de violences structurelles coloniales, et transportés en Europe, et se retrouvant d'abord dans les musées ethnographiques, puis aujourd'hui dans les musées tout simplement en Europe et en Amérique : Il y a ce voyage...

> SAVOY : Qui prend ? Pourquoi ? À quel moment ? Avec quelle force, quelle arme ? Qui porte quoi ? Qui est dissocié de sa propre culture sur son propre dos ? Symboliquement, non seulement on te prend tes objets, mais en plus on te les fait porter toi-même. On te les fait *déporter* toi-même. Non seulement on te prend ce très grand tambour de 250 kilos, qui est là depuis 300 ans dans ce village, et qui a une importance sociale considérable. Non seulement on te le prend, mais en plus on te le fait porter jusqu'à en crever, pour certains. Et

ce au prix du dépeuplement des villages où les gens ne sont plus. Ce sont les hommes, les femmes parfois, voire des enfants qui portent, donc ils peuvent plus s'occuper de l'agriculture etc.

DIAGNE : Et la raison pour laquelle je dis que c'est une mutation extérieure, parce que c'est un voyage, mais qui s'est intériorisé, c'est que ce voyage a profondément transformé ces objets, ne serait-ce que par leur caractérisation à un moment donné comme objets esthétiques.

SAVOY : Toutes conséquences de ces déplacements, c'est ce qui est pour moi la question cruciale, et le plus invisible, à mon avis, dans ces institutions de musées qui sont faites pour montrer autre chose.

Fig. 4: Massamba Guèye. Kader Attia, *Les Entrelacs de l'Objet* | *The Object's Interlacing* (2020, 00:16:18).

GUÉZO : Quand ma fille me demande pourquoi paie-t-on pour voir ce qui est à nous, mon impuissance est de reconnaître que le chasseur a gagné . . . Mais il raconte l'histoire de la chasse en disant qu'il a gagné, sans dire combien d'entre eux, nous les lions, nous avons mangés ou blessés . . . Il faut qu'on puisse me donner la capacité de dire que j'en ai aussi vaincu. Il ne faut plus que j'aie la mésestime de moi-même . . . J'ai vécu avec cette souffrance. Je pense que c'est propre à tout immigré d'avoir perdu quelque chose. C'est cela, la mésestime de soi-même. La peur la plus terrible, c'est de la transmettre aux autres . . .

Massamba GUÈYE : Pourquoi dois-je mettre mon enfant dans une école qui contredit mon savoir ? Moi je sais comment les plantes fonctionnent, je sais comment on fabrique les prédispositions nécessaires à une sociabilité. Mais l'école française dit le contraire. À partir du moment où elle dit le contraire, que vais-je faire ? Je vais écouter celui qui vient de l'autre côté, celui qui a été formé par un européanisme. Mais ce qu'il va dire sur l'histoire de son propre village va contredire ce que moi je sais sur l'histoire de mon propre village. C'est cette confusion-là qui a créé une sorte de névrose intellectuelle. Et donc même sans s'en rendre compte, un intellectuel comme moi ne sait pas qu'il est sous l'emprise de l'inconscient qu'on lui a inculqué.

SARR : Le souvenir que j'ai de ma jeunesse, c'est que le musée n'était pas le lieu des objets. Les objets étaient dans la quotidienneté. Je veux dire . . . On va en Casamance, dans un endroit sacré, on y trouve des masques. Dans une cérémonie, on en trouve aussi, et on n'y fait même pas trop attention, tellement ils appartiennent aux espaces du quotidien. [. . .] Je me rappelle des objets à charge spirituelle, de la sorte de fascination que cela crée, et de champs énergétiques que cela irradie, et qu'on avait bien conscience que ces objets étaient habités, c'est-à-dire qu'on avait bien conscience que ce n'étaient pas des objets, mais que c'étaient des sujets et que ces sujets pouvaient être agissants, et qu'ils étaient dotés de capacités . . . et que tout cela était réel . . .

SAVOY : Les moments d'affections, de tristesse même, c'est toujours dans les moments où j'ai lu des articles où on apprenait que ces pièces avaient été soit disséquées, au XIXe siècle, ou plus récemment passées au scanner, pour savoir ce qu'il y a à l'intérieur. L'idée que le musée européen ou le scientifique européen, avec ses outils d'européen, peut avoir l'arrogance de vouloir faire cracher à l'objet le plus profond de son secret – qui de toutes façons ne se résume pas à la somme des pièces qui se trouve à l'intérieur de lui – ce sont des moments que je trouve d'une très grande violence. Alors je ne détourne pas le regard en disant « non, ne me montrez pas cela », mais ce sont en fait des moments de colère qui ressemblent à quelque chose comme : « Mais laissez l'invisible être invisible ! »

SARR : Les sociétés africaines ont considéré qu'il y a plusieurs ordres, et que dans le visible, il y a l'invisible, et que ces objets-sujets sont aussi là pour témoigner de la présence de l'invisible dans le visible. Fondamentalement, et c'est ce qui est intéressant, c'est que l'objet est juste un support pour rendre présentes un certain nombre de ressources et de puissances spirituelles qui sont là. La mise en rituel est une opération par laquelle cet objet qui est un signifiant vide est doté d'un souffle, d'une anima et de capacités agissantes et ce n'est plus un objet.

DIAGNE : C'est une cosmologie de la vie. Dans les religions traditionnelles ouest-africaines que je connais, le principe était qu'exister signifie être une force et que l'univers dans lequel on existe est un univers de forces vitales, dont la finalité de chaque force est de devenir encore plus forte. Autrement dit, ce sont des cosmologies qui visent une vie toujours encore plus surabondante.

Les Entrelacs de l'Objet | The Object's Interlacing — 75

Fig. 5: Awa Cheikh Diouf. Kader Attia, *Les Entrelacs de l'Objet | The Object's Interlacing* (2020, 00:25:32).

Awa Cheikh DIOUF : Je crois qu'un objet inanimé est juste un objet. Ce qui peut faire l'intérêt de cet objet-là, c'est sans doute le discours qu'il y a autour, et le symbole que cet objet peut représenter pour une communauté. Je crois que ces objets qui sont partis portaient un certain discours créé par la communauté, créé autour des valeurs de cette communauté, et donc c'est sans doute plus ce discours-là qui peut être considéré comme les éléments immatériels, et qui à mon avis accompagne les objets. Donc réclamer ce bien immatériel, c'est en même temps réclamer les objets qui vont avec.

> GUÈYE : Vous prenez un masque Bambara, vous le transportez dans un espace européen, américain, un autre espace. A partir du moment où la famille gardienne de ce masque perd son statut social, du fait du déplacement de l'objet qui lui conférait un statut social, vous ne pouvez pas ramener un objet sans ramener la partie d'immatérialité que confère l'objet.

SARR : Les communautés savent quels étaient les usages des objets et en savent plus que les anthropologues. Et ces savoirs-là, ces régimes documentaires-là, on doit aussi les remettre ... Donc le fait que les objets reviennent, c'est aussi une circulation sémantique : Ce n'est pas que le retour de l'objet, c'est la reprise du travail autour de la compréhension de la fonction fondamentale de l'objet, donc de la compréhension de nous-mêmes.

> GUÈYE : Parmi les procédés qu'on a récupérés des recherches sur la colonisation, le procédé le plus pernicieux a été celui du bâillonnement. Le bâillonnement, c'est l'interdiction du discours, et l'interdiction du discours a traversé toutes les communautés : parce que l'on dit que votre structure sociale n'est plus la structure reconnue ; que votre espace politique de décision n'est plus l'espace politique de décision ; que votre tribunal n'est plus un tribunal ; que l'on fait taire le chef, le shaman, le guérisseur, et le griot parce qu'on leur dit que leur parole est inutile. Et même lorsqu' ils parlent, ils ne disent pas la parole essentielle, parce que la parole essentielle devait avoir pour effet de structurer ou de donner des indications. La colonisation a donc fait taire la parole normale et a fait émerger une parole importée.

DIAGNE : Quand j'ai dit que les objets d'arts africains dans leur forme portaient une philosophie, exprimaient une philosophie, ce que j'ai essayé d'exprimer par là, c'est que non seulement ils prennent leur signification quand on les replonge dans la religion – ou plutôt dans la cosmologie – qui leur a donné naissance. Autrement dit, ils expriment cette cosmologie de la vie dont j'ai parlé tout à l'heure, cette cosmologie dans laquelle tout ce qui existe est considéré non seulement comme vivant, mais comme une force agissante. Cela veut dire que c'est une cosmologie où il n'y a rien d'inerte ! Donc que l'on prenne la force des forces, les divinités, les ancêtres, les humains vivants, les animaux, les plantes ou même les minéraux, on ne rencontre jamais un degré zéro de vie ou un degré zéro de force agissante.

SAVOY : On s'est habitués à l'idée que la nature, les fleuves ont des droits, que les objets ont des droits, que l'objet agit . . . Je le sais aussi pour des raisons historiques. Autour de 1800, il y avait au Louvre par exemple une Provençale, une femme, qui tombait en extase devant l'Apollon du Belvédère : Elle se mettait à trembler, elle venait tous les jours . . . Ils ont fini par la mettre dans un établissement psychiatrique autour de 1800, parce que ce n'était pas possible au musée : Tu ne peux pas te laisser aller, tu ne peux pas être l'objet de l'objet au musée. Tu peux seulement être neutre, tu peux contempler, tu peux t'agacer du fait qu'il y ait du bruit, etc. Mais tu ne peux pas te mettre à genoux, et te mettre à trembler, à pleurer, et être autant affectée par l'objet.

Fig. 6: Bénédicte Savoy. Kader Attia, *Les Entrelacs de l'Objet* | *The Object's Interlacing* (2020, 00:13:26).

Kader ATTIA : Senghor aurait dit « la raison est hellène et l'émotion est nègre ». Comment, d'un point de vue philosophique, considères-tu l'émotion générée par ces créations que l'on appelle aujourd'hui « arts anciens d'Afrique » ?

DIAGNE : Alors justement c'est bien que l'on y revienne . . . Il faut toujours revenir à cette phrase de Senghor, parce que c'est à cause d'elle qu'il a été le plus critiqué. On lui a dit : « Pourquoi accorder la raison aux Hellènes, donc aux Grecs et aux ancêtres des Européens, en disant que les Africains, quant à eux, sont plutôt du côté de l'émotion ? » Dire que l'émotion est nègre comme la raison est hellène, ce n'est pas nier que les Nègres aient une raison, ou que les Hellènes d'ailleurs soient des êtres d'émotion . . . C'est simplement dire que les œuvres produites dans le monde africain noir sont à l'émotion ce que les œuvres produites dans la statuaire gréco-romaine sont à la raison analytique. Et Senghor établit une différence entre ce qu'il appelle « une raison œil » : la raison contemplative, qui pour bien saisir la réalité la tient à distance de soi. D'abord on tient la réalité à distance de soi, et ensuite on la décompose en ses éléments constitutifs pour la comprendre. « Je suis le sujet qui comprend ou qui connaît ; toi tu es l'objet qui est là en face de moi, et qu'il faut que je comprenne, et te comprendre c'est savoir comment tu es fait, quels sont les éléments qui entrent dans ta constitution. » C'est cela la raison qui analyse . . . Et Senghor oppose à cela ce qu'il appelle « une raison étreinte » : une raison qui embrasse, où le sens privilégié n'est plus le sens de la vue mais celui du toucher. Et il estime justement que c'est une autre approche de la réalité : Ce n'est plus une approche par séparation entre un sujet et un objet, mais par sympathie du sujet et de l'objet. Le sujet entre en quelque sorte dans l'objet, et est en sympathie avec lui, coïncide avec lui, et étreint en quelque sorte l'objet. Le modèle de cela – ce qui montre que ce type d'approche de la réalité existe – c'est l'Art . . . Et il dit qu'au fond, cet objet nous le voyons moins qu'il ne nous touche . . . Senghor utilise l'expression « être dans une attitude rythmique avec lui », c'est-à-dire être en rythme avec l'objet que l'on regarde. Ce qui est une manière de dire que le contact est presque physique : On danse ensemble, on est en relation d'étreinte. Et c'est cela qu'il appelle « émotion », en donnant à ce mot son poids étymologique. É/motion : c'est-à-dire « motion » le mouvement, « é » qui me fait sortir de moi. Et pour lui c'est cela la signification profonde de l'art . . . L'art nous touche plus que nous le voyons.

SAVOY : Quand tu prends un objet, tu ne prends pas seulement un objet bien sûr : Tu prends l'autre, tu prends une part de l'autre. Et pas seulement si tu lis l'essai sur le don de Marcel Mauss sur l'autre se donnant, tu l'as aussi dans les discussions politiques autour de 1815, quand la France doit rendre à l'Europe entière les chefs d'œuvre qu'elle s'était appropriée sous Napoléon, et qu'elle résiste beaucoup, les autres disent : « Tant que vous n'aurez pas rendu ce que vous avez pris à l'Italie, à l'Allemagne, aux Pays-Bas etc. Tant que vous ne l'aurez pas rendu, vous ne serez pas d'accord avec le fait que les frontières se sont réduites. » C'est à dire que tant que tu as les œuvres que tu as prises quand tu étais un empire napoléonien, tant que tu les as chez toi, tu es l'empire. C'est seulement quand tu les rends, que tu comprends que tu es redevenu un petit état bourbon royaliste. Cela me paraît extrêmement important de le dire et de le redire, parce que cela a été dit dans le contexte européen, ce n'est pas seulement une théorie postcoloniale, ce n'est pas spécialement une épistémologie très lointaine. C'est que l'objet que tu possèdes, ce n'est pas seulement l'objet, mais c'est le signal de ta domination sur beaucoup d'autres choses. Or il me semble que personne ne le dit explicitement, mais en réalité c'est cela, la véritable raison. La vraie raison, c'est qu'on a du mal à penser la restitution de ces objets, parce que penser la restitution de ces objets, c'est être obligé de se confronter au fait qu'on ne soit plus un empire, qu'on ne soit plus qu'une petite surface sur une surface mondiale bien plus considérable etc. Ça c'est un effort psychologique énorme. Et c'est peut-être cela, ce fascisme larvé : C'est de ne pas arriver à se dire : « voilà, on est petit », ou en tous cas : « on est plus petit qu'on aimerait être », et il faut gérer cela.

SARR : Aucune société fondamentalement ne s'accomplit si elle ne se réapproprie pas ses ressources symboliques. Parce que c'est là le lieu, le vrai gisement de tout : de la créativité, de la productivité et de l'inventivité. Et le symbolique est absolument fondamental. Et ce continent a quand même produit énormément de ce point de vue-là. Il l'a même disséminé dans le monde, y compris lorsque ses enfants étaient dans les cales, étaient réduits à la plus grande des inhumanités. Ceux qui ont traversé l'Atlantique dans la cale des négriers ont transporté des cultures dans les ailleurs, même lorsqu'on niait leur humanité. Le continent a affecté le monde dans ses ressources symboliques. Là est le vrai gisement cette fois-ci d'avoir un geste choisi et conscient qui consiste à dire : « J'ai ces ressources, je les remets dans un bain, dans un bouillon, dans une forge, et je recrée à nouveau avec un souffle nouveau, je les reféconde ». Cela est pour moi la grande révolution culturelle : ce geste de se réapproprier est un geste double. Il ne s'agit pas juste de reprendre et de ramener, mais de le réinscrire dans un geste de créativité.

DIOUF : Vous savez, je crois que l'art fait partie des éléments les plus essentiels de la souveraineté, et ces œuvres-là font partie du patrimoine africain, et en tant qu'éléments du patrimoine, ce sont aussi des éléments de souveraineté. Et de ce point de vue-là, je crois qu'il est quand même intéressant de pouvoir les retourner à leur lieu d'origine, pour que les populations qui en ont fait la production puissent pouvoir en disposer.

Fig. 7: Serge Guézo. Kader Attia, *Les Entrelacs de l'Objet | The Object's Interlacing* (2020, 00:02:48).

GUÉZO : Dans les années 1980, je crois, la première fois où j'ai entendu parler des objets en tant qu'enjeux, c'est quand on y a fait référence dans le journal télévisé de TF1. Je ne sais plus quel journaliste l'a fait, et il a cité le cas du Bénin et du président du Bénin Mathieu Kérékou. On était à l'époque en pleine révolution, et en général on parle rarement ou jamais même du Bénin.

> SAVOY: Ce qui me parait vraiment intéressant, et ce sur quoi je travaille aussi beaucoup en ce moment, c'est de comprendre d'une part pourquoi, alors qu'on était très très près de la restitution, que plusieurs états, dont la France, recommandaient des restitutions, qu'en Allemagne aussi – c'était juste avant l'arrivée d'Helmut Kohl au début des années 1980 – le ministère des affaires étrangères avait dit en 1982 qu'on allait faire des restitutions symboliques en 1984, au moment des 100 ans de l'anniversaire de la conférence de Berlin, la conférence du Congo, on en était tout près tout près – et puis ça n'a pas marché!

GUÉZO : Donc ils ont nommé le président Kérékou en disant que la France réfléchit à restituer leur patrimoine aux pays africains, et quel ne fut mon choc d'entendre le président dire que cela ne servait à rien que cela vienne, parce que nous n'avions pas les capacités et les moyens de pouvoir les entretenir ... J'ai pris cela comme quelque chose de méchant, parce qu'il n'était pas Fon, il n'était pas de cette ethnie.

> SAVOY : Le moment où ça échoue en Allemagne comme en France, c'est le moment où en France arrive la gauche au pouvoir, Mitterrand etc., et ça se met à échouer. Mais c'est le moment où ici en Allemagne arrive Kohl au pouvoir. Donc on voit bien que ce n'est sûrement pas une dynamique politique, qui amène cet échec, mais c'est autre chose. [. . .] À mon avis, d'après ce que j'observe dans les archives, du côté français il y a un rôle assez important du marché de l'art, qui, dans les années 1980, est extrêmement actif sur ces questions d'art africain, et avec une collusion assez forte entre les milieux politiques, les milieux économiques, et les milieux des collectionneurs. C'est quelque chose qui n'existe pas du tout en Allemagne, en tout cas qu'on ne voit pas et dont on ne sent pas la trace, mais il y a une mobilisation massive systématique très forte et très efficace des musées qui s'opposent complètement. Ici en Allemagne, ils s'opposent de manière très organisée. Ils font des réunions, il y a des procès-verbaux de réunions, et tout cela se retrouve dans les archives pour empêcher que cela avance, notamment en proposant des choses concrètes comme par exemple de ne plus utiliser le mot « restitution », de le substituer, et le terme proposé à l'époque était « transfert ». Donc on va arrêter de dire le mot « restitution », ça suscite des émotions trop fortes, et ça a des implications juri-

diques trop fortes. On va donc dire « transfert », on va cesser de publier les inventaires, des catalogues qui pourraient « susciter des envies » de la part de ceux qui sont privés de ces patrimoines. On va, à chaque fois que les émotions montent (puisque c'est un sujet émotionnel), toujours remettre sur le terrain juridique.

SANKALE : En droit, nous savons que la propriété est subdivisée en trois éléments qui sont, puisque nous aimons les formules latines : l'usus, l'abusus et le fructus . . . L'usus c'est le droit d'user de la chose, l'abusus c'est le droit de le vendre, et le fructus c'est le droit d'en tirer les fruits (le louer). Donc, si on restitue quelque chose, on transfère une propriété à quelqu'un, on lui transfère ces trois droits là . . . Cela veut dire que les personnes à qui l'on restitue ces objets sont en droit demain de dire : « Bon, finalement, moi je les revends à un marchand si j'en ai envie. » . . . Et personne n'a le droit de dire quoi que ce soit !

SARR : Ce que je trouve intéressant, c'est que bien que la réflexion n'ait porté que sur les collections publiques, il y a des externalités sur les collections privées. Les marchands d'art ont été les plus opposés au travail sur la restitution, et au départ, je ne comprenais pas pourquoi. Ayant creusé la question, j'ai compris deux choses : Certains musées s'approvisionnent dans les marchés de l'art. Si les musées sont amenés à restituer les pièces dont on aurait démontré que la provenance est problématique, du coup, ce marché perd de son attractivité, parce que l'on va acheter une pièce cher, mais si l'on est censé la restituer un jour, le marché peut s'effondrer parce qu'il fonctionne par signaux. Et là c'est l'économiste qui parle.

SANKALE : Nous savons que c'est impossible, parce que l'Histoire s'est déroulée et que les populations mêmes auxquelles nous rendons ces objets ne se sentent peut-être plus du tout concernées par ces objets-là parce que le temps est passé, les croyances, les convictions et les pratiques religieuses, etc. ont dû changer. Donc il faut bien se rendre compte que tout cela est une charge symbolique plutôt qu'autre chose.

GUÉZO : Quand on parle du retour des objets, où vont-ils retourner ? Est-ce qu'ils vont retourner dans ce musée ? Aujourd'hui, on nous accuse d'être incapables de pouvoir entretenir ces musées, qu'il y a des incendies, qu'il y a des vols . . . Peut-être que quelque part, la colonisation a atteint son objectif : nous détourner de nous-mêmes . . .

Fig. 8: Malik NDiaye. Kader Attia, *Les Entrelacs de l'Objet* | *The Object's Interlacing* (2020, 00:51:58).

GUÈYE : Je pense que la restitution des biens est vraiment une réparation irréparable. Pourquoi ? Parce que lorsqu'on vous arrache votre téléphone portable, lorsque la police vous ramène votre téléphone portable, ils ne vous ramènent pas juste votre objet, ils vous ramènent le perpétuel souvenir de l'agression. A chaque fois que vous avez le téléphone portable, que vous l'ouvrez, vous vous souvenez de l'agression. [. . .] Le pire c'est lorsque le voleur efface le contenu de votre téléphone portable, lorsqu'il met ses propres photos. Et lorsque qu'à chaque fois que vous ouvrez votre portable, vous voyez le visage de votre voleur, le visage de votre pilleur. C'est ce qui va se passer avec ces biens culturels, qu'ils vont revenir en étant tripotés, en étant réparés, en étant vernis . . . Des dieux qui n'auraient jamais dû être touchés par des mains, ont été touchés par des mains, des objets de culte qui n'auraient dû sortir de la cour ont été exposés à la vue de tout le monde, des objets qui étaient en relation avec le cosmos divin ont été enfermés dans des cases de verre, parce qu'ils ont une valeur financière pure.

Malik NDIAYE : Dans le cadre de mon travail d'historien de l'art, je me suis beaucoup intéressé à la mémoire de l'objet, pour rompre avec une certaine épistémologie qui prend l'objet à distance, qui aseptise, qui est d'ailleurs le travail de l'historien ou du scientifique, souvent là où l'artiste ne fait pas cette rupture épistémologique mais entre dans l'objet, pour essayer de le travailler, de le changer, de lui inculquer une certaine âme. L'historien – c'est son métier – doit plus ou moins prendre de la distance, et j'ai essayé de trouver une position intermédiaire au profit de l'objet. J'ai essayé, à partir des théories sur le sens, sur la signification de l'objet, de montrer que cet objet-là que l'on appréhende avec nos méthodes d'analyse, ne vient pas neutre, vient de quelque part . . . Alors ce quelque part c'est son parcours, c'est sa trajectoire, c'est son pedigree, le pedigree de l'objet, qui est composé de son passage entre plusieurs mains. Chaque main l'a regardé, l'a palpé, et chaque homme l'a tenu entre ses mains, et l'a regardé, a chuchoté quelque chose, l'a interprété d'une certaine manière. Un conservateur l'a mis dans un espace pendant plusieurs années . . . Un historien a mis son image dans un article . . . Des spectateurs l'ont vu en famille . . . Des visiteurs dans un musée, ils ont certainement proféré quelque chose, ont dit quelque chose, ont sorti des interprétations devant cet objet . . . Alors, pourquoi ne pas prendre quelque chose que l'on ignore souvent pourtant de l'objet et qui est ce passage entre plusieurs temporalités, plusieurs mains, plusieurs contextes, et le mettre au profit de l'objet . . . C'est-à-dire prendre l'objet et lui donner la parole.

DIOUF : Sur ces questions-là qui sont plutôt philosophiques, je crois que la restitution a un sens pour les femmes, dans la mesure où avec les religions révélées, ce statut de femmes fortes qui avaient des pouvoirs de décisions, qui avaient des biens propres, ce sont des choses que nous avons perdu au fur et à mesure que les gens se sont convertis au Christianisme et à l'Islam. Donc si ces choses-là, qui étaient attachées un peu aux femmes, revenaient, cela pourrait aussi constituer dans une certaine mesure une forme de réappropriation de ces valeurs-là, du statut de la femme en tant que responsable, pouvant exercer un certain pouvoir dans la communauté.

> DIAGNE : La fois où j'ai fait l'expérience d'un traumatisme s'exprimant, c'est la frustration que l'on peut sentir chez les Diola dans le sud du Sénégal parce que chez eux, le traumatisme précisément des objets spoliés, des objets partis, s'est accompagné de la capture et du départ en exil de la dernière reine qui avait été une résistante contre le colonialisme français : Aline Sitoe. Aujourd'hui le corps d'Aline Sitoe est encore absent ! On parle du retour de ses restes ; on n'est pas sûr de l'endroit où elle est morte. Donc si tu veux, sur ce corps absent d'Aline Sitoe s'est cristallisé en quelques sortes toute la blessure, le traumatisme et l'humiliation que représentaient non seulement la subjugation coloniale de la Casamance, mais également le départ de ce qui étaient les objets les plus sacrés de la communauté.

SARR : La question de l'Histoire est pour moi fondamentale de plusieurs points de vue. Il y a d'abord cette histoire qui manque, cette trace qui manque. Et je trouve que Karima Lazali l'a bien décrypté dans son texte *Le trauma colonial* dans le contexte de l'Algérie, où il manque une parole – y compris pour les générations qui n'ont pas vécu la guerre d'Algérie. Il y a quelque chose qui ne leur a pas été transmis et qui crée un malaise et impacte leur subjectivité. C'est-à-dire que nous sommes porteurs de mémoires plus anciennes que nous, et quand ces mémoires ne sont pas articulées, elles nous impactent même si nous n'avons pas vécu le temps historique. Alors que quelqu'un comme moi, la perte dont je parle s'est instituée pendant que je n'étais pas un sujet : Je n'étais pas là . . . C'est donc une perte imaginaire, et pourtant c'est une perte qui installe chez moi une trace qui manque. Ce sont donc des questions sur lesquelles tu travailles : la trace qui manque, la réparation, etc. . . . ! Il est absolument fondamental qu'on se ressaisisse de ces traces qui manquent, et qu'on fasse un travail là-dessus : le travail de reprendre les objets, leur histoire, de compléter . . . ! Parce que parfois, l'histoire manque.

> NDIAYE : On ne sera jamais quitte ! Il y a des choses que rien ne pourra racheter. L'Histoire est tellement complexe et tellement dense, les stratifications sont tellement nombreuses que toute la richesse du monde occidental ne

pourra jamais réparer ces choses-là. Je veux dire, tout le massacre des Indiens en Amérique : Comment réparer cela ? Toute la question de l'esclavage : Comment réparer cela ? Et bien, il y a des compensations qui ont pu être faites pour certains crimes, mais en réalité, cela n'enlève en rien le crime. Ça ne peut pas réparer. « Réparer » est un verbe qui – à mon avis – triche, trompe, parce qu'on a l'impression que c'est de l'ordre de la mécanique, comme on répare quelque chose qui va redémarrer, mais en réalité, ce n'est pas le bon verbe. C'est pourquoi cette question de réparation, je la mets de côté par rapport à la question de la restitution.

GUÈYE : Lorsque les biens reviendront, l'immatérialité de ces biens-là doit être mise en avant, parce que c'est cela qui va convaincre les populations africaines de la nécessité de reprendre ces biens. Parce que lorsqu'on prend une divinité qui était dans un village dit animiste, partie depuis 200 ans, et qui doit revenir dans un village devenu totalement chrétien ou totalement musulman, c'est à dire qui récuse toute forme de représentation physique dans l'objet, est ce qu'on va replacer cet objet dans ce village ? Qui a disloqué ce village-là ? À quoi cela servira-t-il ? C'est pourquoi il faut réfléchir à ces paramètres immatériels, même dans la politique de positionnement de ces objets dans tel ou tel lieu. C'est pourquoi ils doivent être dans l'un de ces trois lieux : Premièrement, les lieux médiatiques, dans les médias. Il faut donner une très grande place à cet immatériel-là dans la construction des émissions, dans la construction des contenus des émissions pour savoir comment toucher les personnes afin qu'elles acceptent le retour des biens. Deuxième espace : l'espace muséal ou l'espace de confinement de ces objets pour les protéger. Lorsqu'un objet ne peut plus aller quelque part, pour l'installer – par exemple que ce soit un objet de la communauté Diola, Haoussa ou Dogon, il faut aller voir dans ces villages-là comment ces objets étaient installés et sacralisés ou désacralisés. Une fois que le processus est maîtrisé, cela peut servir de parcours artistique, et ce parcours artistique va créer une conformité entre l'objet dans son espace social et l'objet dans son espace muséal. Je pense que le dernier élément est simple : Vous me ramenez un bien, quel est le discours immatériel que vous avez construit sur le bien ? Il faut déconstruire ce discours immatériel-là, sinon on reproduira.

Fig. 9: Felwine Sarr. Kader Attia, *Les Entrelacs de l'Objet | The Object's Interlacing* (2020, 00:11:19).

SAVOY : Moi mon impulsion n'est pas une impulsion de scientifique du XIXe siècle qui veut absolument savoir ce qu'il y a derrière le mur. Et j'aurais plutôt volontiers tendance à proposer qu'on ait la connaissance qu'il y a quelque chose que l'on ne connaît pas derrière le mur. Donc ça on peut en parler . . . Parlons-en ! Faisons de la publicité scientifique etc. en disant : « Voilà, on sait qu'il y a quelque chose là derrière, mais on ne va pas aller voir. On ne va pas démailloter la momie. On ne va pas aller faire un scan de cette petite pièce magique pour savoir s'il y a un grain d'or, un texte ou un brin d'herbe à l'intérieur de son ventre, etc. » Non, laissez-les comme ça ! J'aime bien savoir que le savoir s'arrête.

SARR : Que faisons-nous des différentes couches successives de sens que ces objets ont désormais ? Et je fais l'analogie des gens qui partent en exil. Je prends mon propre cas : J'ai vécu au Sénégal jusqu'à l'âge du bac, et je suis allé faire mes études en France, j'y ai vécu 15 ans, et je suis revenu. Quand je reviens, je suis le même et en même temps je ne suis plus le même. L'ipséité, donc la partie de moi qui s'est transformée, qui a accueilli des souffles du monde : Qu'est-ce qu'on en fait ? Je pense que lorsque je reviens, je peux la réinjecter dans un processus quand même créatif, dans la société dans laquelle je suis. Et que justement c'est ça qui est intéressant, c'est ma résocialisation. Je ne redeviendrai pas celui que j'étais et je ne serai pas comme une brique qui retrouve sa place dans un édifice, celle qui était la mienne. Mais je suis amené justement à réinventer des espaces, à me réinventer, et puis à réinventer une « relationalité ». Et je pense que c'est ce qui est intéressant. Ces objets quand on les ramène, certains probablement peuvent retrouver des sanctuaires avec des usages de la communauté réinventés, mais la plupart sont des matériaux pour une réinvention.

DIAGNE : Ces objets sont devenus de véritables métisses, de véritables hybrides qui accumulent les identités.

SANKALE : Dodds, né au Sénégal, métis, né de deux parents métisses nés au Sénégal, il était quoi ?

DIAGNE : S'interdire des explorations au nom de l'appropriation culturelle, et dire qu'il faut que chacun garde son territoire, etc. . . . C'est une forme de purisme insupportable, qui est non seulement une insulte à l'imagination créatrice, je crois, et à la capacité justement de cette imagination créatrice d'être très plastique, mais c'est une insulte à ce qui fait l'humanité de l'humain. Et cela a des conséquences qui peuvent être tout à fait désastreuses sur le plan éthique et politique.

SARR : Ce voyage retour n'est pas un retour du même : C'est le retour d'un même différent. Et la différence dans ce même est intéressante, cette différence, il faut l'adresser. Et comment on en fait un matériau créatif pour justement continuer de constituer toujours le même différent. Et je me dis que si nous étions tous intelligents, c'est une occasion formidable qui nous est donnée de dire que ces objets peuvent être les médiateurs de nouvelles relations, puisqu'il y a une part de nous importante, mais il y a une part de vous aussi dedans. Ils sont en quelque sorte des objets métisses créoles. Et qu'est-ce qu'on fait des enfants métisses ? Et bien on peut en faire des jonctions, des lieux de synthèse heureuse. C'est pour moi une option éthique et philosophique qui est la plus intéressante, si on sort de la binarité. Si en face ils reconnaissent l'historicité et la légitimité de ces objets, et que d'ici on reconnaît que leur voyage et leur translocation les a affectés, et que désormais ils incorporent une part de l'autre, et qu'il y a quelque chose à faire avec cette part de l'autre qu'ils ont incorporée.

Jonas Tinius & Angelica Pesarini

(Ir)reparability Begins in the Body: Towards a Museum of Disrepair

Abstract: This chapter is based on a workshop we conducted with PhD candidates attending the Summer School *Restitution, Reparations, Reparation – Toward a New Global Society?* held at Villa Vigoni, Italy. It offers reflections on the situated and embodied experience of talking, thinking, and conceptualising repair and heritage. Starting from the work of the French-Algerian artist Kader Attia, we envisaged the possibility of a "Museum of Disrepair" and invited PhD students to analyse the impacts of such a potential site. Attia's idea of "irreparability" was at the centre of our investigation, and we thought about the notion of "repair" in relation to the racialised body, wounded by histories of colonialism and whiteness. As the analysis shows, repairing damages does not mean to erase the physical evidence of the injury, hoping for the disappearance of the violence. Rather, it is essential to acknowledge pain and damage, and to link the injury with its visible scarification. Restitution, as we argue, is only an element of a wider discourse on reconciliation, decolonisation, and infrastructural changes to Europe's narrative of world.[1]

Keywords: Kader Attia, critical heritage, decoloniality, embodiment, irreparability, museums, repair, reparations

1 (Ir)reparability Begins in the Body

> **Reparations begin in the body**, and that is where our poems must begin; our poems must teach us new ways to use our bodies, must watch with us and walk with us and burst through us as new light, even if it hurts, even if it means we have to relearn self-love through the eyes of a truer more unified self. *Harmony Holiday* (2016)

---

[1] The authors would like to thank the editors of this volume as well as Markus Messling and Christiane Solte-Gresser for the invitation to partake in the event and the subsequent publication. Jonas Tinius was supported as postdoctoral researcher of the project *Minor Universality. Narrative World Productions After Western Universalism*, which received funding from the European Research Council (ERC) under the European Union's Horizon 2020 research and innovation programme (Grant agreement No. 819931). Excerpts of this chapter have previously appeared in the Italian monthly *Art e Dossier* (see Tinius 2021b).

∂ Open Access. © 2023 the author(s), published by De Gruyter. This work is licensed under the Creative Commons Attribution-NonCommercial-NoDerivatives 4.0 International License.
https://doi.org/10.1515/9783110799514-005

In September 2021, we walked up a steep hill on the coastal flank of Lake Como to sit on a bench overlooking the former property of the German entrepreneur Heinrich Mylius, now known as *Villa Vigoni*, the German-Italian Research Centre for European Dialogue (see Fig. 1). Mylius purchased this property in 1829, before his heirs bequeathed it to the German Federal Republic. On the occasion of the first international summer school titled *Restitution, Reparations, Reparation – Toward a New Global Society?*, which sealed the beginning of the cooperation between the Cluster for European Studies (CEUS) of Saarland University and Villa Vigoni, we had been invited to convene a panel on repair, heritage, and museums.

On the first few days of the Summer School, while being lavishly hosted within rooms replete with paintings, sculptures, and an ever-distracting view onto Bellagio, a conversation we had with the legal consultant (*consulente legale*, or *Justiziar*) of Villa Vigoni, Julian Stefenelli, kept on echoing across our encounters. The discussion about the Villa and its owners made us swiftly realise that the history of the Villa itself was embedded in complex questions of care and repair. Stefenelli provided us with a series of public court-case write-ups related to the confiscation of German properties on Italian soil. Proceedings published around this issue from a previous conference held in Villa Vigoni provided further background.[2] At heart, Villa Vigoni – "the most attractive German object of execution" (Peters and Volpe 2021, 14) – became subject to a complicated international conflict, since the Italian Constitutional Court denied the German Republic its immunity from civil jurisdiction over claims to reparation for Nazi crimes committed during World War II, which, in turn, challenged the International Court of Justice's Jurisdictional Immunities Judgement of 2012 (Peters and Volpe 2021, 4). Most recently, in 2015 (and again in 2019), these cases concerned a group of Greek citizens, whose ancestors had been the victims of German violence during WWII. They sued the German state in Italy and asked for reparations related to war crimes. This led the Italian state to mortgage (provisionally) German property on Italian soil, such as Villa Vigoni, as an insurance for such possible repayments (see Tomuschat 2017). Villa Vigoni became implicated – twice – in such legal processes, intricating it in a possible reparation. It was at risk, in other words, of becoming a subject and object of

---

2 See Volpe, Peters, and Battini (2021) for an overview of the question of post-World War II reparations, immunity, and reconciliation between Germany and Italy. In their book, the editors analyse in particular the consequences of the Italian Constitutional Court's Judgment 238/2014. "With this judgment", Peters and Volpe (2021: 4) argue, "the . . . Italian Constitutional Court (ItCC) denied the German Republic's immunity from civil jurisdiction over claims to reparation for Nazi crimes committed during World War II (WWII), indirectly challenging the International Court of Justice (ICJ)'s Jurisdictional Immunities Judgment of 2012 and paving the way for a series of domestic proceedings against Germany."

Fig. 1: Villa Vigoni, German-Italian Centre for European Dialogue. Photo: Jonas Tinius.

possible reparations for intergenerational and international injury. In other words, the place in which we spoke was itself a symbolic site of thinking about repair, reparation, and redress in a multi-national European context.

Eventually, these cases were dismissed, because the Villa was used exclusively for "sovereign, non-commercial purposes" (Pavoni 2021, 95). It was, however, the interpretation of the dismissal that struck a nerve with our preparations for the summer school. The judicial mortgaging of the Villa was considered to inflict more symbolic harm than financial reparation would solve. Villa Vigoni, after all, was already a site for repairing and dialogue between two nations. As Paulus (2021, 341) notes, this act of confiscation of a German property with the purpose of cultural mediation would therefore have come "with the added irony that this precious centre of German-Italian friendship would thereby risk to be transformed into its opposite." It was its status, purpose, and practice as a site of dialogue that kept it from being used as a medium to redress and confront a violent past (see also Boggero and Oellers-Frahm 2021, 296). The Villa thus embodies symbolic reparation as an unfinished and often unsatisfactory process of repair (see also Tharoor 2021). The narratives of the location rendered painfully clear that while repair, reparation, redress, and restitution are often thrown together in conversation, they evoke a series of often but not always overlapping concerns. More precisely, we wish to emphasise that reparations (financial or otherwise) and restitution may form part of a process that addresses past injuries and injustices, but the process of repairing should begin by recognising the potential impossibility of healing. In this respect, institutions may incorporate, house, mediate, and become vessels for expression of pain, injury, and conflict as well as for redress and repair.

This contribution responds to the editors' concern for multilateral government policies and agreements that have re-initiated international debates about 'postcolonial' restitution and reparation. It responds specifically to this volume's preoccupation with how restitution, reparation, and the politics of memory are grappled with in the context of heritage developments, museum work, and through artistic practices – and how artistic and poetic practices can offer forms of reflection about repair and irreparability beyond reparation. In particular, it is concerned with the notion of repair as theorised by French-Algerian artist Kader Attia, whose own work over the past decades has conceived of the conceptualisation of repair and irreparability as a prism to think through colonial legacies in the present. The 2022 Berlin Biennale, led by his artistic direction, is but one example of how one may work in the field of art and curatorial practice in museums and enact visions of a world society after Western universalism (see Tinius 2022). In this contribution, rather than focusing on a single artwork or a particular museum site, we ask what an hypothetical 'museum of disrepair' can do to think about repair and reparation. To do so, it builds on the anthropology of art, curation, museums, and difficult heritage and considers the relational and symbolic importance of opening up rather than immobilising conflict. It also brings into conversation ideas of the racialised body intended as a site on which colonial histories are inscribed, and the impacts of the "white look" (Fanon 1952 [2008]) operating within visual registries of colonial violence.

Given our situatedness as authors, it is also an autoethnographic reflection on the bodies in dialogue through which we experienced the summer school. A white German anthropologist speaking about reparation on a site that had been confiscated by the Italian government in order to redress German war crimes during WWII, and a Black Italian scholar, who thinks about the wounds inflicted by Italian colonial violence on racialised bodies. For Jonas, repair and reparation are concerns directly tied to his growing up and working in the postindustrial Ruhr region, whose twice-fold destruction during WWI and WWII are the direct result of industrial war mobilisation by the Germans. The reconstruction of this region has to a large extent been achieved through the invited labour of so-called guestworkers principally from the Mediterranean, whose citizenship status in postwar Germany remained unclear for decades and has created tensions about the intergenerational trauma caused by repair. The economic devastation of the working class after the phasing out of coal mining and industry in the region, and its illusions of rejuvenation through the postindustrial creative industries, has continued to solidify the layers of disrepair in this region. Jonas' work on German public theatres departs directly from the concerns of a postwar generation of scholars, teachers, activists, and artists for the recognition of German guilt for its war crimes, and a self-critical accountability of its public (cultural) institutions for the state of distress that migrant and refugee (non-)citizens in this region experience (see Tinius and Wewerka 2020; Tinius 2023, forthcoming). For Angelica, repair starts from the body and the acknowledgement of wounds and scars left by the histories of colonialism and whiteness. She sees reparation in the rehabilitation of certain experiences that have been systematically excluded by processes of knowledge production, and she seeks to draw upon new and alternative ways of knowing, in order to make visible what has been kept invisible, and to make audible the inaudible (Pesarini 2022, forthcoming).

The aim of this chapter is to provide some reflections on the panel and the workshop we conducted with the wonderful students attending the summer school in Villa Vigoni. It also offers a narrative about the situated and embodied experience of talking, thinking, and conceptualising repair and heritage. In our view, repairing damage does not mean erasing the physical evidence of the injury, as if the marks left by violence can simply be repaired, and therefore eradicated. Rather, as the analysis of Kader Attia's work will demonstrate, repairing means precisely to acknowledge pain and damage, and to link injury with visible scarification. In this way, we contend, we can contribute to a collective attempt of "dismantling the opacity of the grand national narrative of the old colonial empires" (Attia 2012b, 12).

2 Feeling the Wound

In preparation for the Summer School in Villa Vigoni, we provided students with a series of readings that offered theoretical positions on the body as a carrier of injuries and wounds inflicted by the colonial discourse, on the non-neutrality of the gaze, and how (ir)reparability begins in the body.

In relation to colonialism and the production of the racial body, it was essential to start our conversation with ideas of 'race', a term used, if at all, with caution in continental Europe, especially in Italy and in Germany, where deeply ingrained ideologies based on ideas of race caused death and violence (see Messling 2016). Given its implications about biological essences and its connections with the collective guilt of the Holocaust (Goldberg, 2006; Spickard and Nandi, 2014) in the aftermath of WWII, European governments eliminated mention of 'race' from the politics and public policy, adopting instead a "colour evasive" approach in the hope that this could prevent a return to biological ideologies of race (Pesarini and Tintori, 2020). In this respect, David Theo Goldberg (2006) illustrates the impacts of this specific form of European racial denial defined by the author as "racial Europeanisation". According to Goldberg, race denial in Europe is a wishful but unattainable evaporation, a frustrating desire buried, and at the same time alive, that has left "odourless traces but ones suffocating in the wake of their at once denied resinous stench" (Goldberg 2006, 334). 'Race', as a social construct, inevitably continues to impact the lives of those who are othered and discriminated against and the erasure of this category not only contributes to the perpetuation of white privilege, but also widens the colour-line divide and enhances systemic racism.

However, rather than focusing on the concept of 'race', we oriented the students' attention towards processes of "racialisation", that is, an understanding of race as an effect of a process of racialisation, rather than as its origin (Garner 2010). It is through an active process of racialisation, as Sara Ahmed (2002) shows, that the racial body has been discursively materialised. Therefore, it is important to reflect on the idea of the performative and phenomenological nature of 'race' and racial categories. Ahmed (2002, 46) illustrates how the existence of the "racial body" is not anchored to the presence of skin colour or hair texture, but rather to the meaning attributed to a certain colour or hair texture.

Drawing on phenomenologist Maurice Merleau-Ponty, Linda Martín Alcoff (2006) argues how 'race' works through the "perception of the visible", or in other words, how it passes through the reading of visual signs inscribed on the body. These signs are made visible and meaningful key signifiers through what Alcoff (2006, 192) defines as "learning processes", suggesting that the perception of race is therefore an ability we learn (Alcoff 2006, 187) rather than something natural. Here lies the performativity of 'race' that draws on Judith Butler's theory of gender performativity. Referring to gender, Butler (1998, 519) claims that the illusion of gender identity is nourished by a "stylised repetition of acts" that gives gender identity consistency. According to Butler (1990, 25), gender is not something preexisting, but it is "performatively constituted" by attributes and expressions that are considered the results of a perceived gender identity (see also Butler 1993). The racialised body, similar to the gendered body, is performatively constituted by discourse rather than being the result of a biological underlying truth. Thus, by 'naming' the racial body within specific sets of discursive regimes, such as normative Whiteness, this body is produced and becomes meaningful. This also implies an intimate connection between *seeing* a body and the knowledge we may presume to have of that body. As Ahmed (2002, 56) argues, "it is by 'seeing' bodily others that they are 'known', and this knowledge serves to constitute the subject (and in this case the white subject) as the who one who knows". The visual is therefore intimately connected to racialising practices through the knowledge we have of bodies. More precisely, the visual is far from being neutral to 'race', but rather, as argued by Butler (1993, 17), "it is itself a racial formation, an episteme, hegemonic and forceful". It is for that reason, too, that we can speak of the non-neutrality of the gaze and the idea of the "white look" as theorised by Frantz Fanon (1952 [2008]).

Fanon (1952 [2008], 84) illustrates how the construction of the Black body has been produced through a long racial historicity, or, as he calls it, a "historical racial schema", constituted by stereotypes, legends, racial and racist myth. In *Black Skins, White Masks* (1952 [2008]), he tells the reader an anecdote that would be fundamental for his theorisation on the white look as it clearly highlights the wounds caused by the white colonial look onto the racialised body. While travelling on a train, Fanon recounts, a French white child points at him, and he excitedly repeats to his mother the same sentence: "Look! A Negro" (Fanon 1952 [2008], 91). In this occurrence, Fanon states that he perceived how his body is given back to him distorted and dissected by the white look:

> The white gaze, the only valid one, is already dissecting me. I am fixed. Once their microtones are sharpened, the Whites objectively cut sections of my reality. I have been betrayed. I sense, I see in this white gaze that it's the arrival not of a new man, but of a new type of man, a new species. A negro in fact! (Fanon 1952 [2008], 95).

The injuries inflicted by the white look on the racialised bodies are numerous, and they may include feelings of pain, shame, and violence (Pesarini 2020). In relation to gaze and shame, it is precisely the fact of "being looked at", the experience of "coming under the regard of another" which defines shame (Bewes 2011, 153). It is through the look of the 'other' that one experiences because this act implies "violation and exposure" (Treacher 2007, 288). Moreover, shame also requires a witness, considering that it is the gaze of the other that shows us our own failure (see Ahmed 2004, 106).

Therefore, the wounding racialising look does not only affect bodies; it also shapes spaces and institutions, landscapes and objects. In the next section, we explore these connections in relation to the work of Kader Attia, whose practice served as a backdrop to our seminar at Villa Vigoni.

2.1 Seeing the Wound

Commenting on the management of difficult heritage sites, the French philosopher and philologist Barbara Cassin often evokes an anecdote about Nelson Mandela. Upon coming to power, he decided to place an inscription at the entrance to a museum: "dans les salles de l'horrible musée édifié au temps de l'apartheid, où les Khoïsan, peuples premiers d'Afrique du Sud, étaient caricaturé en statues de cire atroces de racisme" (Cassin and Fabre 2022, 13). Instead of demolishing the museum, or replacing the sculptures, he decided to place, in writing, the following question at the heart of this site: What do you think of what you see? According to Cassin, this statement obliges the visitor to take a stance, to judge, to situate the problem of colonial injustice in one's own positionality (Cassin and Fabre 2022, 14). Instead of destroying signs of violence, Mandela decided to let people construct a position from the concrete by confronting them with an injury of discrimination and colonial violence (see Cassin 2018). It was a way to leave the wound open instead of erasing its traces.

In his work "Some modernity's footprints" (2018, the Power Plant, Toronto), artist Kader Attia arranges wooden railway sleepers across the space of an empty gallery, seemingly cutting into the walls of the space in an imagined continuation. The old, broken, and porous wooden sleepers are held together by metal staples that seem to keep them from breaking apart, like a long cut held together provisionally by medical plasters or stitches. Among other works in the show, such as prosthetic limbs, the wooden railway sleepers evoke a bygone power, a train about to break through the gallery walls. They are traces of the technologies that enabled colonial invasion in the European colonies in Africa and the Americas, "deep scars etched into unspoiled lands" (Whyte 2018). This work, like so many others in the artist's œuvre, does not seek reconciliation; rather, it reduces the viewer to the moment of confrontation with several layers of scarification. The railway, a symbol of progress, is itself in a state of disrepair, removed from its original function, left in a state of rotten dismembering. The wooden railway sleepers alone do not carry a train, lacking the metal rails, and the soil into which they were etched. They scarred themselves the soil from which they were taken and created lines into (previously untouched) land. In need of repair themselves, they are helplessly held together by metal staples, which signal the superior strength of the industrial metal over the decomposing wood, leaving a pitiful impression. The work thus incorporates two levels of injury and of scarification: that imposed by modernity on the lands it exploits by way of its technologies, and the inevitable rupture of this progress, itself in desperate need of constant repair. This work does not repair itself, rather, it evokes reparation as conscience and awareness of the injury.

This work is symptomatic for Attia of how the modern West deals with injury. In his article "La réparation, c'est la conscience de la blessure" (Attia 2018a), the artist clarifies that for him "reparation" signifies, on the one hand, "d'aspects physiques et concrets de la réparation d'objets sacrés ou profanes, mais toujours rudimentaires – telles que les techniques de la réparation dans les sociétés antemodernes occidentales ou extra-occidentales, de l'Afrique au Japon" (Attia 2018a, 13). Here the artist evokes for instance the art of repair called *kintsugi* on traditional Japanese ceramics, for which "the cracks on the surface of the pots used for the tea ceremony are bathed in gold" (Attia 2018b). As he puts it, this creates "an incredible fusion of injury and repair – by repairing an object so roughly you actually leave the injury visible" (Attia 2018b). In this way, he continues, "repair and the injury are linked forever" (Attia 2018b). He radically opposes the conception of a link between repair and injury to the idea that "we can rationally control everything, even the injury [. . .] to give back an object or a human body its own initial shape" (Attia 2018b). As he puts it, this is the flipside of the non-occidental capacity to leave the injury tied to the scar; there is a kind of "dogme" of "contrôle de la blessure, en s'obstinant à la faire disparaitre complètement, en niant l'histoire de l'objet ou du corps blessé, et ainsi le temps qui s'associe à cette histoire" (Attia 2018a: 13).

In his public lectures, Attia often evokes an anecdote that encapsulates this ideology. He recounted a conversation he had with a curator-conservator at the Ethnological Museum in Berlin, who proudly presented him with an object that was perfectly repaired after shattering, to the extent that the lines of the detailed piecing together were left invisible. All traces of the shock that cracked the object gone; a perfect replica of what was before the incident. That day in his talk, he described this as a "blindness towards injury" and a "paradigm of repairability" that represents not solely the Western obsession with the putting back together of what has been destroyed – "to think that everything can be repaired" (Attia 2018b), but also the inability of Western museological institutions to admit cracks, scars, wounds, gaps. It is a form of "denial of the injury, the denial of the destruction" (Attia 2018b). Confronting this evasiveness towards injury and illness, for

Attia, is not merely a process of practical confrontation, but a more fundamental socio-psychic anxiety.

It is for this reason that it appears for Attia so

> important de travailler sur cette question de la réparation, et *de facto* d'un point de vue aussi physique que théorique, voir politique, pour comprendre la nécessité de ré-évoquer ces blessures immatérielles, de l'esclavage à la colonisation, de la dépossession à l'humiliation, qui perdurent aujourd'hui à travers toute forme d'expression à la fois névrotique, juridique, économique, politique des êtres qui dominent, qui ont le pouvoir sur ceux qui subissent le pouvoir (Attia 2018a, 14).

It is here that he concludes: "Car la réparation c'est la conscience de la blessure, même lorsque la réparation semble irréparable . . ." (Attia 2018a, 14). The question that we pose ourselves in this contribution is how this conception of repair, irreparability, and cultural memory can be translated into a museological conception. How may ideas of embodied scars and the conscience of injury inform the way we think (of) museums containing collections of difficult heritage pertaining to the colonial European past? In the following and final section of this essay, we analyse the way in which museums themselves may incur injuries, and how one might address their state of disrepair.

3 A Museum of Disrepair

The Congolese activist Mwazulu Diyabanza created both international outrage and fascination when he orchestrated a series of spectacular museum "thefts", during which he dislodged art objects from the African continent that were located within European ethnographic museum collections and had been assembled in dubious circumstances.

"We go home". With these words, whispered to the object, Diyabanza accompanies a nineteenth century wooden funerary pole expropriated from Chad during the French colonial period through the galleries of the Parisian Musée du Quai Branly-Jacques Chirac in the French capital.[3] He had dislodged the pole from its display and made for the exit, filmed, and protected by "comrades" (2018). Speaking live to social media while clinging his hands firmly onto the artefact and ignoring the shouting of the guards, he looks into the camera and reiterates his charge: "I have come to recuperate this in the name of unity and

---

[3] This can be watched on YouTube via this link: https://www.youtube.com/watch?v=jyjH-ZIvBDo&t=133s (19 December 2022).

dignity [. . .] We go home, and we do not ask a thief for permission [. . .] What belongs to us, belongs to us" (see footnote 3).

Diyabanza's first action in Paris on 12 June 2020 was followed suit by similarly spectacular, vocal, and live-streamed choreographies in Marseille's Museum of African, Oceanic and Indian Art inside the Vieille Charité (July); in the Africa Museum in Berg en Dal in the Netherlands (September), and in the Louvre (October). He was subsequently arrested, heard in court, and charged with "attempted joint theft of a cultural asset" (Otieno 2020). While Diyabanza and his colleagues faced prison terms and a six-figure fine, he received a minimum sentence of 2,000 Euro. The judges refused to engage with the vast ideological scope of his performance, stating that they are "not competent to judge France's colonial era".[4]

French officials denounced Diyabanza's interventions as threatening negotiations with African countries, following President Emmanuel Macron's launch of reports on restitution and reconciliation three years ago. However, this appears to be the same desperate resorting to "Europe's self-referential legality" (Otieno 2020) that patrimony laws on inalienability have already rehearsed in previous attempts of restitution. His performances have instead raised the curtain on a complicated machinery of justifications, excuses, and anxieties; consequently, the time has come to think of a different future for ethnographic collections, ethnological museums, and, indeed, the entire Western model of the curation of objects signifying historical injury and injustice.

The questions towering over Diyabanza's trial are simple, yet consequential: Who holds court? Who is accused? What is justice? His companions and lawyers argued that they are in fact putting on trial the entire French state and its colonial heritage, enshrined in its modern institutions and the legal framework of national patrimony that protects them as inalienably French. This goes for other countries too, where restitution lags behind the yet unsystematic work of provenance, and the public opening of inventory lists that prevent calls for restitution to be made in the first instance.

So, while the French judges in the Parisian capital attempted to scale down the trial against Diyabanza to a mere case of theft, he goes the other direction: this is a trial against an entire system based on extraction and exploitation, which has, in turn, served to build up not only the social sciences and their legacies of inventing both race and culture, but also art history and its canonised modernist guises. What is rhetorically and symbolically put on trial is European universalism, and

---

4 This is according to a report by AP Archive. Diyabanza's reaction in court can be watched here: https://www.youtube.com/watch?v=iVGBdqRThYg (19 December 2022).

the Western sovereign claim to represent, collect, display, and reason on world heritage. The museums and heritage institutions on trial are those that, while they may pluralise interpretations, continue to narrate a story of world from the epicentres of European imperial modernity.

If thus the crime scene is not the theft of a funerary pole, but the museum itself, the injustice of colonialism and its crimes against humanity, then repair may not be achieved through reparation. Loot may not be mitigated by restitution. And reparation cannot repay injustice. Instead, as Achille Mbembe (2020) posited in a conversation aptly titled "The Paranoia of the Western Mind", the West may need to acknowledge the debt of truth and move towards a "reparative globalism" – although that is only one way of looking at it.

When Mwazulu Diyabanza walks through the courtyard of the Vieille Charité in Marseille during his second attempted recuperation of African heritage, and finds himself locked into the vicinity by observant security and harassed by local bystanders, he turns around and addresses the tourists in the courtyard cafe: "Are you complicit with the Occident's crime against humanity?"[5]

Perhaps, the issue at stake thus is justice and equality on a more than national level. If "reparative globalism" (Mbembe 2020), "a new relational ethics" (Sarr and Savoy 2018), and the "politics of making humanity together" (Diagne 2019) are what is being negotiated, then museums of world heritage are not getting rid of the stains on their histories by simply sharing a few of their most problematically acquired items (Sarr and Savoy 2018; Diagne 2022).[6] In fact, shared heritage can rightly be called a "coward, but genius" invention of the western museum of world (see Tinius 2021a; Tinius and Carroll 2020).[7] Restitution can only be an element, albeit an important one, of a wider discourse on reconciliation, decolonisation, and infrastructural changes to Europe's narrative of world. Justice, then, may exceed the framework of Europe's self-referential legality, and become a form-giving vector (Hofmann and Messling 2021). Reflections on justice can give rise to ethical and aesthetical practices in museal terms (Rotinwa 2020).

---

5 This video, like many others, can be watched on his personal Facebook site called Mwazulu Diyabanza Siwa Lemba official.
6 See the *Restitution Report* by Felwine Sarr and Bénédicte Savoy, published as *The Restitution of African Cultural Heritage. Toward a New Relational Ethics* (2018), accessible via: http://restitutionreport2018.com/sarr_savoy_en.pdf (28 August 2022) and a lecture given by Souleymane Bachir Diagne at the University of Nantes in 2019 under the title "Faire humanité ensemble". It is accessible via: https://www.youtube.com/watch?v=MS-TvPVT7u8 (19 December 2022).
7 A member of the public during an event on restitution during the Manifesta 2020 in Marseille accused the director of the public museums in Marseille of acting thusly. Watch the video and access full documentation of the event here: https://manifesta13.org/programmings/rencontres-tracing-fractures-across-listening-movement-restitution-and-repair/ (28 August 2022).

The future of European museums of world with problematic collections will have to undo a number of assumptions, beginning with their approach to repair and injury. Many proposals have been made, for example, to reconcile old museum infrastructures with their contemporary critique. Notable propositions include those of former director of the *Museum of World Cultures* in Germany's Frankfurt am Main, Clémentine Deliss (2020), to open up storages and create artistic engagements, or the frank account of death-writing about looted objects by Dan Hicks, curator at the *Oxford Pitt-Rivers Museum* (2020), which have together suggested museums as "investments in critical discomfort" (Modest 2020). Such investments may challenge the very infrastructures, personnel, and programming of museums, or reconsider what a museum may do.

In his article "Those Who Are Dead Are Not Ever Gone" (2020), curator Bonaventure Soh Bejeng Ndikung asks whether museums cannot, perhaps, be considered as apoptotic archives that allow for its objects to be rehabituated, resocialised, or even abandoned – asking for a broader and corporeal conception of museum work. Ndikung evokes the metaphor of museum-choking, suggesting that the "coughing from the choking throes of the ethnological museum / world museum / universal museum is becoming loud and blaring" and that the "blows and punches" needed to unblock the windpipe of the Western museum, which devoured its objects "with little focus on mastication", come in multiple ways. Besides the proposed reckoning with its process of devouring and choking, Ndikung makes a proposal that puts to one side the museum and its collection and instead asks for a different, incorporated view on how we view processes of repair and injury in relationship to the museum of world. He proposes "to think of the body as the primary museum" (Ndikung 2020), which puts centre-stage the question "How then does this primary museum of the body encounter the secondary museum, which tends to be those spaces in which 'objects' are conserved?" Put most bluntly: "If the secondary museum becomes a site of concern, of insult, of epistemic violence; a site of the erasure of histories, a site of hubris, then what impact does that have on the beholder, the visitor, the citizen, the human?" (Ndikung 2020).

In our workshop at Villa Vigoni, we confronted students with these thoughts on irreparability, the body, and the primary and secondary museum. We asked them what thinking about injury and irreparability could change in our understanding of these "secondary museums"? Considered as mediators and carries of possible relationships between the body as museum and objects incorporating historical injustice, museums offer ways of pointing to the wound without repair. Thus, we suggested, they are ways of thinking about the state of disrepair of relations between bodies and objects, institutions and societies. Considering that museums of world are thus themselves in a state of disrepair, what would it mean to point to the incompleteness of such museums, the injuries they inflict? Instead of imagining a museum of repair or museums *as* repair, what about a museum of disrepair that points to the incomplete processes of healing?

4 An Open Conclusion: Towards a Museum of Disrepair

Together with the students of the Summer School, we split in pairs, and with some material – cardboard, objects brought by participants, pens, scissors, sticky tape – we imagined possible forms and paths for a museum of disrepair. We asked, among others, the following questions: What would such a museum be called? What – if any – objects would it house? Would *your* objects be in such a museum? How would like to be and feel within this museum? Do you feel like injuring it for the injuries it has caused? Do we even need a museum of disrepair?

The miniature model of the museum, placed in front of Villa Vigoni – a site of negotiation for repair, redress, and the mediation of injury – evoked both refusal and embrace. Half of the students questioned whether a museum as a *site* and a physical *institution* was indeed necessary. If a museum is about the people whose objects it contains or about communities to whom its objects should speak, one student put it poignantly, then why do we not try to make the museum about these communities – "why do we even need objects at all?". "It needs an agora, a place of encounter and dialogue". "Reparations", another student interjected, "are about building new relationships", by which she was referring to the argument of the Sarr-Savoy restitution report (2018), she added. Moreover, it was felt that a museum that is about relationships should change directions itself, somehow be in flux and think about displacement more than fixation. This could be done, another student suggested, by thinking about the story of its collections and the museum itself – "opening up the instability of the institution". To this, another student added that collections could themselves "travel and in that way move the museum itself". A concrete third suggestion was made: "A museum of repair or disrepair", the student remarked, "should contain the history of all the mistakes and inexactitudes of its labels, its decisions, and its descriptions – and show their progressive corrections and changes. We need a museum that shows its own ability to see its mistakes."

A second strand of the discussion erupted when a student began a strand of thought about Bonaventure Soh Bejeng Ndikung's text that we had read earlier that afternoon (see Ndikung 2020). The student remarked: "When someone dies, their descendants continue to honour the deceased and thereby their lives; if museums contain the stories of others, then the museum becomes a body multiple. It is about the creation of life, and not about the conservation of the dead". "Why then", another student responded, "do we think about a museum that looks inwards to bring things into it, rather than looking outward to bring what it has into the world?" The student continued to reflect: "Before asking what kind of museum we want, we have to ask ourselves what part of society this museum – and museums in general – is; in other words, what is the relationship of this museum to the society in which it is built?"

A third and final strand of the discussion erupted itself in violence. "I want to cut the museum into pieces – this cardboard box", one student provocatively interjected, prompting laughter and some shouts of "yeah, yes" among the students. "We should not have objects, but actions!", the student continued, saying that thinking about repair, as we did with Kader Attia, is not about erecting more monuments, but about "inhabiting a future together". "It is a social project, and societies are broken – so the museum itself should be broken, and not be a museum *of* repair."

The students' forceful remarks, concluding into an action of destruction itself, left us wondering how to put together these suggestions as theorisations about a museum conception that take into account our discussion of racialisation, brokenness, and injury. Most evidently, it seems to us that a museum that deals with the impossibility of repair and erasure of injury should itself bear both the marks of pain and scarification. It is not an empty museum devoid of memories of pain, and neither is it a peaceful projection of conciliation and peace. In some way, it should put on display the brokenness of its past, the failures, and the attempts of repair that it has undertaken. A site that, like Villa Vigoni, hosts encounters about its own status, that constantly asks what its purpose is, and challenges its self-evidence. A Museum of Broken Relationships.[8] A Museum of Scars.

References

Ahmed, Sara. "Racialized Bodies." *Real Bodies. A Sociological Introduction*. Eds. Mary Evans and Ellie Lee. Basingstoke: Palgrave, 2002. 46–63.
———. The Cultural Politics of Emotion. Edinburgh: Edinburgh University Press, 2004.
Alcoff, Martín Linda. *Visible Identities. Race, Gender and the Self*. Oxford: Oxford University Press, 2006.
Attia, Kader. "La réparation, c'est la conscience de la blessure." *Décolonisons les arts*. Eds. Leila Cukierman, Gerty Dambury, and Françoise Vergès. Paris: L'Arche, 2018a. 11–14.

---

[8] We discussed the actual crowd-sourced project called The Museum of Broken Relationships with the students, too (see: https://brokenships.com, 20 September 2022).

_____. "Injury and Repair: Kader Attia." Conversation with Gabriele Sassone. *Mousse Magazine* (10 May 2018b). https://www.moussemagazine.it/magazine/injury-and-repair-kader-attia-2018/ (10 September 2022).

Bewes, Timothy. *The Event of Postcolonial Shame*. Princeton, N.J.: Princeton University Press, 2011.

Boggero, Giovanni and Karin Oellers-Frahm. "Between Cynicism and Idealism: Is the Italian Constitutional Court Passing the Buck to the Italian Judiciary?" *Remedies against Immunity? Reconciling International and Domestic Law after the Italian Constitutional Court's Sentenza 238/2014*. Eds. Valentina Volpe, Anne Peters, and Stefano Battini. Berlin: Springer, 2021. 281–309.

Butler, Judith. *Gender Trouble: Feminism and the Subversion of Identity*. New York: Routledge, 1990.

_____. "Endangered/Endangering: Schematic Racism and White Paranoia." *Reading Rodney King, Reading Urban Uprising*. Ed. Gooding-Williams Robert. New York: Routledge, 1993. 15–22.

_____. "Performative Acts and Gender Constitution: An Essay in Phenomenology and Feminist Theory." *Theatre Journal* 40.4 (1998): 519–531.

Cassin, Barbara. "La langue française n'est pas statique, elle est faite pour changer." *Libération* (14 December 2018). https://liberation.fr/debats/2018/12/14/barbara-cassin-la-langue-francaise-n-est-pas-statique-elle-est-faite-pour-changer_1697963/ (13 September 2022).

Cassin, Barbara and Thierry Fabre. "À quoi sert de mettre en place un universel s'il est multiple? Entretien avec Barbara Cassin." *Partager l'universel? D'une rive à l'autre*. Ed. Thierry Fabre. Arles: Arnaud Bizalion, 2022. 7–19.

Deliss, Clémentine. *The Metabolic Museum*. Berlin: Hatje Cantz, 2020.

Fanon, Frantz. *Black Skin, White Masks*. Transl. Richard Philcox. New York: Grove Press, 1952 [2008].

Goldberg, David Theo. "Racial Europeanization." *Ethnic and Racial Studies* 29 (2006): 331–364.

Hicks, Dan. *The Brutish Museums. The Benin Bronzes, Colonial Violence and Cultural Restitution*. London: Pluto Press, 2020.

Holiday, Harmony. "Reparations begin in the body: A crucial look at why the first and most crucial poetic gesture for a black poet in the West is a knowledge and mastery of her body." *Poetry Foundation* (6 October 2016). https://www.poetryfoundation.org/harriet-books/2016/10/reparations-begin-in-the-body-a-look-at-why-the-first-and-most-crucial-poetic-gesture-for-a-black-poet-in-the-west-is-a-knowledge-and-mastery-of-her-body (13 September 2022).

Hofmann, Franck and Markus Messling. Eds. *The Epoch of Universalism 1769–1989 / L'époque de l'universalisme 1769–1989*. Berlin, Boston: De Gruyter, 2021.

Messling, Markus. *Gebeugter Geist. Rassismus und Erkenntnis in der modernen europäischen Philologie*. Göttingen: Wallstein, 2016.

Milo Rau in conversation with Achille Mbembe. "The Paranoia of the Western Mind. Why is it so difficult to recognize a non-European universalism?" *Paranoia TV*, 2020. https://www.paranoia-tv.com/en/program/content/383-milo-rau-in-conversation-with-achille-mbembe-the-paranoia-of-the-western-mind (28 August 2022).

Modest, Wayne. "Museums are Investments in Critical Discomfort." *Across Anthropology. Troubling Colonial Legacies, Museums, and the Curatorial*. Eds. Margareta von Oswald and Jonas Tinius. Leuven: Leuven University Press, 2020. 65–76.

Nandi, Miriam and Paul Spickard. "The Curious Career of the One-Drop Rule: Multiraciality and Membership in Germany Today." *Global Mixed Race*. Eds. Rebecca C. King-O'Riain, Stephen Small, Minelle Mahtani, Miri Song, and Paul Spickard. New York: New York University Press, 2014. 188–212.

Ndikung, Bonaventure Soh Bejeng. "Those Who Are Dead Are Not Ever Gone." *South As a State of Mind* 10 (2020): 36–59.

Otieno, Eric. "Why Restitution Won't Happen If Europe Controls the Terms." *Frieze Magazine* (25 November 2020). https://www.frieze.com/article/why-restitution-wont-happen-if-europe-controls-terms (15 August 2022).
Paulus, Andreas L. "Between a Rock and a Hard Place: Italian Concerns Between Constitutional Rights and International Law." *Remedies against Immunity? Reconciling International and Domestic Law after the Italian Constitutional Court's Sentenza 238/2014*. Eds. Valentina Volpe, Anne Peters, and Stefano Battini. Berlin: Springer, 2021. 337–342.
Pavoni, Riccardo. "A Plea for Legal Peace." *Remedies against Immunity? Reconciling International and Domestic Law after the Italian Constitutional Court's Sentenza 238/2014*. Eds. Valentina Volpe, Anne Peters, and Stefano Battini. Berlin: Springer, 2021. 93–118.
Pesarini, Angelica and Tintori, Guido. "Mixed Identities in Italy. A Country in Denial." *The Palgrave International Handbook of Mixed Racial and Ethnic Classification*. Eds. Peter Aspinall and Zarine Rocha. London: Palgrave MacMillan, 2020. 349–365
Pesarini, Angelica. "You Were the Shame of Race: Dynamics of Pain, Shame and Violence in Shape Shifting Processes." *Shape Shifter: Journeys Across Terrains of Race and Identity*. Eds. Paul Spickard, Lily Anne Y. Welty-Tamai, and Ingrid Dineen-Wimberly. Lincoln (NE): University of Nebraska Press, 2020. 189–219.
———. "Making visible the invisible: Colonial sources and counter body-archives in the boarding schools for Black 'mixed race' Italian children in Fascist East Africa" *Journal of Postcolonial Writing*, forthcoming (2022).
Peters, Anne and Valentina Volpe. "Reconciling State Immunity with Remedies for War Victims in a Legal Pluriverse." *Remedies against Immunity? Reconciling International and Domestic Law after the Italian Constitutional Court's Sentenza 238/2014*. Eds. Valentina Volpe, Anne Peters, and Stefano Battini. Berlin: Springer, 2021. 3–35.
Rotinwa, Ayodeji. "'Restitution is important but it is not essential': the African museums building a homegrown cultural revival." *The Art Newspaper* (27 November 2020). https://www.theartnewspaper.com/analysis/african-museums-restitution (28 August 2022).
Sarr, Felwine and Bénédicte Savoy. *Restituer le patrimoine africain*. Paris: Philippe Rey / Seuil, 2018.
Treacher, Amal. "Postcolonial subjectivity: Masculinity, shame, and memory." *Ethnic and Racial Studies* 30.2 (2007): 281–299.
Tharoor, Shashi. "Können Reparationszahlungen die Schulden der Geschichte jemals begleichen." Transl. Maria-Anna Schiffers. *Rhinozeros. Europa im Übergang* 1 (2021): 68–73.
Tinius, Jonas. "Animated Words, Will Accompany my Gestures". Seismographic Choreographies of Difficult Heritage in Museums." *Moving Spaces. Enacting Dance, Performance, and the Digital in the Museum*. Eds. Susanne Franco and Gabriella Giannachi. Venice: Università Ca' Foscari Press / Edizioni Ca' Foscari, 2021a. 77–92.
———. "Verso un museo postuniversale." *Art e Dossier* 384 (2021b): 26–29.
———. "Il lavoro (im)possibile della riparazione. Kader Attia e la Biennale di Berlino." *Art e Dossier* 401 (Sept. 2022): 18–21.
———. *State of the Arts. An Ethnography of German Theatre and Migration*. Cambridge: Cambridge University Press, forthcoming (2023).
Tinius, Jonas and Alexander Wewerka. *Der fremde Blick. Roberto Ciulli und das Theater an der Ruhr*. Berlin: Alexander Verlag, 2020.
Tinius, Jonas and Khadija von Zinnenburg Carroll. "Phantom Palaces: Prussian Centralities and Humboldtian Horizontalities." *Re-Centring the City. Global Mutations of Socialist Modernity*. Eds. Jonathan Bach and Michal Murawski (with Khadija von Zinnenburg Carroll). London: UCL Press (Open-access), 2020. 90–103.

Tomuschat, Christian. "No Consensus – but Hope at Villa Vigoni". *VerfBlog*, 2017/5/18, https://verfassungsblog.de/no-consensus-but-hope-at-villa-vigoni/ (20 September 2022).
Whyte, Murray. "In Kader Attia's show at the Power Plant, tracks from colonialism's bloody past lead to here and now." *Toronto Star* (14 February 2018). https://www.thestar.com/entertainment/visualarts/opinion/2018/02/14/in-kader-attias-show-at-the-power-plant-tracks-from-colonialisms-bloody-past-lead-to-here-and-now.html (12 September 2022).

Clément Ndé Fongang
Repairing Cultural and Museum Cooperation between Cameroon and Europe

Abstract: How can we recreate conditions for a relationship based on reciprocity and mutuality between Europe and Africa? How do we repair this relationship? Beginning with these questions, this contribution analyses museum and cultural cooperation between Cameroon and Europe from the 1960s to the present day. Building on Kwame Nkrumah's and Ade Ajayi's concepts of decolonization and "Reparation" (with a capital R) on the one hand, and Aimé Césaire's and Philipp Schorch and Noelle Kahanu's concepts of cooperation on the other, the chapter interrogates legal and institutional mechanisms of this cultural cooperation such as the formal agreements on which it is based, as well as participating institutions and their impact in Cameroon today. By addressing museums as one of the many legacies of (post)colonial relations between Cameroon and Europe, the chapter aims to contribute to the debate on the future of the colonial legacy in Cameroon.[1]

Keywords: grassroot, Aimé Césaire, Cameroon, development, museum, bilateral and multilateral cooperation, musealisation/demusealisation, decolonization, Reparation, Jean-Marc Ela

> The ultimate ethnocentrism is one in which recognition of the other is based solely upon the similarity to self (Ravenhill 1986, 34).

1 Introduction

It is almost impossible to talk about museums in Europe and Africa today without bringing up the issue of restitution and reparation. Under the pressure of activists, postcolonial critics and researchers in publications such as the special issue of *Cahiers d'Études africaines* no 173–174 edited by Bogumil Jewsiewicki in 2004, and especially more recently in 2018, after the Sarr and Savoy report, the museum

---

1 Research that led to the publication of this article was supported by a PhD studentship of the project "Minor Universality. Narrative World Productions After Western Universalism", which received funding from the European Research Council (ERC) under the European Union's Horizon 2020 research and innovation programme (Grant agreement No. 819931).

has turned into a theatre of heated discussions on restitution and reparation. The opening of the Humboldt Forum[2] in Berlin illustrates this strikingly. However, as Bénédicte Savoy has pointed out, this debate is not novel, because almost every conversation we are having today about the restitution of looted cultural objects to Africa took place 40 years ago (Savoy 2021, 195). Addressing the failure of restitution in the 1970s, she reveals that museums lied to prevent the return of colonial objects to Africa. And over many years, laws in European countries have declared most of these objects public property, thus making restitution very difficult today (Sarr and Savoy 2018).

This situation has left some African claimants sceptical about Reparation[3] and despairing of any hope that it might take place, viewing it as recolonializing Africa (Ajayi 2004; Bayena and Monteh 2021). This position is fuelled by the rhetoric of refusal[4] held by European museums and governments that characterises the current debate where reason and the will to make humanity together are not shared. Considering all this, Ade Ajayi wrote in 2004 that it should not be expected, however, that convincing arguments for Reparation will be sufficient to persuade people to accept or make amendments. There is, he writes, an old adage that it is almost as difficult to wake the dead as it is to wake someone who is pretending to be asleep. No one is harder to convince than someone who has decided in advance not to succumb to the logic of an argument (Ajayi 2004, par. 1). Another African intellectual to explicitly talk about this aspect of Reparation is Chimamanda Ngozi Adichie. In her opening speech at the Humboldt Forum in 2021, she said, "And so it seems to me that what we are fundamentally grappling with in this space, in all of these questions about the Humboldt Forum, is power, unequal power, how we

---

2 The renovation and opening of the Prussian palace in 2021 were preceded by numbers of critical voices who decried it for perpetuating colonial hegemony over other non-European cultures (see for example AfricAvenir International e.V. 2017).
3 The term "Reparation" in the singular and with a capital R as conceptualised by Ade Ajayi will be used in this essay to refer to both reparation and restitution. According to Ajayi (2004), who coined the term in the context of slavery, Reparation is about redressing the harm done, not about assigning blame, seeking revenge or claiming financial compensation. It is about restoring justice. However, this analysis will be less concerned with reparation for the wrongs of slavery than focus on postcolonial wrongs.
4 I refer to the silence of governments (Savoy and Sarr 2018) and the classical arguments against the restitution of colonial looted artefacts: that the objects have long been part of European culture, European cultural heritage and cultural consciousness (a view that obscures the colonial past and argument about the irreversibility of history); preservation of the collections and conservation of the objects according to the highest scientific standards; the fear of a domino effect after some restitutions; circulation of knowledge and expositions in a globalised world (von Oswald 2018; Savoy 2021). This includes endless planning and talking with urge financial support (Adichie 2021).

navigate unequal power relations" (Adichie 2021, 8:49–9:03). At the same time, many intellectuals regard restitution as an opportunity for Europe to repair and reinvent its relationship with Africa (Mbembe 2018). Against this background, a question arises: how can reparation be made a means of true justice and reconciliation rather than an instrument for geopolitical and strategic power interests, so that it once again enables equal footing in the negotiations between Europe and Africa? How can we recreate the conditions for a relationship based on reciprocity and mutuality (Mbembe 2018) between Europe and Africa? If states have until now been the important main actors of Reparation, how can negotiations be possible in this context?

Rather than providing a definitive and complete answer to these questions, in this contribution I will analyse cultural and especially museum cooperation between Cameroon and Europe in the context of restitution and reparation from a postcolonial perspective. Focusing on media (print and audio-visual media) and scientific writings after the independence of Cameroon in the 1960s to the present, it seeks more specifically to understand the cultural and museum cooperation between the two parties, the conditions under which "negotiations"[5] on Reparation are likely to be conducted, and how they are likely to contribute to repair this relation. In this regard, I consider that reparation also means decolonization in the sense of Kwame Nkrumah and Ade Ajayi. The latter, drawing on Kwame Nkrumah's thoughts, defines decolonisation as the action of erasing the psychological and other effects of the colonial regime (economic exploitation, underdevelopment etc.). These psychological sequelae include a loss of self-respect, confidence and cultural sensitivity (Ajayi 2004, par. 7). On this basis, the study does not consider collaboration or cooperation, as it was developed and spread in the 1960s, as a relationship between the "rich" states of the North and the "poor" states of the South, with the aim of compensating economic, technical and technological backwardness of the latter by the former (Mpegna 2014, 42). Contrarily, it refers to a conception developed by Aimé Césaire at the same time: he defined collaboration as a "rendez-vous du donner et du recevoir" (Césaire quoted in Senghor 1983, 1). Or as Schorch and Kahanu (2015, 112) explain, a "dialogue which does not involve a gestural accommodation of the subaltern part for its eventual assimilation within the dominant whole, but refers to a conscious, methodological co-production and co-interpretation [. . .]". From the outset, this study on cooperation appears to be a subject of international law. However, it does not pretend to replace the work of a jurist, an economist or a political scientist, but it invites the

---

5 Every restitution effected till now seems to go through (diplomatic) negotiations most often with joint declarations as in case with Nigeria and Germany or France and Senegal and Benin.

latter as well as the actors of cooperation between Cameroon and Europe to reflect more deeply on their longstanding relationships by rethinking the premises of their cultural relations. In the same way, this contribution is also a plea for some Cameroonian and African political actors to re-tune their interest not only in Reparation but also in the cultural domain as most of their partners do. This contribution first analyses the legal and institutional mechanisms of the cultural relationship between Cameroon and its European partners. It then examines Cameroonian museums as a result of the relationship between Cameroon and Europe.

2 Agreements on Cultural Cooperation and the Need for Revisions

Since laws and treaties are the basis of state relations and states are the main interlocutors of Reparation, it is worth looking at the cultural cooperation agreements between Cameroon and Europe to understand the conditions and factors that may prevent the two parties from repairing their relationship. When dealing with cultural cooperation between Cameroon and Europe, or its "traditional partners" according to the expression used in Yaoundé, we primarily see the former colonial power, France, with which Cameroon has been having a "privileged"[6] relationship, sometimes close and friendly, sometimes cold and tense, for over 60 years. This section focuses on two moments in these relations: the signing of a series of cooperation accords in 1960 and their revision in 1974. The aim is to review the legal and institutional framework of cooperation between Cameroon and its partners in the cultural sector and the impact this may have on Reparation.

2.1 The 1960 Cultural Convention

In the aftermath of independence, between June 1960 and July 1963, the French government concluded nearly thirty cultural agreements with the 13 new African republics and Republic of Madagascar, known as "Accords de coopération Culturelle" (1960). In the case of Cameroon, however, a "Convention Culturelle" and subsidiary

---

6 Already present in the 1960s, the controversial term "accord" is also used to characterise "how the EU is well ahead of Cameroon's partners, given the volume of exchange, without forgetting French, British, German, Dutch, and Spanish. . . cooperation on the bilateral side" (Presidency of the Republic of Cameroon).

agreements were signed in 1960. These agreements cover socio-cultural sectors, namely education, scientific research, language and cultural activities and information (broadcasting and press). For the young African states, these agreements and conventions were vital to affirm their sovereignty and cultural autonomy, and to mark the egalitarian and reciprocal nature of cultural exchanges, as expressly formulated in the preambles to the documents. But this was not in fact the case: as France shouldered most of the responsibility, the symmetry only existed on paper.

As Guy Feuer (1963, 901) argues, the main purpose of this series of agreements is above all to organise French assistance to the young independent states. This assistance was both technical and financial. In return, French authorities were obviously granted important prerogatives ("privileges") intended to enable them to perform their obligations as effectively as possible, while protecting their own interests. This situation is reflected in the agreements by practical provisions. Most importantly, the preamble to the 1960 Franco-Cameroonian Cultural Convention emphasized that French is the official language of Cameroon as in other former French colonies. This was justified by the claim that the French language, in contrast to the multitude of local dialects in Cameroon, should serve as an instrument of development and national unity. The convention on cooperation in the field of scientific and technical research stipulates that the various levels of education in the African states should be coordinated with French education. Other European languages were introduced gradually because of Cameroon's colonial past with Great Britain and Germany, following a 1963 cultural convention. On October 1, 1961, with the decision of Western Cameroon, until then under British rule, to join the Republic of Cameroon, English became one of the two official languages. At the same time German was reintroduced into the Cameroonian educational system as a direct consequence of the Élysée Treaty signed a few months earlier, in January 1963, for "la réconciliation du peuple allemand et du peuple français, mettant fin à une rivalité séculaire" (de Gaulle and Adenauer 2012 [1963], 22). Spanish, Latin, etc. were introduced automatically with the application of the French educational system in Cameroon (Fogang Toyem, 2016). By so doing, this language policy continues to hinder and even threaten the existence of Cameroonian culture, as Bahoken and Atangana (1976, 14) write: "not only is language the instrument in and through which the spirit of the community is forged, but it is also one of its specific manifestations."

In order to perform its mission and implement its cultural foreign policy, the French government used a number of structures in its former colonies, but museum did not play a significant role here. The term "museum" remained in shadow. The French foreign policy in Cameroon focused mainly on language, education and culture. Belmond Mpegna's study on French institutions in Cameroon from the 1960s to 2000 sheds light on the political dimension of the founding of French cultural institutions in Cameroon. The Centre culturel François Villon in Yaoundé and et Centre culturel Blaise Cendras in Douala were established in 1962.[7] They aimed to promote and disseminate French culture on the one hand and, on the other, to prevent Cameroon from falling under the political and cultural influence of the English-speaking world through the Anglophone part of Cameroon (British Cameroon) and to compete with the British Council (Mpegna 2014, 55). Four Franco-Cameroonian alliances were also opened in the regions with low penetration of French, notably in ex-British Cameroon, in Buea and Bamenda, and in Ngaoundéré and Garoua. Their mission was to extend the French language throughout Cameroon. In the education sector, the French Inspectorate of Education and the French Foundation for Higher Education were responsible for running and overseeing education in Cameroon. The research and technical institutions include the Office de recherche scientifique et technique d'outre-mer (ORSTOM), the Institut de recherches agronomiques tropicales (IRAT) based in Dschang and Guétalé and the Institut Pasteur. This French cultural policy was financed by the Fonds d'Aide et de la Coopération (FAC), a special fund created in 1959 to help Africans fight against underdevelopment. According to Mpegna (2014, 231), the "collaboration" was merely unilateral. Despite the reciprocity clauses in Article 4 of the Cultural Convention, Cameroon had no institutions in France or in other partner countries. Educational institutions were a monopoly of the Metropole. Other accompanying accords guarantee France either a monopoly or quasi-monopoly on higher education or at least a priority on the choice of staff members not directly involved in higher education (Mpegna 2014; Feuer 1963).

A specific feature of the 1960–1963 conventions is the strong presence of the ideas of solidarity and association. Indeed, the emphasis on these ideas not only underlines the equality between the co-contracting parties, but more importantly highlights their "communauté d'esprit" and the practical intermingling of their institutions (Feuer 1963). These ideas are expressed in the names of the institutions, such as "Alliance Franco-Camerounaise", or in the conventions by the frequent use of the term "en commun". According to Guy de Lusignan (1970, 79), through these agreements and conventions, the French president de Gaulle aimed to gather all former French colonies into a Franco-African community in order to save what remained of colonisation. Therefore, the cultural conventions were merely a legal condition for maintaining the French language and culture in France's former

---

7 In 2012, the François Villon cultural centre in Yaoundé and the Blaise Cendras cultural centre in Douala merged with the Service de Coopération et d'Action Culturelle of the French Embassy to become the Institut français du Cameroun (IFC).

African colonies, and for developing an intellectual and political elite in the French cultural tradition.

The importance of reviewing these first agreements and cultural conventions of the so-called independent Cameroon is obvious, because they form the basis of the current cultural relationship between Cameroon and France and Europe in general, and in some way contribute to the establishment of the highly contested network Françafrique (Deltombe et al. 2011). Although these accords do not explicitly address the museum component, we will see that they also prove to be crucial in defining the current cultural policy in Cameroon. However, it should be noted that the signing of these accords did not go smoothly. When they were concluded, many African states, including Senegal and Madagascar, and various independence movements expressed distrust, as they saw these agreements as colonial pact legitimating neo-colonialization. It was undoubtedly with the aim of defining a cultural policy anchored in African realities that African countries, including Cameroon, signed the *Pan African Cultural Manifesto* in 1969.[8] The acts of contestation of these neo-colonial and unilateral accords multiplied and intensified until the revisions of 1974.

2.2 The new 1974 Agreements

In Cameroon, the leaders of The Union of the Peoples of Cameroon (UPC) who were fighting for "total and immediate independence" already suspected that France did not want to "liberate" Cameroon, just like the other nations in the French sphere of influence (Mouna Mboa 2016). The fight led to the genocide committed against Bamiléké and Bassa people that remains unresearched to this day.[9] This critique,

---

8 This strong aspiration for sovereignty and autonomy clashes with other global projects. Few months after the adoption of the Manifesto, a Meeting of experts on problems of cultural policies in Africa (Dakar, 6–10 October 1969) was convened by UNESCO as part of the framework for preparing the Intergovernmental Conference on the Institutional, Administrative and Financial Aspects of Cultural Polices held in Venice in September 1970. The objective of the meeting was to identify and discuss problems confronted by African countries in the formulation and implementation of cultural policies (Máté Kovács 2009, 25–26).
9 Still debated by many experts, estimates of the death toll range from 100,000–400,000 people killed between 1959 and 1964. Cameroon attained independence amidst this genocide in 1960. This bloody repression lasted until 1971 and people are still very traumatized today and carrying the wound of it. Studies show this massacre paved the way for the cosy relations enjoyed between French political leaders and their African counterparts. In 2015, French President Hollande acknowledged colonial-era massacres in Cameroon, while critics called for an apology. See Deltombe et al. (2011) as well as Okello (2015).

although well expressed at the United Nations in the late 1950s, did not make the French leaders change their policy, as they loudly proclaimed that Cameroon's independence would be total. As indicated above, from 1960 to 1970, France enjoyed the exclusivity and primacy of Cameroon's foreign policy and was its main provider of socio-cultural and development aid. But after 1970, as Cameroon's leaders became aware of this deception, they decided to take Cameroonian cultural life out of its dependence on French cultural centres and Franco-Cameroonian alliances and worked on to diversifying their diplomatic partners.

This decision to place Cameroonian relations in the context of common international law led to what Belmond Mpegna (2014, 84–85) described as a period of recession (1970–1991) in the history of French-Cameroonian relations, during which the 1963 Conventions were amended. In the cultural sector, this period of recession was marked by a series of measures that included the withdrawal of Cameroon from the Francophone community, the refusal to participate in Francophone summits, the renegotiation of agreements and the signing of new cooperation accords. It is during this period that the Cameroonian authorities carried out a radical cultural revolution by strengthening the existing institutions and above all by establishing the National Council for Cultural Affairs in 1973. The latter was a standing advisory body responsible for shaping cultural policy.

Following the revisions of 21 February 1974, Cameroon gained a greater autonomy in the technical sectors, education, cultural activities and especially the orientations of cultural policy. France's influence diminished: technical assistance and aid for cultural activities disappeared in the 1980s, and French aid in the Cameroon cultural field decreased. However, this decrease was otherwise compensated by aid for structural adjustment (initiated by the Bretton Woods institutions in 1988), particularly in the form of loans through the French Development Agency. When the current president Paul Biya took office on 6 November 1982, he continued this recession or distancing policy towards France and the Breton wood institutions while intensifying the diversification of Cameroon partners as his predecessor Ahmadou Ahidjo initiated. This policy is expressed in his statements. During an official visit to the Federal Republic of Germany in 1986, he said about France: "le Cameroun n'est la chasse gardée de personne, ni d'aucune grande puissance" (Biya quoted in Moussa 2015). Several months later in 1987, he also declared that "le Cameroun n'ira pas au Fmi". But this lasted until 1991, when he was stopped dead in his tracks by two major world events. On the one hand, the economic crisis at the end of the 1980s forced him to open negotiations with the Breton Woods institutions for the setting up of drastic structural adjustment programmes. Before long, Cameroon had a huge debt to its donors. On the other hand, the fall of the Berlin Wall and the disintegration of the Soviet bloc led to worldwide standardisation and the imposition of democracy at the Baule Conference. The resumption of Franco-Cameroonian relations was therefore "unavoidable" (Mpegna 2014, 168). France appeared to Cameroon to be the only ally that could save it from the political and economic stagnation into which it had fallen. Cameroon therefore slowly joined organisations and groupings that had a French influence, either directly or indirectly. For example, Cameroon re-joined La Francophonie in November 1991. A new approach was adopted by Yaoundé. Paul Biya even told journalists on the steps of the Elysée Palace, after a meeting with the French president François Mitterrand: "Je ne crois pas démentir la pensée du président qui pense que je suis le meilleur élève" (Biya quoted in Moussa 2015). France once again became Cameroon's leading bilateral donor. From the French side, the interest remains to oust the growing influence of the United States in the 1990s which openly supports the opposition party in Cameroon (Mpegna 2014).

The instruments of French-African and French-Cameroonian cooperation were readapted or created. For example, the Priority Solidarity Fund (FSP) replaced the FAC, Agence Française de Dévelopement replaced the French Development Fund (CFD) in 1992, and the French National Research Institute for Sustainable Development replaced the ORSTOM (Mpegna 2014, 169). The dissemination of French language and culture was also to be achieved through audiovisual media, including Radio France International, TV5 and Canal France International. Today, 90% of the channels broadcast and offered to Cameroonians by satellite are French or Francophone. The domain of school and academic scholarship has experienced an exponential development (Mpegna 2014, 165–211).

This brief overview of the legal-institutional framework of cultural cooperation between Cameroon and its traditional partners, mainly France, has brought to light unilateral, asymmetric and damaging relations where the authorities in Yaoundé tend to adopt a policy of diversification in order to escape foreign powers influences. This political situation reminds us of what Albert Gouaffo (2011) said about Cameroonians remembering Germany to heal themselves from French or English colonial violence. Reparation would therefore consist in freeing oneself from this psychological and political confinement. The study of the 1963 and 1974 accords also reveals that the relationship between the donors and Cameroon was marked by a discourse of assistance, development and development aid. What are the implications of these agreements for Cameroon and its relations today?

2.3 Some Consequences of the Agreements in the Present

The effects and the legacy of the colonial and neo-colonial relationship are numerous and visible in Cameroon. The violence perpetrated in the colonial and present post-colonial periods affects Cameroon's cultural sector and to some extent the current debates on Reparation, which is not simply a cultural but a political and economic issue.

In general, Cameroon's cooperation with its partners, France in particular, has not been very satisfactory. Indeed, several studies describe the climate of this relationship as marked by mistrust, mutual incomprehension, opacity and non-transparency. The ex-post evaluation Final Report (2009) on the French cooperation instruments in Cameroon reveals that this situation is due to the divergent priorities of the two partners, the omnipresence and influence of the Western donors on Cameroon's strategic discourse and to the unconcern and negligence of the Cameroonian government. Similarly, the Paul Ango Ela Linear Report (2016) on cultural enterprises and creative industries in Cameroon observes that the government has abandoned its responsibilities to its partners and deplores the almost "non-existent" contribution of the government to the development and promotion of Cameroonian art and culture. A partial explanation of this can be found in the unequal and unilateral past agreements that have paved the way for French and foreign domination through their cultural cooperation institutions, leaving Cameroonian cultural and educational life in agony. As a result of this "surrealistic" situation (Mefe 2004, 20), artists and cultural actors only have to rely on the West as a "Messiah" to get funded. Tony Mefe (2004, 20) explains:

> Les seules bibliothèques sérieuses sont celles des centres culturels étrangers. Il en va de même pour ce qui a trait aux arts du spectacle : salles de spectacles adaptées, matériel de sonorisation et d'éclairage professionnel, techniciens de spectacle etc. Impossible pour une compagnie artistique d'obtenir quoi que ce soit dans ce domaine sans passer par les Centres culturels français, les Alliances françaises et l'Institut Goethe.

This foreign dependence, coupled with the scarcity of local funding, creates frustration owing to the inability of bilateral and multilateral partners to respond favourably to all requests and the "artistic vagueness" in the choice of projects that receive funding. There is no denying that, as a Guinean proverb says, the hand that gives is always above the hand that receives. Many critics therefore argue that Cameroonians should look after their own interests fairly and respectfully rather than expecting or asking for favours or assistance, and this even in the process of reparation. As Ade Ajayi puts it: "Je pense que nous irons plus loin en exigeant que justice soit rendue plutôt qu'en négociant avec les nations industrialisées, c'est-à-dire en demandant des faveurs à des gens qui utilisent depuis longtemps la philanthropie pour servir leurs propres intérêts" (Ajayi 2004, par. 30).

The monopoly of Cameroon Western partners over institutions in the realms of culture, education and communication has crafted certain narratives about Cameroonians that are often unflattering, to say the least, and often demeaning. It has also led to a general amnesia of the past and the loss of cultural identity and landmarks. This amnesia makes it difficult for researchers to trace the provenance of the many looted objects in the European museum, adding to the doubts and criticisms about the provenance research, which is seen as "empty promises" (Häntzschel quoted in Oswald 2018) to Africa, and as a tedious and endless task due to the number of objects to be examined and the amount of time devoted to each one of them (Kalibani 2020). After the departure of African focal objects during the colonial period, which contributed to the alienation and deculturation of subordinated populations and the breakdown of their psychological equilibrium (Savoy and Sarr 2018, 7), the neo-colonial relationships between post-independence Africa and Europe also pursue the same colonial objective (Ajayi 2004, par. 2). The Cameroonian educational system for example, which is modelled on the French system, as well the cultural sector and media dominated by Cameroon's partners conditioned the development of an intellectual and political elite in the French cultural tradition (Mpegna 2014, 51). As a result, many Cameroonians in particular and Africans in general have adopted Western culture at the expense of their own culture. This could explain both the ignorance of the past and of these cultural objects (Gouaffo 2019), and consequently the way some Cameroonians and Africans mockingly reject their own cultural treasure as "strange" (Mataga 2018, 58) and the indifference of some African governments and the African Union (Kalibani 2020). So far, the Cameroon government has not taken a stand on this question of reparation. An important act of Reparation should thus be questioning our knowledge and stopping the policy of influence that has been causing trauma and wounds over the centuries and threatening culture by extension, not least because, as it is said, every culture is unique and any disappearance impoverishes all of humanity.

The spectre of the colonial past still haunts even the present debate on Reparation, and forms of reparation have been instrumentalized for geopolitical and strategic power interests, thus hindering the reinvention of new dynamics based on equality between Europe and Africa. The programmed death of the educational and scientific field in Cameroon, as in some African countries, entitles some countries of the North to establish, maintain and boast themselves as the only true research centres. The few true research places in Cameroon are the international cooperation agencies that organise conferences, seminars, workshops, scholarship, projects, etc. Such organisations include the DAAD, the French Institute, the Alexander von Humboldt Foundation, ICOM, UNESCO. Besides this, there are other factors relevant in the negotiations. Many researchers argue that the lack of transparency from European museums (Sarr and Savoy 2018, 58), the near centralisation of research on Reparation in Western countries, the inaccessibility of data to both the general African population and African researchers and specialists (Kalibani 2020) and restrictive visa policies[10] guarantee researchers in Europe a monopoly on research on African heritage in Europe despite the fact that they have less ability to understand the meaning of these objects in their cultural context (Kalibani 2020). Similarly, with regard to restitution, some negotiations and returns have been effected since the publication of the Sarr and Savoy Report (2018), especially in Senegal, Nigeria and Congo. The example of the return of 26 objects to Senegal garnered widespread media coverage and has been highly encouraging. However, the conditions leading up to this restitution have raised concerns. Once again, the negotiations were one-sided, thus raising questions about France's willingness to actually repair its relationship with Senegal. A documentary by Nora Philippe, published on ARTE in 2021, reveals this:

> Leonie Simaga, Narrator : Dans leur indépendance, les États n'orchestrent pas les restitutions sans monnayages diplomatiques. Ces retours servent de lourds intérêts financiers, industriels et militaires. Pour un seul sabre revenu, la France négocie des centaines de million d'armements et l'externalisation des mesures migratoires subsahariennes. Œuvrons-nous véritablement au service d'un avenir commun (01 :17 :18)?

> Gabin Djimassé, Historian, Abomey : Seule la France peut nous dire : « Nous disposons de tel nombre d'objets venus de chez vous ». C'est le répertoire que le Qais Branly veut bien nous donner que nous connaissons. Une chose est claire, eux-mêmes ils ont parlé de plus 3000 pièces. Malheureusement, ils ont choisi nous restituer 26 et ces 26 c'est encore eux qui les ont choisis (01 :19 :05–40).

In view of this context, some researchers prefer to remain suspicious, even dubious, because they consider restitution to be a trap or an opportunity in the hands of Western powers to pursue their geopolitical struggles. Similarly, Bayena and Monteh (2021, 38) note that

> [. . .] the concept of restitution has created more problems for Africa and the Third World (victims of most stolen art) than it has solved. The numerous judicial procedures, expenses and international laws associated with the localization, identification and eventual restitution of stolen or illegally transferred antiquities look more like calculated devices designed to frustrate Africans and other plaintive nations.

Another consequence that is important to mention here is the link between reparation, development and democracy. Reflecting on these concepts historically, Bogumil Jewsiewicki observes that from the use of argumentation based on the notion of Reparation, the notion of development has rapidly replaced it over time

---

[10] An example of this policy is the recent case of Schengen visa refusal in early 2022 to three Cameroonian academics who were to travel to Germany to participate in a workshop on the restitution of colonial objects at the Fünf Kontinente Museum in Munich (VAD 2022).

in North-South relations, so that in the relations between nations and communities, development and reparation refer to the same basic notions (Jewsiewicki 2004, par.1). Taking this further, Ajayi argues that the condition for achieving this economic development was political independence and democratic institutions (Ajayi 2004, par. 6). This thought is enshrined and operationalised in the above-mentioned accords. As a discourse of promoting greater dependence and underdevelopment for Africa emerges (Ajayi 2004, par.12), its effects have been the negation, devaluation and inferiorisation of African practices through Western hegemonic values. A development standard has been decided by Western partners and donors, which the new African governments have to strictly follow. In the same vein, the model of cultural policy institutionalised after the Second World War, and closely linked to the construction of the nation-state especially in Europe and Canada (Poirrier 2011, 13–14), was imposed on the newly independent states, including Cameroon. The main important aspects of this cultural policy are the "development of culture" and the "democratisation of culture" (Heumen Tchana 2014, 17). Under the accords of the 1960s and 1974, reform programmes and managers and technocrats training have been launched to guarantee legitimacy and good governance in Cameroon, conditioned by political measures that are sometimes difficult to take. Unfortunately, the aspirations of neither leaders nor the people are very rarely at the centre of concerns (Paul Ango Ela Report 2016; Ex post evaluation Final Report 2009). Many political and economic experts have observed that political independence has not led to the economic stability and democratic institutions of growth and social transformation that were expected. Rather, they have brought wars over the colonial legacy in Cameroon as it is the case for the so-called Anglophone Crisis.[11] One of the challenges for Cameroonians would consist of an internal reparation both for external and "internal colonisation" (Jewsiewicki 2004, Introduction) while addressing postcolonial and colonial legacies in order to reinvent oneself from a truly Cameroonian base, that is from the grassroot or as Jean-Marc Ela (1998) calls "le monde d'en-bas".

---

11 The "Anglophone crisis" can be seen as a clash over two external (colonial) cultures, which shows how imperative it is to address colonial legacies in post-colonial Cameroon. The historian Verkijika G. Fanso (2017) explains this conflict in The Conversation, an online newspaper, as follow: "Anglophones have long complained that their language and culture are marginalised. They feel their judicial, educational and local government systems should be protected. They want an end to annexation and assimilation and more respect from the government for their language and political philosophies. And if that doesn't happen, they want a total separation and their own independent state."

It has been shown above that the 1960 cultural convention was not de facto negotiated on equal footing and, thus, that it maintains inequality between European and particularly France and Cameroon, which led to its revision in 1974. Through a number of institutions, Cameroon's European partners have implemented a policy of influence, assimilation and cultural alienation. Such cultural action has harmful consequences on Cameroonians' lives, notably the obscuring of Cameroon's history, the forgetting of cultural objects, the loss of identity, poverty, trauma, genocide and wars. Hence the urgency and necessity for each party to wake up from its slumber and take responsibility for reinventing the dynamics of new equitable and mutual relationships. This requires, among other things, self-questioning, revision of existing accords and reflexions on the legacy of this violence, for instance in the museum.

3 Rethinking Museum and Cultural Cooperation between Cameroon and Europe

Immediately after independence in 1960 and 1961, establishing institutions for nation building was a priority. At the beginning, museums did not play a significant role. It was only in 1970 that the term "museum" was included in legislation. Yet since 2000, museums have multiplied. How can this increase be explained? In which environments is this proliferation taking place? And what are the implications of this expansion for Reparation?

3.1 Museums in Cameroon: Genesis and Evolution

Addressing the question of museums brings us back to the relationship between Cameroon and Europe and how to deal with the colonial history and legacy today – because the museum as an institution of collection and exhibition, education, scientific research and delectation (Ousman 2018, 14) was introduced in Cameroon, as in other African countries, in the contexts of colonial violence.

The case of the Bamoum Kingdom Museum illustrates this point. As Loumpet shows, in the 1920s, King Njoya, the monarch of the pre-colonial Bamoun kingdom, initiated an exceptional initiative to establish a museum. The initiative was a reaction to the strategy of destabilization and destruction of the socio-political organization and its symbols perpetrated by the French colonial administration that took over from Germany in 1916. It was meant that "the royal objects and symbols of secret societies should be exhibited in public, in order to demystify them and empty them of their power of evocation and subjugation" (Loumpet 2018, 48). Alongside this initiative, the colonial administrations established other museums not for the native population, but mainly for the European colonial population. Of course, at that time, the local populations rarely visited them, not only because they were banned from such civilized milieu, but also because they saw the exhibitions of their masks and sculptures as "retrograde images of themselves" or "mockery or secularisation of their beliefs, which instilled fear and stigmatisation" (Loumpet 2018, 43). Later in 1944, the French created the Centre Camerounais de l'Institut Francais d'Afrique Noire (IFAN), a French research institute based in Dakar, with a satellite research centre in Douala. This was followed by the establishment of regional museums in Bamenda, Douala, Fumban, Maroua, Bafoussam, Mokolo and Buea (Bayena and Monteh 2021, 32).

In post-independence Cameroon, the new government attempted to readapt the existing museums for its political purpose. Most of the colonial museums either disappeared completely or were transformed into national museums. Informed by the Western model, the young government quickly saw the museum as a medium and a place to promote national consciousness and contribute to national unity. Some intellectuals and politicians therefore strongly called for a "National Museum". But the project would run into difficulties for three reasons. First, as Laurence-Anick Zerbini points out, the museum was used by the Europeans as an instrument of cultural alienation or propaganda tool to legitimate their presence in Africa while assigning it a new objective to educate the indigenous population (Zerbini 1991, 16–17), who were said to be illiterate. This European presence, especially from France, puts a greater strain on the new government which contrarily sees the building of a museum "as a form of self-congratulation for their regimes" (Loumpet 2018, 43). The second reason has to do with the type of museum to be built. The museum proponents were divided on the type of museum: a national museum or decentralised regional museums? This discussion was held among scholars and political authorities. On the one hand, proponents of a national museum proposed the creation of a dynamic national museum where all cultural objects of the national territory would be conserved. This vision of the museum, advocated mainly by Engelbert Mveng, is in line with the ideas of the designers of the Cameroonian national unity policy, promoted by President Ahmadou Ahidjo, which aims at the fusion of cultural identities (Ousman 2018, 17). On the other hand, backers of regional museums, notably Issac Paré, since 1963, defended the idea of conserving material culture in the regions where the collections are produced. He argued that local cultural diversities would be preserved by creating a national centre for monitoring and coordinating the various activities of local museums, which would play an educational role in the regions and create local tourist attractions (Paré 1964). The third reason, which is often poorly documented, is related to those who question the raison d'être of museums in general. For these opponents, a national museum or regional museums were not absolutely necessary, but rather it was imperative to reflect on other forms of preservation and promotion of culture adapted to the socio-cultural context of Cameroon without copying the recommendations of the UN and European partners. Madelaine Ndobo, for example, drew the attention of her contemporaries:

> Nous ne partageons pas simplement l'idée de vouloir massifier toutes les cultures autochtones dans un musée, fût-il national, car cela peut entrainer un « effacement catastrophique de l'épistème traditionnelle » et provoquer un effet contraire aux ambitions des pouvoirs politiques. Gardons-nous d'oublier que ce musée ne sera jamais « un musée de l'ONU », et qu'il pourrait par contre s'avérer comme « un lieu de lutte » des identités individuelles et collectives (Ndobo 1999, 807).

It should be noted that the project of "massifying" cultures in a museum, as Ndobo warns, also raises the issue of "collecting"[12] objects from populations and kingdoms, which could not only reproduce the violence perpetuated by the colonists during the collection missions, but also lead to institutional amnesia (Zerbini 1991, 15). After all, this group meant that the museum can neither exhibit nor represent all of Cameroon's cultural and ethnic diversity (more than 250 cultures) like the Western universal museums to which it refers. This vision is still held today in Africa. For example, George Okello Abungu argues that "in many circumstances, though, this is evident more in theory than in practice, since representing the entire world under one roof is an almost impossible feat – even for the so-called universal or encyclopaedic museums" (Ubungu 2018, 26). Equally, this insight questions the Western conception of the museum which creates the absence of certain arts or crafts in museums since their interest is in material culture considering only the aesthetic value of the object as an art object. As Zerbini (1991, 16) writes, "L'Art est sauvé mais la Culture et l'Histoire, elles, sont perdues." By so doing, the African museum becomes, as one of the most important museum critics Alpha Konaré writes, "rien d'autre qu'un mouroir de biens culturels, un cimetière d'objets, un autre instrument d'aliénation Culturelle" (Konaré 1987 quoted in Zerbini 1991, 16).

Although Engelbert Mveng's vision corresponds to Ahmadou Ahidjo's policy, because it strengthens national unity, it was only later in 1972, the date of the

---

[12] Felwine Sarr and Bénédicte Savoy recently argue that the vocabulary of "collecting" and of "harvesting" imply an undeniable cynicism. The term implies that art could be picked up, harvested, gathered, as if it had no legitimate owner, as if it could be reborn. However, the two authors remind us that the very principle of culture is "generated and regenerated by the transmission, reproduction, adaptation, study and transformation of knowledge, forms and objects within societies" (Sarr and Savoy 2018, 14).

unification of Cameroon, that it was adopted. Article 36 of Decree No. 72/425 of 28 August 1972 on the transfer of the Directorate of Cultural Affairs to the Ministry of Information and Culture, recognises the museum as a component of Cameroonian cultural heritage. But, as Ndobo (1999, 794) notes, this remains a declaration of intent. The government's decision to open the national museum only came in 1985. During this time, as many museum actors observed with disapproval, the state largely supported popular culture (Ndobo 1999; Ousman 2018). In doing so, building museums remained a private initiative. Between 1990 and 2000, there was an explosion of new community museums in the west of Cameroon, where each chiefdom opened its own museum, often in cooperation with European museums or non-governmental organisations (Loumpet 2018, 43).

3.2 From 2000 to Present: Musealisation

After 2000, a phenomenon of "musealisation" (Loumpet 2018) took place in Cameroon, as nearly 80% of the Cameroonian museums were established during this period (Heumen Tchana 2017, 418). The study by Mahamat Abba Ousman (2018) commissioned by the UNESCO's Multisectoral Regional Office for Central Africa presents a museum map of Cameroon made up of eight public museums under the exclusive competence of the Ministry of Arts and Culture and forty-eight private and community (chiefdom) museums. It should be recalled that this last category, mostly known as "cases patrimoniales" (Djache Nzefa et al. 2012, 35), is considered a recent Cameroonian peculiarity because they are transformation of Chiefdom collections into museums.[13] This proliferation of museums is motivated, on the one hand, by socio-economic, educational and scientific considerations and, on the other, by tourism as well as global and political concerns.

Because of the economic depression of the 1980s caused partly by the sharp fall in coffee and cocoa prices, the loss of power and authority of the chiefdoms that globalisation marginalised through increasing economic decline (Bayena and Monteh 2021) and the desire to save the populations from acculturation, some Cameroonians and in particular the *Fon* (kings), see museums as new sources of

---

13 In several chiefdoms, palace or community museums, *cases patrimoniales* present thematic exhibitions. These are living museums within the chiefdoms, from which, for certain ceremonies and rituals, objects of high symbolic value are brought out, supporting the identity of the group or the chiefdom. They are occasionally taken out to the sacred forest, activated and used in various rites, then deactivated and returned to the museum. These museums are non-interactive because the touching or photographing of objects is considered to be potentially dangerous to the visitor (Djache Nzefa et al. 2012).

revenue and a way of accomplishing their role as a cultural guard to preserve their ancestral value and culture (Djache Nzefa 1994; Djache Nzefa et al. 2012). Within this context, numerous museum projects have been carried out, notably the Programme of the Road of Chiefdoms (Programme de la Route des Chefferies (PRDC)), initiated by the Cameroonian diaspora in France in cooperation with the cities of Nantes, Dschang and Région Pays de Loire. The aim of this program is to create a unique cultural and tourist centre nationwide in order to encourage populations to re-appropriate their heritage while contributing to their economic and social development (Djache Nzefa et al. 2012). To meet this challenge, the PRDC operates largely thanks to international subsidies acquired through calls for projects which cover 60% of the total budget. In 2019, 14 cases patrimoniales have been established.

Another important factor to mention here is ideological-political. As mentioned above, the obsession of post-independence cultural policy-makers was with the construction of a national identity. The Western museum model had to fulfil this function. The intended or unintended contribution of Western bilateral, multilateral or intergovernmental partners has a great influence on Cameroon's cultural policies (Heumen Tchana 2014, 17). For example, with its philosophy of conserving African heritage and making museum an institution of research and education for the general population, UNESCO has a strong influence on national policies; the International Centre for the Study of the Preservation and Restoration of Cultural Property (ICCROM) which set up a specific programme and a dedicated training centre to develop museums in Africa; and the European Union whose aim of cultural cooperation is to promote cultural identity and foster the individual creativity of ACP (African, Caribbean and Pacific) countries and establish the means for production and dissemination (Loumpet 2018, 45). Inspired or advised by its Western partners, Cameroonian actors have thus made the "democratisation of culture" and "culture and development" mainly advocated by UNESCO an important aspect of their cultural policy (Heumen Tchana 2014, 17). These conceptualisations have been concretised over the years through numerous sensitisations, research, training and education programmes. These programmes are accompanied by enormous financial, technical and advisory support for Cameroon's state and institutional partners in this musealisation process. Thus, many studies and programmes have been carried out to win and develop public loyalty (Heumen Tchana 2009) in order to reduce disparities between different sectors of the population (Mpegna 2014, 17), paradoxically with an institution that is essentially discriminatory and bourgeois. This raises the question: What kind of culture are we talking about? If we develop what already exists, how can the programmes not consider diverse Cameroonian cultural expressions? How does it sound when programmes aim at teaching people about their spiritual creations and democratising their own creations? For whom are these museums really created?

A last but not exhaustive reason behind this proliferation is the desire for global recognition or belonging to the global culture, because it is believed museums are "institutions of world-cultures" (Loumpet 2018). This frantic struggle for global recognition requires adaptation to a certain norm or standard that the Western partners have unilaterally established. According to Bayena and Monteh the progressive museumization of Africa's royal collections inextricably embraced alien values and devalued African religious objects. "At best, the situation moved from devaluation through commoditization to desecration. Notwithstanding such sacrileges, the dream of many colonial and post-colonial local communities is to see their collections recognized as museums" (Bayena and Monteh 2021, 33). Still, this struggle for "global" recognition has had a rather minimal result as George Okello Abungu (2019, 64) deplores: "It is also clear that the ICOM museum definition, which provides guidance on what museums can or cannot be, has seen little change over the years, except for small additions such as 'tangible and intangible heritage', and has remained pretty static, despite the changing global environment and changing dynamics." Drawing from the above abstractions, one is tempted to ask why other possibilities are not considered, for example, starting from the bottom up (Ela, 1998). Is collecting objects from the population to preserve in museums, albeit for research, economic and tourist purposes, and in the name of recognition and universality, not in itself a violence? How otherwise could the mistrust or resistance of the populations for whom these museums are intended be explained?

3.3 From Musealisation to Demusealisation

The musealisation process is confronted with passive resistance from the communities they are dedicated to, what Germain Loumpet (2018) calls "demusealisation". Despite the role of public sensitization by national and international bodies on the one hand and African diaspora elites on the other, the population continues to feel alienated from these programmes. Most often people have a different relationship with these museum objects because they are magicoreligious, customary, and/or mystical, but they also see these objects taken out of their socio-cultural context as bearing little relevance to the living cultures of their communities (Bayena and Monteh 2021). Furthermore, museum practices alter their social fabric by creating, on the one hand, an omnipresent "modern culture", inherited from colonisation, which is the prerogative of the literate and widely disseminated by the mass media and the school system, and on the other hand, an "authentic culture, now called traditional or folk culture" (Zerbini 1991, 6), which is lived by a part of the Cameroonian people and is conveyed by the national languages. This is also the result of the dispossession of the grassroots group by the elite group and the hyper-centralisation on the latter.

This critical view is also present in academic milieu where musealisation is seen as an expansion of Western culture and the folklorisation of Cameroonian cultures, and this current challenging museum situation as an inability of museums to integrate into Africa's modern culture. For example, Noël and Geromini draw attention to an obvious risk of folklorisation of chiefdoms to the detriment of their significance in Cameroonian society as well as the heritage preserved in these socio-political and cultural sites. The Programme Route de la Chefferie is also concerned about the infatuation of art dealers with chiefdoms as their popularity grows (PRDC 2011), while Hugues Heumen Tchana (2017b) draws attention to the dangers of Eurocentrism. He argues that the proliferation of museum collections raises a number of questions about the aims and purposes of these collections, and the intervention of external forces, namely European agencies, raises the concern of a neo-colonial relationship. He also points out that the current state of academic museology in Africa is determined more by imported forces than by endogenous African factors and advocates for the creation of African universities that explore Africa's own epistemologies and techniques and respond directly to societal needs. This musealisation is also worrying in that the number of museums has increased and, paradoxically, other forms of cultural expression have almost disappeared and other cultural sectors have closed down:

> En moins de 15 ans, soit de 2003 à 2017, 28 musées ont été créés au Cameroun parmi lesquels 14 dans les Grassfields Cameroun paradoxalement, les autres secteurs qui était privilégiés ont fermé. Presque toutes les salles de cinéma ont fermé, pas de Palais de la Culture, les bibliothèques sont à la traîne, les dépôts d'archives sont poussiéreux à travers le Cameroun (Heumen Tchana 2017a, 418).

Recently, Thomas Laely et al. edited a collective book on museum cooperation between Africa and Europe. The book acknowledges "the paternalistic view of African museum institutions, embedded in the intercontinental museum cooperation approach presented" and calls for a "new paradigm" (Laely et al. 2018, 3). In Cameroon, however, the very existence of museums is being debated to the extent that their practices of collection, representation and preservation do not fit the Cameroonian socio-cultural context. Thus, the imperative need to reflect on the possibilities and dynamics by questioning this colonial heritage and to take up one of the great challenges by putting the "world from below" (Ela 1998) with its everyday practices, its new and existing innovations and with the corresponding socio-cultural tools and methods at the centre of the concerns.

4 Conclusion

This study has examined some factors that can contribute to repairing the relationship between Cameroon and Europe by specifically exploring museum cooperation in the context of reparation and restitution of looted objects and by focusing on the actors involved, namely the European and Cameroonian laws, museums and state actors. I have identified several factors that may prevent the two parties from repairing their relationship, namely the persistence of the colonial discourse, non-updated accords, non-transparency, inertia, one-sided negotiations when talking about restitution and instrumentalizations for geopolitical and strategic power interests. The unbridled quest for economic and material development objectives is causing the social structure to be altered and the chiefdoms, places of power, to be transformed into purely touristic sites. In the quest for development, many palaces and the art have been transformed into a purely commercial activity, of massive production to satisfy the market demand. This situation has led to a rupture between the economic, social, political and spiritual orders, which should be repaired.

Several proposals have been made so far to the Cameroonian side as well as to its partners. But the fact is that some of them are still "pretending to be asleep". Far from making a string of proposals here, I would like to come back to two aspects: the partners must take courage to address their painful stories, and to ensure respectful relations above all, yet restitution and reparation, too, because restitutions as a result of two-sided negotiations are the condition for a common future. At present, the question of culture in Africa and in Cameroon in particular needs to be addressed on its own terms. If research has shown that the museum, whether ethnographic, popular arts and traditions, scientific or technical, is foreign to African culture, it is up to Cameroon to explore frankly, boldly and courageously the existence and contribution of museums and to open up other possibilities that correspond to the country's culture. As Felwine Sarr exposes in *Afrotopia* (2016), it is a question of reconceptualising everything and inventing a new utopia by asking the fundamental question: What does it mean to live well and to live better? In view of the above, it seems to me that reparation is necessary on two levels: internally and externally. The first should be carried out among Cameroonians, i.e., by decolonising their knowledge and practices and deeply questioning their needs, in order to regain courage and confidence. This internal reparation also concerns the Westerns, who should question their position in the world and their capacity to inhabit the world with others. Then Cameroon and Europe could redefine new dynamics for their relations. And restitution and decolonialization appear to be important steps for reparation as Albert Gouaffo explains:

> La décolonisation et la restitution des biens culturels volés par dans les musées européens sont liés. Après quatre siècles d'exploitation coloniale et de relation d'asymétrie postcoloniale, les Africains et les Européens sont arrivés à un point où des relations entièrement nouvelles doivent être entièrement renégocier. L'art africain présent aujourd'hui dans les musées européens en est l'occasion. Vivre dans la justice, la fraternité, l'humanité est-il réservé aux seuls pays du nord ? Les symboles de l'excellence sont-ils des idéaux universels de l'humanité ? Donc l'Afrique a besoin des relations avec ses partenaires qui la libèrent et non l'asservissent (Gouaffo 2021).

There is no doubt that embarking on this path of freedom and reparation is not easy, but courage, hope and wisdom seem to be essential on this route for the ultimate sake of our humanity.

References

Abungu, George Okello. "Museums: Geopolitics, Decolonisation, Globalisation and Migration." *Museum International* 71.1–2 (2019): 62–71. DOI: 10.1080/13500775.2019.1638030.

Adichie, Chimamanda Ngozi. "Festrede. Humboldt Forum." 22 September 2021. https://www.youtube.com/watch?v=gMRv5xhMCo4 (22 March 2022).

AfricAvenir International e.V. *No Humboldt 21!: Dekoloniale Einwände gegen das Humboldt-Forum.* Berlin: AfricAvenir International e.V, 2017.

Ajayi, J. F. Ade. "La politique de Réparation dans le contexte de la mondialisation." *Cahiers d'études africaines* 173–174 (2004): 41–63.

Association for African Studies in Germany (VAD e.V.). *Protests against visa refusal for Cameroonian scholars by the German embassy.* 13 January 2022. https://www.vad-ev.de/vad-protests-against-visa-refusal-for-cameroonian-scholars-by-the-german-embassy/ (22 March 2022).

Bahoken, Jean Calvin and Engelbert Atangana. *Cultural policy in the United Republic of Cameroon.* Paris: The Unesco Press, 1976.

Bayena, Ngitir Victor and Rene Ngek Monteh. "The Survival of Community Museums in Cameroon." *Himalayan Journal of Humanities and Cultural Studies* 2.2 (2021): 25–34.

De Gaulle, Charles and Konrad Adenauer. "Déclaration commune du 22 janvier 1963." *Dokumente/Documents. Zeitschrift für den deutsch-französischen Dialog / Revue du dialogue franco-allemand* 4 (2012): 22–25.

De Lusignan, Guy. *L'Afrique noire depuis les indépendances : l'évolution des États francophones.* Paris: Fayard, 1970.

Deltombe, Thomas, Manuel Domergue, and Jacob Tatsitsa. *Kamerun. La guerre cachée de la France en Afrique noire (1968–1971): Une guerre cachée aux origines de la Françafrique (1948–1971).* Paris: La découverte, 2011.

Djache Nzefa, Sylvain. Ed. *Les chefferies bamiléké dans l'enfer du modernisme: réflexion sur l'état actuel des chefferies bamiléké. Une chefferie de demain: renaissance, recherche et affirmation d'identité.* Couëron, Vincennes: Menaibuc-Dila, 1994.

Djache Nzefa, Sylvain, Estelle Piou, Flaubert A. Taboue, and Anita Kamga Fotso. "La sauvegarde et la valorisation du patrimoine culturel au Cameroun." *La Lettre de l'OCIM* 139 (2012): 30–39. DOI: 10.4000/ocim.1026.

Ela, Jean-Marc. *Innovation sociale et renaissance de l'Afrique noire: Les défis du « monde d'en-bas*. Paris: Harmattan, 1998.

Evaluation ex post Rapport final. Les outils de la coopération française avec le Cameroun: 2001–2007. Ministère des affaires étrangères et européennes and Agence française de développement. Paris: 2009.

Feuer, Guy. "Les accords culturels passés par la France avec les États africains et malgache." *Annuaire français de droit international* 9 (1963): 890–905.

Fogang Toyem. "Enseignement des langues étrangères dans les lycées et collèges en Afrique: de la problématique d'acculturation a la justification des échanges culturels dans une didactique de l'allemand en contexte camerounais." *Plumencre* (21 May 2016). http://plumencre.e-monsite.com/actu/opinion-sur/enseignement-des-langues-etrangeres-dans-les-lycees-et-college-d-afrique.html (22 April 2022).

Gouaffo, Albert. "Se guérir de la violence coloniale? Jean Ikelle-Matiba et Réné Philombe face aux colonialismes français et allemande." *Violences postcoloniales. Perceptions médiatiques, représentations littéraires, actes du colloque du 17–18 juin 2005 à Saarbrücken*. Ed. Isaac Bazié and Hans-Jürgen Lüsebrink. Münster: LIT, 2011. 49–63.

———. *Enjeux éthiques de la communication interculturelle pour la paix en Afrique*. Atipik: November 2021. https://www.youtube.com/watch?v=fRvuglUluwI (20 March 2021).

Heumen Tchana, Hugues. *Conquête et fidélisation des publics au musée national de Yaoundé au Cameroun*. Master Thesis. Alexandria: Université Senghor, 2009.

———. "Reouverture du Musée National du Cameroun Expositions fonctionnement et perspectives." *African Humanities* 2 & 3 (September 2017a): 413–446.

———. "Dangers of Eurocentrism and the Need to Indigenize African and Grassfields Histories." *CAA News Today Global Conversations 2017* (18 May 2017b). https://www.collegeart.org/news/2017/05/18/global-conversations/ (22 April 2022).

Jewsiewicki, Bogumil. "Réparations, restitutions, réconciliations Entre Afriques, Europe et Amériques." *Cahiers d'études africaines*, 173–174 (2004). https://doi.org/10.4000/etudesafricaines.4510.

Journal officiel de la République Fédérale, no. 1434 du 17 mars 1961 portant publication de la Convention Culturelle.

Journal officiel de la République du Cameroun, no 6140 du 13 novembre 1960; convention no 2285 du 27 juillet 1960 relative à la coopération Franco-camerounaise en matière d'information.

Accord Franco-Camerounais de Coopération et d'Assistance Technique du 13 Novembre 1960.

Décret n° 64/AF/60 du 05 février 1960 portant publication d'une convention générale relative à la coopération en matière de recherche scientifique et technique entre la France et la République fédérale du Cameroun.

Journal officiel de la République Unie du Cameroun, n° 7 du 30 Déc. 1974: décret no 74663 du 11 juillet 1974 portant ratification des accords de coopération franco-camerounaise.

Kalibani, Mèhèza. "Objets spoliés, exposés puis dissimulés: la gestion des inventaires par les musées ethnographiques allemands et les défis pour les chercheurs africains dans le débat sur la restitution du patrimoine africain." *L'Afrique en mouvement, en question* (23 December 2020). https://jcea.hypotheses.org/1181 (22 April 2022).

Kovács, Máté. *Cultural Policies in Africa. Compendium of reference documents*. Madrid: Spanish Agency for International Development Cooperation (AECID) and Observatory of Cultural Policies in Africa (OCPA), 2009.

Laely, Thomas, Marc Meyer, and Raphael Schwere. *Museum Cooperation Between Africa and Europe: A New Field for Museum Studies*. Kampala and Bielefeld: Fountain Publishers and Transcript Verlag, 2018.

Linear Report, 2nd Conference on cultural enterprises and creative industries in Cameroon Yaounde. Fondation Paul Ango Ela (FPAE) 27–29 April 2016, http://fpae-cameroun.org/wp-content/up loads/2017/08/RAPPORT-LINEAIRE-ASSISES-CULTURELLES-2017-.pdf (22 April 2022).

Loumpet, Germain. "Cooperation between European and African Museums: A paradigm for Démuséalisation." *Museum Cooperation Between Africa and Europe: A New Field for Museum Studies*. Eds. Thomas Laely, Marc Meyer, and Raphael Schwere. Kampala and Bielefeld: Fountain Publishers and Transcript Verlag, 2018. 43–53.

Mataga, Jesmael. "Shifting Knowledge Boundaries in Museums Museum Objects, Local Communities and Curatorial Shifts in African Museums." *Museum Cooperation Between Africa and Europe: A New Field for Museum Studies*. Eds. Thomas Laely, Marc Meyer, and Raphael Schwere. Kampala and Bielefeld: Fountain Publishers and Transcript Verlag, 2018. 57–68.

Mbembe, Achille. "La restitution des œuvres est l'occasion pour la France de réparer et de réinventer sa relation avec l'Afrique." *Le Monde* (28 November 2018). https://www.lemonde.fr/idees/article/2018/11/28/achille-mbembe-la-restitution-des-uvres-est-l-occasion-pour-la-france-de-reparer-et-de-reinventer-sa-relation-avec-l-afrique_5390009_3232.html (4 January 2022).

Mefe, Tony. "Financement de la culture au Cameroun: soutien aux actions, absence d'infrastructures." *Africultures* 60.3 (2004): 19–25.

Mouna Mboa. "Coopération Cameroun-France: Plus de 50 ans d'accords iniques et cyniques." *237online* (8 May 2016). https://www.237online.com/cooperation-cameroun-france-plus-de-50-ans-daccords-iniques-et-cyniques/ (13 April 2022).

Moussa, Njoya. "Paul Biya et ses quatre homologues français." *Le Jour* (3 July 2015). http://www.camer.be/43318/30:27/cameroun-paul-biya-et-ses-quatre-homologues-francais-cameroon.html (20 March 2022).

Mpegna, Belmond Nicaise. *La politique française de coopération culturelle en Afrique – l'exemple du Cameroun*. Paris: L'Harmattan, 2014.

Ndobo, Madeleine. "Les musées privés et publics au Cameroun." *Cahiers d'Études Africaines* 39.155–156 (1999): 789–814.

Noël, Jean-François and Vincent Geromini. "La Route des Chefferies dans l'Ouest camerounais: entre vulnérabilité du patrimoine et développement touristique." *Vulnérabilité et résilience* (Colloque), Université de Versailles Saint-Quentin-en-Yvelines, November 2019.

Okello, Christina. "Hollande acknowledges colonial-era Cameroon massacres but critics want apology." *RFI* (5 July 2015). https://www.rfi.fr/en/africa/20150705-hollande-acknowledges-colonial-era-cameroon-massacres-critics-want-apology/ (17 April 2022).

Oswald, Margareta von. "The 'Restitution Report': First Reactions in Academia, Museums, and Politics." Weblog (18 December 2018). https://blog.uni-koeln.de/gssc-humboldt/the-restitution-report/ (4 January 2022).

Ousman, Mahamat Abba. *Les musées au Cameroun: État des lieux et besoin en formation*. UNESCO: 2018.

Paré, Issac. "La place du musée dans le plan de développement économique et social de l'Afrique." *Abbia* 7 (1964): 49–65.

Poirrier, Philippe. "Pour une histoire des politiques culturelles dans le monde. Introduction." *Pour une histoire des politiques culturelles dans le monde (1945–2011)*. Ed. Philippe Poirrier. Paris: Comité d'Histoire du Ministère de la Culture, 2011. 13–18.

Presidency of the Republic of Cameroon. *Cameroon's diplomacy – Introduction*. https://www.prc.cm/en/cameroon/diplomacy/190-introduction (5 January 2022).

Programme de la Route Des Chefferies. Au cœur du développement des peuples du Cameroun à travers la protection du patrimoine culturel. *EPA-Porto-Novo* (8 February 2011).

Ravenhill, Philip. "The past and the future of museology in sub-saharan Africa." *ICCROM Newsletter* 13 (January 1986): 34–36.
Restituer? *L'Afrique en quête de ses chefs-d'œuvre*. Dir. Nora Philippe. ARTE, 2021. https://www.arte.tv/fr/videos/097591-000-A/restituer-l-afrique-en-quete-de-ses-chefs-d-oeuvre/ (17 April 2022).
Sarr, Felwine. *Afrotopia*. Paris: Philippe Rey, 2016.
Sarr, Felwine and Bénédicte Savoy. *On the Restitution of African Cultural Heritage, Toward a New Relational Ethics*. Transl. Drew S. Burk. Paris: 2018. http://restitutionreport2018.com/sarr_savoy_en.pdf (13 April 2022).
Savoy, Bénédicte. *Afrikas Kampf um seine Kunst. Geschichte einer postkolonialen Niederlage*. München: C.H. Beck, 2021.
Schorch, Philipp and Noelle Kahanu M.K.Y. "Anthropology's Interlocutors. Hawai'i Speaking Back to Ethnographic Museums in Europe." *Zeitschrift für Kulturwissenschaften* 9.1 (2015): 110–113.
Senghor, Léopold Sédar. "La culture africaine." *Revue des Sciences morales et politiques* 559 (1983): 1–13
Verkijika, G. Fanso. "History explains why Cameroon is at war with itself over language and culture." *The Conversation* (15 November 2017). https://theconversation.com/history-explains-why-cameroon-is-at-war-with-itself-over-language-and-culture-85401 (17 April 2022).
Zerbini, Laurence-Anick. *Problèmes et perspectives: le musée en Afrique*. Master Thesis. Grenoble: École Nationale Supérieure de Bibliothécaires & Université des Sciences Sociales Grenoble II, 1991.

Patricia Oster
Les statues considérées comme des protagonistes des histoires européennes d'interdépendance et de désunion

Résumé : Les statues dans l'espace public, en tant qu'objets de vol et de restitution, sont souvent l'expression des histoires d'interdépendance et de désunion européennes. Ceci sera étudié à travers différents exemples : une sculpture d'Urs Fischer (Fondation Pinault, Bourse de Commerce) dans le contexte d'un panorama mondial réalisé pour l'exposition universelle de Paris en 1889, la statue en bronze d'Henri IV sur le Pont Neuf, objet d'un curieux échange franco-allemand, le quadrige de Berlin sur la porte de Brandebourg, devenu otage de l'Histoire, et la représentation littéraire des statues comme témoins du passé dans le roman *L'Ile aux musées* de Cécile Wajsbrot. L'article est issu d'une intervention de Patricia Oster, tenue dans le cadre de l'école d'été internationale « Restitution, réparations, *reparation* – Vers une nouvelle société mondiale ? » (09.09–13.09.2021) à la Villa Vigoni, centre italo-allemand pour le dialogue européen.[1]

Mots-clés : statue ; Urs Fischer ; Cécile Wajsbrot ; Ile aux musées ; Napoléon ; Henri IV ; quadrige de la porte de Brandebourg

Par leur présence physique dans l'espace public, les statues se révèlent être un palimpseste européen condensé. Objets de spoliation et de restitution, elles deviennent les surfaces de projection de connotations inédites multiples dans le contexte des histoires d'interdépendance et de désunion européennes. Dans l'art et la littérature, elles servent de figuration conceptuelle. Pour Urs Fischer, la statue est une allégorie de l'Europe déchue de sa position illusoire de centre du monde, en quête de formes d'apparence nouvelles dans la dissolution. Si les statues restent généralement à l'horizon de l'appréhension dans l'espace public, chez Cécile Wajsbrot elles sont un thème et affirment résolument leur présence dans le texte. Douées d'une mémoire absolue, elles apparaissent comme les prota-

---
[1] L'article a été traduit par Monique Rival. La traduction de l'article a été financée par le projet "Minor Universality. Narrative World Productions After Western Universalism", financé par le Conseil Européen de la Recherche (ERC) (Programme–cadre de recherche de l'UE "Horizon 2020", convention n° 819931).

Traduction : Monique Rival

gonistes de processus culturels dans le *terrain vague* du musée, témoins muets, souvent victimes de vol et de destruction.

1 Les statues comme protagonistes des histoires européennes d'interdépendance et de désunion sur fond de panorama mondial

En mai 2021 a été inauguré dans l'ancienne Bourse de Commerce de Paris le nouveau Musée d'art moderne du grand collectionneur d'art François Pinault. C'est à l'architecte japonais Tadao Ando que l'on doit la modernisation de cet édifice construit en 1767. Tadao a placé dans le bâtiment circulaire de l'ancienne Bourse de commerce, classé aux Monuments historiques, un cylindre de béton monolithe ouvert, de neuf mètres de haut. Au-dessus de ce cylindre, le regard s'ouvre sur une peinture de plafond de 140m de circonférence et dix mètres de haut, courant sous la coupole de verre (Fig. 1). Comme la Tour Eiffel, ce panorama global de la Bourse du commerce, inaugurée en 1889, était une contribution à l'Exposition universelle de Paris la même année. Il dépeint de manière frappante la conception du rapport entre l'Europe et le reste du monde dans l'imaginaire du 19e siècle. Le commerce florissant de l'Europe avec cinq des sept continents – l'Amérique, la Russie et le Nord, l'Asie et l'Afrique – y est illustré dans un amalgame de références culturelles (Lignier 2021, 70–76). Les réseaux de circulation internationaux semblent converger du monde entier vers l'Europe.

L'Européen rappelle ici le protagoniste au nom très parlant de Passepartout – emprunté au roman de Jules Vernes *Le tour du monde en 180 jours*, texte qui relate aussi l'accessibilité totale du monde. Les Européens sont ici très clairement représentés en commerçants, conquérants et découvreurs –, Christophe Colomb étant figuré comme une apparition divine au-dessus de l'Amérique. L'Europe elle-même apparaît comme un continent éminemment complexe. Des colonnes corinthiennes signalent ses racines antiques – mais on relève aussi une allusion à la guerre d'Indépendance de la Grèce avec des hommes en costumes de la Garde royale grecque. Des cheminées d'usines fumantes illustrent la puissance industrielle moderne de l'Europe, de grands navires sa puissance commerciale. Une place est aussi accordée au monde rural, avec une scène de vendanges pour évoquer le paysage méditerranéen par exemple.

Ce panorama présente le monde comme horizon de l'Europe, et figure même pour ainsi dire une restitution authentique de la conscience européenne d'hori-

Fig. 1 : L'Europe dans la peinture de plafond de la Bourse de Commerce, Paris, 2021. Photo: Patricia Oster.

zon. Une réflexion de Peter Sloterdijk dans son essai *Si l'Europe s'éveille* illustre parfaitement ce contexte :

> L'amalgame européen entre la science et le colonialisme a d'abord fait naître l'image politique et géographique de la Terre – comme si la fonction naturelle de la globalité du monde était d'être reconnue parmi les centres d'intérêts européens et de se faire pénétrer par les mesures adoptées en Europe. [. . .] Le monde n'est que l'horizon, donné par la nature, des ambitions européennes les plus extrêmes (Sloterdijk 2003, 12–13).

Dans ce panorama du monde du 19e siècle, les privilèges panoptiques de la vieille Europe sont flagrants. Dans le nouveau musée, ils sont délibérément confrontés à une installation de l'artiste suisse Urs Fischer, placée très précisément sous le panorama, au centre du cylindre de béton (Fig. 2). Il s'agit d'une reproduction à l'identique de la célèbre sculpture maniériste en marbre « L'Enlèvement des Sabines », œuvre du sculpteur italo-flamand Giambologna, datée de 1583 et conservée dans la Loggia dei Lanzi à Florence, qui illustre à son tour une légende fondatrice romaine transmise par Tite-Live. Tout en se plaçant ainsi dans un contexte de tradition européenne, Fischer le contourne de manière subtile : sa parfaite réplique en cire de la statue est dotée, comme une bougie, d'une mèche enflammée. Ainsi, dans un processus continu de fusion, la Sabine kidnappée se débattant dans les bras d'un Romain est-elle détruite sous les yeux des visiteurs. Cette statue est entourée de reproductions, également en cire, de sièges d'horizons culturels les plus divers qui soient – jusqu'à une chaise en plastique de notre époque –, qui fondent elles aussi lentement sous nos yeux. Sous le grand panorama peint, synthèse de la domination de l'Europe face à l'horizon du monde, la statue, entourée de sièges d'époques et de cultures diverses, peut ainsi devenir l'allégorie de l'Europe déchue de sa position illusoire de centre du monde, en quête de formes d'apparence nouvelles dans la dissolution.

Fig. 2 : Urs Fischer dans la collection de François Pinault de la Bourse de Commerce. Photo: Patricia Oster.

Le musée lui-même expose des œuvres d'art contemporain prestigieuses du monde entier, chacune y affirmant individuellement son droit, élargissant du même coup le champ des possibilités de nouvelles transitions vers le monde global. J'aimerais en donner ici quelques exemples : les œuvres de l'artiste anglaise Lynette Yiadom-Boakye, originaire du Ghana, les œuvres de Xinyi Cheng de Wuhan, celle de l'artiste latino-américain Antonio Obà, de l'Américain Kerry James Marshall, membre du mouvement américain pour les droits civiques et qui révolutionna les portraits des Noirs, et les artistes allemands Martin Kippenberger, Thomas Schütte et Florian Krewer.

Devant ce décor original emblématique de la domination coloniale, deux exemples de la cartographie européenne, se trouve l'installation intitulée *Minimum Security*, de l'Américain David Hammons, enraciné dans la culture urbaine afro-américaine, qui suggère une austère cellule de prison tridimensionnelle, dont la porte s'ouvre et se referme de temps à autre en grinçant. Ici encore je citerai Sloterdijk :

> La cartographie de l'Europe jouait un rôle dominant dans l'effort, caractéristique des temps modernes, visant à donner aux politiciens, marchands et bourgeois cultivés, dans les citadelles de l'Occident, une vue d'ensemble et dénuée de mystère sur le globe terrestre, dont on venait tout juste de découvrir la forme réelle, avec ses continents et ses océans. On est en droit d'affirmer que les fabricants de globes européens ont accompli pendant des siècles une prestation décisive pour la faculté de représenter concrètement la terre habitée dans son ensemble ; ils ont assouvi le besoin d'une supervision quasiment divine, qui a entretemps été transposée sur les optiques des satellites. C'était sans aucun doute une passion typiquement européenne que de combler les taches blanches sur les cartes géographiques des continents lointains (Sloterdijk 2003, 12).

L'installation minimaliste de Hammons met en regard l'image des phantasmes européens d'expansion, clairement illustrés dans le décor original de la Bourse de Commerce, avec l'incarnation de l'inhumaine oppression. Ainsi s'affirme une fois de plus, sous une autre forme, la tension entre le grand panorama du monde et la statue de cire qui se désintègre lentement au centre du musée pendant toute la durée de l'exposition.

L'Europe, qui apparaît comme un conglomérat complexe dans le panorama global, est envisagée comme une unité à l'horizon du monde. Cette unité est-elle un phantasme ? Dans ce contexte, au centre imaginaire du musée, la sculpture présente un intérêt particulier redoublé. Car en effet, avec cette représentation de l'Enlèvement des Sabines, c'est un mythe fondateur de l'Europe, expression pour une part d'une histoire européenne de désunion, qui se dissout lentement. Mais dans cette sculpture s'affirme par ailleurs une histoire complexe d'interdépendance européenne, qui va de Tite-Live à Urs Fischer en passant par Giambologna. Dans ce qui suit, je propose d'approfondir cette idée des statues comme protagonistes de certaines histoires européennes d'interdépendance et de désunion.

2 Les statues en tant que protagonistes des histoires européennes d'interdépendance et de désunion

Pour en revenir à la réplique en cire de l'œuvre de Giambologna, la statue suppose un espace qui est toujours un espace public. Elle peut donc devenir surface de projection de connotations sans cesse renouvelées. Ce qui peut être corroboré par l'exemple d'une autre statue de Giambologna à Paris, laquelle préside en propre à une histoire de sculpture européenne germano-franco-italienne (Oster 2013, 383–396). Cette statue du roi français Henri IV de Giambologna se trouve aujourd'hui encore sur le Pont Neuf. Elle est due à l'initiative d'une reine de France, l'Italienne Marie de Médicis qui, ayant assisté en 1604 à Florence à l'inauguration de la statue équestre du cardinal Ferdinando de Medici, du même Giambologna, eut l'idée de faire ériger à Paris une statue semblable de son époux, Henri IV (Dubost 2016, 129–159). Cette statue ne fut cependant réalisée qu'après la mort du roi à Paris en 1635. Henri IV était un souverain aimé de son peuple. C'est à lui que l'on doit l'idée « d'une poule au pot pour chaque Français le dimanche » – de même que la légendaire formule « Paris vaut bien une messe », après sa conversion au catholicisme pour pacifier la France. C'est pourquoi la statue, connue dans le langage populaire sous le nom de *Cheval de Bronze*, devint immédiatement un lieu de vénération du roi défunt. Où l'on voit d'emblée qu'une statue dressée dans un espace public peut devenir surface de projection, en même temps qu'elle est l'expression d'une histoire d'interdépendance européenne. Car une statue équestre italienne, inspirée en son temps des statues de l'antiquité romaine, devenait non seulement le modèle du premier monument équestre parisien mais aussi l'emblème d'un roi juste et bon. Ceci n'ayant pas empêché que, dans la foulée de la ‚Cancel culture' de la Révolution française, la figure en bronze d'Henri IV soit renversée de son socle, fondue et réutilisée plus tard pour la statue de Napoléon sur la colonne Vendôme.

Napoléon est le mot-clé qui nous conduit maintenant – avant de revenir à la statue d'Henri IV à Paris – à Berlin. Après sa victoire sur la Prusse, Napoléon fait son entrée triomphale à Berlin et le Quadrige de la Porte de Brandebourg suscite aussitôt sa convoitise. Cet ensemble sculpté appartient lui aussi à une longue tradition européenne. Pour cette œuvre au service d'un projet prussien, le sculpteur

Schadow s'était inspiré de l'art grec antique. Le char de combat, fréquemment requis dans les courses ou les marches triomphales et souvent conduit par Victoria, la déesse de la victoire, est soustrait de son contexte original et transféré dans un contexte architectural tout autre. Car le Quadrige de la Porte de Brandebourg est au premier chef l'élément matériel de tout un système symbolique dans lequel s'affiche le pouvoir du roi prussien. Il est dirigé vers l'avenue *Unter den Linden*, où est prévu dès 1741, après l'arrivée au pouvoir de Frédéric II, l'aménagement du Forum Fridericianum, nouveau centre culturel et scientifique du royaume prussien. Dans la figure qui conduit le Quadrige, Schadow a voulu combiner la Niké grecque Victoria avec Irène, la déesse de la paix. Après l'entrée de Napoléon à Berlin, le Quadrige berlinois, déclaré butin de guerre, fut démonté en 1806 et transporté par bateau à Paris. À Berlin, voir la Porte de Brandebourg « nue » était chaque jour un crève-cœur pour les sujets prussiens, l'absence du quadrige étant unanimement ressentie comme un signe d'humiliation nationale.

En tant qu'objet d'art spolié, le quadrige acquiert une fonction radicalement nouvelle : il devient le symbole du triomphe sur la Prusse et de surcroît une œuvre d'art destinée à entrer dans le musée qui, selon la volonté de Napoléon, doit faire de Paris la capitale artistique du continent. Ce musée, qui touche aussi à un aspect intéressant des débats sur les questions de restitution, n'existant pas encore à l'époque, le quadrige fut d'abord stationné aux *Menus Plaisirs*, où étaient par ailleurs entreposés les décors de l'opéra.

Dans le contexte de notre sujet concernant les statues en tant que protagonistes des histoires européennes d'interdépendance et de désunion, je me permettrai ici une petite digression pour évoquer un autre quadrige, volé par Napoléon en Italie cette fois, notamment parce que cet exemple d'imbrication européenne nous fait remonter jusqu'au 1er siècle après J.C. Dès 1797 et la prise de Venise, Napoléon avait en effet spolié et fait transporter à Paris les chevaux de la basilique Saint Marc, qui, avant de devenir le butin des Vénitiens, avaient orné l'hippodrome de Constantinople jusqu'en 1204. Mais un premier transfert les avait déjà conduits de Rome, où ils ornaient manifestement l'arc de triomphe de l'Empereur Néron, à Constantinople, puisqu'ils sont datés du 1er siècle après J.C. Dans une lettre de 1364, Pétrarque décrit comment, sur une invitation du Doge, il s'était trouvé assis sur la tribune qui trônait au-dessus de la Place Saint Marc, directement à hauteur des chevaux :

> Déjà le Doge en personne, entouré d'un immense cortège de dignitaires, avait pris place dans la façade de l'église, au-dessus du vestibule ; depuis cette tribune de marbre, il avait tout sous ses pieds : c'est à cet endroit que se tiennent les quatre chevaux de bronze et d'or – œuvre d'exécution ancienne, et d'un artiste remarquable, quel qu'il fût – qui vus d'en haut, semblent hennir et frapper du sabot comme des chevaux vivants (Pétrarque 2003 [1364], 64).

Comme le quadrige prussien, les chevaux volés à Constantinople avaient valeur d'emblème de pouvoir pour le doge. Et Napoléon, ici encore, avait manifestement succombé à l'envie de transporter cet emblème de la République de Venise – visible aux yeux de tous sur la Basilique Saint Marc – à Paris.

Le char de la Porte de Brandebourg comme les chevaux du char de Constantinople, plus tard transférés dans la façade de la basilique Saint Marc, étaient entourés d'une aura de puissance qui conduisit à leur vol pour humilier les vaincus. À chaque vol, cette aura grandit et s'enrichit de nouvelles connotations de sens.

En 1808, Napoléon fit installer les chevaux vénitiens sur l'Arc de triomphe entre le Louvre et les Tuileries, qu'il avait fait ériger en hommage à sa Grande Armée sur le modèle de l'Arc de Septime Sévère à Rome ; après sa défaite, ils furent restitués à l'Italie et remplacés à Paris par une copie.

La défaite de Napoléon en 1814 eut aussi des conséquences pour le quadrige brandebourgeois. Les Prussiens préparèrent aussitôt son retour triomphal à Berlin pour l'intégrer de nouveau dans le système de pouvoir prussien originel. Mais entre son statut d'œuvre d'art spoliée à Paris et de symbole de la victoire de la Prusse sur Napoléon, le quadrige – emballé dans des caisses – échappe pour une brève séquence à tout système de signification et se prête à de nouvelles connotations. Soustrait à son contexte original de la Porte de Brandebourg, il est lesté d'une nouvelle virtualité, œuvre d'art emballée dans différentes caisses, chaque caisse contenant une œuvre d'art en soi, un char de combat et quatre somptueux chevaux distincts. Dans sa fonction référentielle de cheval, l'un d'eux va attirer l'attention. S'il existait en tant qu'élément du quadrige dans une caisse, le voilà maintenant *Zuhanden*,[2] à-portée-de-main, pour citer un jeu de mots de Heidegger. Car, en 1814, on a de toute urgence besoin d'un cheval majestueux pour la statue équestre d'Henri IV, détruite pendant la Révolution. Le *Cheval de Bronze* doit retrouver sa place sur le Pont Neuf pour l'accueil de Louis XVIII, qui se revendique de la lignée d'Henri IV.[3] Après la Révolution, il parut en effet opportun au nouveau roi de se présenter à son peuple non comme un successeur de Louis XIV mais plutôt du roi bien-aimé Henri IV. La gazette allemande contemporaine *Göttingischen Gelehrten Anzeigen* se fait l'écho de cette aventureuse combinaison :

---

2 On peut lire dans *Être et temps de Martin Heidegger* : « Je dringlicher das Fehlende gebraucht wird, je eigentlicher es in seiner Unzuhandenheit begegnet, um so aufdringlicher wird das Zuhandene, so zwar, daß es den Charakter der Zuhandenheit zu verlieren scheint. Es enthüllt sich als nur noch Vorhandenes, das ohne das Fehlende nicht von der Stelle gebracht werden kann. Das ratlose Davorstehen entdeckt als defizienter Modus eines Besorgens das Nur-noch-vorhandensein eines Zuhandenen » (Heidegger 1957, 73).

3 Dans ce contexte, voir la représentation détaillée dans « Pariser Exil, das die Pferde und die Siegesgöttin aus Berlin über sich ergehen lassen mussten » (Savoy 2011, 374).

Au même moment, le vœu avait été exprimé de reproduire la statue unseren Kontexkd'-Henri IV [. . .] Mais de telles statues de métal ne se réalisent pas en un tour de main, elles requièrent des années de travail. On décida donc le 18 avril d'improviser une statue de plâtre. On possédait des dessins de la statue détruite ainsi qu'un buste similaire d'Henri IV ; seul le modelage du cheval en grand pouvait causer des difficultés et nécessiter un délai. Par chance, le quadrige berlinois déjà emballé n'était pas encore expédié, et l'on reçut de sa Majesté le roi de Prusse l'autorisation de déballer l'un des chevaux et de l'utiliser pendant 3 jours pour les moules du plâtre. Aussitôt dit, aussitôt fait et le cheval, restitué au bout de trois jours, partit avec les trois autres pour Berlin. Sculpteurs, plâtriers, charpentiers et forgerons se répartirent alors la tâche, qui du cheval, qui du cavalier, qui du harnachement et des socles de bois ; le 3 mai aux environs de midi, tous les échafaudages et parements de bois furent enlevés et la statue apparut terminée à la stupéfaction générale (*Göttingische Gelehrte Anzeigen* 1822, 1997–1998).

Etienne Jouy relate ce grand événement de 1814 : « Lorsque la voiture royale s'arrêta devant la statue d'Henri IV, qui semblait avoir été replacée là par enchantement, un concert mélodieux fit entendre les airs chéris du peuple. Tous les yeux, tous les cœurs, se portaient alternativement de Louis XVIII à Henri IV, dont les traits semblaient revivre sous le plâtre » (Jouy 1823, 31).

En 1818, la statue de plâtre provisoire fut remplacée par une statue de bronze, réalisée cette fois avec le matériau obtenu de la fonte de la statue de Napoléon sur la Place Vendôme.[4] Cet épisode montre clairement les changements possibles de la signification affectée à une statue en espace public dès lors qu'elle s'affranchit de tout système connoté et se libère virtuellement. Ainsi le cheval prussien inspiré d'un cheval de quadrige grec antique acquiert-il une nouvelle fonction dans la statue équestre « italienne » d'Henri IV, qui sert à son tour de légitimation au roi français Louis XVIII.

Mais l'histoire du quadrige ne s'arrête pas là. Sa restitution avec le rapatriement du char par les troupes de Blücher à Berlin en 1814 inspira aux Berlinois l'amusante expression « Retourkutsche », ou retour du carrosse, qui signifie aujourd'hui « rendre la pareille ». Une autre caricature dépeint ce triomphe sous une forme drastique : « La perfidie les a enlevés – La bravoure les a ramenés » – d'une part des chevaux efflanqués, vainement poussés par Napoléon vers Paris et d'autre part la déesse de la Victoire lançant ses fiers chevaux vers la Porte de Brandebourg, pour ainsi dire « castrée » par Napoléon.

---

4 Voir la reproduction de la « Vue de la Galerie Henri IV dans l'exposition des produits de l'industrie française en 1819 » au Louvre, Lithographie de F. Villain, Paris Bibliothèque nationale de France, département des estampes et de la photographie, Inv. Va 218 1; A 16365, reproduite dans le livre de Bénédicte Savoy, *Kunstraub* (Savoy 2011, 379). Karlheinz Stierle a thématisé ce processus de transfert dans le contexte de l'histoire du concept de Renaissance (Stierle 1987, 466 sq.).

Le quadrige s'insère alors dans un nouveau contexte. Schinkel remplaça la couronne de laurier de la conductrice de Schadow par une croix de fer ornée de feuilles de chêne et couronnée d'un aigle, transformant ainsi la messagère de paix en déesse de la Victoire pour célébrer le retour à Berlin de la sculpture transportée à Paris, et la victoire sur les troupes napoléoniennes. Le vol du quadrige et son transport triomphal après la victoire sur Napoléon en ont fait – et du même coup de la Porte de Brandebourg – un symbole politique des efforts de liberté et d'unité nationale. Pendant la Deuxième Guerre mondiale, la Porte de Brandebourg fut très gravement endommagée et le quadrige totalement détruit, à l'exception d'une tête de cheval. Il existait cependant un moulage en plâtre qui permit sa reconstitution après la guerre. Entre-temps, il avait acquis une valeur de symbole politique telle que le Sénat de Berlin et le conseil des magistrats s'accordèrent, au milieu des années 1950, pour une reconstruction conjointe de la Porte de Brandebourg, et ce malgré les énormes tensions entre les quatre secteurs de la ville après-guerre. Un nouveau quadrige fut recréé dans la partie ouest de Berlin à partir des moulages en plâtre, puis remis à sa place sur la Porte de Brandebourg, orienté vers l'est – sans aucun symbole prussien néanmoins. Le drapeau rouge russe qui y flottait jusque-là fut retiré.

Désormais la Porte de Brandebourg et le quadrige, qui n'étaient plus des emblèmes des revendications de pouvoir prussien, marquaient la frontière entre Berlin-Est et Berlin-Ouest et du même coup la frontière entre les états du Pacte de Varsovie et de l'OTAN. Symbole de la guerre froide jusqu'à la réunification de l'Allemagne, la Porte de Brandebourg devint le symbole de la réunification allemande et de l'Europe après 1990. Après la chute du mur, elle pouvait devenir l'incarnation d'une Allemagne réunifiée (Jurt 1993, 45–58, à propos de la symbolique de la Porte de Brandebourg, notamment p. 51).

3 Les statues en tant que protagonistes d'une communication européenne

Revenons une fois encore aux statues. L'exemple des statues de Giambologna et de l'histoire européenne d'interdépendance de sa statue équestre sur le Pont Neuf, qui s'y trouve aujourd'hui encore – tout comme nous pouvons admirer aujourd'hui sur la Porte de Brandebourg le cheval du quadrige après son escapade sur le Pont Neuf – ont montré que les statues peuvent devenir l'expression d'un palimpseste européen condensé. C'est cette dimension des statues, qui perdurent dans le temps et l'éprouvent, que l'écrivaine française Cécile Wajsbrot a placé au centre de son roman *L'Île aux musées* (2008), dans lequel elle fait des statues de

Berlin et Paris les sujets du discours. Bien avant les débats sur les questions de restitution des œuvres d'art, elle fait parler les statues des musées parisiens et berlinois de leur provenance et de leur expatriation de par le monde entier.

Cécile Wajsbrot est née en 1954 à Paris dans une famille de juifs polonais ; son grand-père a été assassiné à Auschwitz et sa mère a échappé de justesse à la razzia du Vélodrome d'hiver en juillet 1942. « L'essentiel de mon travail [. . .] », explique-t-elle en synthèse, « consistait dans la recherche du passé et de ses effets sur le présent. » À ses yeux, la littérature est apte à transmettre le passé et le présent : « ramener à la surface tout ce qui est habituellement caché, le laisser remonter à la surface comme ces objets que la marée rejette sur la plage, après qu'ils avaient disparu pendant des jours, des semaines, des années ».[5]

Son roman *L'Île aux musées* commence par un portrait : « C'est un homme seul dans l'avenue monumentale qui traverse le parc Tiergarten et mène à la porte de Brandebourg. » Cet homme seul n'est cependant pas un humain ; dès la deuxième page, il se révèle qu'il doit s'agir d'une sculpture qui devient dès lors l'objet d'une réflexion poétique :

> Là, entre la colonne de la Victoire et la porte – [. . .] – au milieu des voitures rapidement garées, sa forme harmonieuse s'élève d'un socle de marbre. Au milieu de l'agitation, du chaos, il invite au silence de la contemplation et attire le regard par sa simplicité – nul artifice, nulle décoration ne vient distraire, [. . .] le visage rond des statues romaines. Les deux bras sont levés et les mains repliées en porte-voix entourent une bouche grande ouverte dont le cercle décrit la courbe d'une parole lancée au loin. Il n'a pas de nom, seulement une fonction, il est celui qui appelle, *der Rufer*, mais le cri, loin de déformer son visage, montre la force du mot, sa portée (Wajsbrot 2008, 7).

L'autrice fait explicitement de ce personnage du crieur, qui doit son existence à un processus complexe de transfert culturel européen, le centre d'intérêt de son roman. Le motif du « Rufer » réfère à la figure antique du Stentor, dont la voix retentissait comme celles de cinquante hommes. Il est rapporté dans l'Iliade qu'Héra prit son apparence et sa puissante voix pour conduire les Grecs au combat devant Troie. Si le puissant volume de sa voix était mis au premier plan dans le contexte antique, sa fonction change dans celui de l'œuvre d'art de Gerhard Marcks. Le silence méditatif qui semble environner ce « crieur », et que Cécile Wajsbrot souligne intentionnellement, fait clairement apparaître cette divergence.

---

[5] Cécile Wajsbrot a inventé un discours urbain qui réfléchit dans sa forme très particulière la ville comme un palimpseste du souvenir. Dans ses romans *Nation par Barbès* (2001), *Caspar Friedrich Strasse* (2002), *Fugue* (2005) et *L'Île aux musées* (2008), les métropoles Paris et Berlin sont au centre de l'expérience de recherche et de perte de soi de ses protagonistes (Oster 2009, 237–256). À propos de Cécile Wajsbrot, cf. Böhm (2010).

Dans la version moderne sculptée, le stentor à la voix puissante devient une posture suggestive, un lanceur d'appel anonyme. Le « visage rond des statues romaines » (Wajsbrot 2008, 7) conserve néanmoins présent – du moins dans la perspective de Wajsbrot – le contexte antique. Dans le contrat proposé par Radio Bremen à Gerhard Marcks en 1967 pour un nouveau média et dans un contexte de sens tout à fait inédit, l'antique figure du Stentor se prête pour ainsi dire à de nouvelles fonctions. Gerhard Marcks voyait dans son crieur l'incarnation du droit à la liberté d'expression. Cécile Wajsbrot fait remarquer dans une allusion à Marcks qu'il avait été déclaré artiste dégénéré et que ses œuvres étaient stigmatisées par le totalitarisme. L'artiste Marcks fait de la puissante voix une voix libre. En 1989, à l'occasion du centenaire du sculpteur, une reproduction en bronze de sa sculpture de trois mètres de haut a été dressée à portée de vue du mur de Berlin et de la Porte de Brandebourg. Cette œuvre fut financée par une fondation privée de banques et par la maison d'édition Axel-Springer. Le choix pour cette réplique en bronze d'un emplacement à proximité du mur signale un nouveau cadre politique de référence que Cécile Wajsbrot ne manque pas de relever. La sculpture du crieur/Rufer se laissait aisément intégrer dans un nouveau contexte politique, cet appel muet se prêtant sans cesse à de nouvelles interprétations. Les sponsors ont fait graver la leur dans le triple socle de granit. Mais une fois encore, cette voix n'était pas la leur puisqu'ils recourent en l'occurrence à une citation du poète Pétrarque qui, au 14e siècle, lors de la guerre civile entre les états-cités d'Italie du Nord, aspire à la paix : « I'vo gridando : pace, pace, pace »[6] (Wajsbrot 2008, 9). Le Stentor, qui ne se distinguait à l'origine que par la puissance de sa voix, se voit pour ainsi dire sans cesse attribuer de nouveaux appels : à la liberté de l'appel se substitue maintenant un cri pour la paix. Mais Cécile Wajsbrot ne s'en tient pas à ces processus de transferts culturels qui conduisent de la Grèce à Berlin en passant par l'Italie.[7] Elle semble vouloir amplifier la force de la voix du crieur près du mur berlinois, suggérant que son appel aurait conduit à la chute du mur : « Six mois après l'installation de l'homme éternellement immobile à la bouche éternellement ouverte, le mur de Berlin tombait » (Wajsbrot 2008, 9).[8]

Dans le roman de Wajsbrot, le crieur endosse la fonction d'un prologue. Son appel ouvre l'espace à l'appel muet d'un collectif de statues entre Berlin et Paris, dont l'autrice fait retentir les voix :

---

6 « Je vais, criant : paix, paix, paix. »
7 Rémi Brague parle de la « Secondarité culturelle », qui caractériserait l'identité européenne. La sculpture décrite par Cécile Wajsbrot semble tout particulièrement l'illustrer (Brague 1993, 157).
8 À propos des transformations de Berlin après la chute du mur, voir Oster (2014, 45–59).

« Nous montons la garde. Même si personne ne nous prête attention – et peut-être est-il plus facile de veiller quand personne ne regarde. [. . .] Nous sommes en pierre, en bronze, nous sommes en granit ou en marbre, nous sommes sur les ponts, en haut des édifices ou devant les musées, nous sommes dans les jardins, [. . .] – mais immobiles, le regard fixe » (Wajsbrot 2008, 10).

La complexité de cette œuvre, qui se place dans la tradition du *nouveau roman*, réside dans le floutage de la différence entre les vivants et les protagonistes de pierre du roman. Si le livre raconte d'une part l'histoire d'une Française et d'un Français qui quittent l'un et l'autre Paris pour cause de problèmes divers dans leur couple respectif et se rencontrent en visitant *L'Île aux musées* de Berlin un week-end de Pâques, le texte évoque aussi par ailleurs le discours des statues de l'île, qui relatent leur propre existence tout en observant le couple. Cécile Wajsbrot met ici en scène des *regards croisés* entre les humains et les statues. Les humains observent au musée des œuvres d'art, dont le regard se porte aussi sur les touristes français et qui commentent leur comportement. Le texte ne marquant pas de distinction entre les différents discours, le lecteur est constamment contraint de veiller lui-même aux inflexions de voix. Si, dans l'espace public, les statues restent d'ordinaire à l'horizon de l'appréhension, elles sont ici thématisées et affirment opiniâtrement leur présence dans le texte. En parallèle à l'histoire du couple sur *L'Île aux musées* de Berlin, le livre raconte aussi l'histoire des partenaires restés à Paris. Ici aussi le discours des protagonistes se mêle au discours des statues qui commentent ce qui se passe sur les places et dans les parcs parisiens. Il semble n'y avoir aucune différence entre les statues en France et en Allemagne, le musée suggère un *terrain vague* intemporel. Ainsi la touriste française constate-t-elle au Musée de Pergame : « [. . .] ici on a n'a aucune idée du temps, on est sans territoire, on pourrait aussi bien être au Louvre » (Wajsbrot 2008, 41).

Les statues partagent la même destinée au-delà des frontières nationales. Oui, elles apparaissent dans le texte comme des témoins muets, souvent victimes de spoliation et de destruction. Le transfert d'art dicté par des intérêts de recherche semble purement arbitraire dans la perspective des personnages :

« Vous nous avez dégagées de la terre où nous dormions. Par bloc vous nous avez transportées, nettoyées – puis identifiées, tentant de nous assembler, de reconstituer ce gigantesque puzzle que vous appelez le grand autel de Pergame. [. . .] Vous nous restaurez, vous nous exposez, nous étudiez, vous nous copiez depuis des siècles mais ce que nous sommes vraiment, ce que nous avons vu, d'où nous sommes nées, vous ne le savez pas [. . .] (Wajsbrot 2008, 32).

Cécile Wajsbrot dote les statues parlantes, qui commentent et réfléchissent ce qui se passe, d'une mémoire absolue. Ainsi est-elle en mesure de confronter leur contexte originel au système de signification actuel qui les entoure. Des cartes géographiques, des systèmes politiques, des noms ont changé, toute tentative de reconstruction fait courir le risque d'une réécriture des traces encore présentes dans la mémoire des statues : « Nous sommes là depuis longtemps, plus longtemps que vous ne croyez mais loin, si loin de nos villes d'origine. Nos cartes ne coïncident pas avec les vôtres ni les frontières ni les noms de pays et parfois, s'il est resté quelque chose, une trace de nos époques, votre nom a recouvert le nôtre » (Wajsbrot 2008, 30).

En regard de l'art romain, il apparaît cependant clairement que les statues volées soustraites à leur contexte originel peuvent servir de tremplin pour l'innovation : « Imitatio, interpretatio aemulatio – tels étaient les principes de l'art romain. À chaque bataille gagnée, ils ramenaient des statues. Conscients de leur infériorité, ils copiaient, et en copiant, ils interprétaient et s'éloignaient un peu de leur modèle, leur imagination, leur force de création, s'en trouvait stimulée et ils pouvaient à leur tour inventer » (Wajsbrot 2008, 76).

Si d'un côté les statues jadis déplacées participent, dans le roman de Cécile Wajsbrot, d'un héritage européen antique commun, leurs souvenirs divergent considérablement à partir de leur transfert à Berlin ou Paris, les statues servant alors de médium pour mettre en scène l'histoire franco-allemande dans une perspective de distanciation. Ainsi les statues de *L'Île aux musées* se souviennent-elles du projet de complexe muséal consécutif à la restitution des trésors spoliés par Napoléon ; elles furent les témoins des autodafés de 1933 et des atrocités du Troisième Reich, elles ont vécu les bombardements de Berlin, l'époque du Mur, la répartition des œuvres et le retour de tous les trésors artistiques dans les musées restaurés de la Museumsinsel (*Île aux musées*) après la Chute du mur, qui vit aussi la destruction de nombreuses statues de Lénine. Avec l'exemple du buste en marbre d'Acellino Salvago, d'Antonio Tamagnino, nous pouvons suivre un transfert culturel littéraire au cours duquel le buste d'un fier prince de la Renaissance, qui avait trouvé place dans un musée berlinois et avait été endommagé par un incendie pendant la guerre, est devenu l'incarnation même des humains victimes de la guerre et des déportations. Chez Cécile Wajsbrot, les statues du musée évoquent son souvenir et sa destinée :

> Le marbre du buste était parfait et la ressemblance étonnante – la ressemblance avec la vie car personne ne sait plus quelle allure avait cet aristocrate italien. Il est sur le point de parler, disiez-vous, on a l'impression qu'il surveille, disiez-vous, l'arrivée de l'ennemi ou d'un personnage important. Maintenant il reste une partie du visage, un œil, et à peine une oreille, un peu de front et la moitié du crâne. Il reste la forme du visage. L'autre œil n'est plus qu'une orbite, la bouche, une cavité. Il n'y a plus de nez, le cou est décharné, le col arraché, et le haut de la toge, les premiers plis. . . Il n'y a plus d'expression, plus rien. Le buste était avec nous, dans un bunker du parc pour échapper à votre guerre [. . .] Mais une nuit [. . .] une lumière vive – un incendie. La plupart d'entre nous ont péri, attaquées par les flammes, carbonisées, désintégrées (Wajsbrot 2008, 203–204).

Wajsbrot décrit de nombreuses œuvres d'art moderne qui rappellent le destin de la population juive, comme l'installation de 1988 « Der verlassene Raum » (« La pièce quittée »), de Karl Biederman, en souvenir du pogrome de la Nuit de Cristal, le 9 novembre 1938 : dans un parc, une gigantesque table et deux chaises dont l'une est renversée :

> Sur une petite place d'allure presque champêtre que viennent faire cette table et ces chaises ? Quelqu'un d'une maison avoisinante est-il en train de déménager ? A t-il posé ses meubles en attendant le camion qui viendra les prendre ? Ou veut-il s'en débarrasser, les donner à une association caritative ? Mais le bureau n'est pas en bois, son plateau n'est pas recouvert de cuir comme on pourrait le croire, il est en bronze, comme les chaises, comme le motif de parquet dessiné au sol. Il s'agit d'une sculpture – il faut tout reconsidérer. Une chaise rangée derrière un bureau ou une table au tiroir fermé, une autre renversée. Renversée dans la bousculade par ceux qui durent fuir précipitamment ? Renversée par des agresseurs ? Les passants arrivent trop tard pour sauver quoi que ce soit. Les gens sont partis. Ils viennent de partir ou d'être emmenés et voilà fixé le moment qu'on ne voit jamais – l'instant après. L'appartement vide après qu'on l'a quitté, l'expression de quelqu'un après un au revoir, ce qu'on laisse définitivement quand on part sans se retourner (Wajsbrot 2008, 121).

Ailleurs, à Paris, les statues se souviennent du projet des Tuileries de Catherine de Médicis, des sanglants désordres de la Révolution française, des combats de rues pendant la Deuxième Guerre mondiale et de l'évacuation des peintures du Louvre au château de Chambord, de l'occupation allemande, du regroupement des œuvres dites d'art dégénéré au Jeu de Paume et de l'autodafé de beaucoup de ces œuvres dans les jardins des Tuileries. Les statues parisiennes se souviennent aussi de la lente et longue restitution d'œuvres d'art spoliées à la population juive, que leurs propriétaires n'ont bien souvent jamais revues. Si, dans le texte, les propos des humains et ceux des statues se confondent constamment sans transition, c'est précisément cette notion de transition catégoriale qui est requise au niveau de l'*histoire* pour ramener au premier plan la destinée humaine derrière l'histoire des statues. Les statues parisiennes relatent sur un ton neutre en apparence le sauvetage des œuvres d'art par un groupe de résistants, qui n'empêchera pas le départ suivant d'un train de déportés : « Vous l'appelez le train d'Aulnay – parce qu'il fut arrêté en gare d'Aulnay par un groupe de résistants. Tous les tableaux qu'il contenait furent récupérés, Picasso, Braque, Bonnard – le dernier convoi de déportés – puisque c'est votre mot – part après le dernier convoi d'œuvres d'art. Et personne n'essaya de l'arrêter » (Wajsbrot 2008, 144).

Il devient tout à fait clair dès lors que chez Cécile Wajsbrot, les statues, qui se distancient explicitement du discours des humains, deviennent des figures de projection du destin juif. On est en même temps frappé, dans ce contexte précisément, qu'il ne soit pas fait de différence déterminante entre l'Allemagne et la France. Les statues se souviennent d'histoires différentes, mais les destructions et les atrocités ont aussi lieu à Paris, le train en partance pour le camp de concentration quitte Paris sans être retenu par les résistants français. Il s'agit aussi à l'évidence d'une confrontation avec le phénomène de la collaboration, longtemps tu en France. Si Cécile Wajsbrot, spécialement sensible à ce silence en tant que Juive française, donne une voix aux statues muettes, c'est aussi pour parler d'une histoire d'implication franco-française. Son roman prend pour ainsi dire le relais du crieur qui intervient ainsi une fois de plus dans un nouveau système de signification.

Un crieur est nécessaire au dialogue intra-européen et au dialogue de l'Europe avec le monde. Les statues montrent à quel point les histoires d'interférence de l'Europe sont profondes – mais aussi comment s'attisent en elles les histoires de désunion. Cécile Wajsbrot les appréhende comme des témoins de notre passé européen, mais elles soulèvent aussi des questions de restitution et de réparations avec lesquelles l'Europe tente de reconsidérer son rapport au monde, de concilier le regard vers le passé et le regard vers l'avenir.

Références

Böhm, Roswitha et Margarete Zimmermann. Éds. *Du silence à la voix. Studien zum Werk der Cécile Wajsbrot*. Göttingen : V&R unipress (Formen der Erinnerung), 2010.

Brague, Rémi. *Europe. La voix romaine*. Paris : Criterion, 1993.

Dubost, Jean-François. « Henry IV au Pont-Neuf. Genèse, hésitations sémantiques, et détournement d'une effigie royale (1604–1640). » *Henry IV. Art et pouvoir*. Éd. Colette Navitel. Tours : Presses Universitaires de Rennes, 2016.

Göttingische Gelehrte Anzeigen, 200. Stück (16. Décembre 1822) : 1995–2000.

Heidegger, Martin. *Sein und Zeit*. Tübingen : Niemeyer, 1957.

Jouy, Etienne. « Le Franc Parleur », n° II (14 mai 1814). *Œuvres complètes*. Vol. 4. Paris : Didot, 1823.

Jurt, Joseph. « La Nouvelle Allemagne : Quels symboles? ». *Actes de la Recherche en Sciences Sociales* 98 (1993) : 45–58.

Lignier, Sarah. « Le Monde en 1400 mètres carrés ». *La Collection Pinault à la Bourse de Commerce*. « Ouverture » [Catalogue de l'exposition]. Éd. Claude Pommereau. Paris : Beaux Arts & Cie, 2021, 70–76.

Oster, Patricia. « Transfuges entre Paris et Berlin. Stadterfahrung und Stadtdiskurs bei Cécile Wajsbrot ». *Observatoire de l'extrême contemporain. Studien zur französischsprachigen Gegenwartsliteratur*. Éd. Roswitha Böhm, Stephanie Bung et Andrea Grewe. Tübingen : Narr, 2009, 237–256.

_____. « Kunst als Medium des Kulturtransfers. Methodische Reflexionen am Beispiel von Cécile Wajsbrots Berlinromanen ». *Zwischen Transfer und Vergleich*. Éd. Christiane Solte-Gresser, Hans-Jürgen Lüsebrink et Manfred Schmeling. Stuttgart : Steiner, 2013, 383–396.

_____. « Sophie Calle à la recherche des signes perdus ». *Après le Mur : Berlin dans la littérature francophone*. Éd. Margarete Zimmerman. Tübingen : Narr, 2014, 45–59.

_____. « Laudatio auf Cécile Wajsbrot ». *Académie de Berlin*. 2016. https://www.academie-de-berlin. de/prix/laudationes/prof-patricia-stierle-laudatio-auf-cecile-wajsbrot (02 septembre 2022).

Pétrarque. *Lettres de la vieillesse, Rerum Senilium.* Vol. II, 4–7. Ed. Elvira Nota. Paris : Les Belles Lettres, 2003.
Savoy, Bénédicte. *Patrimoine annexé. Les biens culturels saisis par la France en Allemagne autour de 1800*. Paris : Éditions de la Maison des sciences de l'homme, 2003.
Sloterdijk, Peter. *Si l'Europe s'éveille*. Trad. Olivier Mannoni. Paris : Mille et une nuits, 2003.
Stierle, Karlheinz. « Renaissance – Die Entstehung eines Epochenbegriffs aus dem Geist des 19. Jahrhunderts ». *Epochenschwelle und Epochenbewußtsein*. Éd. Reinhart Herzog et Reinhart Koselleck (Poetik und Hermeneutik XII). München : Fink, 1987.
Wajsbrot, Cécile. *L'Île aux musées*. Paris : Denoël, 2008.

Part III: **Commemorative Politics and the Public Sphere**

Troisième partie : **Les politiques de la mémoire et le domaine public**

Hannah Katalin Grimmer
To Represent the Non-Representable. A Mnemonic Restitution of the Body in Claudia Fontes' *La Reconstrucción del Retrato de Pablo Míguez*

Abstract: The extent of atrocities committed during Latin American civil-military dictatorships is not quantifiable; more precisely, the gap left by *detenidos desaparecidos* is difficult to grasp. This chapter illustrates the importance of cultural expression within post-conflict societies and aims at further including visual arts in Memory Studies. I argue that through art, people whose lives were erased by the military and who left no physical traces can be represented. The site-specific sculptural artwork by the Argentinian artist Claudia Fontes is taken as an example to elucidate a method that opposes the (in-)visibility of crime and victim and what Diana Taylor conceptualized as *percepticide*. Through an in-depth analysis of the sculpture as well as its relation to the place where it is located, this chapter demonstrates what a possible mnemonic restitution can look like.

Keywords: visual arts, sculpture, Claudia Fontes, Memory Studies, *detenidos desaparecidos*, percepticide, Southern Cone, Argentina

¿Adónde van los desaparecidos?	Where do the disappeared go?
Busca en el agua y en los matorrales.	Search in the water and in the bushes.
¿Y por qué es que se desaparecen?	And why do they disappear?
Porque no todos somos iguales.	Because we are not all the same.
¿Y cuándo vuelve el desaparecido?	And when does the disappeared return?
Cada vez que los trae el pensamiento.	Every time the thought brings them back.[1]

1 Introduction

The song "Desapariciones" [*disappearances*] by the Panamanian singer Rubén Blades first appeared on his album "Buscando América" in 1984, one year after the end of the civil-military dictatorship in Argentina. With three simple questions,

---

[1] Taken from the song *Desaparecidos* by the Panamanian singer Rubén Blades (*1948). All translations from Spanish, unless otherwise noted, are mine.

ə Open Access. © 2023 the author(s), published by De Gruyter. This work is licensed under the Creative Commons Attribution-NonCommercial-NoDerivatives 4.0 International License.
https://doi.org/10.1515/9783110799514-008

Blades illustrates how difficult it is to approach the subject of the so-called *detenidos desaparecidos*,[2] and even more so, to find a form of representation of these missing people. Not all people are equal, so some are not meant to belong to the community of the nation-state and their lives are not considered worth living – this was one of the prominent beliefs of the military in the Southern Cone during the 1970s and 1980s. How this discourse has been counteracted in an artistic way and the question of how the *disappeared* may thus return – or rather be made visible – is the topic of this chapter.

As an example, I will discuss a particular artwork as a possible process of representing or depicting a person who has *been disappeared*. The site-specific sculpture *La Reconstrucción del Retrato de Pablo Míguez* (2000/2010)[3] by Argentinian artist Claudia Fontes is a mnemonic work located in the Parque de la Memoria in Buenos Aires. The historical incident spatially and visually integrated into the present by Fontes is the *desaparición forzada [forced disappearance]*[4] of people during the civil-military dictatorships in the Southern Cone of Latin America. The present that is revealed in the work is the continuing *absence* of countless people.

Today, at a time where the field of Memory Studies has become increasingly transdisciplinary and international, not only the approaches but also the subjects of investigation are diverse. Artistic confrontations of violent pasts play a vital role within this area, but it is noticeable that the analytic focus lies on discursive media (Erll 2017, 7). The aim of this chapter is to broaden this perspective by taking into account visual art as another form of expression and response that counters speechlessness in the face of violence, terror, and death. The research approach

---

2 *Forced disappearance* was a brutal practice during the civil-military dictatorships in the Southern Cone, directed against supposed communists, so-called 'internal enemies' (Jelin 2012). It was a 'war' in which people who were considered harmful to the state (conceived as a national body) were captured and then *disappeared* (Huneeus 2004; Huyssen 2003). The Spanish *detenido desaparecido*, translated as "detained disappeared", is used to refer to the whole system and not to a specific group of people, therefore the Spanish term is not gendered.
3 From now on referred to as *Reconstrucción*.
4 In February 1975, the United Nations defined the method of *forced disappearance* with the term "persons unaccounted for" and, referring to the developments in Chile, supplemented it by "missing people" (Bolte 2011, 77). In 1981, the Federación Latinoamericana de Asociaciones de Familiares de Detenidos-Desaparecidos (Fedefam) was founded and in 1983 August 30th was declared 'International Day of the Disappeared.' In 1998, with the *Rome Statute* the International Court of Justice in The Hague recognised *forced disappearance* as a crime against humanity (Gatti 2017, 19). In 2003, the UN founded the Working Group on Enforced or Involuntary Disappearances and since 2010 the Committee on Enforced Disappearances exists, through which the International Convention for the Protection of All Persons from Enforced Disappearance globally recognised August 30th as the day of the *disappeared*.

adopted here is based on cultural studies, which assign equal relevance to forms of knowledge that emerge beyond university hierarchies, allowing social and political – as well as artistic – knowledge to be integrated into the academic sphere (Richard 2015, 196–197).

This chapter seeks to work with theoretical principles developed within Memory Studies and to highlight their benefits for the analysis of visual art. To this end, a historical and theoretical framework will be outlined in a first step. In a second step, I will analyse how the concrete artwork *Reconstrucción* and the concrete site of memory, Parque de la Memoria, enter into dialogue and, furthermore, how international discourses are integrated in the process.[5]

2 *Forced Disappearance* and its Linguistic Perfidiousness

In 1979, the Argentinian General Jorge Raphael Videla (1925–2013) posed the question what a disappeared person is. At that time, the military junta he headed had been in power for three years. Very cynically, he gave the answer himself: "It is an unknown quantity, a disappeared person, they have no being, they are not there, neither dead nor alive, they have disappeared" (Jinkis 2006).[6] This statement delivered at a press conference on December 14th, 1979 (Vaisman 2018, 190) is remarkable in multiple ways: Not only did the dictator speak directly about a system established to remove 'unwanted' people, so-called subversives, but these remarks were also printed in a major Argentinian daily newspaper. Videla described the practice of *forced disappearance* with linguistic perfidiousness and thereby laid the foundation for this verbally obfuscated system. The problem of Videla's wording needs to be elaborated on more precisely as it contributes to my argument on the relevance of visual art within Memory Studies.

Videla spoke about people who were imprisoned and then *disappeared* from the place where they were held captive. By omitting the term 'forced,' he suggested

---

[5] I would like to express my sincere thanks to Professor Astrid Erll for her advice in developing the ideas in this chapter, as well as to Philipp Idel, Sophie Buscher, and Emily Wick.
[6] Videla's discourse was published in the newspaper *El Clarín* in, 1979. The part I am referring to here is: "En tanto esté como tal, es una incógnita el desaparecido, si el hombre apareciera, bueno, tendrá un tratamiento X, y si la desaparición se convirtiera en certeza de su fallecimiento, tiene un tratamiento Z, pero mientras sea un desaparecido no puede tener ningún tratamiento especial, es incógnita, es un desaparecido, no tiene entidad, no está, ni muerto ni vivo, está desaparecido."

that the *detenidos desaparecidos* – the victims – were themselves responsible for their *disappearance*. If one wants to adequately understand this dictatorial method, a neologism needs to be created: *someone has been disappeared* (Bolte 2011, 79). Besides, it should be emphasised that Videla used the words "no está." The intransitive verb *estar* means 'being' in the spatial, conditional, or temporary sense, while "no es" from the verb *ser* refers to existence in general. Instead of saying that the person affected does no longer exist, Videla implied that one was merely not present. It follows that making people *disappear* also meant making them (in)visible.[7] As I will show, *forced disappearances* have produced social phantasms. Since then, memorial practices aim at exorcising the spectre of the violent past (Huffschmid 2015, 443). Deconstructing dictatorial language is part of these practices.

The linguistic analysis allows to understand two paramount components of this system: first, existing words are insufficient to articulate the fate of the *detenidos desaparecidos* (Gatti 2006, 28). Second, Videla's statement points to its consequences: people remain *disappeared* to this day, their relatives are left in a state of ongoing uncertainty. The military dictatorships continue to exert a strong influence on the societies of the Southern Cone.[8] The case of the *detenidos desaparecidos* has led to a hardly comprehensible situation in which alternative methods must be developed to establish collective forms of communication (Kansteiner 2002, 188). Even if the principle of making people *disappear* without a trace is not tactically used for the first time during the military dictatorships of the 1970s and 1980s,[9] Argentina is a special case: Videla's statement illustrates that the term *detenido desaparecido* is introduced as an autonomous category (Gatti 2017, 17) for people outside of society (Gatti 2011, 99); they are characterised by a refusal of any ontologisation. The N.N., the Latin *Nomen Nescio*, has become the characteristic of human identity (Gatti 2017, 17). Only memories of the *detenidos desaparecidos* remain, and they need to be (re-)produced incessantly to be part of a collective

---

7 Throughout the chapter, the (in) of invisible is in brackets as is *disappearance* in italics. This is to point out that the military's attempt was doomed to failure. Even if the bodies of the *detenidos desaparecidos* were no longer visible, those left behind gave form to their memories in a variety of ways. In this chapter, only one specific way of creating a representation of memories is analysed.

8 In many Latin American countries, controversies about the recent past and former lines of conflict still hold considerable conflictive potential and collective memories prove disparate tendencies (Jelin 2012, 103). Human rights organisations are still working tirelessly to shed light on the crimes. Unfortunately, there is not sufficient space here to discuss how the two lines of the Madres de Plaza de Mayo conceive the existence of their *disappeared* children (Huffschmid 2015, 271).

9 Already in the 1930s in El Salvador as well as in the 1960s in Guatemala and Brazil people are *disappeared* (Bolte 2011, 77). In Mexico the first case of *forced disappearance* is registered in 1969 (Huffschmid 2015, 17).

memory (Richard 2007, 144). These memories must be articulated in multiple ways to create a material basis and to be enduring and transferable from generation to generation. To this day, different approaches and unconventional medialisation strategies are needed to question this forcefully created (in-)visibility (Bolte 2011, 36). When there is no evidence, traces need to be searched and identified, which then testify to the absence of what has caused the absence (Krämer 2007, 14). Argentinian artist Claudia Fontes ascertains, pursues, and depicts these traces in *Reconstrucción* (2000/2010). It is a site-specific sculpture located in the Río de la Plata, off the coast of Buenos Aires.

3 Basic Premises of Memory Studies

Let me begin my analysis with a very concise definition of memory that will serve as a basis for all considerations in this chapter:

> They [memories, H.K.G.] are subjective, highly selective reconstructions, dependent on the situation in which they are recalled. *Re*-membering is an act of assembling available data that takes place in the present. [. . .] Individual and collective memories are never a mirror image of the past, but rather an expressive indication of the needs and interests of the person or group doing the remembering in the present (Erll 2011a, 8, emphasis in original).

Erll's definition clarifies that memories are always personal and that remembering is an open process in which interpretations of specific events of the past are dealt with (Richard 2001, 29). Extending this basic definition, to capture the concept of memory on which this chapter is based, I would like to briefly mention three general theoretical premises of memory research.

First, the human ability to remember relies on what the German language calls "Gedächtnis" (Plate and Smelik 2013, 4). It is the indispensable, organic-physical prerequisite and forms the underlying infrastructure of "Erinnerungen" (Assmann 1997, 33). In this constellation, 'Gedächtnis' appears as a static factor, while remembering, "Erinnern", always has to be understood as an active process. Second, memories require external support to be preserved. Materialisation can be carried out in a variety of media (Erll 2010a, 389), ranging from monuments and memorials to writings, museums, artworks, and anniversaries (Assmann 1997, 33). Third, individual memory is always socially embedded, as French sociologist Maurice Halbwachs clarifies with the term *frame of memory*. He understood these frames of memory as instruments needed for any collective memory to reconstruct the past in a meaningful way and in accordance with the dominant thoughts of the epoch (1985 [1925], 22–23). The assumption is that what individuals remember is attached to the social group to which they belong (Dimbath 2013, 31). It must be emphasised that, while speaking of memory cultures, it should not be disregarded that every collective phenomenon manifests itself only in actions and statements of individuals (Kansteiner 2002, 180). In this regard, a continuous mediation based on various kinds of media between the level of individual and collective memory takes place (Erll 2011a, 113).

Within Memory Studies, the movement of memories holds a central position, which is also helpful for understanding the mnemonic specificities of the Southern Cone. In this case, I would like to use the term *Travelling Memory* devised by Astrid Erll (2011b).[10] It illustrates that memories 'move' in a metaphorical sense, bound to "people, media, mnemonic forms, contents, and practices" (Erll 2011b, 12). Memory culture is no longer conceptualised as exlusively national, as the view on borders changes. To differentiate the various dimensions of movement, Erll suggests three levels. First, the social level, in the form of people and relations; second, the material level through artefacts and media; and third, the mental level, based on culturally shaped ways of thinking (Erll 2010b, 4).[11]

The concept of Travelling Memories permits the elaboration of three aspects of *forced disappearance* and its systematic character: First, national cultures of memory are ambiguously delineated and hence memories of the dictatorial experiences in Argentina as well as in the other countries of the Southern Cone may be similar. Second, national memory cultures are internally heterogeneous, so that different and also divergent collective memories coexist. Finally, Travelling Memories can be used to look at communities that function beyond the national (Erll 2011a, 65).

Memories can be shared across national borders, especially because similar experiences exist within the Southern Cone (Jelin 2010, 63–64). Civil-military dictatorships were established during the 1970s in all countries of the region.[12] This gave rise to a belligerent, ideological public discourse of crisis, in which 'communist,' 'subversives,' or 'guerrillas' (Bolte 2011, 81) – considered to be nonhuman (Taylor 1997, 83) – posed a danger to society. The military presented itself as an authority that protected society, propagating an ideology of purifying the 'national body' (Huyssen 2003, 98) which was embedded in a broader context of the discourse of the Cold War. A new social structure was to be formed for which *forced disappearance* was a crucial method. An agreement between the military secret services of

---

10 Erll draws on James Clifford's idea of *travelling cultures* (2011a, 65–66; Erll 2011b, 11).

11 The focus on movement within Memory Studies cannot be overlooked, as the number of terms used to describe it illustrates, e.g.: "global memory" (Assmann 2010), "screen memory" (Huyssen 2003: 14), "global template" (Levy/Sznaider 2001), "transnational memory" (Rigney and de Cesari 2014).

12 Military dictatorships involved in the *Operación Condor* were Paraguay 1954–1989, Brazil 1964–1985, Bolivia 1971–1978, Uruguay 1973–1985, and Chile 1973–1990.

Argentina, Bolivia, Brazil, Chile, Paraguay, and Uruguay, known as *Operación Condor*, was decisive (Ferreira Navarro 2014, 154): The aim of this operation was to make people *disappear* in all countries involved. The perfidious execution methods of the military dictatorships had been partly unknown to the public until secret archives were discovered in 1992 (Ferreira Navarro 2014, 153).[13] Furthermore, in the mid-1990s, former Argentinian corvette captain Adolfo Scilingo confessed that people who were meant to be made unseen had been thrown into waters, after they had been narcoticised or killed (Franco 2018, 37), and that *disappearance* in the water was considered a not very violent and 'Christian death' (Verbitsky 1995, 13). This procedure was named *vuelos de la muerte* [death flights] and forms the central historical background for the realisation of the artwork analysed in this chapter.

4 The Park of Memory and a Description of the Artwork

The Parque de la Memoria – Monumento a las Víctimas del Terrorismo de Estado [Park of Memory – Monument to the Victims of State Terrorism] is a fourteen-hectare public space located on the coastal strip of the Río de la Plata in Buenos Aires. It was created in 1998 and forms a memorial project in which human rights organisations, the University of Buenos Aires, and the executive and legislative bodies of the city [Poder Ejecutivo y Legislativo de la Ciudad] worked together (Parque de la Memoria 2022). Today there are ten sculptures and the PAyS Hall[14] for temporary art exhibitions that also includes a Centre for Documentation and a digital archive (Parque de la Memoria 2022). Symbolising a place of crimes, the park was built outside of Buenos Aires, in proximity to the former torture center Escuela de Mecánica de la Armada (ex-ESMA) (Huyssen 2003, 100). It is situated close to the airport Jorge Newbury, from which many of the so-called death flights took off (Bell 2014, 81–82).

The design for *Reconstrucción* was created in 1999 as part of an international competition organised by the government of Buenos Aires; the sculpture was

---

13 Given these records, human rights organizations assume 50,000 murdered, 35,0000 *detenidos desaparecidos* and 400,000 prisoners (Ferreira Navarro 2014, 174).
14 PAyS is the acronym for "Presentes, Ahora y Siempre" ["Present, Now and Forever"] (Bell 2014, 90). By linking past, present and future, it refers to *Nunca más*, the paradigm which will be thematized below.

installed in 2010.[15] The work is built in the water of the Río de la Plata with a distance of about 70m to the coast. The sculpture measures 1.70 x 0.50 x 0.70 meters and is life-sized. It is the stature of a boy turning his back towards the viewer. The standing figure is attached to a floating steel platform, of which only four

Fig. 1: Claudia Fontes, *Reconstrucción del retrato de Pablo Míguez*, 2000/2010. Mirror of polished stainless steel. 1,70 x 0,45 x 0,40 m. Río de la Plata, 70m off the coast, Parque de la Memoria, Avenida Costanera Norte, Rafael Obligado 6745, Buenos Aires. Photo: Guadalupe Miles, courtesy of the artist. http://claudiafontes.com/project/reconstruction-of-the-portrait-of-pablo-miguez/.

---

15 In the post-dictatorial setting of the Southern Cone, controversies about recent pasts continue to harbour considerable conflict potential and collective memories show disparate tendencies. Jelin notes that several lines of conflict were considered closed in the 1990s but were in upheaval again with the turn of the millennium. Relevant factors were, for example, the arrest of Pinochet in Chile, the Peace Commission in Uruguay, attempts to reopen cases in Brazil, and truth trials concerning child abductions in Argentina. In the 2010s, other constellations emerged again: in Argentina, trials for the unconstitutionality of the laws *Punto Final* [Full Stop Law, 1986] and *Obediencia Debida* [Law of Due Obedience, 1987] became more numerous; there were active trials in Chile, and memory museums in Chile, Uruguay, and Paraguay opened. The process of reprocessing the past is ongoing (Jelin 2012, 103).

rounded, buoy-like elements rise above the water. The steel construction moves with the current in a constant, calm way. The material is stainless, highly polished silver steel. The surface texture is even, an impression of skin or fabric is created by convex and concave bulges that alternate. The depicted boy holds his right forearm on his back and embraces the left arm from the inside at the level of the elbow. His left leg is set slightly forward. The gaze is directed into the distance. The beholder stands on the bank of the river, has a direct view on the sculpture and, like the sculpture, looks in the same direction at the river. The steel functions as a mirror reflecting its surroundings, the water of the Río de la Plata, and the sky. As a result, the appearance of the sculpture changes depending on the weather. In comparison to the surrounding river, the figure looks small, and the plastic forms create a filigree impression (Fig. 1).

5 Against Percepticide – a Mnemonic Restitution of the Body

The sculpture is based on the image of a real boy, Pablo Míguez. The artist's intention to depict the stature of a boy as realistically as possible about 30 years after his *forced disappearance* was almost impossible due to the military's iconoclastic methods (Bolte 2011, 199). Like in the case of Pablo Míguez, they made not only people, but also private photographs of them *disappear* (Bell 2014, 151). Gatti emphasises that this was an attempt to erase people's identity and individuality in their entirety (2011, 99). This specific form of de-presentation and the societal consequences can best be understood with the term *percepticide* coined in this context by Diana Taylor (1997, 119–138). Taylor thus refers to the two levels that were inherent in the procedure: A person was *disappeared*, and a society had to pretend not to know about it. Even though it was known that the military made people '*disappear*,' it was better not to be a witness, which turned seeing into a "dangerous" (Taylor 1997, 122) act. Taylor characterises this process of "self-blinding of the general population" (Taylor 1997, 123) by the dichotomies of "given-to-be-seen" and "given-to-be-invisible" (Taylor 1997, 119). This had lasting impacts on social cohesion (Taylor 1997, 119) as it shaped the entire social structure by fear and mistrust. A highly theatrical society was established, predicated on the ability to render the visible (in)visible. Perhaps, the fact that one knew what was happening but was not allowed to see it made it even more frightening (Taylor 1997, 132). Accordingly, Taylor describes the social coexistence during the Argentinian dictatorship as follows:

> The military spectacle made people pull back in fear, denial and tacit complicity from the show of force. Therein lay its power. The military violence could have been relatively invisible, as the term *disappearance* suggests. [. . .]. People had to deny what they saw and, by turning away, collude with the violence around them (Taylor 1997, 123, emphasis in original).

Forced disappearance meant the negation of the former existence of a person (Gatti 2017, 17; Mandolessi 2018, 51). These crimes, given the absence of the *corpus delicti*, could neither be accused nor condemned; there were no traces of *disappearance* (Fortuny 2010, 8–9). This dichotomy could not be resolved and the negative chain – no body, no murderer, no crime, no judgment, no corpse, no funeral, and no grief (Mahlke 2012, 200) – remained unchanged with the official end of the dictatorship in 1983. Accordingly, it is pertinent when Colombo and Schindel (2014, 1) ask: "What happens when state crimes do not leave traces and when there are no recognizable graves? How can the absence be made visible?" *Disappearance* often implied an unspeakable and inexplicable fate (Bolte 2011, 253) and therefore had traumatising effects on individuals as well as societies.

To foster an understanding of this situation, it is helpful to establish a spectral discourse (Caruth 1995, 8–9; Mandolessi 2018, 59). In Latin America, the notion of the ghostly was already part of the discursive construction of the *detenidos desaparecidos* during the dictatorships (Bolte 2011, 105), as the discourse of Videla cited at the beginning of this chapter illustrates by the usage of expressions such as 'unknown,' 'no entity,' or 'neither dead nor alive.' Besides, the spectral discourse makes it possible to elaborate more on the temporal component of *forced disappearance*: Given that spectres are object and metaphor of a past that remains present (Pilar Blanco and Peeren 2013, 1), the spectral is "a metaphor for the concept of temporal diffraction" (Hristova et al. 2020, 779). This perspective represents a crucial development, allowing an understanding in which past violence is not thought of as a presumably finished "state of exception" (Hite and Jara 2020, 248). Rather, it enables us to understand *forced disappearance* as a traumatic experience for both the individual and society. Trauma in this sense should be conceptualised as defined by Craps: It is a past that does not cease to structure the present (2010, 473). The importance of the spectral discourse gives evidence of "the liminal nature of disappearance and its effects" and allows us to emphasise the "presence of that past" as well as the difficulties "in the attempts to tame it" (Crenzel 2020, 254).

Traumatic experiences do not have privileged access to collective memories (Kansteiner 2002, 187); these experiences only enter commemorative structures if a corresponding socially shared and structured framework is created (Kansteiner 2002, 187–188). I regard artworks as an attempt to create a possible framework and (re-)presentation of (in-)visibilised people. They can do so without necessarily having to resort to forensic means. With the arts, it is possible to consider the fundamental system behind *forced disappearance*: The intention is not to "express a mimetic, literal, and almost naïve representational gesture" (Schindel 2014, 193); rather, the unrepresentable is thought through the impossibility of representation (Gatti 2006, 34). In that sense, art is conceived as a cultural force (Bal 2006, 19) that can seek to represent memories and to open a space for discourse.

Against this backdrop, the sculpture *Reconstrucción* is a strategy of materialisation to create lasting memories. Due to the difficulties involved in the process, the title of Fontes' work is instructive: *Reconstrucción* means reconstruction/restoration; it refers to something that once existed. With this title, Fontes alludes to the protracted process of investigating, researching, and developing an image of Pablo Míguez and the difficulties in materialising the '*disappeared*' body. By working on the story of a child Fontes did not know personally, she points to the need for active remembering within societies, which goes beyond a personal level. Thus, she links her own approach and her recreation of Míguez' story to a collective level of remembrance. To generate a picture of the boy who was,

Fig. 2: Claudia Fontes, *Reconstrucción del retrato de Pablo Míguez*, 2000/2010. Mirror of polished stainless steel. 1,70 x 0,45 x 0,40 m. Río de la Plata, 70m off the coast, Parque de la Memoria, Avenida Costanera Norte, Rafael Obligado 6745, Buenos Aires. Photo: Graciel Díaz, courtesy of the artist. http://claudiafontes.com/project/reconstruction-of-the-portrait-of-pablo-miguez/.

together with his mother, *disappeared* at the age of 13 on May 12th, 1977 (Franco 2018, 39–40), the artist worked with witnesses, relatives, friends, artists, forensic institutes, as well as former prisoners and other 13-year-old children – a method she described as an act of collective memory work. The posture that the sculpture demonstrates is based on a photograph of Míguez' father at the age of 13 (Fig. 2). A computer specialist assisted Fontes in reconstructing the boy's profile using the three remaining photographs showing Míguez, and naval engineers were responsible for the design and realisation of the platform. The sculpture was finally positioned on January 14th, 2000. Only two people involved in the work knew Míguez personally: his father and the journalist Lila Pastoriza, who had been imprisoned in the ESMA at the same time (Bell 2014, 151). In reaction to percepticide, Fontes strives all-embracingly to create a paradoxical visibility and to work retrospectively against the iconoclastic methods of the military regime.

6 The Sculpture and the River – Site-Specificity, Affectivity, and the Beholder

The sculpture is situated close to the largest object in the parc, the *Monumento a las Víctimas del Terrorismo de Estado*. The monument consists of four stelae on which plaques with names of the *detained disappeared* are placed. In addition, there are empty plaques which, on the one hand, symbolise the still unidentified people, and on the other hand offer space for further names when new information is discovered (Huyssen 2003, 108). The Argentinian monument, additionally, forms the void – or gap – between the city and the river itself, thus fulfilling a metonymic function. As a negative aesthetic (Huyssen 2003, 106),[16] the excavated 'rampart' appears like a gigantic wound on the earth (Bell 2014, 85). Moreover, it functions as an arrow pointing to the actual grave, the river (Torre 2002, 401–404).

Stepping out of the monument and approaching the river produces a sensation for which I would like to adopt Mieke Bal's term "affective syntax" (2006, 9). According to Bal, this concept suggests that affective potency unfolds not only in the individual object, but also in its spatial arrangement, and the temporal order of its reception (ibid.). What happens in this succession of reception resembles a filmic cut (ibid., 11). This implies that the monument and *Reconstrucción* emphasise different aspects of *forced disappearance* (Bell 2014, 95): The monument refers to the sheer mass of *detenidos desaparecidos*, independent from their biography and social

---

[16] Its design is reminiscent of Daniel Libeskind's extension of the Jewish Museum in Berlin.

background, while the sculpture takes up a concrete example of *disappearance*. After experiencing the monument, being confronted with the depiction of a single human figure standing alone on the water evokes surprise: At first glance, the sculpture might be frightening, as I have argued above regarding the notion of a spectral discourse; it is the past that does not cease to remain subtly present in the present. The fragile impression of the sculpture is reinforced by the contrast to the massiveness of the monument and by the vast surroundings of the river (Fig.3).

Fig. 3: Claudia Fontes, *Reconstrucción del retrato de Pablo Míguez*, 2000/2010. Mirror of polished stainless steel. 1,70 x 0,45 x 0,40 m. Río de la Plata, 70m off the coast, Parque de la Memoria, Avenida Costanera Norte, Rafael Obligado 6745, Buenos Aires. Photo: Claudia Fontes, courtesy of the artist. http://claudiafontes.com/project/reconstruction-of-the-portrait-of-pablo-miguez/.

Therefore, the location of the statue in the river is an important choice (Franco 2018, 43), as the sculpture imparts to the water its connotation as an anonymous mass grave (Huffschmid 2015, 272), becoming itself a kind of gravestone. Consequently, the Río de la Plata turns into the last 'resting place' of the *detenidos desaparecidos* (Franco 2018, 43), especially for those who remain to be identified. Hence, the water of the river is turned into a symbol of the irretrievable bodies thrown from airplanes (Franco 2018, 103), but the liquid quality of the river is unable to give the deceased the stability that earth does (Schindel 2014, 189).

The river can also be understood as a 'contact zone,' a place where the past 'emerges' in the present and enables a dialogic-discursive interaction with it (Assmann 2009, 337).[17] In addition, the art-historical concept of site-specificity proves helpful in understanding the sculpture. Michael Archer defines it as follows:

> Site-specificity implies neither simply that a work is to be found in a particular place, nor, quite, that it is a place. It means, rather, that what the work looks like and what it means is dependent in large part on the configuration of the space in which it is realized (Archer 1994, 3).

In both its form and content, the work refers to the place in which it is located (Krystof 2014, 270). Beyond the physical and perceptual aspects, the specificity of the site can be associated with the social, political and identity characteristics that define the location of the work (Szmulewicz 2012, 43). Regarding *Reconstrucción*, it is the environment of the park that gives the sculpture its appearance and its meaning. A museum space, with its own traditions, logics and conventions would undermine the sculpture's logic. Even though Fontes' sculpture is inscribed in the victim-centred discourse of memory, it does not subordinate itself completely to the surrounding space, and therefore its reception can only be understood through the relationship between the viewer, the work, and the place it occupies (Crimp 1986, 43).

The reception of the sculpture depends on the weather conditions. It is sometimes hardly possible to see it, which points to the fact that the individual fate is often in danger of being overlooked. The highly polished steel leads to an even stronger connection with its surroundings: When the weather is bad, it reflects the mud-coloured water in which it is located; when the weather is good, it reflects the sun's rays. Sunshine makes the sculpture appear almost golden.[18] Therefore it communicates intensively with its *Umraum* [environment], the water surrounding it, whereby a "dialogical spatial relationship" (Prange 2010, 141) is created. The depiction as a *Rückenfigur* [back figure] accentuates the relevance of the water. The motif of the back figure is derived from painting, but as Fontes negates a spatial-temporal reception by positioning her work in a place the viewer cannot physically reach, the reception is comparable. This motif encourages the viewer to place themselves in the position of the person portrayed, to assume their perspective. Additionally, it directs the viewer's gaze in the same direction the sculpture faces.

---

17 For further analysis on the water and the significance of the place where the park is located, see especially: Huyssen 2003, Schindel 2014, Bell 2014, Franco 2018.
18 In this respect the sculpture also contains Christian connotations: The disciples in the boat are afraid because they believed that they were seeing a ghost when Jesus walked on the water (Katholische Bibelanstalt 2016: Matthew 14).

As a beholder looking at the figure of Míguez, one is invited to activate one's own capacity to imagine the face of the boy and the cruelty of the dictatorship, and to consider the consequences for the people left with uncertainty about what happened to their friends and relatives. This can be considered a *Leerstelle* [void] as introduced to art history by Wolfgang Kemp, expressing that the viewer is always present in an artwork in order to complement it: Work and viewer enter into a dialogical relationship (2015, 146). According to Kemp, it is not a matter of imagining oneself as a direct eyewitness, but rather of an ideal observer who gets involved in the message of the work (1992b, 325–326). Therefore, Kemp speaks of the 'implicit observer' (1992a, 22). Despite the figurative representation of Míguez, his face – the most characteristic feature of a person and the best possible guarantor of individuality (Bal 2006, 12) – remains unknown. Paradoxically, this might render the sculpture less personal than the monument (Bell 2014, 95). In this way, it allows to actively involve the beholder; the artist herself states that the moment one tries to (re-)construct the boy's face, it becomes clear that he is an exemplary presence of a *detenido desaparecido* (Fontes in Baulo 2018).[19] The viewers are asked not to remain in a superior, distanced viewing position (Platter 2016, 222), but to imagine the topic at hand.

Fontes' sculpture can be impactful without knowing about the people thrown in the waters. The large number of sculptures in the park reinforces diversity and the park sets out a thematic, mnemonic framework. As Susanna Torre states, it is more of a sculptural park than a memorial as it detaches the works from their historical contexts, referring to more general topics such as pain, shock, and absence (2002, 401–404). As a result, the park is accessible to everyone, regardless of their knowledge about the events during the Argentinian military dictatorship – although it is likely that visitors are aware of it. Bridget Franco emphasises that the visitor's inclusion in the reception of *Reconstrucción* requires them to reflect on the historical significance of the military dictatorship, as well as its influence on contemporary coexistence and the economic system (Franco 2018, 41–43). To my understanding, it is true that the sculpture demands that viewers make up their own minds, but I would not want to limit this to the Argentinean context. This would create an overdetermination of *Reconstrucción*, almost excluding viewers from other historical contexts from a productive reception. The perception of works of art, no matter how political their content, does not keep anyone from making their own political statements. Torre's conception of an inclusive sculptural park is more appropriate

---

[19] It is remarkable which significance the artist continues to have today for the fate of Pablo Míguez because of this work. Human rights organisations contact her with questions and requests, so that she has become a quasi-member of the family (personal conversation with the artist, April 2022).

in this respect as it considers the suffering caused by civil-military dictatorships in general, even beyond the experience of *forced disappearance*. Furthermore, James E. Young's *Forms of Memory* (1997) seems to be useful for understanding the park as a whole. In his point of view, monuments and memorials should not be mistaken for representations of collective memory, as they are not necessarily unifying.[20] Rather, they are places of "collected experiences" where the intended message is completed by different opinions, current developments in memory politics, and the reception of the respective viewer (Young 1997, 16).

7 Travelling Concepts

Supplementary to the national perspective, the park elucidates a transnational moment that plays a significant role within the internationalised human rights discourse in Argentina (Baer and Sznaider 2015, 334). *Never again* is the title of the report elaborated by the Comisión Nacional sobre la Desaparición de Personas [National Commission on the Disappearance of Persons] (CONADEP, 1986), declaring remembrance a duty to prevent violence (Jelin 2010, 69; 2015, 32). The paradigm of *Never Again* was inspired by the Dachau concentration camp memorial site; it bears witness to the fact that the paradigmatic *Nunca más* in the Southern Cone is influenced by the Shoah (Huyssen 2003, 99) from which all other uses of *Never again* are derived (Baer and Sznaider 2015, 332). It functions as a medial carrier of memory, as a Travelling Memory (Erll 2011b). Despite its site-specificity, Fontes' work is "transcending time and space" (Baer and Sznaider 2015, 329).[21] The use and context-dependent interpretation of such paradigms, nevertheless, harbours the danger that the generalised commandment of *Never again* veils the atrocities of today's world and that, as a consequence, the Shoah is reduced to a

---

20 In this context, it is important to bear in mind that the construction of the park was accompanied by various disputes within human rights organisations. Of the Madres de la Plaza de Mayo, only the Línea Fundadora has supported the park (Bell 2014, 82; see also Franco 2018).

21 It is crucial not to disregard the fact that despite the 'mobile' character of memories, there is no universalising moment. The example of *Nunca más* can even include antagonistic moments (Baer and Sznaider 2015, 332). Further, Jelin questions the consistently positive connotation of remembering. Neither does the commitment to remembering a violent past necessarily lead to the prevention of violence in the present, nor is there an absolute connection between memory in transition and the democratisation of a country (2012, 19). The omnipresence of *Nunca Más* can even lead to a routinisation which covers the conflictual nature of memory (Jelin 2012, 19; Richard 2001, 29). At worst, only standardised narratives are repeated that have little influence on commemoration (Jelin 2012, 67).

"screen memory" (Huyssen 2003, 14). Therefore, the question should be asked to what extent publicly ritualised remembrance can also constitute a strategy of forgetting (Huyssen 2003, 14). At this point, however, I would like to emphasise that in the Parque de la Memoria, attempts to counteract this danger are made, since the area is used for diverse events in which people from every generation and social background are included. Even more importantly, the park's social potential consists in the fact that it does not focus on specific people and their respective biographies, but on diverse people whose social beliefs and ideas contradicted those of the military regime (Huyssen 2003, 104). Political affiliations play no role and no heroisation takes place: The commonality of the people to be remembered is based exclusively on the fact that they were victims of the dictatorship. This makes the park an integrative project.

8 Conclusion

In reference to the Shoah, Aleida Assmann states that "memory artists" (2009, 260) have nothing left to reconstruct after a catastrophe. Through the process of developing and realising *Reconstrucción*, it seems that Fontes is vehemently working to contradict this statement. The artist uses the site-specific sculpture to restitute a body to a person erased from society – in a literal sense by being *disappeared* and in a symbolic sense by the iconoclastic procedure of destroying personal photographs.

The mnemonic function of the sculpture can be summarised in three aspects: (1) Memories are inevitably dependent on present conditions and are always shaped by subjective factors (Erll 2011a, 8). Thus, each viewer will create a different image of Míguez. (2) Memories are never constant or uniform, but subject to constant change (Erll 2011a, 126). Since the sculpture is mounted on a floating platform, it adapts to the movement of the river. Likewise, it symbolises a constant change within (official or private) memory discourses. (3) There is no purely individual memory and although the artwork is dedicated to a single person, it reverberates beyond the context of the dictatorships of the Southern Cone.

Over and above, by placing a figurative representation of a person in the Río de la Plata, Fontes creates a mnemonic place. In this way, she succeeds in bringing to the surface a story that would otherwise remain (in)visible; therefore, this sculpture is a trace and mnemonic materialisation for *detenidos desaparecidos*. The fact that *Reconstrucción* is a vertical, anthropomorphic sculpture reminds of monuments, but the artist undermines this impression in two ways: First, she reinterprets the pedestal and installs her work on a mobile platform 70 meters away from the shore; second, she presents a shiny *Rückenfigur* [back figure] whose face cannot be seen. Thereby the artist withdraws her work from the clarity that the title suggests and includes a spectral component that requires an understanding and interpretive beholder. The "affective syntax" (Bal 2006, 9) was used to capture the way the work is perceived while walking along the path through the park.

Fontes' work does not attempt to evoke consternation or sentimentality; it stands symbolically for the fate of the *detenidos desaparecidos* and their relatives. Pablo Míguez is no more or less memorable than other *detenidos desaparecidos*. At the same time, Fontes acts neither as a witness nor as a political actor who wants to evoke certain reactions; she neither commits the viewers to a certain gesture of memory nor does she confront them with a moral "responsibility of seeing" (Platter 2016, 279). By pointing out that people were murdered without their bodies identified to this day, she counteracts the percepticide (Taylor 1997, 119–138). *Reconstrucción del Retrato de Plabo Míguez* invites the viewer to the task of active engagement: As to "remember means to read traces; it demands imagination, attentiveness of the gaze, construction" (Huyssen 2013, 39).

References

Archer, Michael. "Toward Installation." *Installation Art*. Ed. Nicolas De Oliveira, Nicola Oxley, Michael Petry, and Michael Archer. London: Smithsonian Institution Press, 1994. 11–31.

Assmann, Aleida. "Gedächtnis, Erinnerung." *Handbuch der Geschichtsdidaktik*. Ed. Klaus Bergmann, Klaus Fröhlich, Annette Kuhn, Jörn Rüsen, and Gerhard Schneider. Seelze-Velber: Kallmeyersche Verlagsbuchhandlung, 1997. 33–37.

_____. *Erinnerungsräume. Formen und Wandlungen des kulturellen Gedächtnisses*. München: C.H.Beck oHG, 2009.

_____. "The Holocaust – a Global Memory? Extensions and Limits of a New Memory Community." *Memory in a Global Age. Discourses, Practices and Trajectorie*. Ed. Aleida Assmann, and Sebastian Conrad. Basingstoke: Palgrave Macmillan, 2010. 97–117

Baer, Alejandro, and Natan Sznaider. "Ghosts of the Holocaust in Franco's Mass Graves: Cosmopolitan Memories and the Politics of 'Never Again'." *Memory Studies* 8.3 (2015): 328–344.

Bal, Mieke "Affect and the Space We Share: Three Forms of Installation Art." *The Next Thing. Art in the Twenty-First Century*. Ed. Pablo Baler. Plymouth: Fairleigh Dickinson University Press, 2013. 67–80.

_____. "Einleitung. Affekt als kulturelle Kraft." *Affekte. Analysen ästhetisch-medialer Prozesse*. Ed. Antje Krause-Wahl, Heike Oehlschlägel, and Serjoscha Wiemer. Bielefeld: transcript Verlag, 2006. 7–19.

Baulo, Maria Carolina. "Walking the Edges: A Conversation with Claudia Fontes." *International Sculpture Center. Hamilton* 37.1 (2018): https://sculpturemagazine.art/walking-the-edges-a-conversation-with-claudia-fontes/ (07 April 2022).

Bell, Vikki. *The Art of Post-Dictatorship. Ethics and Aesthetics in Transitional Argentina*. Oxon, New York, NY: Routledge Taylor & Francis Group, 2014.
Benjamin, Walter. *On Photography*. Transl. Esther Leslie. London: Reaktion Books Ltd, 2015.
Bolte, Rike. *Gegen(-)Abwesenheiten. Memoria-Generationen und mediale Verfahrensweisen kontra erzwungenes Verschwinden. Argentinien 1976–1996–2006*. Dissertation, Humboldt-Universität Berlin, 2011.
Caruth, Caty. "Introduction." *Trauma. Explorations in Memory*. Ed. Caty Caruth. Baltimore, MD: John Hopkins University Press, 1995. 3–12.
Colombo, Pamela, and Estela Schindel. "Introduction: The Multi-Layered Memories of Space." *Spaces and the Memories of Violence. Landscapes of Erasure, Disappearance and Exception*. Ed. Estela Schindel, and Pamela Colombo. New York: Palgrave Macmillian, 2014. 1–17.
Craps, Stef. "Learning to Live with Ghosts: Postcolonial Haunting and Mid-Mourning in David Dadydeen's 'Turner' and Fred D'Aguiar's 'Feeding the Ghosts'." *Callaloo* 33.2 (2010): 467–475.
Crenzel, Emilio. "The Ghostly Presence of the Disappeared in Argentina." *Memory Studies Journal* 13.3 (2020): 253–266.
Crimp, Douglas. "Serra's Public Sculpture: Redefining Site Specificity." *Richard Serra, Sculpture*. Ed. Rosalind Krauss, and Richard Serra. New York: Museum of Modern Art, 1986. 40–56.
del Pilar Blanco, Maria, and Esther Peeren. *The Spectralities Reader. Ghosts and Haunting in Contemporary Cultural Theory*. London: Bloomsbury Publishing, 2013.
Dimbath, Oliver. "Soziologische Rahmenkonzeptionen. Eine Untersuchung der Rahmenmetapher im Kontext von Erinnerung und Vergessen." *Formen und Funktionen sozialen Erinnerns. Sozial- und kulturwissenschaftliche Analysen*. Ed. René Lehmann, Florian Öchsner, and Gerd Sebald. Wiesbaden: Springer VS, 2013. 25–48.
Erll, Astrid. "Literature, Film, and the Mediality of Cultural Memory." *Cultural Memory Studies: An International and Interdisciplinary Handbook*. Ed. Astrid Erll, and Ansgar Nünning. Berlin: De Grutyer, 2010a. 389–398.
──────. "Cultural Memory Studies: An Introduction." *Cultural Memory Studies: An International and Interdisciplinary Handbook*. Ed. Astrid Erll, and Ansgar Nünning. Berlin: De Grutyer, 2010b. 1–15.
──────. *Memory in Culture*. Hampshire: Palgrave Macmillan, 2011a.
──────. "Travelling Memory." *Parallax* 17.4 (2011b): 4–18.
Ferreira Navarro, Marcos. "Operación Condor. Antecedentes, formación y acciones." *Ab Initio* 9 (2014): 153–179.
──────. "Travelling Memory in European Film: Towards a Morphology of Mnemonic Relationality." *Image & Narrative* 18.1 (2017): 5–19.
Fortuny, Natalia. "Memoria fotográfica. Restos de la desaparición, imágenes familiares y huellas del horror en la fotografía argentina posdictatorial." *Amerika. Mémoires, identités, territoires* 1 (2010): https://doi.org/10.4000/amerika.1108 (07 April 2022).
Franco, Bridget. "Floating Status and Streams of Consciousness: Memory Work in Argentina's Río de la Plata and Río Salí." *The Image of the River in Latin/o American Literature: Written in the Water*. Ed. Elizabeth Rivero, and Jeanie Murphy. Lanham, Boulder, New York, London: Lexington Books, 2018. 35–54.
Gatti, Gabriel. "Las narrativas del detenido-desaparecido (o de los problemas de la representación ante las catástrofes sociales)." *CONfines de Relaciones Internacionales y Ciencia Política* 2.4 (2006): 27–38.
──────. "El lenguaje de las víctimas: silencios (ruidosos) y parodias (serias) para hablar (sin hacerlo) de la desaparición forzada de personas." *Universitas Humanística* 72 (2011): 89–109.

───. "Prolegómeno. Para un concepto científico de desaparición." *Desapariciones. Usos locales, circulaciones globales*. Ed. Gabriel Gatti. Bogotá: Siglo del Hombre Editores; Universidad de los Andes, 2017. 13–32.

Halbwachs, Maurice. *Das Gedächtnis und seine sozialen Bedingungen*. Berlin, Neuwied: Suhrkamp, 1985 [1925].

Hite, Katherine, and Daniela Jara. "Presenting Unwieldy Pasts." *Memory Studies Journal* 13.3 (2020): 245–252.

Hristova, Marije, Francisco Ferrándiz, and Johanna Vollmeyer. "Memory Worlds: Reframing Time and the Past – An Introduction." *Memory Studies Journal* 13.5 (2020): 777–791.

Huffschmid, Anne. *Risse im Raum. Erinnerung, Gewalt und städtisches Leben in Lateinamerika*. Wiesbaden: Springer VS, 2015.

Huneeus, Carlos. "Pinochet: Institutionelle Faktoren und politische Führungen im Autoritarismus." *Chile heute. Politik, Wirtschaft, Kultur*. Ed. Peter Imbusch, Dirk Messer, and Detelf Nolte. Frankfurt am Main: Vervuert, 2004. 227–251.

Huyssen, Andreas. *Present Pasts. Urban Palimpsests and the Politics of Memory*. Stanford, California: Stanford Univ. Press, 2003.

───. William Kentridge, and Nalini Malani. *The Shadow Play as Medium of Memory*. Milano: Edizioni Charta, 2013.

Jelin, Elizabeth. "The Past in the Present: Memories of State Violence in Contemporary Latin America." *Memory in a Global Age. Discourses, Practices and Trajectories*. Ed. Aleida Assmann, and Sebastian Conrad. Basingstoke: Palgrave Macmillan, 2010. 61–78.

───. *Los trabajos de la memoria*. Lima: Instituto de Estudios Peruanos, 2012 [2002].

Jinkis, Jorge. "'Ni muerto ni vivo'." *Página1* 2. (2006): https://www.pagina12.com.ar/diario/psicologia/9-70866-2006-08-05.html (07 April 2022).

Kansteiner, Wulf. "Finding Meaning in Memory: A Methodological Critique of Collective Memory Studies." *History and Theory* 41.05 (2002): 179–197.

Katholische Bibelanstalt. *Einheitsübersetzung der Heiligen Schrift* (2016): https://www.bibleserver.com/text/EU/Matth%C3%A4us14%2C22-33 (07 April 2022).

Kemp, Wolfgang. "Kunstwissenschaft und Rezeptionsästhetik." *Der Betrachter ist im Bild. Kunstwissenschaft und Rezeptionsästhetik*. Ed. Wolfgang Kemp. Berlin: Reimer, 1992a. 7–27.

───. "Verständlichkeit und Spannung. Über Leerstellen in der Malerei des 19. Jahrhunderts." *Der Betrachter ist im Bild. Kunstwissenschaft und Rezeptionsästhetik*. Ed. Wolfang Kemp. Berlin: Reimer, 1992b. 307–332.

───. Der explizite Betrachter. Zur Rezeption zeitgenössischer Kunst. Konstanz: Konstanz University Press, 2005.

Krämer, Sybille. "Was also ist eine Spur? Und worin besteht ihre epistemische Rolle? Eine Bestandsaufnahme." *Spur. Spurenlesen als Orientierungstechnik und Wissenskunst*. Ed. Sybille Krämer, Werner Krämer, et al. Frankfurt am Main: Suhrkamp, 2007. 11–33.

Krystof, Doris. "Ortsspezifität." *DuMonts Begriffslexikon zur zeitgenössischen Kunst*. Ed. Hubertus Butin. Köln: Snoeck Verlagsgesellschaft, 2014. 270–275.

Levy, Daniel and Natan Sznaider. *Erinnerung im globalen Zeitalter: Der Holocaust*. Frankfurt am Main: Suhrkamp, 2001.

Mahlke, Kirsten. "A Fantastic Tale of Terror: Argentina's 'Disappeared' and Their Narrative Representation in Julio Cortázar's 'Second Time Round'." *Literature and Terrorism. Comparative Perspectives*. Ed. Michael Frank. Amsterdam: Rodopi, 2012. 195–212.

Mandolessi, Silvana. "El tiempo de los espectros." *El pasado inasequible. Desaparecidos, hijos y combatientes en el arte y la literatura del nuevo milenio*. Ed. Jordana Blejmar, Silvana Mandolessi, and Mariana Eva Perez. Buenos Aires: EUDEBA, 2018. 49–69.

Parque de la Memoria. *Sobre el parque* (2022): https://parquedelamemoria.org.ar/parque/ (07 April 2022).

Plate, Liedeke, and Anneke Smelik. "Performing Memory in Art and Popular Culture: An Introduction." *Performing Memory in Art and Popular Culture*. Ed. Liedeke Plate, and Anneke Smelik. New York: Routledge, 2013. 1–23.

Platter, Johanna. *Mitleiden, Mitwissen, Mitfühlen. Über das Moment der körperlichen Wahrnehmung in den Werken von Teresa Margolles und Doris Salcedo*. Dissertation: München, 2016.

Prange, Regine. "Sinnoffenheit und Sinnverneinung als metapikturale Prinzipien. Zur Historizität bildlicher Selbstreferenz am Beispiel der Rückenfigur." *Ambiguität in der Kunst. Typen und Funktionen eines ästhetischen Paradigmas*. Ed. Verena Krieger, and Rachel Mader. Köln: Böhlau, 2010. 125–168.

Richard, Nelly. *Residuos y metáforas. Ensayos de crítica cultural sobre el Chile de la Transición*. Santiago de Chile: Editorial Cuarto Propio, 2001.

———. *Fracturas de la memoria: arte y pensamiento crítico*. Buenos Aires: Siglo veintiuno editores, 2007.

———. "Akademische Globalisierung, Kulturwissenschaften und lateinamerikanische Kulturkritik." *Lateinamerikanische Kulturtheorien. Grundlagentexte*. Ed. Isabel Exner, and Gudrun Rath. Konstanz: Konstanz University Press, 2015. 191–205.

Rigney, Ann, and Chiara de Cesari. *Transnational Memory. Circulation, Articulation, Scales*. Berlin, Boston: De Gruyter, 2014.

Schindel, Estela. "A Limitless Grave: Memory and Abjection of The Río de la Plata." *Spaces and the Memories of Violence. Landscapes of Erasure, Disappearance and Exception*. Ed. Estela Schindel, and Pamela Colombo. New York: Palgrave Macmillian, 2014. 188–201.

Smulewicz, Ignacio. *Fuera del cubo blanco. Lecturas sobre arte contemporáneo*. Santiago de Chile: Metales Pesados, 2012.

Taylor, Diana. *Disappearing Acts. Spectacles of Gender and Nationalism in Argentina's 'Dirty War'*. Durham, NC, London: Duke University Press, 1997.

Torre, Susana. "Vom Bau von Mahnmalen." *Experimente mit der Wahrheit. Rechtssysteme im Wandel und die Prozesse der Wahrheitsfindung und Versöhnung; Documenta 11_Plattform 2*. Ed. Okwui Enwezor. Ostfildern-Ruit: Hatje-Cantz, 2002. 387–406.

Vaisman, Noa. "Posmemoria y memoria desaparecida en dos obras de la posdictadura argentina." *El pasado inasequible. Desaparecidos, hijos y combatientes en el arte y la literatura del nuevo milenio*. Ed. Jordana Blejmar, Silvana Mandolessi, and Mariana Eva Perez. Buenos Aires: EUDEBA, 2018. 185–202.

Verbitsky, Horacio. *El vuelo*. Buenos Aires: Ed. Planeta, 1995.

Young, James Edward. *Formen des Erinnerns. Gedenkstätten des Holocaust*. Wien: Passagen Verlag, 1997.

Sahra Rausch
Repairing the 'Suffering of the Others'? The OvaHerero and Nama Genocide between Recognition and Misrecognition

Abstract: In July 2015, the German government used the term "genocide" in an official statement to refer to the mass killings of the OvaHerero, Nama, Damara, and San committed between 1904 and 1908 in the former colony 'German South West Africa'. The acknowledgement of past crimes in the present is often understood as a 'moral obligation'. However, this use of the term *genocide* was merely to be understood as a linguistic adjustment which rejected the OvaHerero's and Nama' claims for reparations. In this paper, I explore the construction of 'morality' and moral standards in Germany's postcolonial memory politics and how they affect the recognition of Germany's colonial past. Comparing the recognition of 2015 with the debates over the "reconciliation agreement" in 2021, the paper reveals the discrepancy between the recognition of the genocide and the misrecognition of the 'suffering of the others'. By conducting a discourse analysis of newspaper articles, press releases as well as governmental statements and initiatives by opposition parties, I reconstruct the ambivalences of the rhetorical recourse to morality: On the one hand, the recognition of the genocide becomes a moral obligation. On the other hand, the OvaHerero's and Nama's demands for reparation are discursively placed outside Germany's moral understanding of how to acknowledge colonial crime. As a result, the established *moral collective ideal* is identified as the 'nation's' aim of 'successfully' coming to terms with its colonial past, thus perpetuating the misrecognition of the 'suffering of the others'.

Keywords: recognition, reparations, memory politics, (universalised) morality, collective ideals, genocide, German colonialism, German South West Africa, Herero, Nama

---

Note: This paper draws on the results of my doctoral thesis submitted in 2022 to the Department of Social and Cultural Sciences at Justus Liebig University Giessen, Germany, entitled: "Verstrickte Emotionen: Transnationale Perspektiven auf postkoloniale Erinnerungspolitiken in Deutschland und Frankreich seit den 1990er Jahren".

∂ Open Access. © 2023 the author(s), published by De Gruyter. This work is licensed under the Creative Commons Attribution-NonCommercial-NoDerivatives 4.0 International License.
https://doi.org/10.1515/9783110799514-009

1 Introduction

At a press conference in 2015, a spokesperson of the German government announced that the Federal Republic would henceforth refer to the crimes committed by Germany's colonial army against the OvaHerero and Nama between 1904–1908 as genocide. 'German South West Africa' was declared a *Schutzgebiet* ('Patronage') of the German Reich in 1884 (Krüger 2011 [2004], 17). In reaction to the constant resistance to German expansion and land appropriation, the German Empire's colonial troops (the so-called *Schutztruppe*) started a war against the local communities, such as the OvaHerero, Nama, Damara, and San, leading to the first genocide of the twenty-first century (Zimmerer 2011 [2004], 45). Although the OvaHerero and Nama have been advocating for an official recognition since the 1990s (Kößler 2015, 236–237), the mass killings of thousands of people were only reluctantly regarded as genocide in Germany and described as such (Bürger 2017; de Wolff 2021).

It was not until the 1990s – and due to the end of the Cold War (cf. Levy and Sznaider 2001, 234) – that recognition of past crimes gradually became the constitutive moment in Western memory politics. The sociologist Natan Sznaider (2011, 252) relates this shift to a universalisation of Holocaust remembrance which resulted in a "new system of universalised sympathy for the suffering of others". Arguing in the same vein, the political scientist Elazar Barkan (2001, xi) observes a change in "moral rhetoric" which explains the preponderant focus on the victims of historical crime. Grounded in an increased 'sympathy' towards the 'victims', 'perpetrators' are more willing to come to terms with historical injustice and be in accordance with what Barkan (2001, xi, 315–316) calls a "new international morality". Henceforth, victims and their descendants dispose of the "moral superiority" (Barkan 2001, 316) that is necessary to make 'perpetrator' societies comply with their claims.[1] The proclaimed "exten[sion] of sympathy to the weak" would thus establish new, globally valid moral norms making it a duty to work through historical crimes (Barkan 2001, 315). However, the OvaHerero's and Nama's still ongoing struggle for recognition and reparation indicates that there is a need for elaboration on how

---

[1] The historian Yvonne Robel (2013, 81) states that taking responsibility for past crimes depends on the establishment of the victim. Conversely, the victim status requires the definition of the 'perpetrator'. This perpetrator-victim-dichotomy not only levels historical ambiguities; it also allows for the transference of these statuses to subsequent generations which proves to be historically problematic (Trouillot 2000). On the other hand, the self-designation as a victim helps marginalised groups to make their demands *recognisable* (Robel 2013, 81). Due to these ambiguities, I use inverted commas to highlight the term as a self-chosen designation of the OvaHerero and Nama if I am not referring to the victims of 1904–1908.

marginalised memory groups achieve 'moral superiority' to make their 'suffering'[2] relevant to remember.

This paper is premised on the assumption that neither all pasts nor all victims of historical violence meet the conditions to be *recognised*. To unravel the unequal power relations that are usually concealed when universalised moral norms are invoked, I reconstruct the production of moral standards regarding the *(mis-)recognition* of the genocide of the OvaHerero and Nama. After 2004's commemorations of the anniversary of the genocide in Namibia, debates over its recognition only became a topic in media coverage when a spokesperson of the German government declared on 10 July 2015 that the term 'genocide' would henceforth be applied to the crimes committed in former 'German South West Africa'. In 2016, the government's positioning was further confirmed by promising an official apology to the Namibian government. In 2021, former Foreign Minister Heiko Maas (SPD) eventually announced the conclusion of a "reconciliation agreement" with the Namibian government. On the one hand, I analyse the ways in which the 'suffering of the others' is produced in the course of this development and the demands of OvaHerero and Nama for recognition are either accepted or rejected. On the other hand, I concentrate on the negotiations of how 'repairing' colonial injustice is conceived of in German memory politics and on the question of how this understanding discursively changes from 2015 to 2021.

To do so, I analyse newspaper articles, governmental statements as well as press releases from representatives of the OvaHerero and Nama and their German allies. Choosing newspaper articles of the German daily press daily press as a main source enables me to systematically scrutinise all relevant postcolonial memory events in the period under review and to integrate print media of the right and left leaning political spectrum. It can be assumed that the national daily press is widely accessible across Germany (Meyen 2013, 33), which, emphasises its "dual role" as a "public arena" in which political opinions are reflected and historical knowledge is actively produced (de Wolff 2018, 414). In detail, my corpus consists of articles from *Süddeutsche Zeitung* (SZ), *Frankfurter Allgemeine Zeitung* (FAZ), *Frankfurter Rundschau* (FR), Die WELT, *die tageszeitung* (taz), and *Neues Deutschland* (ND). If frequently cited, I also incorporate articles from other sources, such as the weekly *Die ZEIT*. Altogether, I analyse 113 newspaper articles in the years 2015 and 2016 and 54 articles between May and August 2021.

---

[2] I use the term 'suffering' in quotation marks in order to highlight its constructedness and to point out that historical crimes are appraised differently in the present. Especially colonial pasts first need to be recognised as 'painful' to be considered 'relevant to remember' (Robel 2013, 74).

By putting in perspective the debates of 2015/2016 and 2021, the analysis argues that the 'suffering of the others' is discursively produced through the way it is mediatised. This paper shows how, in the process of naming the genocide, rhetorical references to moral registers prevent further concessions in memory politics. One major finding is that the German government rejects all reparatory demands for colonial crime. Instead, the *Bundesregierung* pursues the misrecognition of the OvaHerero and Nama as legitimate representatives by exclusively granting increased investments in development cooperation. On the other hand, the analysis of media reporting suggests that working through Germany's colonial past has progressively turned into a *moral duty*. Despite the discursive shift, the paper emphasises the discrepancy between the recognition of past crimes and the recognition of the 'suffering of others'. In the following, I therefore develop my argument that marginalised historical crimes first need to be made discursively 'relevant to remember' before their reappraisal is made a moral collective ideal.

2 Recognising the 'Suffering of Others' as a Moral "Collective Ideal"?

In 1994, and thus in the decade in which Barkan (2001, xi, 315–316) locates the change in "moral rhetoric", philosopher Charles Taylor (1994) published his essay *The Politics of Recognition*. Widely cited, the text is considered the starting point for the theories of recognition formulated in the following years (Butler 2004; Fraser and Honneth 2003; Honneth 2016 [1994]). Taylor starts from the observation that minorities and marginalised groups increasingly demanded recognition and equal rights, which made the "politics of recognition" the constitutive moment of the present (Taylor 1994, 25). Taylor argues that the recognition of the self and the 'other' is fundamentally linked to the formation, confirmation, or rejection of identities. In his understanding

> our identity is partly shaped by recognition or its absence, often by the misrecognition of others, and so a person or group of people can suffer real damage, real distortion, if the people or society around them mirror back to them a confining or demeaning or contemptible picture of themselves. Nonrecognition or misrecognition can inflict harm, can be a form of oppression, imprisoning someone in a false, distorted, and reduced mode of being (Taylor 1994, 25).

However, by focusing predominantly on the formation of identities, Taylor is neglecting the question of *who* has the power to recognise or misrecognise the 'other'. The philosopher Judith Butler (2004) draws our attention to the unequal power relations that determine the 'struggle for recognition'. In her analysis of US-American obituaries, Butler shows that the war casualties caused by US military are not mentioned, making their deaths "not worth a note" and consequently non-recognisable (Butler 2004, 34). Applying Butler's thinking to the field of memory studies, Robel states that commemorating means "in a figurative sense, 'we hereby recognise the relevance to remember'" (Robel 2013, 74). Creating 'relevance to remember' depends on speaking about past crimes and considering them important for the present. By speaking about it, historical violence is rendered intelligible. Therefore, processes of recognition are always performative since they establish and confirm the relevance of the past in the present and generate the obligation to remember (Robel 2013, 74). Turned into an obligation, remembering becomes a "collective ideal" that societies strive for.

Coined as a term by French sociologist Émile Durkheim, "collective ideals" are based on established moral rules, making social groups both the "addressee" and the "creator" of morality (Durkheim 1973 [1922], 134). Crucial to his concept is the idea that morality can never be analysed without considering the power relations inherent in the production of collective ideals established in and by societies as the anthropologist Ann Laura Stoler (2009, 101) emphasises. However, most scientific approaches advocating for a moral obligation to come to terms with historical injustice are less interested in the production of moral norms as sociological facts. Instead, proclamations for an "international morality" (Barkan 2001) or a "transcultural empathy" (Craps and Rothberg 2011, 518) follow the normative moral standards constituting a 'language of reconciliation' (cf. Deslaurier and Roger 2006, 19; cf. Sznaider 2011, 248) which obscures the globally effective power asymmetries. Referring to Weber and Durkheim, Stoler argues that "the harnessing of affect in the state's shaping of what constituted morality and who had the right to assess it" has always been the core of colonial governance (Stoler 2009, 69). Therefore, Stoler emphasises that consent to rule is achieved "by adjudicating what constituted moral sentiments (that is, affectively informed good reason)" (Stoler 2009, 69). According to this, societies only *sense* a duty to remember past crimes when their commemoration has become a moral collective ideal that societies agreed on consciously and voluntarily (Durkheim 1973 [1922], 165). This means that the social norms underlying the collective ideal also define the rules by which past crimes are assigned with "moral authority" (Miles 2004, 371) or not.

In conclusion, three elements are essential for the present analysis of the processes of recognising the OvaHerero and Nama genocide in German memory politics: Firstly, the visibility of the 'suffering of others' is a prerequisite for recognition, which, as Butler illustrated in her analysis of US-American obituaries, is only possible if the conditions for its recognisability are fulfilled discursively (Butler 2004, 86–87). Secondly, the 'relevance to remember' colonial violence mostly depends on the societies of the 'perpetrators' because demands for recognition are predominantly directed towards them, which necessarily perpetuates power asymmetries. As we will see in the following analysis, the German government seeks to find acknowledging words, but "word with less power, words that did less" (Ahmed 2004, 117) and which wouldn't change the political status quo. Thirdly, the moment of performativity is central, since the recognition of the 'relevance to remember', as Robel writes (Robel 2013, 74), might change the importance of the formerly marginalised past in the present. The following analysis of the unofficial recognition of the genocide in 2015/2016 shows in which ways the conditions of recognisability are discursively constituted and altered over time.

3 "Well, then make it News!": The Unofficial Recognition of the OvaHererero and Nama genocide in 2015/2016

It was not until Namibia gained independence from South Africa in 1990 that the OvaHerero were able to advocate for the recognition of the genocide committed between 1904 and 1908 in former 'German South West Africa' (Kößler 2015, 236–237). In Germany, however, the genocide gained greater public attention for the first time in 2004 (Bürger 2017, 11; de Wolff 2021, 255–259). On the occasion of the 100th anniversary of the "Battle of Waterberg", then Federal Minister for Economic Cooperation and Development, Heidemarie Wieczorek-Zeul (SPD) admitted that "[t]he atrocities of that time were what today would be called genocide" (Wieczorek-Zeul, 14th August 2004). Although being of far-reaching symbolic value, Wieczorek-Zeul's speech did not have any political consequences. Both the term genocide and the request for forgiveness were declared the minister's private opinion (Kößler 2015, 257; de Wolff 2021, 266–272). Parliamentarian motions put forward by opposition parties which sought to have the genocide recognised failed in 2004 (Bündnis 90/Die Grünen), 2007/2008 (Die LINKE), and again in 2012 (SPD and Bündnis 90/Die Grünen) (Robel 2013, 125–126).

In the following, I first refer to Michael Rothberg's (2009) understanding of "multidirectionality" to show how the recognition of the Armenian genocide created the discursive context in which the naming of the OvaHerero and Nama genocide became inevitable. Second, I point out the German government's strategy to link the naming of the genocide with higher investments in development cooperation. With the aim to avoid the payment of direct compensations to the Namibian government and/or the Namibian communities, development cooperation is portrayed as the only means of memory politics to work through the past. Finally, I argue that the debates over the recognition of the genocide in 2015/2016 produce a divergence between the recognition of the genocide and its 'victims', thus perpetuating a misrecognition of the 'suffering of the others'.

During the press conference on 10th July 2015, the spokesperson of the Foreign Ministry, Martin Schäfer, indicated that the use of the term genocide for the crimes committed against the OvaHerero and Nama would henceforth correspond to the official language of the Federal Government (Press Conference of the *Bundesregierung*, 10 July 2015). The chosen framework of a press conference highlights the diplomatic delicacy of the term since Schäfer's statement is not equivalent to an official statement by a representative of the Federal Government. This is due to the fact that the Namibian and German governments have been working on a joint statement since 2014 in order to "gain a common understanding of what has happened" (Press Conference of the *Bundesregierung*, 10 July 2015).[3] Avoiding to anticipate the results of these negotiations, Schäfer uses the term genocide only as a quotation in reference to previous statements on that matter. First, he quotes from Wieczorek-Zeul's 2004-speech, in which she classified "the atrocities of that time" as genocide. Consequently, her statement would now define "the political guideline [. . .] of the now acting Foreign Minister" as well as "the basis for the ongoing talks with our Namibian partners" (Press Conference of the *Bundesregierung*, 10 July 2015, 10). Since Schäfer himself refrains from using the term, the interviewing journalist insists on clarification: "The Federal Government says: It was genocide. – That would be a news story", to which Schäfer replies: "Well, then make it news" (Press Conference of the *Bundesregierung*, 10 July 2015, 11). How can this surprising – albeit still unofficial – naming of the genocide be explained?

This rather unexpected shift in official positioning was caused by another memory political decision taken by the government: the recognition of the Armenian genocide by the *Bundestag* on 24 April 2015. On the occasion of the 100th anniversary of the genocide against the Armenians, the *Bundestag* held a commemorative event in which the term genocide was repeatedly used by all political camps (*Gedenken an Völkermord an den Armeniern* 2015, bundestag.de). The remembrance of the Armenian genocide and the discussions about its official recognition provided a context in which the crimes against the OvaHerero and Nama could also come into focus in German media coverage (de Wolff 2021, 293). Only two weeks after Schäfer's press statement, then President of the German Parliament Norbert Lammert (CDU) publishes an article in the weekly newspaper *Die ZEIT* in which he connects

---

3 All translations of German newspaper article, governmental statements, and press releases are mine if not stated otherwise.

both genocides. In his article, Lammert expresses his surprise that the debates in the 100th commemorative year of the Armenian genocide were conducted with so much passion, while the "direct" "German guilt for the atrocities in the colonies" are hardly remembered (Lammert 2015, 9 July, Die ZEIT, 16). Following a brief description of the historical events in 'German South West Africa', Lammert concludes that "the suppression of the Herero uprising was a genocide". Consequently, those who "speak of the Armenian genocide [. . .] must not remain silent about the German genocide against the Herero and Nama". Lammert concludes: "[L]ike the Turks, we too bear responsibility for how we deal with this history" (Lammert 2015, 9 July, Die ZEIT, 16). The consequence of not working through colonial injustices would undermine the moral standards that have been established in German memory politics. In May 2015, the historian Jürgen Zimmerer emphasises the moral collective ideal by stating that "dealing critically with one's own past, relentlessly exposing the dark sides of one's own history [. . .] was part of Germany's self-image after 1945". The misrecognition of the genocide thus "calls into question the success story of German memory politics as a whole" (Zimmerer 2015, 9 July, taz, 4). Against the background of the clear attitude towards the genocide of the Armenians in 2015, the German government's refusal to recognise the genocide of the OvaHerero and Nama jeopardises the collective ideal of a successful coming to terms with the past. The fact that the Federal Government cannot meet the moral standards is particularly evident in media coverage since newspaper articles leave no doubt that the crimes committed in 'German South West Africa' must be termed a genocide.

The analysis suggests, on the one hand, that the multidirectional references to the recognition of the Armenian genocide as well as German Holocaust remembrance created the discursive conditions that enabled the unofficial naming of the OvaHerero and Nama genocide. However, the genocide was not officially recognised by a representative of the Federal Republic, even though this wording had been declared the new 'political guideline'. The official justification was that the dialogue between Namibia and Germany had not yet been completed. More significant, however, may be the fact that Germany wants to avoid paying reparations demanded by the Namibian government as well as the OvaHerero and Nama. Therefore, Germany translates its historical and moral responsibility towards Namibia into increased investments in development cooperation.

3.1 Germany's "Political and Moral Responsibility": Repairing Colonial Crime with Development Aid?

The article published by Lammert in 2015 illustrates how the process of recognising the genocide is equated with increasing investments in development projects. Even if Lammert argues that naming the genocide is not enough and that it would need more than development aid to work through Germany's colonial past, he relegates the obligation to historical reconciliation to Namibia. For instance, Lammert refers to the construction of a documentary centre to reappraise the history of Namibian resistance in cooperation with the National Archive in Windhoek and the restauration of the Memorial Park Cemetery in Swakopmund. Interestingly, there is not a single mention of how Germany itself should work on its colonial legacies; he even minimises Germany's role as a colonial power by stating that it wasn't among the "leading" ones. In the same vein, Lammert points out that "Germany's special responsibility for its former South West African colony" is already expressed in the highest development aid budget per capita for Namibia (Lammert 2015, 9 July, Die ZEIT, 16). Eventually, Lammert acquits the former colonial power from dealing with the genocide by construing development cooperation as a reconciliatory gesture to come to terms with the past.

The insistence on the payment of development aid underlines the asymmetrical power relations between Namibia and Germany as well as between the OvaHerero and Nama and the German government. As development cooperation is always carried out on the terms defined by the donors, it is thus the German government that specifies the conditions of a successful cooperation (Böhlke-Itzen 2005, 103ff.). Consequently, the power divides between North and South remain intact. Understanding the 'special historical and moral responsibility' towards Namibia in terms of development cooperation eventually denies the admission of 'historical guilt' which would equip the descendants of past crimes with the "moral authority" (Miles 2010, 371) to make their claims be heard. That the German government still defines the conditions of how to come to terms with its colonial past is particularly visible in its persistent refusal to pay reparations for the genocide.

When the German Foreign Office declared 'genocide' to be the official term for the mass killings of the OvaHerero in 2015, the alliance "Völkermord verjährt nicht!" demanded that the recognition of the genocide must be followed by a "formal apology" to the descendants as well as direct participation in the "negotiations for reparations" (Press Release of the alliance "Völkermord verjährt nicht", 10 July 2015). The OvaHerero's and Nama's press statement illustrates those conflicts of interest concerning the negotiation of the recognition of the genocide not only exist between German and Namibian representatives, but also between the Namibian government and the OvaHerero and Nama communities. Paramount Chief Vekuii Rukoro repeatedly emphasises that the "extermination order" was directed solely against the OvaHerero which substantiates their request that the descendants of the former victims and not to the Namibian government should receive reparations (Putsch 2016, 8 June, WELT ONLINE). Instead, the OvaHerero and Nama have not been recognised as official negotiating parties to this day. Interestingly, in 2015/2016, the press statements of the alliance "Völkermord verjährt nicht!" do not coherently employ the terms "reparation", "compensation" and *Wiedergutmachung*. The interchangeability of the terms can be explained by the unclear legal status and the different financial, material, or symbolic demands that reparations can encompass (Barkan 2001, 324). By using the term *Wiedergutmachung*, for instance, the OvaHerero and Nama refer to the historical context of Germany's *Vergangenheitsbewältigung* after the Second World War ("coming to terms with its past", extensive definition in: Jesse 1997, 12). By doing so, the OvaHerero and Nama try to inscribe the genocide in 'German South West Africa' into German memory politics. Although media reporting is taking up on the reference to the German *Wiedergutmachungspolitik* for Nazi crimes, it uses it as a justification why the OvaHerero's and Nama's demand for compensation cannot prevail (cf. Rausch 2022). Repeatedly, legal constraints are evoked according to which "individual compensation" is only possible for those directly affected, but not for the descendants of the victims. Consequently, German special envoi Ruprecht Polenz (CDU), who negotiates with Namibia on behalf of the German government, explains to the press that compensation claims cannot be "inherited" (Vates and Geyer 2016, 14 June, FR, 6). But it is not until 2016 that the German government clearly distinguishes the different meanings of "reparation" to eventually rule out any reparatory claims put forward by the OvaHerero and Nama. In the response to a *Kleine Anfrage* (Question to the government) by Die LINKE, the Federal Government specifies that "reparations" (*Reparationen*) can only be considered as "intergovernmental compensation for war damage" (*Drucksache* 18/9152, 9). "Compensations" (*Entschädigungen*), on the other hand, are equated with the principle of *Wiedergutmachung*, which, however, "refers to the compensation paid by Germany to victims of the Holocaust and other Nazi injustices since the end of the Second World War". Accordingly, *Wiedergutmachung* is not applicable to "the historical background and context of the German-Namibian dialogue" (*Drucksache* 18/9152, 10).

At this point, it is crucial to note that the German government establishes a morally justified understanding of the term genocide in order to exclude reparatory claims that could cause a precedent in international law. Correspondingly, the Federal Government further states in its answer to Die LINKE that "in a historical-political public debate, the definition according to the Genocide Convention" of 1948 can "serve as a benchmark to refer to the historical event as genocide in a legally *non-binding way*" (*Drucksache* 18/9152, 3; emphasis S.R.). As a result, the *Bundesregierung* employs the term genocide in a way that explicitly excludes any consequences under international law. Regarding possible reparation claims, the Federal Government specifies: "The material claims [. . .] put forward by some representatives of the Herero and Nama ethnic groups [have] no legal basis in the view of the Federal Government" (*Drucksache* 18/9152, 9). Only two days after the Government's reply to the *Kleine Anfrage,* the spokesperson of the Federal Foreign Office, Sawsan Chebli (SPD), officially speaks of genocide for the first time in her press statement. Furthermore, she announces a joint statement by the German and Namibian government which is to contain a "common language on the historical events" and the formulation of a "German apology as well as its acceptance by Namibia" (Press conference der *Bundesregierung*, 13 July 2016).

The promise to render an apology, however, required the naming and thus the recognition of the genocide. Consequently, connecting recognition and apology only became possible after having ruled out any possible use of the term in the context of international law (Eveleens 2016, 14 July, taz, 2; von Bullion 2016, 14 July, SZ, 5). The German government's initial refusal to name the genocide, to formulate an apology as well as the continuous rejection to pay compensations highlight that German memory politics are solely responding to its 'own' moral registers. As a result, a rupture emerges between the recognition of the historical events as genocide and the *misrecognition* of the 'suffering of the others'.

In spring 2016, when the first round of negotiations between the German and Namibian special emissaries Ruprecht Polenz and Dr. Zedekia Ngavirue starts without involving the main OvaHerero and Nama groups, a press release issues the slogan: "There can be no reconciliation without the consent and forgiveness of those whose resistant ancestors were murdered, displaced and dispossessed during the genocide" (Press Release of the alliance "Völkermord verjährt nicht", 16 March 2016). Nevertheless, the Federal Government confirms in the aforementioned answer to Die LINKE that there would be no direct negotiations with the "affected ethnic groups" (*Drucksache* 18/9152, 5). How is the German press reporting on the exclusion of the OvaHerero and Nama from the German-Namibian negotiations, and to what extent are their demands recognised or misrecognised?

3.2 "Not about Us without Us" – The Misrecognition of the 'Others'

In 2015/2016, newspaper articles on German colonialism increased considerably because of the (still unofficial) recognition of the genocide and the negotiations with Namibia. Equally, the demands of the OvaHerero and Nama have gained in visibility since postcolonial initiatives have induced a "change of opinion" on a national scale (Kößler and Melber 2016, 18 June, ND, 25). The analysis shows that both statements by opposition parties and by activists are repeatedly quoted, such as those expressed by Berlin based Herero activist Israel Kaunatjike, the Paramount Chief of the OvaHerero Vekuii Rukoro, and Esther Muinjangue as chairperson of the *OvaHerero Genocide Foundation* as well as the Namibian MP and representative of the *Nama Genocide Technical Committee* Ida Hoffmann. Precisely, their exclusion from the ongoing negotiations is critically commented, which is illustrated by article headlines such as *Excluding those affected* (taz, 14 July 2016, 2), *'Not about us without us!'* (ND, 17 October 2016, 12), *'We do not forget'* (FR, 10 August 2016, 18), *Victims' representatives demand money from Berlin* (FAZ, 11 July 2016, 1). However, media visibility is not equivalent to the recognition of the OvaHerero's and Nama's demands (cf. de Wolff 2018, 418).[4] For example, one article in the *FAZ* attributes incompetent conduct of negotiations to the Namibian government and questions the representative legitimacy of the Paramount Chief Rukoro:

> At the same time, however, the lack of progress is also due to the Namibian government's inability to unite the divided Herero, Nama and OvaMbanderu. One of the most eloquent Herero leaders, for example, the self-proclaimed 'Paramount Chief' Vekuii Rukoro, is demanding billions and wants to negotiate directly with Berlin (Scheen 2016, 8 July, FAZ, 32).

The above quoted *FAZ* article presents the Namibian government as incapable to govern because it would lack the capacity to unite the divergent demands of the different interest groups. The recurring reference to the internal Namibian conflicts not only makes the OvaHerero and Nama responsible for the delays in the dialogue process, but also reduces dealing with the past to a Namibian matter. Furthermore, the OvaHerero and Nama are accused of instrumentalising the past in order to improve their own economic position in the Namibian society. The *FAZ* calls it a "political calculation" and argues that the "Herero activist Rukoro openly admits [that] 'economic success [. . .] inevitably [translates into] political influence'" (Scheen 2016, 8 July, FAZ, 32). Repeatedly, Rukoro is portrayed as a 'choleric' man who is not willing to compromise, which disqualifies him as a serious negotiating partner. His reparation demands are consequently characterised as excessive and "unworldly", which is highlighted by stressing the "high" development aid that Namibia already receives. The articles reproduce common colonial and racist dichotomies by constructing rationality as Western and attributing emotionality to the 'others'. The *misrecognition* of the OvaHerero and Nama is reproduced by employing colonial and racist imaginaries, in which 'white' journalists direct

---

[4] Other persons and groups are hardly mentioned in media reporting, apart from the above mentioned OvaHerero and Nama representatives. Kaya de Wolff (2021, 370) argues in her dissertation *Post-/koloniale Erinnerungsdiskurse in der Medienkultur* that German media discourses reproduce an exclusively *white* perspective on the OvaHerero and Nama genocide.

their objectifying and racialising gaze at the 'others'. The failure to recognise the experience of the victims' descendants results in the failure to recognise the Ova-Herero's and Nama's demand for reparations. Nevertheless, media coverage, in contrast to the Federal Republic's official positioning, unanimously demands an unambiguous naming of the genocide. However, the divergence between a *recognition of the genocide* and the *misrecognition of the 'others'* as legitimate representatives of their interests is consolidated.

In summary, the recognition debate in 2015/2016 has highlighted the ambivalences between discursively produced moral collective ideals and a normative invocation of the moral obligation to come to terms with colonial violence. On the one hand, the rhetorical commitment to moral responsibility marks the attempt to find words that do not change the memory-political status quo. Due to political pressure, the German government had to accept an adjustment of language, but it agreed to do so only on the condition that no financial compensation would be granted. Thus, although the moral rules shift to the effect that naming the genocide is unavoidable, the socially imposed collective ideal does not include the obligation to pay compensation. The repeated rhetorical reference to a morally justified responsibility is set in opposition to a political and legal reappraisal of the colonial past. Ultimately, the German government seeks to find words that would have less political consequences, words with "less power", as cultural scientist Sara Ahmed strikingly phrased it (Ahmed 2004, 117). The following section asks to what extent the recognition of the 'suffering of others' becomes a morally accepted collective ideal in the debates over the "reconciliation agreement" announced in May 2021 by the German government.

4 An (Im-)Possibility to Repair Colonial Crime? Debates over the "Reconciliation Agreement" in 2021

On 28 May 2021, a press release published by German Foreign Minister Heiko Maas announced that a "reconciliation agreement" between the governments of Namibia and Germany had been concluded. By the end of the legislative period in September 2021, according to the schedule of the Foreign Ministry, the agreement would be signed by the two parliaments, and Head of state Frank-Walter Steinmeier (SPD) would have rendered an official apology in the Namibian parliament. When presented to the Namibian parliament in early June, opposition parties reacted critically to the outcome of the negotiations and called for renegotiations

(*Namibias Opposition ist erzürnt* 2021, 10 June, FR, 9). As a result, the conclusion of the negotiations before the federal elections in September 2021 had already become unlikely by the beginning of June, the reasons being that the German government still refused to pay reparations.

In this regard, Maas' statement leaves no doubt that the *Bundesregierung* pursues memory politics in terms of development cooperation as the following excerpt from the press statement shows:

> Our aim was and remains to find a shared path towards genuine reconciliation in memory of the victims. This includes being unreserved and unflinching in naming the events of the German colonial period in what is now Namibia and in particular the atrocities between 1904 and 1908. We will now officially call these events what they are from today's perspective: a genocide.
>
> Given Germany's historical and moral responsibility, we will ask Namibia and the descendants of the victims for forgiveness.
>
> As a gesture of recognition of the immeasurable suffering inflicted on the victims, we want to support Namibia and the victims' descendants with a substantial programme to the tune of 1.1 billion euro for reconstruction and development. The communities affected by the genocide will play a key role in shaping and implementing this programme. Legal claims for compensation cannot be derived from it (Press release of the Federal Foreign Office, 28 May 2021, emphasis S.R.).

Maas' press release confirms the German government's position that the recognition of the genocide would not result in any claims under international law, since the criminal offence of genocide only acquired international validity with the adoption of the UN Genocide Convention in 1948. The socialist newspaper *ND* quotes a press release of the association *Berlin Postkolonial*, which criticises "the continuing non-recognition of the genocide under international law". The newspaper continues that "the Federal Government falls 'even behind the position' of then Federal Development Minister Wieczorek-Zeul (SPD) in 2004" by recognising the genocide "from today's perspective" (*Deutschland erkennt seine Verbrechen in Namibia an – irgendwie* 2021, 28 May, nd-aktuell.de).

The demand for a recognition under international law has never been put forward so clearly by activists before. On 16 May, a joint press release of the Paramount Chief Vekuii Rukoro (Ovaherero Traditional Authority – OTA) and the Nama representative Gaob Johannes Isaack (Nama Traditional Leader Association – NTLA) states:

> Germany still has NO intention to recognise that what von Trotha did constitutes genocide in terms of international law, therefore, Germany did not commit a crime against humanity and has no intention to apologise for ANY crime of GENOCIDE – especially not to the descendants of the Victim Communities! (Press statement of the alliance "Völkermord verjährt nicht!" and Joint Press Statement by Paramount Chief Advocate Vekuii Rukoro (OTA) and Gaob Johannes Isaack (NTLA), 17 May 2021, capitalisation in original).

The reason for this reference to international law is "the continued refusal of reparations by the Federal Republic of Germany", as stated in the German press statement of the alliance "Völkermord verjährt nicht!". In contrast to 2015/16, the debate is shifting from recognising the genocide in official statements to its recognition under international law, placing the demand for material reparations centre stage. However, the German government's willingness to recognise and apologise for the genocide is still translated into development projects. Therefore, the OvaHerero and Nama associations, such as the OTA or the NTLA, now insist on the term 'reparations' because it is the descendants of the affected groups that should be legitimate addressees to work through the past. The newspaper *taz* therefore concludes that the "obligation to make amends" can only be met if the genocide is recognised under international law (Johnson 2021, 29/30 May, taz, 7).

Following the critical reactions of the OvaHerero and Nama, the question of how to repair colonial crime dominates media reporting in 2021. Although most articles consider reparations to be unlikely, the fact that they are being discussed renders them intelligible in memory political terms. The journalist Bernd Dörries states that "[t]he genocide in Namibia [. . .] has been treated for many decades as a legal problem, not as a human and moral one. The idea was not to set a precedent for the suffering of other peoples" (Dörries 2021, 28 May, Süddeutsche.de). Dörries points to the ambivalences in the discursive construction of "law" and "morality" as divergent and even opposite realms. By this token, the German government rationalises the legal framework as a non-negotiable given. However, the naming of the genocide in 2015/2016 initiated a shift of moral registers. A change of the moral collective ideal – which now consists of working through Germany's colonial past – could therefore result in a reassessment of the current legal framework (cf. Goldmann 2020). Albeit the German government continues to refuse paying reparations, the analysed newspaper articles increasingly challenge existing legal norms and unanimously demand at least financial compensation in their reporting in 2021.

In contrast to 2015/2016, the discourse analysis shows that most of the articles – no matter of which political spectrum – support the OvaHerero's and Nama's demands for compensatory payments. Nevertheless, a recognition of the genocide under international law is still considered unlikely. For example, the *FR* states that "once again there is no talk of direct compensation for the Herero and Nama" and that "Berlin's hesitant steps towards reparations [. . .] are observed with suspicion not only in Windhoek" (Dieterich 2021, 29 May, FR, 13). The government's reasoning is the same as in the 2015/2016 recognition debates: Neither the term "reparation" nor "compensation" are used. According to the *FAZ*, the aim is to prevent a precedent "that other countries could invoke against Germany" (Bröll and Haupt 2021, 29 May, FAZ, 2). For this reason, "[t]he billions now agreed on [. . .] should be understood *merely* as a political-moral obligation" as the *FR* underscores (Huesmann

2021, 29 May, FR, 7, emphasis S.R.). The *SZ*, in turn, states that "the German state [has] not managed to apologise adequately for the crimes and to compensate the people" (*Aktuelles Lexikon 'Deutsch-Südwestafrika'* 2021, 18 May, SZ, 4), and the above-quoted article published in *FR* estimates that "even in its overdue acknowledgement of guilt [. . .] the Federal Government [has] scrupulously taken care to exclude the question of compensation for the almost complete extermination of the ethnic groups" (Huesmann 2021, 29 May, FR, 7). These excerpts suggest that the exclusively morally justified "gesture of recognition" which aims at increasing the expenses for development cooperation is perceived as insufficient.

Correspondingly, the OvaHerero's and Nama's demand for a "reparation agreement" instead of a "reconciliation agreement" cannot solely be explained by the request for direct compensation, but also needs to be understood as a strategy to inverse the power dynamics at play. In fact, agreeing on reparations would enable the OvaHerero and Nama to define the concrete amount and the conditions of the payment (cf. Selz 2021, 22 May, nd-aktuell.de). Instead, Germany still defines the conditions under which the past is worked through by dictating the terms under which development aid is paid. In this regard, the *SZ* even criticises the German-Namibian dialogue process as such by asking: "A 'negotiation' on whether to accept historical facts? That means one sets conditions. One makes demands. How can one, especially as the legal successor of the perpetrators, come up with such a presumptuous idea?" (Steinke 2021, 30 May, Süddeutsche.de). For this reason, the *SZ*-journalist considers it "absurd" that the German government is pursuing the strategy of preventing the recognition according to the Genocide Convention. Ultimately, the analysed newspaper articles follow the OvaHerero's and Nama's definition of how a just working through of Germany's colonial crimes should look like: First, it would require the acknowledgement of historical guilt, second, the formulation of an official apology and third, financial compensation (but not necessarily reparations) paid to the descendants. The *FAZ* therefore issues the corresponding slogan: "Whoever asks for forgiveness is in debt. He must first acknowledge his guilt and secondly explain what follows from it" (Bröll and Haupt 2021, 29 May, FAZ, 2).

In conclusion, criticism expressed by the OvaHerero and Nama, German activists as well as the Namibian opposition are even more visible in the analysed newspaper articles in 2021 in comparison to 2015/16. The German dominance in the dialogue process is not only criticised, but also denounced as a postcolonial power asymmetry. In reaction to the massive Namibian criticism of the one-sided conduct of the negotiations, the *SZ* concludes that "reconciliation cannot be achieved against the will of those people whom one wants to ask for forgiveness. The fact that now apparently numerous descendants of the victims are angry is not a good sign, and it puts the planned trip of the Head of State to Windhoek into the distant future" (Perras 2021, 8 June, SZ, 8). In fact, Foreign Minister Maas and Head of State

Steinmeier have postponed their travels to Namibia to issue an apology for an indefinite period (Melber 2021). The unforeseen public pressure, also exerted by the Namibian opposition parties, thus seems to have changed the OvaHerero's and Nama's negotiating position. In January 2022, the OTA and NTLA have launched another petition calling "to restart the failed German-Namibia intergovernmental negotiations on the genocide of our ancestors WITH US" (Petition on change.org 2022, Capitalisation in original). It remains to be seen how the new government will respond to the demands of the OvaHerero and Nama.

5 Conclusion: Practices of Misrecognition

The discourse analysis in this article showed that the German government attempted to realise the recognition of the OvaHerero and Nama genocide as a solely linguistic readjustment, which would prevent further political consequences. Consequently, the understanding of morality was ambiguously constructed: On the one hand, moral standards were called upon to justify the official naming of the genocide and Germany's increased commitment in development cooperation. On the other hand, however, the OvaHerero's and Nama's demands for reparations were discursively placed outside the moral collective ideal, thus perpetuating a continuous misrecognition of their 'suffering'.

The multidirectional framework created by the recognition of the Armenian genocide pressured the German government to also take a stand regarding the genocide in the former 'German South West Africa'. By declaring 'genocide' the official term to be applied regarding the mass killings of the OvaHerero, Nama, Damara, and San, the understanding of 'political and moral responsibility' towards Namibia expanded discursively. Henceforth, Germany's efforts in development cooperation are conceived of as a memory political tool to come to terms with the colonial past. Consequently, taking responsibility for the past is defined in moral terms, which decidedly dismisses legal and political actions. The future-oriented development cooperation not only excludes the historical re-evaluation of German colonialism, but it also legitimises the rejection of the reparation claims pronounced by the OvaHerero and Nama. The analysis of German media reporting between 2015 and 2021 highlighted the discrepancy between an increasing willingness to recognise the genocide on the one hand, and a persistent misrecognition of the OvaHerero and Nama as affected groups on the other.

However, the *Bundesregierung* also legitimised the term 'genocide' for media use by officially speaking of genocide, thus enabling the enunciation of further memory political demands: Whereas the OvaHerero and Nama have been demanding the recognition of the genocide, an official apology, and the payments of compensation since the 1990s, these three components became increasingly mediatised in the analysed newspaper articles from 2015/16 onwards. As a result, media reporting agrees that the recognition of the genocide must be followed by an official apology while also considering financial compensations to the descendants of the victims. After all, the official naming of the genocide made colonial violence discursively intelligible. Instead of successfully relegating the colonial past to the sphere of development cooperation, the naming concluded in a process for recognition which eventually ascribed "relevance to remember" to the genocide (Robel 2013, 74). Yet, naming colonial violence describes neither a starting nor an end point in negotiating memory politics; instead, it highlights its performative character enabling processes of recognition as well as of misrecognising of (post-)colonial memories. What this paper intended to show is that the production of moral collective ideals does not necessarily result in the recognition of the 'suffering of the others'. Rather, the memory political interest consists of living up to the nationally established moral standards of 'successfully' coming to terms with the colonial past.

References

Primary Sources

Anonymous. "Opfervertreter in Namibia fordern Geld von Berlin." *Frankfurter Allgemeine Zeitung* 1 (7 April 2016).
Anonymous. "Deutsch-Südwestafrika: Aktuelles Lexikon." *Süddeutsche Zeitung* 4 (28 May 2021).
Anonymous. "Deutschland erkennt seine Verbrechen in Namibia an – irgendwie." *nd-aktuell.de* (28 May 2021).
Anonymous. "Namibias Opposition ist erzürnt." *Frankfurter Rundschau* 9 (10 June 2021).
Antwort der Bundesregierung auf die Kleine Anfrage der Fraktion DIE LINKE. Sachstand der Verhandlungen zum Versöhnungsprozess mit Namibia und zur Aufarbeitung des Völkermordes an den Herero und Nama. Drucksache 18/9152 (2016): 1–16.
Bröll, Claudia, and Friederike Haupt. "Kein Schlussstrich, sondern ein Beginn." *Frankfurter Allgemeine Zeitung* 2 (29 May 2021).
Bundesregierung. *Regierungspressekonferenz vom 10. Juli.* https://www.bundesregierung.de/breg-de/aktuelles/pressekonferenzen/regierungspressekonferenz-vom-10-juli-847582, 2015. 1–14 (24 November 2021).
Bündnis „Völkermord verjährt nicht!" *Schluss mit den Geheimverhandlungen zum Genozid in Namibia.* https://genocide-namibia.net/2016/03/16-03-2016-pressemitteilung-schluss-mit-den-geheimverhandlungen-zum-genozid-in-namibia/#page-content, 2016 (13 April 2022).
Deutscher Bundestag. *Gedenken an Völkermord an den Armeniern: Zusammenfassung der Parlamentsdebatte.* https://www.bundestag.de/dokumente/textarchiv/2015/kw17_de_armenier-369868 (28 July 2021).

Dieterich, Johannes. "Neue Ära." *Frankfurter Rundschau* 13 (29 May 2021).
Dörries, Bernd. "Eingeständnis eines Verbrechens: Meinung." *Süddeutsche.de* (28 May 2021).
Eveleens, Ilona. "Unter Ausschluss der Betroffenen." *taz* 2 (14 July 2016).
Huesmann, Felix. "Namibia hätte lieber Reparationen." *Frankfurter Rundschau* 7 (29 May 2021).
Lammert, Norbert. "Deutsche ohne Gnade." *Die ZEIT* 16 (9 July 2015).
Maas, Heiko. *Foreign Minister Maas on the conclusion of negotiations with Namibia.* 2021. https://www.auswaertiges-amt.de/en/newsroom/news/-/2463598 (20 March 2022).
Johnson, Dominic. "'Erster Schritt' stößt auf Kritik." *taz* 7 (29 May 2021).
Kaunatjike, Israel, and Sima Luipert. *Renegotiate the genocide agreement WITH US, the surviving Nama & Ovaherero NOW! Petition.* https://www.change.org/p/abaerbock-renegotiate-the-genocide-agreement-with-us-the-surviving-nama-ovaherero-now (21 March 2022).
Kößler, Reinhart, and Henning Melber. "Vom Völkermord zur Versöhnung." *Neues Deutschland* 25 (18 June 2016).
Perras, Arne. "Europas dunkle Seite." *Süddeutsche Zeitung* 8 (8 June 2021).
Putsch, Christian. "Namibischer Stamm beklagt Rassismus." *WELT ONLINE* (8 June 2016).
Scheen, Thomas. "Der Preis des Völkermords." *Frankfurter Allgemeine Zeitung* 32 (8 July 2016).
Selz, Christian. "Billige Entschuldigung Vom deutsch-namibischen 'Aussöhnungsabkommen' haben die Nachfahren der Völkermord-Opfer nichts." *nd-aktuell.de* (22 May 2021).
Steinke, Ronen. "Nicht aufrichtig." *Süddeutsche.de* (30 May 2021).
Vates, Daniela, and Steven Geyer. "Namibia-Resolution soll bald kommen." *Frankfurter Rundschau* 6 (14 June 2016).
von Bullion, Constanze. "Entschuldigung für Herero-Massaker." *Süddeutsche Zeitung* 5 (14 July 2016).
Wieczorek-Zeul, Heidemarie. Rede von Bundesministerin für wirtschaftliche Zusammenarbeit und Entwicklung bei den Gedenkfeierlichkeiten zum 100. Jahrestag der Herero-Aufstände. Namibia. https://politische-reden.eu/BR/t/683.html, 2004 (13 April 2022).
Zimmerer, Jürgen. "Mit aller Macht die Augen verschließen." *taz* 4 (9 June 2015).

Secondary Sources

Ahmed, Sara. *The Cultural Politics of Emotion.* Edinburgh: Edinburgh University Press, 2004.
Assmann, Aleida. *Der lange Schatten der Vergangenheit: Erinnerungskultur und Geschichtspolitik.* München: Beck, 2014 [2006].
Barkan, Elazar. *The Guilt of Nations: Restitution and Negotiating Historical Injustices.* Baltimore: Johns Hopkins University Press, 2001.
Böhlke-Itzen, Janntje. "Die bundesdeutsche Diskussion und die Reparationsfrage – ein ganz normaler Kolonialkrieg?" *Genozid und Gedenken: Namibisch-deutsche Geschichte und Gegenwart.* Ed. Henning Melber and Janntje Böhlke-Itzen. Frankfurt am Main: Brandes & Apsel, 2005. 103–120.
Bürger, Christiane. *Deutsche Kolonialgeschichte(n): Der Genozid in Namibia und die Geschichtsschreibung der DDR und BRD.* Bielefeld: transcript, 2017.
Butler, Judith. *Precarious Life: The Powers of Mourning and Violence.* London: Verso, 2004.
Craps, Stef and Michael Rothberg. "Introduction: Transcultural Negotiations of Holocaust Memory." *Criticism* 53.4 (2011): 517–521.
de Wolff, Kaya. "Postkoloniale Erinnerungskonflikte in den Medien." *Deutschland postkolonial? Die Gegenwart der imperialen Vergangenheit.* Ed. Marianne Bechhaus-Gerst and Joachim Zeller. Berlin: Metropol, 2018. 408–432.

———. *Post-/koloniale Erinnerungsdiskurse in der Medienkultur: Der Genozid an den Ovaherero und Nama in der deutschsprachigen Presse von 2001 bis 2016*. Bielefeld: transcript Verlag, 2021.
Deslaurier, Christine and Aurélie Roger. "Mémoires grises. Pratiques politiques du passé colonial entre Europe et Afrique." *Politique Africaine* 102.2 (2006): 5–27.
Durkheim, Émile. *Erziehung, Moral und Gesellschaft: Vorlesung an der Sorbonne 1902/1903*. Transl. Ludwig Schmidts. Neuwied am Rhein, Darmstadt: Luchterhand, 1973 [1922].
Fraser, Nancy and Axel Honneth. Ed. *Umverteilung oder Anerkennung? Eine politisch-philosophische Kontroverse*. Transl. Burkhardt Wolf. Frankfurt am Main: Suhrkamp, 2003.
Goldmann, Matthias. "'Ich bin Ihr Freund und Kapitän'. Die deutsch-namibische Entschädigungsfrage im Spiegel intertemporaler und interkultureller Völkerrechtskonzepte." *MPIL Research Paper Series* 2020.29 (2020). https://doi.org/10.2139/ssrn.3672406.
Honneth, Axel. *Kampf um Anerkennung: Zur moralischen Grammatik sozialer Konflikte*. Frankfurt am Main: Suhrkamp, 2016 [1994].
Jesse, Eckhard. *Vergangenheitsbewältigung*. Berlin: Duncker & Humblot, 1997.
Kößler, Reinhart. *Negotiating the Past: Namibia and Germany*. Münster: Westfälisches Dampfboot, 2015.
Krüger, Gesine. "Das goldene Zeitalter der Viehzüchter: Namibia im 19. Jahrhundert." *Völkermord in Deutsch-Südwestafrika: Der Kolonialkrieg (1904–1908) in Namibia und seine Folgen*. Ed. Jürgen Zimmerer and Joachim Zeller. Berlin: Weltbild [Ch. Links] 2011 [2004]. 13–25.
Levy, Daniel, and Natan Sznaider. *Erinnerung im globalen Zeitalter: Der Holocaust*. Frankfurt am Main: Suhrkamp, 2001.
Melber, Henning. *Koloniale Asymmetrien der Gegenwart. Zum deutsch-namibischen 'Versöhnungsabkommen'*. https://geschichtedergegenwart.ch/koloniale-asymmetrien-der-gegenwart-zum-deutsch-namibischen-versoehnungsabkommen/ (9 August 2021).
Miles, William F. S. "Third World views of the Holocaust." *Journal of Genocide Research* 6.3 (2004): 371–393. https://doi.org/10.1080/1462352042000265855.
Rausch, Sahra. "'We're equal to the Jews who were destroyed. [. . .] Compensate us, too'. An affective (un)remembering of Germany's colonial past?" *Memory Studies* 15.2 (2022): 418–435. https://doi.org/10.1177/17506980211044083.
Robel, Yvonne. *Verhandlungssache Genozid: Zur Dynamik geschichtspolitischer Deutungskämpfe*. Zugl.: Bremen, Univ., Diss., 2012. München: Fink, 2013.
Rothberg, Michael. *Multidirectional Memory: Remembering the Holocaust in the Age of Decolonization*. Stanford, California: Stanford University Press, 2009.
Stoler, Ann Laura. *Along the Archival Grain: Epistemic Anxieties and Colonial Common Sense*. Princeton, NJ: Princeton University Press, 2009.
Sznaider, Natan. "Suffering as a Universal Frame for Understanding Memory Politics." *Clashes in European Memory: The Case of Communist Repression and the Holocaust*. Ed. Muriel Blaive, Christian Gerbel and Thomas Lindenberger. Innsbruck: StudienVerlag 2011. 239–254.
Taylor, Charles. "The Politics of Recognition." *Multiculturalism: Examining the Politics of Recognition*. Ed. Amy Gutmann. Princeton: Princeton University Press 1994. 25–73.
Trouillot, Michel-Rolph. "Abortive Rituals: Historical Apologies in the Global Era." *Interventions* 2.2 (2000): 171–186. https://doi.org/10.1080/136980100427298.
Zimmerer, Jürgen. "Krieg, KZ und Völkermord in Südwestafrika: Der erste deutsche Genozid." *Völkermord in Deutsch-Südwestafrika: Der Kolonialkrieg (1904–1908) in Namibia und seine Folgen*. Ed. Jürgen Zimmerer and Joachim Zeller. Berlin: Weltbild [Ch. Links] 2011 [2004]. 45–63.

Part IV: **Reparation through Literature**

Quatrième partie : **La réparation par la littérature**

hn. lyonga
and I mean / *and* I am saying

Context: First published in early 2022 as a poetic intervention via a VR installation at Kottbusser Tor, Berlin, in cooperation with barazani.berlin – Forum Kolonialismus und Widerstand and art center VIERTE WELT – Temporary Monuments, *and* I mean / *and* I am saying opened up a virtual memory space in which experiences of state violence and resistance to it were made visible.

I am saying
there are many ways of dying in a foreign country
with a dream in my mouth

I am saying
somewhere in the world a black girl is beingheld
in a room againstherwill

I am saying
paperwork and powers that be

I am saying
stamps signaturesand envelops

I am saying
duldung

I am saying
white establishments continue to taunt
abuse and traumatize

I am saying
politics of exclusion disguises itself
as formalities

I am saying
hierarchies whitenessand racist structures

I am saying
everyday bodies collapse
under the weight of governments

I am saying
one day I will have to explain to my nieces
how *blackpeopledie* in germany

I am saying
there are any number of ways
a black person can die while in policecustody

I am saying
in germany a person can go up in flames in a police cell
or die from gunshot wounds at a local *jobcenter*
or tortured and stretched across a hospital bed

I am saying
wholebodies go missing

I am saying
we are tired of writing our names on banners
and building coalitions to stayalive

I am saying
the writing is on the wall & it is glaring

I am saying
state apparatuses come up with newer ways
of eluding proper investigation in police brutality cases

I am saying
the power to evade justice

I am saying
politicians withflyers

I am saying
It has been sixteenyears
and I am not eligible to vote

I am saying
my prayers begin and end
with – I do not want to die face-down
with shoeprints around my neck (& a sigh)

I am saying
sound

I am saying
gunshots&churchbells

I am saying
I am not sure I will return home in time
to bury my grandmother without forfeiting my *aufenthaltstitel*

I am saying
highbloodpressure and the shock of a rejectionletter
can culminate into something deadly

I am saying
my life is a dichotomy of being
trapped in something that seems secure
& being transfixed by the very protection it promises

I am saying
in our household bureaucracy is a subject
it is visceral enough to exist on its own

I am saying
in the many years my body has undergone bureaucratic processes
I have learned

I am saying
when you love something enough
you live with the fear of losing or becoming it

I am saying
I am becoming

I am saying
this story has roots
and names and names and names

I am saying
we have names you will commemorate

hn. Iyonga
Half-Hymns, Prayers, and Fortifications

Context: This writing pays homage to broken magnolia limbs sowed deep into the earth with caskets, fractured recollections of falling things, and people whose names I have long omitted. To people who exist in fringe imaginations simply as antecedents or as dearly departed. Grandparents, great-grandparents, uncles, and aunts whose bodies have returned from whence they came. It monumentalizes their lives, lived in the Bakweri tradition of southwest Cameroon. Dancing across the topics of black faith traditions and practices, personal error as a potential cause of death, life in the diaspora, and immigration politics in the West, it asks the question – what answers can we find about ourselves in the memories we hold of our ancestors?

Keywords: prayers, fortifications, *and* I mean / *and* I am saying, Baptist church traditions, Cameroon, memory culture, virtual memory, life and death, burial rites, tradition, history, the West, immigration politics, loss, error

When I sat down to write an essay that would simultaneously commemorate and give some insights into '*and* I mean / *and* I am saying' and the numerous voices and desires that appear in it, I knew I had to think hard and deeply about many things. Among the things I considered, the voices of my ancestors remained the most piercing and unwavering. I thought about my great-grandmother's face, her favorite earrings, and how they hoofed, shingled, and announced her every arrival. I thought about my motherland, its many complexities, and the tribe of people I hailed from. The sweet smells of jasmine blossoms and sharpened palm-frond leaves we kept and carried on Sundays to the only Baptist church we knew came right back to me. Like the harmattan that ushered in a shift of perspective on things, other recollections and thoughts came with them. I thought about the person who first articulated and then later bestowed me with the name 'Iyonga' at my cradle. And about the people at whose feet I was given my first words, people whose plate I was fed from, whose arms and embrace steered me clear of peril and despair, people whose voices sang me to sleep and gave me a sense of purpose. I thought about where these people are today and about how their lives have and have not advanced since my absconding to the West. I also thought about prayers, half-hymns, departures, and deaths.

In the little town of Mutengene in the southwest region of Cameroon, where I was born, people took prayers very seriously. The act of praying was used to show dedication and respect to and for the elements that live inside and outside of our bodies. Here, people had blessings, psalms, and fortifications for each other. How we beseeched and sang; we prayed leaning in at dinner tables with heads and whole bodies genuflected in curiosity towards what was in the bowl before us. We prayed over a child's head, and at the foot of a tree, and in the morning, before a visit to the farm, after the first crow of a cock that invites the morning into a lamp-lit room. We prayed in sanctums and hallways, reading and singing scriptures. Some prayed with leaves and snuff in their mouths, wearing damask, wax printed motives, lace from Ibadan, and cowries from the sea. Here, people read from leaves, palms, and lips. It is how they knew what the earth beneath their feet was trying to tell them on any given day. It was there that I learned that a welcome embrace and a goodbye kiss were both prayers and acts of fortification. That, when you kiss a face and bid it goodbye, you fortify the person it belongs to. You lay gently a well-meaning curse that will linger on for all of eternity when you say; *I will keep a candle burning until you return again.* With respect, love, and dedication, a course is matched by a promise of return. A departing body allies with a multitude of elements, bodies it knows at its core and all the places it is leaving behind. Hands envelop each other and new bonds take their place.

    I have lived in Germany for sixteen years now and I have lost and buried loved ones in my mind from a distance. It has happened too often, so that a kind of notable routine has developed. It goes like this: A phone call arrives at any time to announce the departure of a dearly loved one. The call is usually brief and to the point. You are told what your contribution will be. And it is seldom something small. In most cases, it is something financial, grand and conspicuous enough to say; *he/she has a relative that lives abroad and thus can afford the finer things in life and death.* The nonchalance and effrontery in the caller's voice doesn't bother you anymore because you have learned to bury the disrespect. When the cause of death is uttered, it is usually in a manner so passive it leaves the listener wanting for more. The responsibility is usually to buy the casket and to foot the bill for each and every entertainment the burial rite requires. The call receiver says; *I'll see what I can do* – and the call comes to a close. A body descends into a chair or a bed or a shower in an attempt to find a kind of soft landing, a place where it can mourn and hold the gravity of what it has just been told. That night, your mind does not sleep. Your body refuses to remove itself from the place it was when the message arrived. And suddenly an excel sheet of names appears in your mind and you check yet another name off the list. Your mind writes a eulogy that ends with – *and I am sorry I could not be there for you like you needed me to.*

In one of the most emotionally wrenching conversations I have had with my mother, I learned about the extent to which we have suffered losses. I also discovered that the sadness I felt and continue to feel as I respire in a country far away from the people I used to know lies in a single and simple truth. The people I love continue to vanish in death. We have lost things of no significance and things of great importance. Lands, homes, opportunities, desires, and people have been lost. We have lost over thirty family members including my father since my mother arrived in Germany some twenty years ago. And we have felt and continue to feel every last one of their losses. In this conversation, some other things came up. Guilt, regrets, and questions. The guilt of not being able to say goodbye or holding and kissing a loved one's hand as they cross their own very peculiar finish-line, the many regrets that come with an understanding that there will never be a second chance at making this wrong right and questions like; was it worth it, to be away for so long – will the people we have lost ever forgive us for leaving them behind – can we make peace with the choices we have made – can we find answers in the memories we hold of our ancestors?

When my father died, I was told it was an error – an error of his own making; that he could have survived if he had just tried a little harder. Was it carelessness or ignorance, I asked? When I didn't get an answer that evening, it was Mbanga soup, plantains, my mother's love and support, and my grandmother's hands that held my heart together. I was ten years old and thought an error is nothing that should cost a person their life. An error shouldn't leave a ten-year-old fatherless and wondering. An error shouldn't leave whole communities in a state of unrest.

Today, my walls are stacked with images of people; alive and dead. This ever-growing collection of photographs of black and white, cracked and stained sepia, of women, men, and children standing or sitting in front of doorways, kitchen stalls, and wooden or brick houses goes back over a century. It is a free-form tree of sorts with no actual shape and boundaries to it. There are no dates of birth and death or names, only faces and stories, because I want to preserve their memories in no terms of limitation. In these images, their eyes reflect many things. Tree branches shooting up sea surfaces under blue, white, and grey skies, traces of mountains with low and high altitudes, the turmoils and the taste of earth itself, vanishing past, present, and futures, and things words fail to capture entirely.

When I burn candles, and sage, and pray at their feet as they have and continue to do over mine for three decades now, I see faces I recognize from dreams and stories told at the foot of trees. And I realize that everybody looks like everybody I have said goodbye to in the past, present, and future. My body adjusts to their loss and mine too becomes part of a buried history in place and time. And to the vast infertile lands their departure has left behind – to the vast infertile lands my departure left them with. You see, violence repeats itself. Life takes its course. Nothing ends. Things continue as they reconfigure into newer things. Prayers become half-hymns we use to fortify ourselves and the people who understand where we have been. It is how I divorce myself from feeling the absolute terror of all that is now lost to me. It is how I register faces, bodies, and the narratives that belonged to them as my body mourns their loss.

Ibou Diop
Qui répare qui ? Comment et pourquoi ? Une éthique et esthétique de la relation

Résumé : La littérature africaine comme lieu de mémoire accompagne le processus de développement du continent africain. Par une analyse subjective, ce texte essaie de revisiter et de raconter l'histoire de cette littérature. Se basant sur une rhétorique de la réparation, cette réflexion passe une analyse historique de la littérature et de l'esthétique noire pour fonder son discours. La question de la réparation rejaillit depuis quelques années dans les débats intellectuels. Il est, aujourd'hui, souvent discuté dans les contextes de la restitution du patrimoine culturel africain. Est-il possible toutefois de réparer sans se pencher sur les thématiques telles que l'esclavage, le racisme et la colonisation, qui sont systématiquement liées à cette dernière ? Le projet colonial s'est accompagné d'une destruction massive physique et symbolique du patrimoine culturel africain et d'un projet de destruction de l'humain africain. C'est de ce projet d'effacement, qui accompagnait l'esclavage et l'aliénation du corps et de l'âme noire, que découle le racisme à la fois systématique et endémique. C'est-à-dire, encré dans un discours scientifique, ethnographique, historique, artistique et littéraire de subordination, le corps et le sujet noir furent le lieu par excellence d'expression d'une certaine violence d'où découlerait par conséquent l'anéantissement des identités africaines et de leurs relations avec le monde. Écrire ou penser alors sur la réparation après des siècles de colonialisme et de la *colonialité* du présent, c'est revenir sur la relation des nations du monde, sur les politiques de la relation et sur l'éthique de l'esthétique. Passé, présent et futur.

Mots-clés : mémoire ; identité ; patrimoine africain ; esclavage ; littérature africaine ; colonialisme ; colonialité ; exploitation ; destruction ; traumatisme

La question de la réparation rejaillit depuis quelques années dans les débats intellectuels. Il est, aujourd'hui, souvent discuté dans les contextes de la restitution du patrimoine culturel africain. Est-il possible toutefois de réparer sans se pencher sur les thématiques telles que l'esclavage, le racisme et la colonisation, qui sont systématiquement liées à cette dernière ? Le projet colonial s'est accompagné de destruction massive physique et symbolique du patrimoine culturel africain et d'un projet de destruction de l'humain africain. Comme le retient Achille Mbembe (2018) : « Le droit de conquête n'imposait pas seulement la défaite militaire des peuples sauvages. Il fallait aussi les déposséder matériellement et effacer symboliquement les liens qu'ils entretenaient, à travers leurs objets, avec le cosmos. » Et c'est de ce projet d'effacement qui accompagnait l'esclavage et l'aliénation du corps et de l'âme noire que découle le racisme à la fois systématique et endémique.

C'est-à-dire, encré dans un discours scientifique, ethnographique, historique, artistique et littéraire de subordination, le corps et le sujet noir furent le lieu par excellence d'expression d'une certaine violence d'où découlerait par conséquent l'anéantissement des identités africaines et de leurs relations avec le reste du monde. Frantz Fanon n'affirmait-il pas déjà au 1er Congrès des Artistes et Écrivains Noirs en France en 1956 sur le thème *Racisme et Culture* qu' « Il n'est pas possible d'asservir des hommes sans logiquement les inférioriser de part en part. Et le racisme n'est que l'exploitation émotionnelle, affective, quelquefois intellectuelle de cette infériorisation » (Fanon 2017, 723). Écrire ou penser alors sur la réparation après des siècles de colonialisme et de la *colonialité* du présent, c'est revenir sur la relation des nations du monde, sur les politiques de la relation et sur l'éthique de l'esthétique. Passé, présent et futur. Delà retient Paul Gilroy :

> C'est pourquoi j'ai choisi l'image d'un navire voguant entre l'Europe, l'Amérique, l'Afrique et les Caraïbes comme point de départ et comme symbole de cette entreprise. . . . Cette image attire immédiatement notre attention sur le « Passage du milieu », sur les divers projets de retour rédempteur à la patrie africaine, et sur la circulation d'idées, de militants et d'artefacts culturels et politiques essentiels, qu'il s'agisse de pamphlets, de livres, de disques ou de chœurs (Gilroy 1993, 19).

En effet, inscrit – par une politique occidentale de la domination – sur une tradition de la soumission et de l'exploitation, l'Afrique et les corps qui l'habitent furent pendant des siècles dépouillés de leurs richesses humaines, matérielles et immatérielles. Dans le but d'une fragilisation et d'une destruction massive de son devenir, l'Occident tentait ainsi par un vaste projet de refuser à l'Afrique son humanité. Ce refus s'articule sur l'approche politique, économique et culturelle que les puissances coloniales avaient sur le reste du monde. En effet, en adoptant une attitude de reniement, l'Europe archiva les connaissances non occidentales, théorisa la supériorité de la notion de la race blanche, essaya d'effacer tout ce qui concurrençait ou remettait la suprématie de l'Occident en question. Loin d'adopter la philosophie du rajout, de la complémentarité ou du parallélisme, cette Europe-là, avec la France, l'Allemagne, l'Angleterre, le Portugal et l'Espagne en tête, inaugura l'ère du morcèlement d'une plus grande partie de l'humanité.

Ce qui fut alors appelé la balkanisation traça les frontières entre les peuples et nations, détermina de nouvelles identités, structures et réalités sociales. Ce système qui accompagna la politique de domination des territoires entre autres non occidentaux, creusa les barrières entre les peuples, anima des conflits intra-ethniques et renforça les traumatismes de séparations. Même si cette balkanisation créa toutefois de nouvelles alliances, elle reste une des principales causes des conflits actuels sur le continent africain. Réparer alors ces blessures (post)coloniales, c'est revenir sur les liens de l'Afrique, des Africaines et Afro-descendantes avec le reste du monde. Nombreux sont aujourd'hui les intellectuelles et intellectuels d'ascendance africaine qui par leurs plumes ont essayé de mettre des mots, des pensées et des perspectives sur cette histoire.

Ainsi, si nous acceptons que la littérature en général soit un réservoir de savoir et que celle africaine en particulier puise dans les plaies de l'histoire et transcende les réalités pour proposer par les textes classiques et modernes des perspectives de vie et de survie, nous acceptons aussi que c'est dans la reconnaissance et l'acceptation de l'autre que se situe le projet de déconstruction, de prise de position et « d'affirmation d'une volonté d'être réintégré dans la famille humaine », comme l'atteste Bernard Mouralis (1993, 11). Et que c'est par cette participation que le discours et le récit africains prennent place dans le monde à venir. Ainsi, dans la création et la conservation d'une mémoire discursive les écrivaines et écrivains comme Chinua Achebe, Cheikh Hamidou Kane, Aminata Sow Fall, Ken Bugul, Léonora Miano ou Fatou Diome – indépendamment de leur lieu de réflexion – pensent et théorisent les zones de contacts. Traduisant les réalités et les transformations des sociétés qu'ils engendrent, ils visitent les mutations sociales, fouillent dans le passé précolonial et colonial pour peindre une humanité vraiment humaine. Et c'est dans cette perspective que nous pouvons lire et comprendre des textes classiques comme *Le monde s'effondre* de Chinua Achebe. Publié en effet pour la première fois en 1958 sous le titre *Things Fall Apart*, ce récit est un texte majeur de la littérature africaine et le premier titre d'un cycle de trois romans qu'écrit Achebe entre 1958 et 1964.

La force de ce roman réside dans la description très poussée qu'il fait des fondements structurels de la communauté des Igbos. Thématisant la colonisation et son rôle dévastateur au Nigéria, ce livre revisite la tradition et la modernité pour nous renseigner sur une société nigériane en pleine mutation. Témoignant sur la vie des populations avant et après la colonisation occidentale, ce livre retrace le projet colonialiste, la mission civilisatrice de l'homme blanc et les mutations qu'elle engendra, tout en se focalisant sur la perspective du dedans. Issu effectivement de la tribu des Igbos, le personnage principal Okonkwo incarne les valeurs qui lui ont été inculquées par la société qui l'engendre. Les croyances, les rites initiatiques, les cérémonies funéraires, nuptiales, liées à la production agricole ou à la justice, les valeurs collectives, les relations avec les autres communautés, les sacrifices humains sont racontés dans ce texte par un langage simple et accessible. À la manière d'une description sociologique et psycho-sociale, le narrateur, dans un discours pudique, explique comment le social détermine le sujet. Dès lors, la critique de la colonisation n'empêche pas l'auteur d'évoquer les limites et les servitudes de la société traditionnelle africaine, à travers notamment des personnages du texte.

En effet, le destin d'Okonkwo est intimement lié à celui de son peuple. Fils d'une tradition et héritier d'un destin tragique, il incarne la transition de deux réalités qui n'ont pas survécu au choc de la rencontre. En somme, une société dans ses réalités les plus justes et dans ses transformations les plus palpables. En outre, si la rencontre – avec l'occident dans ce livre – est teintée d'une certaine violence et d'exploitation sans précédent, nous acceptons aussi que ces mêmes problèmes influent aujourd'hui encore sur la relation de ces deux continents.

Ce qui nous amène à retenir que cette littérature est le lieu de jonction où les cultures se traduisent et se rencontrent. Elle est aussi le lieu d'un essai de réconciliation avec le passé. Ainsi, c'est dans ce projet de réconciliation qu'Alioune Diop retient dans son texte éditorial aux actes du 1er Congrès des Écrivains et Artistes Noirs, « Nos taches » :

> Hommes de culture du monde noir, nos tâches sont nombreuses et exaltantes. Les assumer en toute lucidité et passionnément, c'est exercer dès maintenant notre part de responsabilité dans la gestion du monde – et préparer une renaissance culturelle qui réponde aux douloureuses et profondes aspirations des peuples vers la paix. Et c'est enrichir les ressources de résistance à la dictature – ce vrai mal des peuples – que l'Occident n'était guère préparé à vaincre, puisqu'il vivait d'exercer sa dictature sur les autres peuples (Diop 1957, 6).

Conscient alors de leur rôle déterminant pour une nécessaire renaissance de l'humanité, les Écrivains et Artistes Noirs tentèrent par la culture et les réalités noires de réparer le monde. Le réparer face à un Occident qui n'avait plus rien à servir ou à proposer au monde. Ainsi, pensant cette réparation entre les cultures et les traditions du monde, étant le fruit des rencontres culturelles et transversant par leurs histoires des mondes différents, les actrices et acteurs du monde Noir proposèrent, depuis au moins après la Seconde Guerre Mondiale, par une production intellectuelle et artistique des issues pour un monde à venir. C'est certainement ce qui fait affirmer à Abbé Meinrad Hegba que :

> Il y a plus : un vieux sage nègre ou indien analphabète mais orné de la culture ancestrale est plus humaniste dans sa sphère qu'un jeune bachelier farci de notions et de formules. Le devoir des *Noirs*[1] est avant tout un devoir de prise de conscience : ils doivent découvrir la richesse de leur culture et apprendre à la savourer. Les civilisations raffinées et admirables de l'Occident seront un exemple mais non un idéal. – Si tu ne saisis pas le fondement métaphysique de la relation pluri-univoque mais très bien au contraire le lieu de filiation qui te rattache à ton père ; si tu ne crois voir que jeux d'imagination dans les symboles algébriques des quantités

---

[1] J'ai remplacé ici le terme « Primitifs » par Noirs avec un N majuscule. Ce terme « Primitif » péjoratif et discriminatoire a marqué l'histoire des peuples Noirs et créé des catégories. Car même s'il est utilisé dans les sciences sociale et qualifie ce qui est relatif aux humains qui ignorent la civilisation et n'ont subi aucune influence technologique, nous acceptons aussi que ce concept participa, pendant des siècles, au processus de deshumanisation de l'homme hors du territoire occidentale.

imaginaire et qu'au contraire tu comprennes que deux piquets qui se recouvrent sont égaux ; si l'éclat de rire est pour toi l'expression de l'administration, ne te ratatine pas, ne te comprime pas, dresse-toi et clame la culture ancestrale à ébranler les assises de la terre (Hegba 1957, 306).

Ce que propose ici Meinrad Hegba transcende la création artistique et traduit les rôles que les intellectuelles africaines et de la diaspora se sont assignés dans leur manière d'appréhender et de faire monde. Filles et fils de différentes civilisations, elles/ils pensent le monde dans ses différences et contradictions. Il faut toutefois retenir ici que la contradiction n'est pas pensée comme source de choc de civilisation, mais comme un moment et un lieu de complémentarité et d'enrichissement. Investissant dès sa naissance les intersites de mémoire, la production intellectuelle et artistique du monde *Noir* travaille dans une perspective décoloniale à la réparation du corps/tissu *Noir*. Elle est ainsi dans ses approches à la recherche de la globalité de l'Être, de la conservation des mémoires, de la documentation et du questionnement du temps et de l'espace dans le but de faire société. C'est certainement ce qui fait écrire à Cheikh Anta Diop dans son texte emblématique « Nations Nègres et Cultures » que : « L'art africain a [. . .] toujours été au service d'une cause sociale comme il doit le rester » (Diop 2003, 519). Pensant en effet l'Homme Noir comme le début de toute civilisation humaine, Cheikh Anta Diop milita pour la vérité historique et la réhabilitation de celle-ci. Cette réhabilitation qui est synonyme de recherches de filiation, de traces et de conservation de mémoire plurielle fonde la création du monde *Noir*. Elle permet aussi d'apercevoir l'envers du décor comme le reconnaît Yacouba Konaté en se référant à l'Art Africain Contemporain et à la Biennale de Dak'Art sur ces termes : « Dak'Art a initié le processus par lequel le vaincu ou la vaincue entreprend de raconter, de réécrire ou de reproduire l'histoire du point de vue du perdant ou de la perdante, puis de se faire une idée de l'autorité et du caractère du vainqueur » (Konaté 2010, 108). Reprenant delà l'envers de la formule de Chinua Achebe,[2] Konaté persiste sur la nécessité d'énoncer, par la participation à une humanité nouvelle, d'autres narrations sur la vie, son passé et son avenir. Cette participation qui est traduite par ses thématiques et approches, par ses formes et fonds dans un discours afrocentriste en opposition à celui eurocentriste, semble être le complément d'énonciation sur la vie et les hommes. Ce qui fait remarquer à Léopold Sédar Senghor en définissant l'Être et l'existant en ces termes :

---

[2] Cette citation attribuée à Chinua Achebe et reprit par des intellectuelles ou intellectuels du Continent africain et de sa diaspora : « *Until the lion learns how to write, every story will glorify the hunter* » reconsidère le rôle des vaincues ou vaincus dans les discours qu'elles/ils posent sur leurs réalités. C'est aussi ce que Chimamanda Adichie actualise dans ce qu'elle appelle « The Danger of a Single Story » dans son TED-Talk devenu viral. L'histoire est pensée ici dans sa faculté de rendre à l'humain sa dignité. C'est-à-dire que l'essentiel du discours sur la vie repose sur la singularité de la subjectivité de leur approche.

Ils reposent sur cette vérité que tout étant ou existant, que tout être est multivalent, composé qu'il est de plusieurs éléments d'énergie, de plusieurs « âmes », dont l'ensemble peut subir des variations d'origine physique ou morale, matérielle ou spirituelle. Variations qui se font selon la loi de *participation* (Senghor 1972, 31–2).

Cette participation, qui s'est aussi exprimée dans ce que Senghor appela le rendez-vous du donner et du recevoir, pense le monde par l'échange et la transmission. Une transmission qui conçoit la participation comme un tout nécessaire dans un vivre ensemble dans la différence.

Fondant ainsi le lien de base de tout processus de conservation des mémoires, des cultures et des traditions, les connaissances et les pratiques artistiques africaines participatives veulent être alors des creusets afin d'accéder à la globalité des êtres et des choses d'un monde en devenir. Ce monde à venir ne peut par conséquent être le résultat d'une expérience temps, mais plutôt un projet de prise de conscience et de questionnement dans le but d'engendrer et de saisir le monde dans sa globalité la plus totale. Fatou Diome retient dans ce sens que : « La mémoire est un faucon qui nous emporte dans ses serres, survoler des contrées lointaines. Rien de ce qui a été n'est perdu, tant qu'il y aura des livres pour consigner la vie » (Diome 2021, 219). C'est ce que Dominic Thomas comprend quand il cite Henry Louis Gates en affirmant :

> Les écrivains noirs [. . .] apprennent à écrire en lisant de la littérature, surtout les textes canoniques de tradition occidentale. En conséquence, les textes noirs ressemblent à d'autres textes occidentaux. [. . .] Mais la répétition formelle noire se répète toujours avec une différence, une différence noire qui se manifeste dans une utilisation spécifique de la langue (Thomas 2013, 107 ; citant Gates, 1988, XXII–III).

Si la langue est toutefois une des caractéristiques les plus spécifiques de cette littérature, nous acceptons aussi qu'elle est le lieu par excellence de conservation de la mémoire et le milieu où les héritages pluriels et polyphones s'enrichissent, s'entrechoquent et se régénèrent. C'est-à-dire qu'en saisissant les traces et *les débris de cultures assassinées*[3] dans les sociétés africaines et afro-diasporiques, les penseurs essaient de sauvegarder les civilisations plurielles issues du continent. En les sauvegardant, ils les réactualisent et les confrontent à d'autres réalités issues d'autres sociétés en particulier et d'autres continents en général. Ce qui nous fait retenir que les pensées africaines et afro-diasporiques furent dès leurs naissances des réflexions sur soi et sur l'entre-soi. Ils sont en ce sens des œuvres inter- et transculturelles. Ils ne disent de ce fait ce qui est, mais ce qui devait être et

---

[3] Terme emprunté à Aimé Césaire. Il l'utilise dans son texte publié en 1955 chez Présence Africaine : *Discours sur le Colonialisme*.

c'est ce qui nous mène à accepter qu'ils essaient – par le texte et à la parole et dans une perspective inclusive – à soigner l'humain et l'humanité.

L'aventure ambiguë de Cheikh Hamidou Kane (1961) en est une des plus parfaites illustrations. Naviguant entre tradition et modernité, entre passé et présent, ce chef-d'œuvre transcende l'Afrique et l'Occident pour puiser dans l'essence humaine. Ce livre qui engendre des lectures plurielles est une évocation à la quête de soi. Une quête de soi qui, tout en puisant dans la tradition africaine musulmane, questionne par une lecture exhaustive la philosophie pascalienne, pour aboutir non seulement à une symbiose des connaissances et des réalités, mais plus encore à l'équilibre, à l'éclatement et aux contradictions des souffles du monde. Glissant le résume ainsi dans sa philosophie de la relation :

> Quand on remonte ainsi dans le Continent, on se rapproche par paradoxe des Îles de la Caraïbe, qui sont plus présentes au Canada ou au Québec (cet infini tourbillonnant) que dans la Louisiane, laquelle est pourtant si antillaise d'histoire et de nature : le peuplement africain, le système des Plantations, l'arrière-plan des langues créoles, l'architecture, la cuisine. Les gens du sud des États-Unis ne savent pas qu'ils participent de cette zone de cultures où le jazz a rencontré le reggae, où les mythes animaliers indiens entrent dans les dictons cajuns et les contes créoles, où le golfe du Mexique et la mer Caraïbe éclatent au Continent. Les Québécois guignent vers ces chaleurs-là (Glissant 1993, 464–5).

Ce qui nous fait témoigner que les civilisations africaines et Afro-diasporiques, dont la littérature est une partie intégrante, ne peuvent pas être considérées comme une expérience du temps mais comme un ensemble de travers de connaissance et de relation. Et à Mbembe et Sarr (2017, 8) de retenir qu'« En cherchant en ce début de siècle à restaurer la parenté d'identité entre l'Afrique et le monde, ce sont les diverses manières possibles d'être du monde, d'être monde, de faire monde qu'il s'agit d'exposer ».

Nous retenons alors que la littérature africaine est un lieu de transmission, de traduction et de questionnement de la cause Noire. Les traces de mémoire qui s'y révèlent, comme chez Glissant ou Kane, sont par conséquent une manière de fixer et de transmettre une existence, une expérience humaine ; ils sont le lieu de réparer le discours sur le monde et les sujets du monde. Ce qui nous amène à dire que les discours, les pensées et les expressions artistiques qui découlent en général de la civilisation africaine sont le fruit d'une prise de conscience d'être, le lieu de réparation de l'humain et une manière de rendre accessible l'univers humain à la communauté mondiale.

Ainsi des textes comme *Le monde s'effondre* de Chinua Achebe, *La soif* d'Assia Djebar, *Harrouda* de Tahar Ben Jelloun ou encore *Le baobab fou* de Ken Bugul, pour ne citer que ces derniers, nous renseignent au-delà de la subjectivité des auteurs et des protagonistes sur la préoccupation des peuples, sur les réalités sociales ; mais surtout ils nous montrent leur part d'humanité pour le devenir du monde. En effet, la soif de liberté, la marginalisation et l'oppression sont au centre des textes de Assia Djebar et Bugul. Achebe, quant à lui, pose un regard critique sur la colonisation. Si les histoires individuelles, telles que traitées dans les textes, nous plongent dans l'intérieur des personnages et de leur environnement, elles nous informent, en outre, sur des expériences plurielles, ou pour le dire avec Césaire (2004, 82) : « C'est une manière de vivre l'histoire dans l'histoire : l'histoire d'une communauté dont l'expérience apparaît, à vrai dire, singulière avec ses déportations de populations, [. . .] les souvenirs de croyances lointaines, ses débris de cultures assassinées. »

Ce qui nous amène à retenir aussi que si l'acte de créer émane de la sensibilité et de la responsabilité de l'auteur, nous acceptons aussi que malgré les expériences partagées, les auteurs africains et de la diaspora africaine expriment par leur « Être » leurs identités pour participer, comme le dira Senghor, à la symphonie du monde. Conscients toutefois de l'impératif de devoir combler le vide qui a été théorisé par l'Occident, ils apportent dans ce qu'ils portent des valeurs « enfouis dans la mémoire collective [des] peuples et même dans l'inconscient collectif » (Césaire 2004, 83). Ainsi, en tournant – avant tout par la poésie, l'art et la théorie – la page du colonialisme, ils et elles n'ont non seulement « contribué à inaugurer une ère nouvelle pour l'humanité tout entière » (Césaire 2004, 87), mais plus encore à redresser par de nouvelles connaissances la marche du monde. Dès lors, la parole dite et écrite dans des langues aussi diverses que le Peuhl (tel que les textes d'Amadou Hampathé Ba, de Djibril Tamsir Niane ou de Cheikh Hamidou Kane), le Bambara (tel que ceux d'Ahmadou Kourouma), le Swahili (d'Alexis Kagamé), le Wolof (d'Aminata Sow Fall ou de Boubacar Boris Diop) ou le Lingala (tel que le dernier livre de Richard Ali A Mutu) deviennent une partie intégrante de nos civilisations. Par la singularité, elle exprime une humanité et une universalité qui sont les nôtres. Elle traduit et transpose des réalités culturelles, politiques et sociales qui s'affirment tout en réclamant une reconnaissance, d'où le texte *Ishindenshin : De mon âme à ton âme* de Felwine Sarr. En outre, c'est dans cette quête d'une humanité nouvelle et à venir que les intellectuelles africaines et de la diaspora articulent par des productions théoriques et artistiques des trajectoires de vies et redéfinissent les relations des *noires* avec le reste de la planète. Il s'agit dans ce sens de prendre sa place et d'être en symbiose avec soi. Héritières de cultures et de réalités différentes, portant en eux des civilisations différentes, ces dernières articulent dans leurs discours le dialogue des civilisations. Accumulant en eux les traumatismes des siècles précédents, victimes de préjugés, du déni de soi et d'exister, les penseuses d'ascendance noire ont la « capacité d'ériger un monde en *dépit de* l'autre, celui qui domine » (Miano 2020, 217), et c'est ce qui fait la grandeur de leurs pensées. Elles renforcent – malgré l'histoire tragique endiguée – « le groupe humain dont [elles] font partie » (Miano 2020, 217). D'où la faculté réparatrice de leur texte.

Références

Césaire, Aimé. *Discours sur le Colonialisme*. Paris : Présence Africaine, 1955.
Diome, Fatou. *De quoi aimer vivre*. Paris : Albin Michel, 2021.
Diop, Alioune. « Nos tâches. » *Contributions au 1er Congrès des Écrivains et Artistes Noirs* (Juin–September 1957) : 3–7.
Diop, Cheikh-Anta. *Nations Nègres et Cultures. De l'antiquité nègre égyptienne aux problémes culturels de l'Afrique Noire d'aujourd'hui*. Paris : Pésence Africaine, 2003.
Fanon, Frantz. *Oeuvres. Peau Noire, masques blancs, L'an V de la révolution Algérienne, Les damnés de la terre, Pour une révolution algérienne*. Paris : La découverte, 2017.
Gates, Henry Louis. *The Signifying Monkey. A Theory of African-American Literary Criticism*. Oxford et New York : Oxford University Press, 1988.
Gilroy, Paul. *L'Atlantique noire : Modernité et double conscience*. Amsterdam : Éditions Amsterdam, 1993.
Glissant, Édouard. *Tout-Monde*. Paris : Éditions Gallimard, 1993.
Hebga, Abbé Meinrad. « Une seule Pensée, une seule Civilisation. » *Contributions au 1er Congrès des Écrivains et Artistes Noirs* (Juin–September 1957) : 302–311.
Konaté, Yacouba. « The Invention of the Dakar Biennal. » *The Biennal Reader* (2018) : 107–16.
Mbembe, Achille. « Oeuvre d'art africain : restitution et réparation sont indissociables. » *Jeune Afrique* (13.03.2018). https://www.jeuneafrique.com/mag/540940/culture/oeuvres-dart-africain-restitution-et-reparation-sont-indissociables/ (20 septembre 2021).
Mbembe, Achille et Felwine Sarr. Éds. *Écrire l'Afrique-Monde*. Dakar : Philippe Rey, 2017.
Miano, Léonora. *Afropea : Utopie post-occidentale et post-raciste*. Paris : Grasset & Fasquelle, 2020.
Mouralis, Bernard. *L'Europe, l'Afrique et la folie*. Paris : Pésence Africaine, 1993.
Senghor, Léopold Sédar. *Pour une idéologie négro-africaine*. Paris : Présence Africaine, 1972.
Thomas, Dominic. *Noirs d'encre. Colonialisme, immigration et identité au coeur de la littérature afro-francaise*. Paris : La découverte, 2013.

Alexandre Gefen
La réparation au prisme des débats sur l'universel

Résumé : Les définitions de la littérature comme art de la forme et usage esthétique du langage ont été critiquées à l'heure de la mondialisation de la littérature car jugées abstraites et liées à un universel uniquement occidental. On se demandera si la notion de réparation, qui semble pouvoir caractériser les littératures situées et engagées dans des formes d'action impliquant communautés et identités, peut constituer une approche alternative du fait littéraire dans sa variété.

Mots-clés : réparation ; vulnérabilité ; littérature mondiale ; *Weltliteratur* ; universalisme

Concept attrape-tout dans nos sociétés fragiles, la réparation est devenue une des manières de définir le pouvoir d'action de l'art et en particulier de la littérature. Après avoir cherché à définir la littérature comme un usage particulier et dérogatoire de la langue, nos approches contemporaines nous rendent sensible à cette capacité du récit ou de la poésie à offrir aide, accompagnement au point d'en faire une des propriétés intrinsèques de la littérature. Mais la notion de réparation est-elle pour autant univoque et peut-elle s'universaliser comme une définition de la littérature ? Le débat est d'importance, tant la réflexion sur la littérature est centrale dans les débats contemporains sur l'universalisme.

« La littérature est une, comme l'art et l'humanité sont une » affirmait en 1949, avec un universalisme triomphant, la théorie littéraire de René Wellek et Austin Warren (1962, 42) en explicitant une idée qui s'est imposée depuis le début du XIXe siècle : la littérature est un universel lui-même au service de l'universel. Si cette conception s'impose au début du XIXe siècle, de la révolution kantienne faisant du jugement esthétique un universel « sans concept » au projet d'une *Weltliteratur* formulée par Goethe en 1827, elle est au cœur des débats contemporains pour lesquels le mot littérature reste tributaire d'une conception occidentale écrasant des pratiques variées. Dès 1955, l'immense *Histoire des littératures* dirigée par Raymond Queneau (1955–1958) adopte le pluriel, suivie en 1992 par le non moins gigantesque *Dictionnaire des littératures françaises et étrangères* de Jacques Demougin. Si *The Biography of 'The Idea of Literature'* du grand historien roumain Adrian Marino réaffirme encore l'unité en 1996 de la littérature occidentale depuis l'Antiquité, la conséquence la plus spectaculaire de cette prise de distance historienne et relativiste des années 1980 a été d'interroger la pertinence même du mot de littérature dont l'unicité est récusée. Soit des alternatives sont proposées (« le littéraire » pour Paul Aron et Alain Viala, le pluriel « les littératures » ou encore « l'écriture » d'après Derrida), soit la portée du mot est réduite au champ historique qui est le sien (Aron et al. 2002). Le passage à une échelle historique et géographique globale a conduit à interroger rétrospectivement l'unité du concept de littérature : à l'intérieur même du monde occidental, son application au monde antique a pu être dénoncée par exemple par Florence Dupont dans *L'invention de la littérature* (1998) et son extension à la hauteur du « monde », concept lui-même problématique, a été par exemple critiquée par Emily Apter dans *Against World Literature* (2013).

Les affirmations unitaires tendent à négliger la diversité des langues et des contextes des acteurs comme le fait remarquer Denis Hollier (1994, XXIV), par exemple. Ni Virgile, ni Shakespeare, ni Cao Xueqin, l'auteur chinois du *Rêve dans le pavillon rouge*, ne disposent du mot littérature ou du moins d'un équivalent exact, et l'action qui consiste à réunir des textes aussi éloignés que la « littérature » assyro-babylonienne, les poèmes des troubadours et les fanfictions sur Wattpad pour les aligner sur le programme *littéraire* des *Fleurs du mal* de Baudelaire n'est pas un geste évident ; ses effets de distorsion ne sauraient être sous-estimés. Assurément, la conception universelle unifiée de la littérature a été émise à partir d'une définition esthétique de celle-ci : qu'il s'agisse de la définir comme un écart à la langue ordinaire, une forme de réflexivité du langage ou encore l'usage d'une fonction poétique spécifique du langage, ces définitions sont incontestablement ancrées dans une tradition philosophique européenne née à Paris, à Londres ou à Weimar. Ces conceptions se sont accompagnées d'une pensée nationale de la littérature, entée sur les langues et cultures européennes, saisies elle-même de manière restrictive dans un idéal monolingue. Dans sa préface à son *Histoire de la littérature française* de 1894 Gustave Lanson n'affirmait-il pas « éliminer l'histoire de la littérature de langue d'*oc* » autant que « l'histoire de la littérature celtique » (Lanson 1894, XII) ? Bref, de la même manière que les définitions de l'universel peuvent être critiquées par les approches qui leur reprochent d'être instrumentales au colonialisme, les ambitions hégémoniques des définitions occidentales de la littérature ont été soumises, d'Edward Saïd à Gayatri Chakravorty Spivak, aux critiques que les épistémologies occidentales et non occidentales ont adressées à cet universel lorsqu'il s'est assimilé à la langue du dominant.

Que ce lien supposé entre littérature et universel soit crucial, on en trouvera inversement preuve dans la manière dont la littérature a été prise à témoin lors des attaques subies par les courants critiques de la recherche et de l'université, des études de genre aux approches postcoloniales. Qu'il s'agisse de réfuter le droit à l'examen critique des conditions de traduction et de mise en scène, de s'interroger sur la responsabilité personnelle des écrivains ou collective des représentations, de disqualifier les écritures politiques ou féministes engagées, ou de s'inquiéter du singularisme et du différentialisme portés par les écritures contemporaines, une conception univoque, abstraite et absolutisée de littérature – supposément celle des Lumières, mais en réalité née avec le nationalisme scolaire du XIXe siècle – est avancée par les défenseurs autoproclamés de l'universalisme « républicain » à la française. Ainsi, Isabelle Barbéris, porte-parole des idées de l'*Observatoire du décolonialisme*, mouvement défenseur des formes traditionnelles de l'universalisme laïque français en matière de culture et opposé à ce titre à la critique postcoloniale, s'en ainsi prend dans *L'Art du politiquement correct* à la « privatisation de la représentation », aux « logiques séparatistes » de l'art contemporain comme à ses ambitions politiques qui ne conduiraient qu'à « parodier » l'exercice de la démocratie. Rapprochant la quête de « diversité » de pratiques « tribales », l'essayiste regrette la disparition de « l'ancienne autorité de l'œuvre d'art » et de « communautés interprétatives communes » (Barbéris 2019) au nom de la démocratisation culturelle. Bergère de l'universel, la littérature devrait rester pure des débats et des intérêts des communautés humaines et se tenir dans une description à distance du monde, en alignant si possible la version du neutre qu'elle porterait sur les intérêts du mâle blanc européen. L'artiste, sacralisé par son rapport aristocratique à l'absolu, serait déclaré irresponsable. La mondialisation par la traduction, processus supposé transparent et lui aussi pur de tout enjeu politique, devrait permettre l'alignement des sensibilités sur des idéaux politiques et éthiques représentés si possible par la littérature et la langue française, dominante sur l'Europe et le monde : voilà la théorie littéraire de ceux qui critiquent aujourd'hui les études culturelles issues des USA, raillent la demande de justice des écrivaines et écrivains, dénoncent le tournant éthique de la critique, accusent en substance les études francophones ou les analyses de lectures intersectionnelles de servir l'islamisme. Les mêmes défendent l'immunité des artistes à tout prix et moquent le narcissisme supposé des uns comme les préoccupations écologiques des autres, renvoyant dos à dos les interrogations identitaires et les questionnements politiques, puis finalement condamnent aussi bien les écritures documentaires que les pratiques de performances, que l'on suive par exemple *L'Enfer du roman : réflexions sur la postlittérature* de Richard Millet en 2010 ou *L'Après littérature* d'Alain Finkielkraut en 2021.

Le risque de telles conceptions, patrimoniales si ce n'est conservatrices de la littérature, est la neutralisation du pouvoir d'interpellation et d'action de la culture, l'aseptisation de la force de transformation de la lecture et de l'écriture. Vouloir toujours dissocier le beau du vrai et du bon, déresponsabiliser les écrivains, les expulser hors de la cité réelle, revient à les désarmer. On peut moquer les *sensitivity readers*, mais se refuser à tirer les conséquences de la lecture et à prendre acte du pouvoir de la fiction, n'est-ce pas désespérer de la culture, de son pouvoir d'énonciation, de transformation ? L'innocuité politique de la littérature et de sa critique, sa dilution dans un universel qui ne serait pas incarné par des voix multiples et concernées, son arraisonnement par l'abstraction, esthétique ou académique, son désengagement des problèmes du contemporain, c'est sa disparition. La France, qui au temps de sa gloire a su exporter sa théorie littéraire formaliste, est aussi l'inventrice de la *French Theory*, critique dont sont issues largement les études culturelles critiques, même si paradoxalement, comme l'a montré François Cusset (2005), elle n'en a jamais tiré profit pour elle-même. Alors que les études littéraires et les formations françaises méprisent parfois les littératures francophones et les littératures non occidentales, celles-ci rayonnent partout ailleurs. Alors que les *cultural studies* les plus variées vont souligner le rôle que la littérature peut jouer pour comprendre la diversité des manières d'habiter les corps et les sexualités, les formes variées de migration et de créolisation, les rapports au vivant et à l'environnement, ou pour illustrer la variété des imaginaires vulnérables en offrant des représentations aux oubliés de la mimésis, une partie de la critique préfère résister aux formes contemporaines concrètes et situées d'*empowerment* par la culture pour défendre un idéal d'universalité abstrait.

En proposant de redéfinir la littérature non par des propriétés du langage littéraire (son ironie, sa réflexivité) ou de l'intention de l'auteur (le désintéressement), mais par les effets de réparation et d'intervention produits par des formes pouvant être aussi différentes que des pièces de théâtre à finalité cathartique, des romans à thèse politiques, des récits de reconstruction ou encore de la poésie thérapeutique, l'idée de réparation peut-elle devenir un dénominateur commun aux littératures du monde et décrire un processus universel sans tomber dans les biais de l'universalisme kantien ? Dans la mesure où la réparation décrit un processus psychologique et participe d'une approche anthropologique de la littérature comme fait culturel, serait-il plus à même à unifier des formes culturelles d'expression extraordinairement variées que l'idée occidentale de la littérature, construction historique datée du début du XIXe et décrivant au contraire la littérature comme désintéressée et intransitive, volontiers nichée dans la tour d'ivoire pour faire face au ciel des idées, ne parvient pas à saisir ? Le concept de réparation a été bien accueilli par les études postcoloniales sensibles à la manière dont le colonialisme a corrodé le tissu relationnel des sociétés traditionnelles qu'il détruisait et à la façon dont les écrivains ont inversement cherché à retisser ces liens par la forme d'attention, d'attribution d'agentivité et de parole permise par la fiction littéraire et la poésie – dans un sens très fort, la réparation n'est-elle pas l'autre nom des processus d'indemnisation et de restitution revendiqués par les sociétés anciennement colonisées ? Dans le champ culturel occidental, la réparation a été aussi associée aux désirs des écrivains de restituer du sens et de la visibilité aux formes de vie minorisées et détruites par les sociétés modernes, l'arraisonnement du monde par l'argent étant un processus de séparation destructeur des sociétés et de la relation à la nature. Contre le principe libéral d'autonomie, la littérature serait une énonciation relationnelle, accompagnée de socialités relationnelles (festivals, ateliers d'écriture, clubs de lecture, etc.) promouvant des formes sociales de réparation (partage du sensible, création de communautés, etc.).

La notion n'est pourtant pas indemne de critiques. Si elle est issue de la mystique juive d'Isaac Louria, la « réparation du monde » (*tikkoun olam* en hébreu, voir Scholem 1974), elle s'est développée dans le contexte libéral anglo-saxon dont elle a en quelque sorte constitué un contrepoison : c'est face aux maux du capitalisme néo-libéral qu'elle a trouvé ses principales ressources d'action, comme j'ai essayé de la démontrer dans mon essai *Réparer le monde. La littérature française face au XXIe siècle* (2017) – pensons simplement aux romans se proposant de produire du bien (*feel good novels*) ou une forme de développement personnel : ce qu'il s'agit d'abord de réparer, c'est la solitude de l'individu dans le monde contemporain à une heure où l'action collective n'est plus de mise. Faire de la littérature un instrument de résilience est donc profondément lié à l'histoire culturelle occidentale : son extension à toute les formes d'intervention psychique sur l'individu ou la communauté (fonction cathartique, apotropaïque, etc.) imposerait de redéfinir la réparation comme l'hyper synonyme des fonctions thérapeutiques des formes symboliques et des rites et donc de perdre son sens spécifique.

Il n'est donc pas anodin que si les résistances à une pensée de la littérature comme action réparatrice peuvent émaner d'une nostalgie aristocratique d'un écrivain ayant les moyens de se situer au-dessus des querelles du monde et de se consacrer, dans une conception sacralisée, à un rituel de production d'une vérité supérieur nommé littérature, on peut objecter que la réparation est l'opposé de la transformation, de la révolution. La réparation vise potentiellement la restitution du passé, et justiciable d'une critique de son conservatisme. La réparation ne rompt pas avec les dominations, elle accepte l'imperfection d'un monde créé par un dieu faible dans son origine mystique ; elle ne le rejette pas. La radicalité critique de la littérature s'émousse clairement à devenir réparatrice et se pense plus aisément comme dévoilement, colère ou scandale. Le geste de rupture propre à l'autonomie esthétique n'est pas sans vertu faut-il donc répéter : il permet de constituer tout objet ou toute personne comme digne d'intérêt, geste que Jacques Rancière nomme une « indifférence générique » (Rancière 1998, 26) : ce n'est plus l'objet représenté qui le qualifie comme littéraire, mais l'attention formelle accordée à la représentation, projet d'autonomie qui conserve sa part révolutionnaire, tout comme l'idée que la littérature puisse se penser comme un geste de résistance aux formes variées de comparution d'une société donnée.

Assurément, notre conception contemporaine de la littérature doit incorporer la littérature comme fin et comme moyen, la littérature comme intervention dans le monde et comme émancipation des contraintes politiques et morales imposées par la société, comme réponse au monde réel et comme rêve d'un autre monde, comme réparation et comme révolution. Telle est la condition pour accueillir sous une même « ressemblance de famille » les hagiographies médiévales comme les récits graphiques d'Art Spiegelman, les récits amateurs des *rantbooks* sur Wattpad comme les *Notes de chevet* de Sei Shōnagon, les romans-feuilletons de l'époque de Balzac comme les garas sardes, le matrimoine comme la littérature hors du livre, le journalisme narratif comme le roman hypertexte, les *Chants de Chu* chinois de l'époque Han comme l'épopée créée par George R. R. Martin, le slam de Grand Corps Malade comme les tragédies élisabéthaines, les *Soundiata Keïta* du Mali comme les tweets d'Aimee Nezhukumatathil, les récits akkadiens de Gilgamesh comme les performances de Wendy Delorme. Plutôt que de penser un idéal littéraire univoque qui serait un universel, on gagne à faire des littératures des voies d'accès à la variété humaine. Même si la notion reste tributaire de l'occident moderne qui l'a imaginé comme contre-pouvoir, faire de la capacité de réparation une propriété fondamentale de la littérature pensée comme le moyen de réalisations différenciées et locales est une manière intéressante de résister à un universalisme faisant de la littérature une catégorie abstraite pensée à partir de ses modèles occidentaux.

Invoquer le concept de réparation participe d'une réflexion visant à vider la littérature de son essentialité et de la repenser à la lumière de l'anthropologie culturelle, des *performance studies*, de l'histoire ou de la sociologie comme de disciplines qui, telles les sciences cognitives, proposent de donner à l'acte de raconter, de versifier ou d'écrire, des formes originales de naturalité. Aujourd'hui, préserver une part d'universel dans le geste esthétique, réparer l'universel si l'on veut, c'est prendre acte de la richesse et de l'ampleur des débats existentiels, moraux et idéologiques dans laquelle viennent désormais s'impliquer critiques et écrivains, plutôt que leur imposer un illusoire désintéressement et de jouer l'universel contre les identités.

Références

Apter, Emily. *Against World Literature. On the Politics of Untranslatability*. London & New York : Verso, 2013.
Aron, Paul, Denis Saint-Jacques et Alain Viala. Éds. *Le dictionnaire du littéraire*. Paris : Presses Universitaires de France, 2002.
Barbéris, Isabelle. *L'art du politiquement correct*. Paris : Presses Universitaires de France, 2019.
Cusset, François. *French Theory. Foucault, Derrida, Deleuze & Cie et les mutations de la vie intellectuelle aux États-Unis*. Paris : La Découverte, 2005.

Demougin, Jacques. *Dictionnaire des littératures française et étrangères*. Vol. II. Paris : Larousse, 1992.
Dupont, Florence. *L'invention de la littérature*. Paris : La découverte, 1998.
Finkielkraut, Alain. *L'après littérature*. Paris : Stock, 2021.
Gefen, Alexandre. *Réparer le monde. La littérature française face au XXIe siècle*. Paris : Corti, 2017.
Hollier, Denis. « On Writing Literary History ». *A New History of French Literature*. Éd. Denis Hollier. Cambridge/London : Harvard University Press, 1994, xxi–xxv.
Lanson, Gustave. *Histoire de la littérature française*. Paris : Hachette, 1894.
Marino, Adrian. *The Biography of 'The Idea of Literature.' From the Antiquity to the Baroque*. Trad. Virgil Stanciu et Charles M. Carlton. Albany, New York : Suny Press, 1996.
Millet, Richard. *L'Enfer du roman : réflexions sur la postlittérature*. Paris : Gallimard, 2010.
Queneau, Raymond. Éd. *Histoire des littératures*. Encyclopédie de la Pléiade. Vol. III. Paris : Gallimard, 1955–1958.
Rancière, Jacques. *La Parole muette : essai sur les contradictions de la littérature*. Paris : Hachette, 1998.
Scholem, Gershom. *La kabbale*. Paris : Gallimard, 1974.
Wellek, René et Austin Warren. *Theory of literature*. New York : Harcourt, Brace & World, 1962.

Ibrahima Sene
Forms and Obstacles of Reparation in Bernhard Jaumann's *Der lange Schatten*

Abstract: A revival of debates on colonialism and its legacies has been observed for decades, both in the former colonies and in the former metropolises, which are increasingly dealing with their own colonial heritage. Beyond political and academic discourse, fiction as a social discourse also responds to and sometimes influences these public debates, as it is the case for the novel *Der lange Schatten* [*The Long Shadow*] (2015) by Bernard Jaumann. The material of this crime novel embodies memories of the restitution ceremony held at Berlin Charité in 2011 and of the shared colonial history between Namibia and Germany. This chapter therefore analyses questions of reparation dealt with in Jaumann's book and the mechanisms of legitimisation or instrumentalisation of historical narratives. Accordingly, the thesis put forward here is that this novel addresses the lack of cohesion between the Namibian government and the Herero and Nama people in contemporary Namibia as an obstacle to the recognition of genocide and thus to reparations.

Keywords: Reparation, restitution, fiction, Berlin Charité, historical narrative, colonialism, Germany, Namibia, *Der lange Schatten*, Bernhard Jaumann, Herero, Nama

1 Introduction

"Reparation has become increasingly important in national and international politics. In international politics reparation claims for historic wrongs such as slavery and colonialism are now prominent issues" (Rombouts 2004, 2). This observation by the legal and social scientist Heidy Rombouts, who in his study *Victim Organisations and the Politics of Reparation* (2004) dealt with the legal framework of a reparation policy for past injustice and atrocities at the example of Rwanda, holds true for social and political debates on the (colonial) past more generally. The focus of this debate regarding reparation claims as a struggle for justice, which has long been conducted in the former colonies, underlines the indispensability and significance of reparation and, furthermore, restitution of looted cultural assets (Sandkühler 2008, 26–27; Howard-Hassmann 2008, 2–3). Finding the right approach in this regard seems to be the challenge we're facing today. Therefore, the implementation of reparation and restitution policy is a central point of reference in current

ə Open Access. © 2023 the author(s), published by De Gruyter. [CC BY-NC-ND] This work is licensed under the Creative Commons Attribution-NonCommercial-NoDerivatives 4.0 International License.
https://doi.org/10.1515/9783110799514-013

academic debates, which also discuss obstacles to both concepts. It should be noted that these debates are also reflected in contemporary (German language) literature dealing with the German colonial past. Like academic and socio-cultural debates, fictional texts also turn to the now pressing issue of how to deal with colonial legacies in contemporary societies. An interesting example of this is Bernhard Jaumann's crime novel *Der lange Schatten* [*The Long Shadow*], abbreviated here as DLS,[1] which deals with the German colonial heritage in the former colony of German South West Africa, which is now the country of Namibia.[2] Bernhard Jaumann, born in Augsburg in 1957, is a German writer. Through his many stays in Namibia, Jaumann grows fascinated with the country and its history, which leads him to report on the country's present in relation to its (colonial) history. He is thus considered a "proven expert on Namibian socio-political constellations in their various historical developments" (Demanou 2020, 144).[3] This assertion, however, is open to debate. It indicates a certain legitimacy of writing about Namibia and authorising views on the 'foreigners.' The concept of staying in the foreign country and using the experiences gathered there as a legitimation of one's writing evokes the issue of writing about the 'foreigners' in postcolonial literature by positioning oneself as a witness through individual and personal experiences as well as reporting on distant territories. Jaumann's expertise might be better posed in relation to literary-aesthetic procedures, namely in forms and strategies of 'historiographising' and 'biographising' (experienced) historical stories of experience or/and fictionalising history, all of which operate under the label of the historical novel. A literary reappraisal of history is neither a search for, nor a mediation of reality, but rather a reconstruction and reinterpretation of history with a specific purpose and function, as memories are always selective or subjective images of past perceptions (Erll 2003, 157). Literature, a collection of what people have experienced and thought, can thus be understood as a medium of memory and a means against forgetting (Erll & Nünning 2005, 258).

The Long Shadow has been the object of many literary and cultural study research projects on German colonialism (Demanou 2020; Göttsche 2018). Adding on to these studies, the present chapter addresses the conditions of a possible reparation

---

1 So far, I am not aware of any translation of the book into English or French. The website galaxus.ch only translates the title and the description of the novel for commercial purposes.
2 The novel is part of a trilogy known as "Clemencia Garises" or Namibia Trilogy that tells the story of Namibia's past in relation to the present, focusing on the legacy of the colonial and apartheid era in a post-independent Namibia. It further includes *Die Stunde des Schakals*. Hamburg: Reinbek/Rowohlt Verlag, 2010, as well as *Steinland. Kriminalroman*. Hamburg: Reinbek/Rowohlt Verlag, 2012.
3 Unless indicated otherwise, all translations into English are my own.

as well as the mechanisms of legitimation or instrumentalisation of the historical narrative in Jaumann's book. As we will see, the novel questions state relations between Namibia and Germany at the (in-)official level and also emphasises disparities and divergences within Namibia. Accordingly, the thesis put forward in this chapter is that the novel focuses on the lack of cohesion between the Namibian government and the Herero and Nama people groups in contemporary Namibia as an obstacle to the recognition of past colonial crimes and thus to reparations. Reparation may take several forms (Doxtader and Villa-Vicencio 2004, XV). Drawing on Olúfẹmi O. Táíwò's (2022) and Souleymane Bachir Diagne's (2021) reflections on the concept of reparation, this chapter will analyse central themes in Jaumann's work, such as the relationship between the Namibian government and the Herero and Nama people groups in relation to (colonial) history, the question of colonial guilt and the reparation demands on the part of Namibia. Although the text does not revisit the question of whether the colonial war or the extermination of the Nama and Herero people in what was then German South West Africa can or should be regarded as genocide, it asks how past crimes can be redressed. The novel can thus be said to represent an unofficial recognition of the events as genocide.

2 Colonialism and Reparation Issues in German-language Fiction

The Long Shadow was published in a particular context. It seems crucial to start with the context of the novel's publication before we can consider the ways in which it deals with the issue of reparation in contemporary Namibia. A few years after the ceremony for the restitution of skulls that had been shipped from the former colony of German South West Africa to Germany, which took place in 2011 at Charité in Berlin,[4] Jaumann's work *The Long Shadow* addresses this subject in the form of a crime novel. The novel takes up the demands for reparation of the descendants of the Herero and Nama who had been murdered in the genocide at the beginning of the 20th century.

Within the general contemporary literary discourse on the remembrance of German colonialism in the German-speaking area, a significant development in the thematic focus of texts on this subject can be noted since the 1970s. The subject

---

[4] Cf. the press statement of Berlin Charité with the title: *Charité gibt zwanzig menschliche Schädel an Namibia zurück* [Charité returns twenty human skulls to Namibia].https://www.charite.de/service/pressemitteilung/artikel/detail/berliner_universitaetsmedizin_ehrt_die_opfer/ (22 April 2022).

matter of the reappraised colonial war and the genocide in the former colony of German South West Africa is an example of this development. The topics dealt with in the earlier fiction were mostly oriented towards a depiction of colonial violence, genocide and thus Namibia as a place of remembrance.[5] However, starting around the 2000s, a change in space and thematic focus can be found, which according to Dirk Göttsche can be seen as "a discrepancy between the political focus on Namibia and the conjuncture of historical narratives about Tanzania (and East Africa)" (Göttsche 2012, 174). In the 2000s, there was an increasing interest in the German colonial presence in East Africa, for example, but also in issues of restitution and reparation (Göttsche 2013). It could be argued that this change results from the rise of another generation of writers who do not belong to the post-war and 1968 generation in Germany. For the German generation of '68, burning issues in fiction about Africa were topics such as revolution, rebellion, (colonial) violence and power relations between the 'Global North and South,' cultural relativism and mutual understanding (Lützeler 2005). Within the framework of German language literature, authors such as Uwe Timm and Hans Christoph Buch referred to those topics in their publications. The idea that literature draws from socio-cultural, economic and political – this is, *social* – realities for the purpose of reconstructing a fictionalised, sometimes simplified, sometimes more complex world is thus clearly perceptible in those novels, as it is in *The Long Shadow*. The material in this novel embodies memories of the restitution ceremony at the Berlin Charité in 2011 and of the shared history of Namibia and Germany. As a result, the fiction is infused with real events and thus sometimes also stimulates a public debate by reappraising social events through literature. The literary reappraisal of these past events, such as the restitution of skulls in Berlin, clearly shows that literature can often be perceived as a mirror of socio-cultural debates. While this coincides with a certain shift in the reception and literary representation of historical facts, literature feeds off the public sphere, which in turn is partly influenced by the debates stimulated by literary texts. Considering the material legacy of colonisation, this novel also shows that the current debate among activists, politicians and museologists about the recognition and restitution of cultural objects shipped during the colonial era is also expressed in literature. Jaumann's work, however, deals more directly with the return of the abducted human remains.

---

5 Examples include: *Sturm über Südwest-Afrika* (1962), *Morenga* (1978), *Die schweigenden Feuer* (1994) *Herero* (2003). Cf. Göttsche (2013).

3 On Fictionalised Narratives in the Novel

Jaumann tells three parallel fictional – or fictionalised – stories in *The Long Shadow* that overlap at the end: that of the excavation of Eugen Fischer's skull in Freiburg im Breisgau (by a Namibian character named Kaiphas); that of the restitution ceremony in Berlin Charité in 2011 in the presence of a Namibian delegation led by the character of the Paramount Chief of the Herero, Kuaima Riruako; and that of the self-abduction of the wife of the Ambassador of the Federal Republic of Germany in the Namibian capital (named Maria Engels, Eugen Fischer's great-granddaughter). In Berlin, meanwhile, a police officer is killed just as a delegation arrives to bring back to Namibia twenty Herero skulls stolen during the German colonial period. The novel is also set in three different spaces, all of which contribute to the reconstruction of colonial history: Freiburg, Windhoek and Berlin. Eugen Fischer is a historical figure. He was one of the most decisive advocates and co-founders of racial hygiene and is considered a pioneer of National Socialist racial theories. During the colonial period and the Third Reich, he conducted ethnological studies drawing on eugenics in particular.[6] By measuring physical characteristics, eugenics played a special role in legitimising white superiority over other "races."

Starting with the excavation of Eugen Fischer's skull and the arrival of the Namibian delegation at the Berlin Charité, the plot of the novel is told chronologically until the return of the Namibian delegation to Windhoek. At this point it should be noted that, although the return of the skull really took place in the Berlin Charité in 2011, Eugen Fischer's skull was never excavated and stolen. It is a fictional reconstruction of the events. Consequently, literature mythologises or invents a part of history with the aim of reconsidering history or completing shadow areas that institutional historiography has not or hardly considered: the social dimensions of history, shaped by individual experiences, regarding private life, the individual and social psychology, the worldviews of the social classes (Lüsebrink 1989, 107–108). This social dimension includes social memory as generational memory, which is also a part of the collective and cultural memory of every society (Halbwachs 1939; Assmann 1997). Most literary texts dealing with family memory emphasise, for example, the use of family documents to trace history. The family has a memory that opposes or confirms the official or even national historical memory. However, *The*

---

6 Cf. Hutton (2005) regarding the politics of race in the Third Reich. Even though the concept of eugenics was mostly used during the National Socialist era, the classification of people into *races* had been used before this time by theorists such as Arthur de Gobineau, or Gustaf Kossinna in his work *Die deutsche Vorgeschichte, eine hervorragend nationale Wissenschaft* (1912).

Long Shadow does not deal with family memory in the form of documents left behind, but with a memory passed down as a burden from generation to generation. The more important connecting element between the past and the present in this respect is the hidden family secret, which the novel reveals through analepsis with the character of Mara Engels.

Significant characters in the novel are Mr. Engels, the ambassador of the Federal Republic of Germany to Namibia and husband of the character Mara Engels; Kaiphas Riruako, a young Namibian supposed to steal the skull; and Clemencia, bodyguard of the family of the German ambassador, whose wife organised her own abduction.[7] Mara Engels' aim was to get her husband – through blackmail from Julius Tjitjiku, Head of Department in the the *Ministerium für Geschlechtergleichheit und Kindeswohlfahrt* [Ministry of Gender Equality and Child Welfare] – to officially recognise the colonial genocide on behalf of the German government. This turns out to be a condition for the adoption of a Herero child, as I will elaborate in the following. The child lives at *The Living Rainbow Children Centre* orphanage in Windhoek, which appears as a political or propagandistic tool to gather money from rich donors. In contrast to these characters, Kuaima Riruako, Paramount Chief of the Herero, was a real person. In the novel, he travels with the delegation to Berlin to return the skulls. Both characters – Kuaima Riruako and Kaiphas Riruako – have the same family name but are two characters with different social backgrounds and motivations. There is also the fictional character of Kawanyama, head of the Namibian *Ministry of Home Affairs and Immigration*, who is the mastermind behind the excavation of Eugen Fischer's skull, and Desmond Haufiku, minister of security. While Mara Engels is presented as Eugen Fischer's German great-granddaughter, Claus Tiedtke represents the members of the German minority in Namibia in his function of a mediator between the two cultures and countries: He is editor of the German-language Allgemeine Zeitung newspaper, published in Windhoek, and travels to Berlin as a companion of the delegation to report on the restitution ceremony (Demanou 2020, 168).

---

7 Clemencia runs a private security service after her job in the civil service. She is involved in the investigation of the self-abduction of the ambassador's wife, having worked for the ambassador's family shortly before the incident. In Bernhard Jaumann's whole Namibia trilogy, Clemencia participates in the investigation of crimes committed in the name of the past by gathering expertise and also being part of the community.

4 Historical Burdens and Cleavages in Fictionalised Namibia

A certain fragility of fictionalised post-colonial Namibia is evident when it comes to the coexistence between 'black' and 'white' communities in *The Long Shadow*. The former are often described and perceived in the novel as victims of colonisation and apartheid, while the latter are perceived as the main heirs of colonisation and seen as guilty. For this reason, the individual, collective, national and ethnic dimensions of the past, or memory of the past, can be examined in the text, all of which being closely linked in the narrative. In Jaumann' trilogy as a whole, the 'white' community is partly embodied by the journalist Claus, who works for the *Allgemeine Zeitung*, Namibia's only German-language newspaper. Claus is a white Namibian of German origin (DLS, 83): "The fact that his mother tongue was accidentally German did not prevent him from considering Namibia as his homeland" (DLS, 11). Claus, who considers himself to belong to the Namibian nation, fully engages in the restitution ceremony both as a journalist and a Namibian citizen, which highlights the ceremony's significance for the Namibian nation as it is portrayed in the text. Landing at the airport, however, the burden of the colonial legacy on relations between 'black' and 'white' Namibians can be seen in the exchange between him and the Paramount Chief of the Herero Kuaima Riruako, who embodies "the spirit of resistance that Namibians have developed to deal with their traumatic colonial past with Germany" (Demanou 2020, 159). The distance between Claus and the delegation increases when they land in Frankfurt. (DLS, 11). Regarding the conversation between Riruako and Claus, Demanou argues:

> Kuaima Riruako's words betray the intolerance of indigenous Namibians towards Namibians of German descent in that he [Kuaima Riruako] makes no distinction between them [Namibians of German descent] and the Germans. In his view, they are all perpetrators who subjugated and slaughtered the Namibian people (Demanou 2020, 159–160).

Riruako considers Claus an heir of the (German) perpetrators in the colonial era and therefore directly guilty, although, according to the narrator, Claus identifies himself as belonging to the Namibian nation. Here one can see that a strict separation, as well as an exclusion of the ethnic Germans from the Namibian nation is taking place: "*you* slaughtered *us* then because *you* had the guns and cannons" (DLS, 16, emphasis mine). The statement points to a form of separation by distinctions based on physical characteristics. Firstly, Riruako uses skin colour or physiognomy as distinguishing criteria. In this case, the foreign group is represented by means of certain attributes or specific physical characteristics that distinguish it from its own group (Amossy 2010, 45) and consequently separate it from the nation. He secondly sees the population of Namibia as exclusively 'black African' and in this perspective excludes any possibility of the presence of another skin colour in Namibia. This shows a racist notion of what should be Namibian, African or European/German, considering that the components of belonging are always changing with the heterogeneity of culture in the present.

Thus, different reactions and behaviours of 'whites' towards 'blacks' in relation to Namibia's past can be noticed in the work. At first, Claus reveals a feeling of foreignness and superiority towards the 'black' Namibians, as he feels pity for them and does not understand the Germans' indifference towards their situation when the delegation has landed in Frankfurt: "And yet he [Claus] almost felt something like pity for these Hereros and Namas who imagined that anyone in Europe would care what had been done to their ancestors" (DLS, 14). The novel demonstrates that this complex relationship between and within different interest groups complicates the issue of reparations. In this sense, the narrator reveals a sense of rejection, with 'white' Namibians partly repressing or rejecting their ancestors' involvement in crimes during the colonial period. In the eyes of many white Namibians, their ancestors were innocent. This view is subject to a mythologisation, misrepresentation or simplification of historical facts that can be refuted or clarified by historical research. Myths represent a glorification of the past, which is sometimes taken out of context and can deviate far from historical reality. A myth can further be seen as an affective appropriation of one's own history, especially as an orientation for the future and a tool for identity formation (Assmann 2006, 41). Considering the different communities' perspectives on the colonial past, tensions become apparent between the different population groups, which the narrator highlights once again at the skull-receiving ceremony in Namibia where almost only 'black people' – with the exception of the diplomatic corps – are present.

As part of a trilogy, the novel draws attention to a continuity of tension between the groups dating back to the colonial and apartheid period, highlighted by the author through topics such as social inequalities, racism and discrimination between "blacks" and whites." The colonial legacy is primarily visible, for example, through the so-called land question or land reforms, where the government described makes a decision for a land reform as part of reparation for colonial injustice. This land reform consequently appears as the main theme in the trilogy's second novel, *Steinland* (2012). In the novel, a German-born Namibian farmer named Gregor Rodenstein is murdered by 'black' Namibian robbers and his son is kidnapped. The novel thus addresses grievances such as corruption, rampant crime and social inequality in Namibia. The novel portrays dispossessed 'black' Namibians living in poverty and difficult economic conditions in the former township of Katutura and, alongside them, 'white' or 'German Namibian' farmers who live on their land as descendants of the former colonialists or German settlers and now regard it as their home. The novel therefore deals with questions of identity and homeland as well as the limits and possibilities of compensation for their loss of land. This fragility of social cohesion in Namibia as it is depicted here is equally relevant in *The Long Shadow*, which emphasises the need for dialogue and cohesion between 'black' and 'white' Namibians with German descendants.

5 Reparation and Forms of Reparation in the Crime Novel

Before considering how the novel includes and deals with the issue of reparation, the contours of this concept need to be defined. The following quote provides an overview of the concept of reparation according to Rombouts:

> In the popular view, reparations are associated with financial compensation, often to individuals. In actuality, however, financial compensation is often given to groups, for collective projects to remedy past ill-treatment. Moreover, reparations include other, more symbolic yet often very important actions, such as acknowledgment of past injuries, apologies for them, and access to the truth about the past events (Rombouts 2004, 1).

In this interesting passage, Rombouts points out the outlines of reparation which should be both symbolic and material in order to compensate for past injustice. Reparation in this regard can be seen as justice for the victims or their descendants. This symbolic side to reparation is also emphasised by Souleymane Bachir Diagne, who underlines the impossibility of reparation as sole financial compensation (Diagne 2020). Beyond the symbolic and material aspect of reparation, the main purpose of any reparation process should be considered: Assuming the traumatic and unjust past (social & economic justice) and (re)constructing a common future to correct the existing prejudices (reconciliation, overcoming structural violence and racism, deconstructing the world system). According to Diagne, one cannot repair the past. He is more concerned with recognition and the will to learn from the past for a better coexistence between the peoples of the world, notably "making humanity together" (Diagne 2021). In this perspective, addressing past injustices with the aim of repairing them means not pointing out *what* was done, but *why* it was done.

Doing this involves educational work besides the material and symbolic reparation. In addition, one notices not only the already mentioned impossibility of repair, but also the visible gap or shift between the social and socio-cultural debates or demands and their implementation in politics by those in power. This raises the issue of addressees and negotiating parties. In this sense, Felwine Sarr and Bénédicte Savoy were commissioned by French President Emmanuel Macron to produce a report on the possible outlines of the restitution of cultural artefacts stolen during the colonial period and reparation for such crimes (Sarr and Savoy 2018). This report first describes the concept of "restitution" before examining the collections acquired during the colonial period and possible methods of restitution, ending with the accompaniment of the returned objects to their places of origin. It proposes methods such as practical fact sheets on legal provisions and methodological recommendations. Indeed, despite the enormous amount of work done by researchers, the question of the right approach remains an open debate. Restitutions are not infrequently contested at state level, arguing not for restitution but for return, which does not imply any moral obligation. As a consequence, Sarr and Savoy stress the need for cooperation between scholars, museum professionals, government officials, parliamentarians, collectors, lawyers, educators, activists, etc. in order to start a process of repair. Reparation remains, as already mentioned, an ongoing process which can assume different forms, such as restitutions, educational work on this issue, compensation, recognition over the generations, or others. Indeed, restitution "in UNESCO's normative international law sense means something like an admission of guilt or a legally proven fact" (Hauser-Schäublin 2021, 69–70). This argument about the interests pursued by each entity, in this case the state (liable to pay or entitled to receive compensation) and the affected communities and descendants of the victims, who demand reparation in the form of justice, is found in the novel *The Long Shadow*.

6 Individual and Collective Forms of Compensation and Reparation

"In their [the Herero's] opinion, the Germans should finally pay off their debt, with words, with deeds and with Euros", according to the narrator (DLS, 13). Several processes can be identified here: first with words, an official apology; and then with deeds, as the Hereros are not satisfied with apologies alone but want to see them accompanied by concerted actions to subsequently demand reparations. These elements can be seen as relevant for any recognition of past crimes (Rombouts 2004, 1). Thus, the novel identifies different forms of reparation. First, the return of skulls stolen during the colonial period appears in the novel as a form of reparation.[8] Restitution means recognising the belonging of the objects to be returned and the conditions under which they were stolen. This leads to a recognition of the damage and pain caused by this theft, and further to a moral reparation (cf. West-Pavlov 2020, 12–13). This restitution thus aims to reconcile, first, the dead with their places of origin and, furthermore, the narrated and sometimes simplified or deformed histories given the circumstances in which the skulls were stolen (cf. Rombouts 2004, 22). The skulls are part of a process of restitution and therefore reparation, but I would like to stress that the symbolic dimension certainly differs between the restitution of cultural objects and human remains whose humanity has been soiled and negated. The theft of cultural objects serves a western exoticism, whereas the removal of human remains was an instrument of legitimation of a supposed "racial" superiority. The skulls in the novel belong to those murdered in the concentration camps during the genocide and are then associated with Eugen Fischer's role during the colonial period and the Third Reich. Along these lines, the character Kawanyama reminds young Kaiphas of the massacres and humiliations perpetrated by the Germans against the Herero people:

> The Germans considered us inferior. In order to prove it with the help of skull shapes they looted our graves. [. . .] More than a hundred years ago, Herero women had to excavate the bodies of their slaughtered men. Since the flesh had not yet decomposed, they had to boil the skulls. Then they got shards of glass pressed into their hands. They were forced by the Germans to use them to scrape bare the bones. The skeletons of their husbands, sons, fathers, brothers. The women, of course, could have slit their wrists with the shards (DLS, 54, 219).

Moreover, colonialism or the (colonial) past may initially be perceived as an individual or even personal burden because of the family legacy of that past. Before colonialism becomes the concern of a nation or state, it is firstly the concern of a person confronted with a system of domination and exploitation in the colonial era, and secondly the concern of a person confronted with the crimes suffered or committed by their ancestors. This past thus weighs on the person because of social (and family) memory. The individual dimension of colonial history becomes apparent as soon as the colonial legacy is transformed into a family history to be repaired. This family memory materialises in the character of Mara Engels, the wife of the ambassador, whose great-grandfather was Eugen Fischer. The latter's role in examining the skulls of the colonised during the colonial period and during the Third Reich was crucial for the perception and representation of 'black' people in Germany with the aim of legitimising a racial hierarchy. Thus, family history is

---

8 As Rombouts would have it: "The first form of reparation is restitution. It aims at restoring the victim to the original situation that existed before the violations occurred" (Rombouts 2004, 27).

linked to national history. Therefore, one detects in the work a willingness to make amends on an individual basis. This can be demonstrated more concretely by the behavior of the characters described in the text. First, Claus commits himself intensively through journalism to bring about non-partisan justice. Mara also identifies with the victims of the colonial era. Aleida Assmann is fully convincing here when she examines in detail the memory processes between victims and perpetrators in her study dedicated to the historian Reinhart Koselleck. While "traumatic experiences of suffering and shame [find] difficult entry into memory because they cannot be integrated into a positive individual or collective self-image [. . .], the outlines of those who were or are responsible for such suffering remain rather vague [. . .]. Suffering strengthens the self-image, guilt threatens to destroy it" (Assmann 2006, 75, 81).

This individual legacy of colonialism appears as a burden that is to be solved in a form of reconciliatory action: Mara Engels' adoption of a child. The child comes from the Herero community, the main victim of German colonialism and thus of the crimes of her grandfather – Eugen Fischer – which Mara Engels would like to make amends for. This sense of guilt that runs through the generations is interesting here. The novel poses the question of how one can be guilty of the crimes of one's ancestors, a question that it also attempts to answer through questions of recognition and reparation. Adoption is supposed to be retribution for colonial crimes. The fictional character Julius Tjitjiku, a Herero himself, blackmails Mara Engels after his decision to help her with the adoption, which he initially rejects as "baby shopping in Africa" (DLS, 78). His aim is to obtain an official recognition of the colonial genocide from the German government by putting pressure on Mara Engels' husband, the ambassador of the Federal Republic of Germany in Namibia. The adoption of the child along with the statement of the German ambassador was also intended to facilitate the excavation and shipping of the skull of Eugen Fischer from Freiburg to Namibia. On Mara's adoption of the Herero boy, Clemencia stresses: "The dead German racist as belated symbolic war booty of the Herero descendants against the traumatised Herero boy as object of reparation of the remorseful racist great-granddaughter" (DLS, 307). What is meant here is that Tjitjiku demands the skull as a price for the adoption. The adoption of the child can also be seen as a form of reparation in this respect. The character of Maria lives with the guilt of her great-grandfather's crimes and tries to make amends by offering the child the possibility of a better future.

The colonial past is perceived as a burden for the characters studied in Jaumann's text, who from a personal perspective seek to initiate reparation by contributing to justice or equality. If the characters individually seek reparation and justice, it would also be interesting to discuss the (in)official positions of the Namibian government in dealing with history and colonial guilt, as well as the positions of the Herero and Nama's delegation in Jaumann's novel.

7 Obstacles and Instrumentalisation of the Historical Narrative in Political-Fictional Discourse

The question raised in the novel is not whether Germany should officially recognise its crimes concerning the colonial past. These past events are recognised as genocide on an individual or private level in Germany by its representatives described in the work, such as the ambassador of the Federal Republic of Germany in the capital of Namibia. Not only does the ambassador's character acknowledge this, but so does Claus Tiedtke. The novel is more concerned with the conditions for reparation and the various obstacles at state level. According to the narrator, Germany does not want to recognise colonial genocide and thus not pay reparations for past colonial crimes for two reasons: firstly, in order not to encourage the other former German colonies in Africa to also demand reparations, for "otherwise others would soon be at the door in Berlin to hold out their hands, namely the politicians from Tanzania, Cameroon, Togo and wherever else the empire had tried to conquer its place in the sun" (DLS, 61). It is worth noting that "it [was] not only about the historical atrocities, but also about current political interests. Like all former colonial powers, Germany tried to deny legally binding responsibilities so as not to set a precedent" (DLS, 61). Secondly, the novel suggests that Germany also particularly did not want to deepen the social inequalities in today's Namibia.

In Jaumann's narrative, the German government's position thus remains unambiguous to avoid any form of accountability. In this sense, as René Demanou has pointed out in his dissertation (Demanou 2020: 164), the role of the ambassador in the novel is to keep the question of reparations or compensation out of discussions with Namibian officials by insisting that Germany pay 'development aid' instead of 'reparations.' This leads to questions about the described (in-)official positions of the Namibian government. The latter's position in the novel includes three important goals: deepening development cooperation with Germany, avoiding 'tribalism' in Namibia and thus prioritising the unity of the nation. According to minister Kawawyama of the *Ministry of Home Affairs and Immigration*, "we [the government] are definitely interested in more intensive development cooperation with the Germans, but just at government level" (DLS, 155). Here, the promotion of development cooperation with Germany is meant for the development of the nation, not just for one ethnic group: "Officially, the Namibian government is well disposed towards the Herero cause [. . .]. Unofficially, things look a little different" (DLS, 155). Although development aid is not associated with an acknowledgment – legal or moral – of injustice committed (Etemad 2008; Kollmannsperger 1965), the colonial experience serves as a justification in terms of solidarity expressed in a series of post-independence partnerships in most African countries (Gülstorff 2017). Such solidarity simultaneously implies an indirect recognition of (colonial) injustice, as the supposed "development aid" points to European or Western responsibility for neo-colonial structures. One notices the attempt to present an image of a selfless Europe, while the system keeps former colonies partly in misery and poverty (Moyo 2009). Development cooperation with Germany thus appears in the novel both as indirect reparation from Germany and as acceptance of this reparation by the Namibian authorities. In this sense, the question arises as to whether the described Namibia, staged by the authorities, does not displace the crimes of the past in favor of economic advantages with Germany. Development cooperation with Germany in this respect can furthermore be seen as a certain blackmail to silence people, which is the role of the fictitious ambassador of the federal government of Germany in Namibia.

The Namibian minister Kawawyama of the *Ministry of Home Affairs and Immigration* is also pursuing two important goals by instrumentalising the young Kaiphas for the excavation of Eugen Fischer's skull. For the government described above, the Herero and Nama are a guarantee of economic stability by maintaining development aid and even cooperation between the two countries. The first objective is therefore to discredit the Herero as radical activists and to keep them out of negotiations on recognition and reparations by Germany, so that the Namibian state is seen as the only reliable interlocutor and the only one capable of redistributing wealth. At the same time, according to the minister, the government does not want to run the risk of the Herero people proclaiming "an independent Herero state" (DSL, 157) with the reparations, which is why the second objective is to avoid a proclamation of an independent Herero state as a result of possible compensations. One of the minister's arguments underlined in the text is the desire to combat all forms of 'tribalism' in Namibia. 'Tribalism,' in his view, would rise if reparations were paid directly to the Nama and Herero people: The government also refuses compensations that go directly to the Hereros, because these leaders see themselves as the elected representatives of the nation.[9] While the government prioritises

---

[9] Here is the minister's detailed opinion in the novel: "As you know, these are the same people who are sceptical or hostile towards the SWAPO government. With increased self-confidence,

development aid, the Herero Paramount Chief, Kuaima Riruako, sees this in the novel as instrumentalisation and hegemony on the part of Germany. He criticises this development aid as an attempt to make amends, with which the German government tries to avoid paying reparations, while the authorities, on the other hand, favor development aid for the development of the country.

This split also appears at the state and political level, marked by disparities and divergences between the government portrayed, dominated by Ovambos people groups, and the Herero and Nama communities. The rivalry reveals the political fragility of the country in the novel, especially the *South West African People's Organisation* (SWAPO) government's fear of *The National Unity Democratic Organisation* (NUDO) party, which is predominantly made up of Herero people. In this sense, the minister emphasises: "There is no Herero nation, there is only one Namibian nation" (DLS, 155).

The novel addresses that it is not in the spirit of the Namibian government to give any of the numerous ethnic groups special rights through payment of reparations. It might seem easy to put the nation first as a solution, as everyone benefits from the aid and thus the country would be developed. Along these lines, the narrator asks "who would now offer himself as a mediator to relieve the historical burdens? [. . .] Exactly, the SWAPO government" (DLS, 258). The losers in this perspective are the Nama and Herero peoples who are discredited. Another winner is the figure of Desmond Haufiku, minister of security. He is portrayed by the narrator as a cunning winner of the situation. He exploits the excavation of Eugene's skull for political purposes to become the successor of the current president. He has special decision-making power and remains in the shadows, so that one can hardly discover or denounce his political maneuvers.

8 Conclusion

Reinhart Kössler's concept of *negotiating the past* (Kössler 2008) describes well Bernhard Jaumann's literary work. In the book, the Namibia depicted not only negotiates an acknowledgment of colonial guilt on the part of Germany, but also

---

international recognition and considerable financial resources behind them, they could cause us great difficulties. Their party, NUDO, would be boosted, votes would be bought, demands for autonomy first on this, then on that, then on all issues would be made. I predict that it would not be three years before the first imbecile proclaimed an independent Herero state." "Do you understand now, Mrs. Garises, why we are gently hinting to the Germans that they should send the Hereros packing, along with their demands? If you don't believe me, ask the ambassador" (DSL, 156–157).

the conditions and the need to demand ways of reconciliation and reparation. This makes the function of Jaumann's text quite clear. *Negociating the past* also means dialogue: putting a certain number of conditions and courses on the table and also accepting compromises by putting forward the general interest of the parties concerned. As my analysis has shown, the novel shows why and whether the literary approach to the subject is particularly predestined to negotiate new forms of memory culture or to problematise them in comparison to other forms or discourses (e.g., in politics, the press, etc.). In this way, the significance of the literary readings of the past is demonstrated. Because of the quest for facts and the clear effort to provide literary fiction with referential material, a historical novel becomes also a fictionalised documentary text narrating shadow areas that have not or hardly been taken into account by institutional historiography: the social dimension of history shaped by individual experiences. Moreover, the examination of colonialism in the present also contributes to reflection on current relations between Germany and its former colonies such as Namibia. The text highlights various groups involved in this dialogue or even in these negotiations on the past. Germany is represented by ambassador Engels and, in an indirect way, by the foreign minister, as well as by Mara Engels as a symbol of guilt and reparation. Next to them is the government of Namibia, represented in an official capacity by minister Kawanyama. The delegation is also involved in the negotiations with the Hereros through the figure of the *Paramount Chief* of the Herero Kuaima Riruako. It is apparent that the novel proposes both symbolic and material forms of reparation but locates this reparation mostly at the individual and non-state level. The German state is not present except in economic cooperation, which the Namibian state also prefers to financial compensation for Herero and Nama communities. Each of the groups or individuals concerned (communities, states and descendants) takes a clear position on the genocide, defends their own interests according to the internal circumstances described in the text and tries to repair the past in their own way. As such, reparation remains an ongoing deconstructive process of being (together) with the consciousness of the unjust and traumatic past and the willingness in doing better.

References

Assmann, Aleida. *Der lange Schatten der Vergangenheit: Erinnerungskultur und Geschichtspolitik*. München: Beck, 2006.
Demanou, René. *Das kulturelle Gedächtnis der Kolonialvergangenheit im globalen Kontext: Betrachtungen zur deutschen und afrikanischen frankophonen Gegenwartsliteratur*. Bielefeld: Aisthesis Verlag, 2020.

Diagne, Souleymane Bachir. *What is Reparation?* Rhinozeros asks . . . Souleymane Bachir Diagne, 2020. https://www.rhinozeros-projekt.de/zeitschrift/das-projekt (22 April 2022).
Doxtader, Erik et al. *To Repair the Irreparable: Reparation and Reconstruction in South Africa*. Claremont: David Philip Publishers, 2004.
Erll, Astrid and Ansgar Nünning. Ed. *Gedächtniskonzepte der Literaturwissenschaft: theoretische Grundlegung und Anwendungsperspektiven*. Media and cultural memory 2. Berlin, New York: De Gruyter, 2005.
Göttsche, Dirk. "History and Memory? Postcolonial politics of memory in Bernhard Jaumann's *Der lange Schatten* and M.G. Vassanji's *The Magic of Saida*." *Memory and Postcolonial Studies: Synergies and New Directions*. Ed. Dirk Göttsche. New York: Peter Lang, 2018. 45–74.
——. *Remembering Africa: The Rediscovery of Colonialism in Contemporary German Literature*. Rochester, New York: Camden House, 2013.
Hauser-Schäublin, Brigitta. "Provenienzforschung zwischen politisierter Wahrheitsfindung und systemischem Ablenkungsmanöver." *Geschichtskultur durch Restitution? Ein Kunst-Historikerstreit*. Ed. Thomas Sandkühler, Angelika Epple, and Jürgen Zimmerer. Köln: Böhlau Verlag, 2021. 55–78.
Howard-Hassmann, Rhoda and Anthony P Lombardo. *Reparations to Africa*. Philadelphia, PA: University of Pennsylvania Press, 2008.
Hutton, Christopher. *Race and the Third Reich: Linguistics, Racial Anthropology and Genetics in the Dialectic of Volk*. Cambridge: Polity, 2005.
Jaumann, Bernhard. *Der lange Schatten*. Hamburg: Rowohlt Taschenbuch Verlag, 2016.
Kössler, Reinhart. "Entangled History and Politics: Negotiating the Past Between Namibia and Germany." *Journal of Contemporary African Studies* 26.3 (2008): 313–339.
Lüsebrink, Hans-Jürgen. "De l'incontournabilité de la fiction dans la connaissance historique. Questionnements théoriques à partir de romans historiques contemporains d'Alejo Carpentier, de Yambo Ouologuem et d'Ousmane Sembène." *Neohelicon* 16.2 (1989): 107–128.
Moyo, Dambisa. *Dead Aid: Why Aid Is Not Working and How There Is a Better Way for Africa*. New York: Farrar Straus and Giroux, 2009.
Rombouts, Heidy. *Victim Organisations and the Politics of Reparation: A Case-Study on Rwanda*. Antwerp: Intersentia, 2004.
Sandkühler, Thomas, Angelika Epple, and Jürgen Zimmerer. "Restitution und Geschichtskultur im (post-)kolonialen Kontext: Facetten einer schwierigen Debatte." *Geschichtskultur durch Restitution? Ein Kunst-Historikerstreit*. Ed. Thomas Sandkühler, Angelika Epple, and Jürgen Zimmerer. Köln: Böhlau Verlag, 2021. 9–33.
Sarr, Felwine and Bénédicte Savoy. *Rapport sur la restitution du patrimoine culturel africain. Vers une nouvelle éthique relationnelle*. 2018. http://restitutionreport2018.com/sarr_savoy_fr.pdf (22 September 2022).
Sarr, Felwine. *Habiter le monde: essai de politique relationnelle*. Montréal, Québec: Mémoire D'Encrier, 2017.
Táíwò, Olúfẹ́mi O. *Reconsidering Reparations: Worldmaking in the Case of Climate Crisis*. Philosophy of Race Series. New York: Oxford University Press, 2022.
West-Pavlov, Russell. *AfrikAffekt: deutschsprachige Romane zum Herero- und Nama-Genozid 1904–1908: ein affekttheoretischer Ansatz*. Tübingen: Narr Francke Attempto, 2020.

Part V: **Reparation and Ecology**

Cinquième partie : **La réparation et l'écologie**

Olivier Remaud
Trouble against Trouble

Background: The two texts translated here, assembled under the title "Trouble against trouble," have first been commissioned by the French journals AOC and Socialter (Remaud 2021a & 2021b). They have followed the publication of my book *Penser comme un iceberg* (2020), recently translated as *Thinking Like an Iceberg* (2022). These two articles have been an occasion for me to develop some of the book's arguments from a different angle. I have chosen to join them here as they emanate from the same interest: narrating new alliances with the living in an uncertain world shaken up by emergencies. Both translations have been effectuated by Jack Cox.[1]

The Glacier and the Human Being

It all starts with a thin, invisible crack. Then a dark slash appears. Then one day an endless, straight line is cutting through the ice. By the time the scientists have seen it on their satellite images, it has already started to race towards the sea. They induce that the line is a deep crevasse, perhaps concealing a network of rivers, and that the Larsen C Ice Shelf is in the process of breaking up. They observe closely as this giant cut develops, at the same time watching the whole northern part of the Antarctic peninsula. As the weeks pass, the hypothesis of a fracture gets clearer. Then in July 2017, a large mass suddenly breaks away from its floating platform. As it begins its voyage into the Atlantic Ocean, the iceberg hardly suspects that it has become the protagonist in a suspense drama.

It has to be said that its proportions are gigantic, almost unprecedented. Its tabular surface is close to 5800 km^2 and its volume is almost 1500 km^3. It quickly splits into two pieces. Then these pieces break up into smaller pieces. The US National Ice Center glaciologists give the initial iceberg the name A68A and continue accordingly with each of its fragments: A68B, A68C, A68D, and so on. This alphanumerical classification reminds them that this is the 68th iceberg ("of a size greater than ten marine miles in length") to leave the Antarctic sector – which stretches from the

---
[1] The translation of this text was supported by the project "Minor Universality. Narrative World Productions After Western Universalism" which received funding from the European Research Council (ERC) under the European Union's Horizon 2020 research and innovation program (Grant agreement No. 819931).

Bellingshausen Sea to the Weddell Sea – and that it is the progenitor of a family of icebergs now dispersed over the waves.

The scientific community closely surveys the erratic trajectories of this little family. When they see that A68A is approaching a landmass, they hold their breath. The news spreads, there's something of a media frenzy, the trouble grows. Everyone thinks that this deviant "Behemoth" is about to end its days colliding with South Georgia Island. It's going to get stuck on the coastal floor and block the penguins, sea elephants, sea lions, and seals from access to their food sources. Its ice keel will have ploughed up and destroyed whole marine ecosystems. The collision is predicted for the end of December 2020.

But fate would have it otherwise, and the predicted catastrophe doesn't happen. Warmer waters, powerful winds, and some rubbing up against the continental plateau have weakened A68A's structure. Not far from the island, the iceberg breaks apart again. It loses 70% of its initial volume. It's too thin to sink, so it travels north on the currents. Today, it has disappeared. It will never strike South Georgia Island, nor any other land for that matter.

The threat will have been nothing but a hypothesis disproved by the facts. There's no doubt that it was a danger for part of the island's fauna and for the seabed. But neither was there any question of stopping it. How could it have been stopped anyway? There was nothing left to do but shiver, watching the flow of images beamed in from the sky. The theatrical effect was involuntary perhaps. A predatory monster nonetheless emerged, capable of massacring everything in its way, like an archaic image of death. Will the imaginary of the iceberg forever bear the mark of the Titanic syndrome? We would do better to look at the causes of this event instead.

There is nothing unusual about the presence of icebergs in the ocean. But climate change is accelerating the rate at which they break off from the masses they were once a part of. The higher global temperatures rise, the less the icecaps can resist and the more icebergs there are. Many studies have shown that the Antarctic peninsula has become fragile. Winds that are too warm are generated in its mountains and flow downwards. The föhn alters the density and stability of the ice shelves. Whereas the deep cold is supposed to return with the autumn, the glacial surfaces shrink even more during this period because of the heat, and their snow loses in porosity. The ice fractures faster (cf. Datta, Tedesco, Fettweis, et al. 2019).

Scientists who know about these factors are afraid that the A68A sequence is the beginning of a general disintegration of the Antarctic ice shelves. This will not be without consequence on a planetary level. These ice shelves are fed by glaciers whose flow towards the sea they halt. If they disappear, the "cork" will be popped, the glaciers from other sectors will rapidly melt and sea levels will mechanically rise. The story of A68A tells of the suffering of a continent on which the shared fate of humans and non-humans hangs.

How should we respond to the "trouble" that such events cause in us? Can we manage to "live with it" without becoming overcome with anxiety and unable to act? Is it possible to get out of the register of the spectacle without giving ourselves up to tragic consciousness? The philosopher Donna Haraway has been asking these questions for years (cf. Harraway 2016). She incites us to put away our Hollywoodian emotions together with our despondency so as to invent narratives, practices, concepts, and even other troubles capable of helping us to better inhabit this roughed-up world. In a recent book, I basically responded to this incitement by asking myself what different stories the worlds of ice tell us (Remaud 2020).

If we look closer, the glaciologists have some for us. We only have to examine their vocabulary. They use the word "calving" to speak about the moment a glacier releases icebergs. The word likens the glacier to a cow or a whale, and the iceberg to a calf. Icebergs are literally born. Glaciologists also talk about the "mother" iceberg that itself breaks up into "daughter" or "sister," sometimes "son" or "brother" icebergs. They weave parental, filial bonds. And then they say that a glacier is "dead" when there's nothing left but a thin layer of snow, implying that it once lived. These are not simple poetic exercises. Words mean something. They express feelings that I would call – after the geographer Yi-Fu-Tuan – "topophilic." They stand in for affective, sometimes all-consuming experiences with spaces and their main characters: a glacier, an iceberg, this particular section of an ice floe, that particular mountain slope.

From words to the reality of ecosystems, there is but a short step. The biodiversity of the glacial plains didn't wait for humans to tremble before them to develop and adapt. Faced with a slimmed-down, fissured A68A, the fauna of South Georgia Island might have perhaps invented solutions for finding other ways to get food. While these blocks of ice do run aground, they can also free themselves and continue on their way. Icebergs also disturb submarine habitats as they rake through them. Specialists in Benthic ecology tell us that they always carry off a few and drop them in other zones. They reconfigure the seabed as they plough it up. They're continually inseminating the ocean depths. They carry nutriments and mineral salts that feed phytoplankton and they are situated at the top of the trophic chain of the polar regions. Beneath the ice floe itself all sorts of species live – nematodes, anemones, soft corals, isopods, star fish and sea cucumbers, sea urchins, shrimp. Without the multitude of microcellular organisms that cling to the submerged walls of the icebergs, those living on the planet would breathe less well, including the penguins on South Georgia Island. Icebergs play a crucial role in the equilibrium of marine ecosystems. They confirm the fact that the ice guarantees the stability of the water cycle that the global network of living beings depends on.

Since the ice is a place of life, why not go further and see it as "animated"? Many indigenous populations in the Arctic have been displaced, eliminated, and forgotten throughout history. They are nonetheless there and demand the right to inhabit their land. But the consequences of global warming can be felt dramatically at these latitudes. The reason is simple: The higher temperatures rise, the less of the sun's rays the Earth's mantle refracts into space. The weakening of the albedo drives these regions into the negative spiral of the greenhouse effect, which keep itself going with its own momentum. This hellish dynamic causes severe drought or uncontrolled ice breakups in other places, such as in the inhabited valleys of the Himalayan mountains. The communities there don't feel responsible for this global situation. But the ice is a part of them and they experience the melt as if a part of their own body was being amputated. The environmental activist Sheila Watt-Cloutier speaks about a "right to be cold" in order to remind us that ice is necessary to the Inuit, who have lived in these regions for centuries. They need it in order to exercise their fundamental rights (cf. Watt-Cloutier 2016).

The ice floes, the glaciers, the icebergs – all these "entities" are still part of daily life in the arctic zones. The epistemic division between "things" and "beings" doesn't exist in traditional cosmologies. The glaciers react to human actions. They possess a special authority over communities. There are norms that organize relations. When approaching a glacier, one goes about it in stages, being sure during the first attempts to never look it "in the eyes." One doesn't risk cooking near its icy walls and one is careful not to accidentally let oil drop on the ground. Above all, one doesn't build dams upstream of it, with the risk of interfering with the equilibrium of its base layer and rousing its anger. An annoyed glacier always begins by grumbling. Then it shouts and leaps out of its resting place like a maddened dragon. It pours over villages, floods them, destroys houses and lives. When it sanctions the errors committed by a clan member, it forces a community to reformulate their rules of conduct over a more or less extended period of time. Prudence is required when faced with a glacier. If one doesn't respect the norm of keeping one's distance, it's impossible to coinhabit peacefully.

These uses of the world move the dividing lines between what is living and what is dead. They resituate us within an extensive memory peopled with surprising figures. We are no longer the only actors. The stories tell of solidarity. They are sometimes happy, sometimes cruel stories, collective archives of felt experience. It's important to listen to them. In them we hear the voices of "things" that have never been "things." The Maori tribes who in the New Zealand parliament on 14 April 2017 won the status of "juridical person" for the Whanganui River were in this way able to reconnect with the living, indivisible entity that colonial law had carved up into creeks and banks sold off to landowners. These tribes have never stopped claiming that "they are the river" and "the river is them" (David 2017).

Anyone who lives near glaciers, or who has regular commerce with one of them, sees them in the same way, as a living being. She feels particular emotions. Every day, she listens to them, observes them, takes note of their chromatic variations, wonders upon waking if they have slept well. She becomes part of their world. Takes up place in their life, like a distant family member. Their biographies get mixed up. She becomes the glacier and the glacier becomes her. Deep down, she wishes for them never to melt. When she sees that their volume is diminishing, even though it belongs to a protected zone (as is the case with the Saint-Sorlin glacier in the Etendard de Grandes Rousses mountain range), she weeps and refuses such an absurdity. She wants the glaciers to be considered on their own terms and saved. These intense familial relationships between humans and non-humans are increasingly the basis for climate justice demands (cf. Yolka 2020).

If we don't hold the worlds of ice and their stories far off from ourselves, in a state of radical alterity, we can better understand their importance. After all, glaciers are a bit like trees, and the ice floe is a bit like a forest. We love them just as much. They appear to be motionless. And yet they move, with the downwards pull of their mass or plunging their roots into the earth. They are both our ancestors and our contemporaries. We depend on the oxygen that they help to generate. This is our common trouble. Rather than saddening us, it thrills us. Rather than paralyzing us, it invigorates us. We are troubled here because we perceive multiple affinities with non-human beings that seem to be so different from us. These bonds draw us irresistibly. They awaken our empathy and act on us like a joyous antidote. They open out horizons of new life, extracting us from the narcissistic alternative of the spectacular and the tragic.

The Earth is a place of places where everything depends on everything else. Our signature is too visible in all this, our footprint too deep. We know this. But we are yet to answer collectively the following question: What would we gain by thinking of matter as something other than inert? We would gain an amazingly rich imagination. Our consciousness of life would be truly broadened. Many of our prejudices would disappear and we could reformulate some of our classic concepts (just think of the notion of society). By replacing the old tools with experiences shared with all those beings who make up our ecosystems and by telling this story of boundless life, we would raise our chances of building new tools. This change in perspective would help us to pool our imaginations so as to reorient our behavior. We would gain a completely new sense of complicity. Becoming interested in non-human beings, including those that are neither fauna nor flora, means inviting the whole Earth into the theatre of the living.

One doesn't slay a Glacier that saves a People

Vancouver, Canada, 29 August 2018. The afternoon stretches out before us, the sky is covered in a faint fog. I meet Julie Cruikshank in Waves Coffee at 492 Hastings Street, right near Simon Fraser University and the old docks. The coffee machine steamers hiss and there's laughter mingling in the background as we choose a seat near a window and pick up a conversation began by correspondence about the anthropology of glaciers, which she is a specialist in. My notebook is full of jottings and questions. In only a few minutes, we're transported to Alaska and Yukon, two of her preferred regions. The high-altitude glaciers shimmer in the sun, the voices of the Tlingit and Athapascan peoples echo in the great fjords, the air is full of the dry, resinous scent of red cedars. As for the crows jumping around on the pavement outside, they are messengers from another time. Night begins to fall, in the store opposite they're pulling down their shutter. The cool air of the street brings us back to the city and its sounds. Before saying goodbye, we check the time of the conference where we will find each other again the next day, we turn once more to what we have been reading lately, we say the name "Queneesh." Suddenly I'm cast back to a few days before, on the east coast of Vancouver Island, between Comox and Courtenay. There, on the painted wall of the Big House of the K'omoks, an enormous whale tells us a legend.[2]

    An old man sleeps and dreams. He hears a voice, telling him that the waters are going to rise and engulf the valley. No one will perish if the advice the voice gives is followed to the letter. The old man, as soon as he wakes up, runs to warn the chief of the K'omoks, who decides to trust the dream and gather everyone for the necessary preparations. The children stop playing, canoes are made, the ceremonial clothes are folded up, not a mask or a rattle is forgotten. Salmon and clams are smoked, cockles are dried, stocks of algae are made, the slaughtered game is prepared, clothes are sewed in a hurry. A kilometers-long rope is woven from cedar bark. After tying this to the canoes, the bravest go off to tie the other end to the glacier overhanging the valley. Then a day of heavy rain sets in. The water level begins to rise without abating. Huddled in their boats, the groups wait. Their familiar objects float off into the distance. Soon they can only see the roofs of the houses. Even the totem poles end up under water. Then it's the trees on the mountain slopes that go under. When they see that the glacier is at risk of being flooded, they are seized with fright. At that moment, the mass comes to life

---

2 The Kumugwe Big House is a living space for honoring the traditions of the K'omoks, the indigenous people of the region, who the European colonizers forcibly Christianized and for a long time prohibited from practicing their religion and their culture.

and separates itself from the peak. It's a gigantic white whale and it keeps the canoes above water with the rope. Cries of joy rise up. The whale is given the name "Queneesh." The rain stops the next day, the water level goes back to what it was, and many dream of going back to the villages. Queneesh returns to its place on the mountain. The whale turns back into the glacier that the K'omoks contemplate today. Since that time, they speak to it, whispering their gratitude.

Like most legends, the story of Queneesh has different sources. The artist Andy Everson, whose ancestors were K'omoks and Kwakwaka'wakw, tells us that its form was fixed in 1994 in order to facilitate its pedagogical transmission and to aid in bringing together local groups (cf. Everson 2000).[3] On the wall of the Big House, a thunderbird sits above the whale and the mammal's white back is the glacier. The conversation with Julie Cruikshank plunged me back into a time that is immemorial, deep, and collective. The biblical myth of Noah's Arc and the story of Utnapishtim in *Gilgamesh* comes to mind. With Queneesh, the story's turn of events and its happy ending are due to a being of ice. The glacier-become-whale-become-glacier compensates for the devastation caused by the flood, returning the valley to the K'omoks. It shortens the exile of a people and strengthens its feeling of solidarity. The legend testifies to a new alliance, not only between humans and non-human entities, but also between humans.

Legends are narrations. They tell us that someone is telling a story. This is an advantage that enhances their effects. Everyone whose turn it has been to tell a story knows this well. We adapt our story to our listeners, we embellish in order to get their attention, we lay out the scene. Daily life becomes like an echo chamber that reverberates with the perceptions of a world where souls are part of a dialogue extending beyond the dissimilarity of their respective bodies, where the borders between beings are porous and undefined. These stories create social cohesion, they describe events that tangle up different times, they give us different perspectives.

In the legend of Queneesh, a glacier turns into an animal. It doesn't go from death to life. It is already alive, and animates itself differently. It doesn't disappear under its metamorphosis. Becoming other here doesn't mean dying. Glaciers can change without perishing. All the glaciologists would agree with this *a priori*. After all, they spend their time demonstrating that these masses know nothing of thermal inertia and react to the variations of their environments.

---

3 I have based my telling of the legend of Queneesh on the appendix to Everson's study and on the versions available on the website *indigenous education* (https://indigenouseducation.comoxvalley schools.ca).

Today, however, the glacier is suffering, and its volume is much reduced. It is no longer able to transform itself into a totem-animal. Passing on the legend of Queneesh can seem a vain endeavor when the consequences of global warming can be seen from the valley with the naked eye. Why tell this story of salvation if the glacier-whale is wasting away, if it is short of breath and suffocating, beached way up there on the mountain?[4]

It's enough to maintain a familiar relationship with a high-altitude glacier, to probe the moraines on its margins, in order to feel the concretions of old landforms. If you observe closely, patiently, you relive the vertical time of layers of snow piling up, densifying, you attune yourself to the pace of matter being laid down, you feel the slow growth of alluvions, you can even make out the imprint of turbulent water on the slopes and the peaks. The smallest groove reveals a sedimented history, the landscapes recuperate their natural wrinkles, the whole ecosystem gets back in touch with its four dimensions. And then everything suddenly becomes clear: Nothing that has been experienced dissipates, none of the developments of the past is really ever effaced, all transformations are possible. In oral cultures, the time of human societies is not distinct from the cycles of other living beings, including the mineral kingdom. Memories, remnants, signs are all juxtaposed with one another and interlock. Every memory is constituted like a glacier. When it surfaces, it brings up with it traces that are thousands of years old. It's one more piece of evidence that the ground between humans and non-humans is common, and that only our speeds differ. This is how legends are born.

When they tell the legend of Queneesh, the K'omoks say over the past and share with other beings a history that makes of them the contemporaries of intermingled temporalities. The glacier-whale is not a thing, not just any object, a simple hydric resource. It is an entity that offers its help to those who know how to protect it, a tutelary authority and a precious conversation partner, an audible voice emanating from the folds of the Earth. Queneesh carries a geological intuition of the living, at odds with the flat, hurried time of the Anthropocene, this isolated time that is constantly losing its strata, this incontinent time of melting that causes us to forget everything.

Legends are good tools for reacting to the climate emergency. They orchestrate changing states of matter that give us back a taste of "thick time," the love of tectonics. What they offer us is an exit from our ignorance of temporal proportions and a reeducation in the "poly-temporality" of the Earth. In borrowing these two expressions from the philosopher Donna Haraway (cf. Caeymaex, Despret,

---

[4] For testimonials by people living in the region and for some recent photographs of the Comox Glacier, see MacKinnon 2016.

and Pieron 2019) and the geologist Marcia Bjornerud (2018), I simply want to remind us that we have a lot of time in us.

But how many decades do the glaciers have left? Scientists use modeling to estimate that the melting dynamic that is already underway will continue until 2050 at the earliest, and that there will be almost no glaciers left by the end of the century if the rates of global warming are not quickly reversed (Zekollari, Huss, and Farinotti 2019).[5] For the indigenous populations living near the glaciers, their complete disappearance will be the beginning of a great silence. One of the effects the ice melt has is depopulation. It destroys interlocutors and dissolves communities of affects between humans and non-humans. Temporalities come apart, the world withers. Is it possible that the chance to listen to their advice has passed?

In the old man's dream, the voice said to make a rope. It knew that the glacier would metamorphose into a whale and save the K'omoks from the flood. Dreams are full of surprising links between living beings with different forms. Doubtless we must say to ourselves that the rope has not been broken yet. It's not so easy to slay a glacier that saves a people.

References

Bjornerud, Marcia. *Timefulness: How Thinking Like a Geologist Can Help Save The World*. Princeton: Princeton University Press, 2018.
Caeymaex, Florence, Vinciane Despret, and Julien Pieron (ed.). *Habiter le trouble avec Donna Haraway*. Bellevaux: Éditions Dehors, 2019.
Datta, Rajashree Tri, Marco Tedesco, Xavier Fettweis, Cecile Agosta, Stef Lhermitte, Jan T. M. Lenaerts, and Nander Wever. "The Effect of Foehn-Induced Surface Melt on Firn Evolution Over the Northeast Antarctic Peninsula." Geophysical Research Letters 46 (2019/7): 3822–3831.
David, Victor. "La nouvelle vague des droits de la nature. La personnalité juridique reconnue aux fleuves Whanganui, Gange et Yam." *Revue juridique de l'environnement* 42 (2017/3): 409–424.
Everson, Andrew Frank. *Renegotiating the Past. Contemporary Tradition and Identity of The Comox First Nation*. Master of Arts, University of British Columbia, 2000.
Haraway, Donna. *Staying with the Trouble: Making Kin in the Chthulucene*. Durham, London: Duke University Press, 2016.
MacKinnon, James Bernard. "The Whale Dying on the Mountain." *Hakai Magazine* (16 February 2016). https://www.hakaimagazine.com/features/whale-dying-mountain (20 September 2022).
Remaud, Olivier. *Penser comme un iceberg*, afterword by Anne-Marie Garat. Arles: Actes Sud, 2020.
_____. "On n'achève pas un glacier qui sauve un peuple." *Socialter* 46 (2021), 66–69.
_____. "Trouble contre trouble: le glacier et l'être humain." *AOC* (03.11.2021). https://aoc.media/opinion/2021/03/10/trouble-contre-trouble-le-glacier-et-letre-humain/ (20 September 2022).
_____. *Thinking Like an Iceberg*, trans. Stephen Muecke. Cambridge: Polity Press, 2022.

---

5 The article deals with the Alps.

Watt-Cloutier, Sheila. *The Right to be cold. One Woman's Story of Protecting Her Culture, the Arctic and the Whole Planet*. Toronto: Penguin Random House Canada, 2016.

Yolka, Philippe. "Les glaciers de montagne à l'épreuve du réchauffement climatique (une protection juridique à inventer)." *Revue juridique de l'environnement* 45 (2020/3): 559–568.

Zekollari, Harry, Matthias Huss, and Daniel Farinotti. "Modelling the future evolution of glaciers in the European Alps under the EURO-CORDEX RCM ensemble." *The Cryosphere* 4 (2019/13): 1125–1146.

Lucia della Fontana
Conte de fées et réparation écologique :
La lucina d'Antonio Moresco

Résumé : Face à la dévastation environnementale, de nombreux penseurs et penseuses proposent d'inventer de nouvelles histoires non destructrices. En puisant aux marges de la culture occidentale, en particulier dans les narrations féministes et chez les peuples autochtones et colonisés, ils et elles cherchent à tisser de nouveaux modes d'imagination collective et de réparation. On introduit dans ce but la notion de « fabulation spéculative » : au lieu de se contenter de récits descriptifs qui constatent l'état des choses, il s'agit de créer un nouveau cadre pour l'action et de reformuler ce qui importe comme réel. En s'appuyant sur l'étude de *La lucina* d'Antonio Moresco (2013), l'article se propose d'explorer le lien qui relie fabulation spéculative et conte de fées pour vérifier si et par quel moyen la littérature peut être un instrument de réparation écologique. Dans ce roman, la dimension surnaturelle du conte de fées déstabilise en effet les catégories par lesquelles nous appréhendons le monde pour saisir le caractère situé, enchevêtré et parfois conflictuel des relations entre humains et non-humains.

Mots-clés : conte de fées ; réparation écologique ; *environmental humanities* ; *speculative fabulation* ; Donna Haraway ; Antonio Moresco ; écocritique

Marqués par la perte et le dépassement des seuils de basculement – le taux de dioxyde de carbone, la fonte des glaciers et le dérèglement climatique, la sixième extinction de masse qui touche toute sorte d'êtres, y compris les peuples et les langues autochtones – les temps que nous traversons appellent à une démarche de réparation. Réparation du tissu écologique, bien sûr ; réparation de l'humain aussi. Mais est-ce que réparer un homme, une femme, équivaut à réparer un milieu ? Si cette analogie peut être questionnée, il n'en reste pas moins que nous sommes enveloppés dans un enchevêtrement de relations : à l'instar des champignons qui poussent dans des forêts détruites (Tsing 2015), l'espace que nous habitons nous relie fatalement aux autres. De plus, nous savons aujourd'hui – les experts nous le disent – que ce qui est en train de se passer est irréparable : nous allons habiter une planète de plus en plus ravagée. Dans un tel contexte, toute tentative de réparation devrait abandonner le projet d'une restauration complète et envisager d'autres façons de penser notre relation avec la nature.

Dans son dernier livre *Staying with the Trouble: Making Kin in the Chthulucene* (2016), la philosophe Donna Haraway réfléchit à la manière dont nous pourrions apprendre à vivre sur une planète endommagée. Face au récit dominant concernant l'exploitation de la nature et le progrès économique, Haraway propose d'inventer de nouvelles histoires non destructrices. En puisant aux marges de la culture occidentale, en particulier dans les narrations féministes et écoféministes et chez les peuples autochtones et colonisés, Haraway cherche à tisser de nouveaux modes d'imagination collective et de réparation. Elle introduit dans ce but la notion de « fabulation spéculative » : au lieu de se contenter de récits descriptifs qui constatent l'état des choses, il s'agit de créer un nouveau cadre pour l'action et de reformuler ce qui importe comme réel (Haraway 2016, 2–3). Il faut libérer l'imagination, martèle Haraway, susciter les possibles qui auraient pu ou qui pourraient être. Pour cela, il est indispensable de contrer ce qu'Isabelle Stengers et Didier Debaise appellent « l'adhésion au probable », à savoir « toute interprétation qui souscrirait au caractère irrésistible du déchaînement capitaliste comme s'il s'agissait de notre destin [. . .] alors qu'il désigne la désertification de nos mondes et notre impuissance à penser que ce à quoi nous tenons puisse avoir un avenir » (Haraway 2016, 87–88).

À Cerisy, en 2013, lors du colloque « Gestes spéculatifs », Haraway fréquente un atelier de narration spéculative avec Vinciane Despret et Fabrizio Terranova (Debaise et Stengers 2015). C'est le début d'une aventure qui débouche sur le dernier chapitre de *Staying with the Trouble*, « The Camille stories, Children of Compost » (Haraway 2016, 134–168). Ici Haraway prend la casquette de l'écrivaine pour relayer des récits multi-espèces, proches du conte de fées et de la science-fiction, dont le but est de promouvoir un épanouissement commun. Aussi imagine-t-elle qu'à partir de la fin de notre siècle se crée une communauté visant à survivre sur une terre encore plus en ruines que la nôtre. Contre l'extinction et la menace anthropique qui les guettent, les Enfants du Compost (tel est le nom de cette communauté) se métissent avec d'autres espèces, chaque enfant ayant trois parents humains et un symbiote non-humain. C'est le cas des Camille, créatures hybrides issues d'un croisement entre humains et papillons monarques, qu'Haraway suit pendant cinq générations. Cela lui permet non seulement de repenser la parentalité, mais de faire monde autrement, le but de ces fabulations n'étant pas la restauration ou la réconciliation entre humain et nature mais plutôt les « modest possibilities of partial recuperation and getting on together. Call that staying with the trouble » (Haraway 2016, 10).

De surcroît, la philosophe américaine n'a de cesse de souligner le caractère pratique de sa pensée et de son écriture : « Theory is bodily, and theory is literal. Theory is not about matters distant from the lived body – quite the opposite. Theory is anything but disembodied. » (Haraway 2020, 464). Chez elle, il n'y a pas de séparation entre le plan symbolique et le plan sensible, bien au contraire. Pour Haraway, fiction est synonyme d'action, de fabrication sémiotique et matérielle. Comme elle a pu l'expérimenter lors des compétitions d'*agility* avec sa chienne Cayenne, le langage affecte l'ontologie en déterminant le rôle et la puissance d'agir que nous accordons aux autres. La subjectivation du monde dépend des mots et des pronoms que nous employons pour les désigner : « The pronouns embedded in sentences about contestations for what may count as nature are themselves political tools, expressing hopes, fears, and contradictory histories. Grammar is politics by other means » (Haraway 1991b, 3). Il ne s'agit pas de jouer le ventriloque et de tout ramener à soi, mais de stimuler la capacité d'agir de tous les interlocuteurs avec lesquels nous interagissons. En ce sens, l'écriture spéculative de Haraway vise à créer des formes de « response-ability » (Haraway 2016, 114) qui nous engagent dans des relations en nous apprenant à devenir et penser avec les autres et non à leur sujet. Comme le remarque Vinciane Despret : « Les histoires de Donna Haraway n'illustrent pas, ce que feraient les anecdotes, mais font exister et assument sans innocence ce qu'elles font exister ; elles n'expliquent pas, elles connectent » (Despret 2012, 37). Si nous voulons entamer une démarche de réparation, c'est par la reconstitution des liens qui nous unissent aux autres que nous devons commencer.

Cette mise en avant du récit et de la fabulation comme moyens de faire exister des possibles et de transformer ce à quoi nous tenons me semble mériter réflexion. En s'appuyant sur l'étude de *La lucina* d'Antonio Moresco (2013), l'article se propose d'explorer le lien qui relie fabulation spéculative et conte de fée pour vérifier si et par quel biais la littérature peut être un instrument de réparation écologique. Dans ce roman, la dimension surnaturelle du conte de fées déstabilise en effet les catégories par lesquelles nous appréhendons le monde pour saisir le caractère situé, enchevêtré et parfois conflictuel des relations entre humains et non-humains.

1 Littérature et écologie : déstabiliser le régime réaliste

Dans son livre *Réparer le monde. La littérature française face au XXIe siècle* (2018), Alexandre Gefen reprend la notion talmudique du *tikkun olam* pour annoncer la sortie du régime esthétique de la littérature occidentale. Ainsi Gefen observe-t-il le passage d'une idéologie de l'intransitivité et de l'autonomie littéraire, fondée sur des principes formels et évitant toute finalité pratique, vers une fonction sociale de la littérature à vocation thérapeutique. En témoigne, d'une part, la prolifération sur le marché de l'édition du storytelling, de la biographie et de l'autobiographie, de la littérature du *care* et, de manière plus générale, d'une littérature éthique visant le bien-être des lecteurs ; d'autre part, du côté critique, l'essor de théories hybrides telles que la neuroesthétique, la biocritique ou le darwinisme littéraire dénote une interdépendance croissante entre la littérature et les sciences.

En même temps, les dangers d'une finalisation et d'un assujettissement de la littérature à la science sont dénoncés par plusieurs intellectuels et par Gefen lui-même lorsqu'il affirme que, bien qu'il puisse être utile de se débarrasser d'une « essentialisation du littéraire » (Gefen et Perez 2019, 5) qui restreint les horizons herméneutiques et épistémologiques, l'interdisciplinarité « érode forcément les aspirations à "l'autonomie" dans un contexte où il est demandé à la littérature d'agir, de consoler, de "produire du lien" et du sens alors que les institutions et les autres prises de discours défaillent » (Gefen et Perez 2019, 4).

Plutôt que de s'attarder sur la question de savoir si la littérature nous fait vivre plus ou moins longtemps et quel type de bénéfice les lecteurs tirent de la lecture, il me semble intéressant, dans la démarche écologique qui est la mienne, de creuser les relations qui unissent la littérature et la science. Car, contrairement à la notion d'influence, qui postule deux champs de connaissance indépendants mais hiérarchisés de telle sorte que la science inspire la littérature et non l'inverse, il s'agit plutôt d'avoir une approche empirique et non encadrée aux textes, afin d'identifier des *trading zones* ainsi que des spécificités respectives. Ainsi, Gefen lui-même finit par admettre que, dans leur relation mutuelle, tant la littérature que l'écologie peuvent gagner en singularité. Après avoir consacré un bref sous-chapitre de *Réparer le monde*, intitulé « Protéger le monde », à la « remédiation écologique de la littérature » (Gefen 2018, 199–202), dans un article paru en mars 2021, il considère que « la littérature écologique a pour le XXIe siècle l'importance qu'a eue la "littérature engagée" pour le XXe : elle en est la "repolytisation" » (Gefen 2021). Le dialogue entre la littérature et l'écologie stimule non seulement l'interdisciplinarité, mais produit également de nouvelles formes de discours difficiles à classer. Au-delà de ses implications réparatrices, donner la parole à la nature pour décentrer l'humain revient alors à renouveler la pratique et la critique littéraire : « Loin d'être un effet de mode, en démontant l'opposition nature/culture, le sens de la supériorité humaine et les faux clivages, en renouvelant des questions littéraires aussi essentielles que celle des genres, des personnages et du point de vue, l'écocritique est une vraie rupture épistémologique » (Gefen 2021). La fracture épistémologique dont parle Gefen se caractérise surtout par la « déstabilis[ation] du régime réaliste » (Gefen 2018, 202). En effet, contre une approche réaliste « which has proved a rather poor way of engaging with the world's active agency » (Haraway 1991a, 199), à mesure que la crise écologique s'intensifie, la littérature semble s'éloigner d'une conception étroite du réel. Le roman réaliste en tant que récit de la vie quotidienne et représentation d'une tranche de vie sociale et historique, tel que théorisé par Auerbach (1968), est écarté au profit d'autres formes narratives comme l'épopée ou le conte de fées. Ainsi les écrivains ont-ils recours à des genres dépaysants, traditionnellement associés à la paralittérature ou au folklore, tels que la science-fiction, la dystopie, la fantasy, le conte de fées ou le récit d'horreur.

De même, sur le versant théorique, certains critiques déplorent l'incapacité du paradigme réaliste, fortement attaché aux « effets de réel », à faire place aux éléments perturbateurs introduits par le changement climatique (Ghosh 2017 ; Benedetti 2021). D'autres, en revanche, montrent que la définition d'Auerbach est trop restreinte. Quoi qu'il en soit, il semble évident qu'il faut désormais ébranler l'opposition tranchée entre réalisme et antiréalisme. On pourrait citer à ce propos la célèbre phrase d'Adorno : « Si le roman veut rester fidèle à son héritage réaliste, et dire ce qui existe vraiment, il doit renoncer à un réalisme qui, en reproduisant la façade, ne fait que se rendre complice de son activité mensongère » (Adorno 2009, 39).

2 Pourquoi le conte de fées ?

Contre un réalisme de façade, face à la destruction de la planète les auteurs revendiquent une expérience de vie qui n'est pas appauvrie mais simplement différente. Pour la raconter, ils font appel à des éléments surréalistes et magiques qui déplacent les frontières du réel. Comme l'observe l'écoféministe australienne Val Plumwood :

> Instrumental culture has prepared an exceptional place for speaking matter (which romanticism did not sufficiently disrupt), as the exceptional context of the fairy-tale, or the irrational space of the eerie and haunted. But if it is the space of everyday wonder and quotidian enchantment (and why aim for less?) that is in need of reclamation and recovery, ethical and philosophical theories that legitimate a rich intentionality for as wide as possible a range of non-human actors and descriptors will probably prove most useful (Plumwood 2017, 18).

Plumwood appelle alors à libérer l'imagination et à franchir la dichotomie qui sépare fiction et non-fiction. Elle prône notamment une écriture « intentionnaliste » et « antiréductionniste » qui, loin de considérer ce genre de phénomènes comme extraordinaires, élargisse notre perception du réel en dissipant l'illusion anthropocentrique et indépendantiste qui érige l'homme au-dessus de tout.

En faisant parler ceux qui sont normalement muets et en octroyant une forme de « agency » aux non-humains, le conte de fées remet en question le cadre « instrumental » auquel nous nous sommes accoutumés. Ce dépaysement cognitif semble à même d'exprimer « la voix de la nature » qui « plonge dans l'abîme de l'inanimé » dont il était question dans *Le conteur* de Benjamin (Benjamin 2011, ch. XVIII). Mais suffit-il de représenter l'autre en lui accordant le don de la parole pour réparer la trame déchirée du vivant ? Si l'anthropomorphisme s'approprie souvent l'identité d'autrui, aboutissant à une forme de réductionnisme qui ramène tout à l'humain, peut-il aussi rendre justice aux non-humains en les représentant dans leur complexité ?

Les mots fable et fabulation, comme les mots italiens « favola » et « fiaba », qui signifient respectivement « fable » et « conte de fées », dérivent du latin *fabula*, à son tour issu du verbe *for, fari* qui signifie parler. À l'origine, la *fabula* avait la même signification que le *mythos* grec, à savoir fable, légende, mythe, histoire, apologue, ouï-dire. Contrairement au mythe, la fable a fini par désigner une histoire fictive ou mensongère. Souvent, les fables ont pour personnages des animaux ou des objets naturels personnifiés. Elles sont atemporelles et anhistoriques et engagent le lecteur en se terminant par un message instructif. En revanche, le « conte de fées », s'il est pris au pied de la lettre, ne devrait désigner que les histoires de fées, ces personnages féminins dotés de pouvoirs magiques auxquels font référence les croyances populaires traditionnelles. Toutefois, les frontières entre fable et conte de fées ne sont pas étanches et se chevauchent souvent, le dernier étant généralement employé avec un spectre sémantique beaucoup plus vaste, à savoir des histoires, désormais destinées à un public d'enfants, dans lesquelles un individu est confronté à des événements surnaturels ou étranges.

Il est intéressant de noter que le conte de fées a une double généalogie : d'une part, le folklore populaire qui, à partir de la fin du XVIIIe siècle, est recueilli en tant qu'expression d'une tradition nationale ; d'autre part, la création aristocratique du conte à la française par Charles Perrault et Madame d'Aulnoy. Si le concept moderne de conte de fées ne semble pas remonter plus haut que le XVIIe siècle en Europe, son origine se perd dans la nuit des temps. C'est Vladimir Propp qui, dans *Les racines historiques du conte merveilleux* (1983), a le premier établi un lien direct entre les contes de fées et la préhistoire. À cet égard, Propp a avancé une théorie ritualiste selon laquelle les origines des contes de fées sont liées aux traditions des communautés primitives : avec le passage d'une société de chasseurs-cueilleurs à une société agraire, les cérémonies de la chasse ont disparu, mais les récits qui les accompagnaient ont survécu sous forme de légendes, de mythes ou de fables. La forêt dans laquelle le protagoniste est abandonné et les autres épreuves qu'il doit affronter sont autant de vestiges des rituels initiatiques accomplis afin d'intégrer la communauté des adultes.

Mais la contribution de Propp va bien au-delà car, dans une œuvre pionnière, *Morphologie du conte*, parue en Russie en 1928, il s'inspire des études d'histoire naturelle de Goethe pour dresser une liste des personnages et des fonctions narratives qui charpentent les contes de fées. Ouvrant la voie aux courants formalistes et structuralistes, Propp identifie 31 fonctions récurrentes qui, recombinées selon un ordre plus ou moins rigide, donnent lieu à des variations infinies. Dans les années 1960, le linguiste lituanien Algirdas Julien Greimas prend le relais en remplaçant la notion de personnage par des catégories actantielles (sujet, objet, destinateur, destinataire, adjuvant, opposant) et en réduisant les fonctions de trente-et-un à vingt, réparties en trois catégories (contractuelles, performancielles, disjonctives ; Greimas 1966). Comme le note Bruno Latour, en incarnant celui ou celle qui accomplit ou subit l'acte indépendamment de toute autre détermination, l'actant n'est pas défini ontologiquement, mais relationnellement (Latour 2015, ch. II). Il remplace avantageusement les notions de personnage et de *dramatis persona* et permet de décentrer l'attention vers d'autres « agencies » non-humaines.

Un autre aspect du conte de fées qui paraît fondamental dans une perspective écologique est sa dimension réparatrice. D'après Propp, le point de départ du conte de fées est toujours une situation adverse. Les circonstances initiales, qui sont d'ailleurs celles où se révèle l'historicité du conte de fées, avec des détails qui nous renseignent sur le quotidien du narrateur ou de la narratrice, se caractérisent toujours par une condition de dommage ou de manque : éloignement, interdiction, famine, pauvreté. Le sentiment d'injustice et le besoin de réparation sont les moteurs de la narration, le dommage ou le manque trouvant satisfaction lors du dénouement heureux, souvent stéréotypé, par exemple le mariage réparateur avec le prince ou la princesse. Ce mécanisme compensateur a été défini aussi bien par Propp que par Greimas comme un passage de fonctions négatives à des fonctions renversant ou dépassant les premières. Comme la devinette, le conte de fées offre un modèle résolutoire : transposer les problèmes en conte de fées, c'est alors envisager une action de réparation.

Plusieurs aspects semblent donc expliquer le recours au conte de fées en période de catastrophe écologique : l'émancipation vis-à-vis du régime réaliste, la capacité à décentrer l'humain en octroyant de la puissance d'agir aux non-humains, la démarche réparatrice qui conclut invariablement le récit (« et ils vécurent heureux jusqu'à la fin des temps »). Mais il y a un autre élément qui mérite d'être mentionné. En tant que production narrative archaïque du monde agricole, le conte de fées est issu d'un univers interconnecté où la nature et la culture ne sont pas séparées. La métamorphose, autre *topos* du conte de fées, exprime notamment la continuité entre les trois règnes minéral, végétal et animal. Italo Calvino, le premier anthologiste des contes de fées italiens, considère à ce propos que « avec la disparition d'une totalité naturelle-culturelle archaïque, le conte de fées meurt, c'est-à-dire qu'il perd la faculté de multiplier ses variantes[1] » (Calvino 1988, 125–126). Contrairement à la prédiction de Calvino, face à la crise environnementale, le conte de fées est aujourd'hui revivifié pour repenser le rapport entre les humains et la nature. Mais, comme nous allons le voir, il ne peut être question de mobiliser le conte de fées pour régresser vers une nature intacte, ni pour glorifier une unité homme-nature prélapsaire. Tout en restant avec le problème (Haraway 2016), il s'agit de faire monde autrement, en commençant par les relations qui nous unissent à ceux et celles qui nous entourent.

---

1 [Con la scomparsa d'una totalità naturale-culturale arcaica la fiaba muore, cioè perde la facoltà di moltiplicare le sue varianti.] Sauf indication contraire, toutes traductions sont les miennes.

3 Antonio Moresco : une écriture visionnaire

Antonio Moresco est né à Mantoue en 1947. À quarante-six ans, après une série de refus de la part des éditeurs, il parvient à publier son premier recueil, *Clandestinità* (1993). En 1998, la parution de *Gli esordi*, premier acte de la trilogie *Giochi dell'eternità*, roman remarquable tant par sa taille que par son ambition littéraire, l'impose sur la scène italienne contemporaine. Dans les années 2000 et 2010, en plus de la trilogie, Moresco publie une série d'ouvrages plus courts comme *Le favole della Maria* (2007), *Gli incendiati* (2010), *La lucina* (2013), *Fiaba d'amore* (2014), *Fiabe* (2017), *Fiaba bianca* (2018a) où il s'inspire des fables et des contes de fées. Parallèlement, depuis les pages de *Il primo amore*, le blog littéraire qu'il codirige avec ses collègues et amis Carla Benedetti, Tiziano Scarpa et Dario Voltolini, Moresco se mobilise contre la destruction écologique : en 2018 paraît *Il grido*, un pamphlet dans lequel il pointe du doigt le caractère mortifère de notre société, qui se dirige aveuglément vers l'extinction d'espèce. En 2019, Antonio Moresco est ainsi parmi les organisateurs de l'évènement « Terrestres : des écrivains sur le Vésuve pour défendre l'environnement » avec Amitav Ghosh et Bruno Latour. Mais est-il possible d'établir un lien entre l'attrait que le conte de fées exerce sur l'auteur et son engagement écologique ?

Depuis ses débuts, l'écrivain italien prend position contre une littérature *mainstream* qui, en se limitant à décrire la réalité telle qu'elle nous a déjà été racontée, conforte le lecteur dans ses convictions. Dans un extrait de *Lettere a nessuno* de 1991, il observait déjà, en reformulant Beckett : « Ce n'est pas une question de réalisme ou de non-réalisme, puisque tant le réalisme que le non-réalisme ne sont pas possibles, ni même théoriquement concevables, pour la simple raison que la réalité n'est pas et ne peut pas être "réaliste"[2] » (Moresco 2018c, 336). Moresco vise notamment le roman réaliste et sa narration anthropocentrique orientée vers le dénouement. À la place du « psychologisme » (Moresco 2018c, 365), il affirme vouloir atteindre le noyau de l'existence. Ainsi, il aborde directement des catégories fondamentales comme la vie, la mort, l'éternité. Face à cette dimension biologique et cosmique, les frontières entre réalité et fiction s'estompent au profit d'une expérience totale qui dépasse la littérature.

C'est dans cette perspective que Moresco a recours aux contes de fées : à l'instar de la philosophie, ces derniers se chargent de poser les questions indispensables qui nous hantent depuis toujours. Moresco insiste alors sur l'origine anthropologique du conte de fées en tant que réservoir intarissable sur lequel repose notre imaginaire

---

2 [Non è questione di realismo o non-realismo, dato che sia il realismo che il non-realismo non sono possibili e neppure teoricamente ipotizzabili, per il semplice fatto che la realtà non è né può essere "realistica".]

collectif et dans lequel chacun peut puiser. En outre, dans le récueil de contes de fées qu'il a collectés pour la maison d'édition Sem, il élargit les frontières du genre en incluant des auteurs tels que Kafka, Campana, Rimbaud et la Bible et tient à préciser : « J'ai également essayé d'étendre le champ du conte au-delà du soi-disant "genre". J'ai fait une intrusion, parce qu'il est nécessaire de briser la petite barrière et la prison du "genre" dans laquelle le conte de fées avec sa vérité et sa puissance a été enfermé[3] » (Moresco 2017, 17).

Loin de s'agir de récits paisibles et enfantins, pour Moresco les contes de fées sont « extrémistes, électifs, prophétiques, emblématiques, sapientiels[4] » (Moresco 2017, 11). Les personnages y font un avec leur destin. Cette verticalité du conte de fées s'exprime dans l'acte métamorphique qui brise les règles de la représentation mimétique pour révéler la radicale unité du monde : la grenouille se transforme en prince, la servante devient princesse, la citrouille se métamorphose en carrosse... Comme l'écrit Moresco, « le conte de fées ne reflète pas mais transperce la réalité[5] » (Moresco 2017, 11). Lieu oxymorique, activité perturbatrice, il est l'endroit où tout redevient possible. Moresco cite à ce propos l'essayiste italienne Cristina Campo, pour qui « La leçon obstinée et inépuisable des contes de fées est donc la victoire sur la loi de la nécessité, le passage constant à un nouvel ordre de relations et absolument rien d'autre, car il n'y a absolument rien d'autre à apprendre sur cette terre[6] » (Campo 1987, 34).

En même temps, dans l'introduction à *Fiabe*, le récueil qu'il a dirigé pour Sem, Moresco considère que les contes de fées peuvent emprunter deux voies : transmettre un message de consolation ou bien être sincères jusqu'à la cruauté. Moresco opte pour la seconde option. Il sélectionne alors des récits cruels, comme le *Conte du genévrier* ou *L'enfant obstiné* des frères Grimm. De plus, il intervient en modifiant certains passages pour rendre les contes plus cruels, comme lorsqu'il conclut *Le roi est nu* d'Andersen par le supplice de l'enfant qui a révélé la nudité du roi. Ce sont des histoires amères qui véhiculent une vision du monde désenchantée. Mais comment la cruauté et la rupture de la loi de nécessité peuvent-elles coexister et même aboutir à une démarche de réparation ? Essayons de le comprendre en analysant un court roman de Moresco paru en 2013, *La lucina*.

---

3 [Ho anche cercato di allargare il campo della fiaba oltre il cosiddetto "genere". Ho sconfinato, perché bisogna sfondare il piccolo recinto e la prigione del "genere" in cui è stata rinchiusa la fiaba con la sua verità e potenza.]
4 [Estremiste, elettive, profetiche, emblematiche, sapienziali.]
5 [La fiaba non riflette ma trafigge la realtà.]
6 [La caparbia, inesausta lezione delle fiabe è dunque la vittoria sulla legge di necessità, il passaggio costante a un nuovo ordine di rapporti e assolutamente niente altro, perché assolutamente niente altro c'è da imparare su questa terra.]

4 *La lucina* : la nature léopardienne et la question du mal

En 2013, dans le sillage de *Gli incendiati* (2010), Antonio Moresco publie *La lucina*, suivi en 2014 par *Fiaba d'amore*. Par opposition à la trilogie monumentale *I giochi dell'eternità*, écrite sur une période de trente ans, ces récits se caractérisent par leur brièveté. À mi-chemin entre le conte de fées et le roman métaphysique, *La lucina* est définie par Moresco comme une « rencontre du troisième type avec mon moi enfantin[7] ». Il y raconte l'histoire d'un homme qui choisit de s'isoler dans un petit bourg situé en zone sismique où la nature a repris ses droits. C'est l'un de ces petits hameaux perchés sur les collines, peu accessibles, parfois menacés par des catastrophes environnementales, qui sont en voie de dépeuplement dans toute l'Italie. Dans cet espace végétal sans bornes, le seul signe de vie humaine aperçu par le narrateur est une petite lumière qui s'allume chaque soir de l'autre côté de la vallée. L'homme décide alors de partir à la recherche de sa source et finit par découvrir qu'elle provient d'une maison en pierre où vit un enfant aussi solitaire que lui.

Premier livre de Moresco à se dérouler entièrement dans un cadre naturel, *La lucina* débute par le choix du narrateur de quitter la ville pour se réfugier au milieu de nulle part : « Je suis venu ici pour disparaître, dans ce hameau abandonné et désert dont je suis le seul habitant » (Moresco 2014, 9). Le choix de s'autoexclure de l'écoumène humain et le fait que le protagoniste soit un alter ego de l'auteur sont deux *topoi* de l'écriture de Moresco. Mais, contrairement à ce que l'on pourrait penser, le rejet de la société au profit de la nature n'aboutit pas à une rencontre pacifiée. Ce n'est pas un hasard si *La lucina* s'ouvre précisément à la fin du printemps, la saison la plus cruelle, d'après T. S. Eliot (2001, 5), au cours de laquelle le contraste oxymorique entre la profusion de la nature et son incessant dépérissement atteint son apogée. Dans la première scène du roman, le narrateur, assis sur une chaise en fer face à un abrupt végétal, observe la nature luxuriante qui l'entoure. Au lieu de l'apaiser, ce spectacle accentue son isolement. À commencer par le syntagme « tourment végétal », répété deux fois aux chapitres 2 et 29, puis repris à travers le polyptote « tourmentés » au chapitre 5, l'élément naturel est aussitôt perçu comme violent et incontrôlable. La référence à la forêt des suicidés de l'Enfer de Dante est évidente, mais l'inspiration à la "nature marâtre" de Giacomo Leopardi est tout aussi présente. On peut citer à ce propos une note célèbre du *Zibaldone* écrite par le poète à Bologne en avril 1826 et surnommée « le jardin de la souffrance ».

---

[7] C'est ce que dit Moresco lors d'une rencontre organisée par la librairie Charybde à Paris le 4 octobre 2014.

Leopardi y décrit un jardin printanier qui, sous des apparences harmonieuses, est régi par la domination du plus fort sur le faible. La mort y règne en maître :

> Entrez dans un jardin peuplé de plantes, d'herbes et de fleurs. Riant, tel que vous l'aimeriez. Dans la plus douce saison de l'année. Vous ne pourrez poser vos yeux nulle part sans y découvrir quelque tourment. Toutes ces familles de végétaux sont plus ou moins en état de *souffrance*. Ici, cette rose est blessée par le soleil, qui lui a donné la vie ; elle se plisse, se languit, se fane (Leopardi 2003, 1849).

Leopardi poursuit en détaillant la souffrance des lys, tourmentés par les abeilles, puis des arbres, dont l'écorce est blessée ou meurtrie, puis des branches cassées et enfin de l'herbe, involontairement lacérée par les pas inconscients du jardinier. Le poète conclut en considérant que « chaque jardin est pareil à un vaste hôpital et si ces êtres sentent ou, si l'on préfère, sentaient, il est certain que pour eux le non-être serait de loin préférable à l'être » (Leopardi 2003, 1850). Dans la description de la nature par Moresco, on retrouve les mêmes éléments que chez le jardin de Leopardi : les tourments végétaux, les arbres blessés, les lys déchirés, les branches cassées. La lutte pour l'existence paraît prendre le dessus :

> Et puis il y a tout ce sous-bois féroce et ces mille et mille formes végétales qui s'entrelacent et se combattent, déjà sous la ligne de la terre, dans les mille et mille radicelles et dans les mille autres formes pressées par leur turgescence chimique et encore sans forme, qui jaillissent de la terre comme des armées avec leurs corps nus encore dépourvus d'écorce, et qui s'inventent leurs premières machines à respirer et à échanger avec l'atmosphère et commencent à grimper en un furieux enchevêtrement muet de formes nées des graines portées par le vent ou par d'autres bombes qui pullulent dans le ventre pourri du monde, et qui entament leur lutte pour grimper vers le haut, vers la lumière (Moresco 2014, 15).

Ces considérations se poursuivent jusqu'au point climacique où le narrateur se demande :

> Pourquoi tout ce grouillement de corps qui tentent d'épuiser les autres corps en aspirant leur sève de leurs mille et mille racines déchaînées et de leurs petites ventouses forcénées pour détourner vers eux la puissance chimique, pour créer de nouveaux fronts végétaux capables de tout anéantir, de tout massacrer ? Où je peux bien aller pour ne plus voir ce carnage, cette irréparable et aveugle torsion qu'on a appelée vie (Moresco 2014, 16) ?

Au début de *La lucina*, la vie se présente sous la forme d'un principe biologique universel qui veut sa propre persistance coûte que coûte. En dépit de ce vitalisme exacerbé dans la première partie du roman, l'isolement du protagoniste est décrit comme absence de vie : « J'avançais en faisant tournoyer de temps en temps mon bâton au-dessus de ma tête et de mes épaules, pour chasser insectes et taons qui venaient bourdonner autour de cette seule personne vivante qui marchait dans leur monde » (Moresco 2014, 19). Le narrateur humain semble la seule « personne » qui dispose d'une puissance d'agir suffisante pour représenter la vie. Cela confirme l'impression de séparation de l'incipit : un narrateur qui observe, une nature observée ; un protagoniste doté de « agency », une nature régie par la loi aveugle de la chimie. Pour l'instant, la sienne est la seule voix qui vient combler le silence : « je demande, je crie, pour me faire entendre tout là-haut, dans cette vastitude végétale silencieuse qui renvoie l'écho de ma voix » (Moresco 2014, 25). Le monde se tait et la nature et la culture restent séparées, ce qui ne fait qu'accroître sa solitude. Mais tout cela va changer.

5 *La lucina* ou la voix de la nature

Moresco ne résout jamais ces contradictions, mais, petit à petit, une métamorphose s'enclenche. Dans la seconde moitié de l'œuvre, la situation initiale est renversée, passant d'un état de détachement vis-à-vis de la nature hostile à une immersion holistique en elle, qui s'opère en abandonnant la perspective anthropocentrique. Une série de rencontres qui sont autant de tentatives plus ou moins ratées de dialogue interspécifique jalonnent ce parcours : deux blaireaux qui fixent le narrateur de leurs « grands yeux cerclés de blanc » (Moresco 2014, 11), un crapaud « qui fuit avec des bonds pesants au bruit de [s]es pas » (Moresco 2014, 12), un châtaignier presque mort, des racines, des hirondelles qui lui répondent (Moresco 2014, 25–26), des lucioles, un rottweiler aux pattes brisées.

Les contes de fées, constate Moresco dans l'introduction aux *Fiabe* rassemblées pour Sem, « n'acceptent pas des explications partielles et superficielles concernant la présence du mal dans le monde[8] » (Moresco 2017, 9). Dans *La lucina*, le dispositif du conte de fées est utilisé pour investiguer les origines du mal qui affecte la nature, humains compris. Si interroger le mal ne signifie pas le réparer, le questionnement engage le processus de réparation. Ainsi, au cours de la narration, la série de rencontres inter-espèces qui ponctuent le périple du narrateur le conduisent à changer de point de vue. Peu à peu, l'observation[9] solitaire du « tourment végétal » est dès lors remplacée par une attitude de plus en plus créative et spéculative. Cette capacité à imaginer permet au narrateur de percevoir de nouvelles connexions et de nouvelles présences qui étaient auparavant invisibles. Il apparait alors que non seulement notre perception de la nature dépend de nos représentations sociales, mais que la violence que nous lui infligeons est relationnelle et rétroactive. Aussi, avant de se

---

8 [Non accolgono spiegazioni parziali e di superficie dell'incombente presenza del male nel mondo.]
9 L'observation se trouve d'ailleurs dans l'étymologie de spéculer, du latin speculum, à son tour dérivé de specĕre, « regarder ».

révéler un compagnon doux et fidèle, la férocité du rottweiler reflète celle des humains qui le dressent pour le combat :

> J'avais reconnu dans cette grosse bête une de ces races de chiens qu'on dresse pour le combat, un rottweiler. [. . .] Je savais comment ces chiens se comportent. Je l'avais lu par le passé, dans les journaux, à l'occasion d'attaques sur des hommes, des femmes, des enfants, agressés et tués ou bien défigurés par les morsures. [. . .] D'un coup, ils vous sautent dessus et vous mordent les mains, les bras, la gorge, le visage, ils vous broient la chair et les os avec leurs dents. Ils ne s'arrêtent pas tant qu'ils ne vous ont pas massacré, ou que quelqu'un d'autre ne les arrête à coups de bâton, assénés sur la tête (Moresco 2014, 20–21).

La conversion de l'observation de la nature marâtre à l'immersion végétale se produit lorsque le narrateur décide de quitter son hameau pour traverser la vallée à la recherche de la petite lumière. Alors qu'au début du roman, face aux spéculations sur la présence d'OVNIs dans la région, le narrateur nie catégoriquement toute existence suprasensible, déclarant avec désillusion : « Il n'y a rien ! Il n'y a rien ! [. . .] Il n'y a, en tous lieux, que cette pullulation désespérée de vie et de mort à travers le temps, l'espace, que cette imagination désespérée » (2014, 41) ; dans une ascension qui est aussi une allégorie du chemin initiatique menant à la rencontre avec son moi enfantin, le narrateur pénètre dans une forêt de plus en plus dense, d'abord en voiture puis à pied, et finit par trouver une minuscule maison en pierre : « à l'intérieur, dans une cuisine, se trouvait un enfant en culottes courtes, la tête rasée. Il soulevait dans ses petits bras un nuage de draps, qu'il s'apprêtait à mettre dans un baquet. De stupeur, je me suis arrêté » (2014, 48).

Cette dernière rencontre est définitive pour la conversion du narateur. La présence inexplicable de l'enfant au milieu de la forêt l'oblige en effet à mettre de côté ses préjugés et à laisser son imagination travailler au-delà de toute frontière précédemment imposée. En apprenant à se servir de la faculté imaginative en tant que moyen de connaissance, le narrateur commence à se comprendre lui-même, à comprendre la nature qui l'entoure, et à comprendre l'enfant. Au premier abord, ce dernier semble être « juste un enfant » (2014, 52), un orphelin vivant seul au milieu de la forêt : il travaille mal à l'école, fait pipi au lit, craint le noir, c'est pourquoi il allume la petite lampe. Mais, peu à peu, le narrateur se rend compte qu'il ne s'agit pas d'un enfant comme les autres. C'est un enfant mort. Il s'est suicidé. Comme dans l'apologue raconté par Ivan dans *Les frères Karamazov*, sa souffrance illustre la douleur et la brutalité humaines. Dans cet univers parallèle où les frontières entre les vivants et les morts sont poreuses, la fréquentation de l'enfant fantôme sort le narrateur de sa solitude. La petite lumière, qu'il essaie maintenant d'apercevoir chaque soir de l'autre côté de la colline, lui apprend la réciprocité : « et peut-être que cet enfant aussi peut voir de là-haut la lumière de chez moi, la nuit [. . .], je me surprends à penser. De l'autre côté de la gorge, au milieu de toute cette obscurité à perte de vue, de toute l'obscurité du monde, comme moi je vois la sienne, d'ici » (2014, 66).

La capacité à « se compromettre dans la relation » (Despret 2012, 43) fait découvrir au protagoniste que la nature, malgré la loi darwinienne qui la régit toujours, est un réseau de relations dont l'humain fait partie et qu'il ne peut saisir que s'il quitte son anthropocentrisme. En effet, *La lucina* se configure comme un véritable voyage initiatique qui, d'une condition de séparation, conduit le narrateur à rencontrer la partie la plus intime de lui-même, incarnée par l'enfant, à travers une immersion végétale où toute distinction entre sujet et objet se trouve neutralisée. Comme le notent Didier Debaise et Isabelle Stengers : « Ce qui perd prise est la tenaille kantienne démembrant l'expérience entre ce qui revient au sujet (connaissant) et à l'objet (connaissable). Mais ce qui perd prise également est l'anthropocentrisme. Car le sens de l'importance ne peut être un privilège humain face à un monde indifférent » (2016, 86). Vers la fin du roman, malgré l'arrivée de l'hiver, les occasions de partage avec les non-humains se multiplient : le rottweiler devient un ami fidèle, la végétation et la maison ne font plus qu'un et le tremblement de terre, autrefois effrayant, est perçu comme une berceuse exprimant la voix de la terre : « Peu avant, il y a eu des secousses de tremblement de terre. Mais faibles. Des vibrations légères qui montaient des profondeurs. Mais si légères, si légères, que je ne saurais dire si elles m'ont réveillé ou si au contraire elles m'ont endormi. Il m'a même semblé avoir un peu souri, reconnaissant leur chère voix dans le noir » (Moresco 2014, 109). Désormais capable d'entendre la « voix de la nature », le protagoniste est prêt à conclure son apprentissage et à embrasser son moi enfantin.

Dans son introduction à *Fiabe*, Moresco observe : « Les contes de fées peuvent être contradictoires. Ils n'obéissent pas à la prétention philosophique qui veut que la raison soit séparée de tout le reste[10] » (2017, 9). En multipliant les perspectives, l'attitude spéculative du conte de fées met en scène puis révèle le caractère illusoire des dichotomies nature/culture, mort/vivant, adulte/enfant, voix/silence, observateur/observé. En même temps, Moresco ne cède jamais à la tentation de peindre une nature salvatrice, ni de faire table rase de l'humain au profit de celle-ci. À l'instar de ce que note Vinciane Despret à propos de l'écriture de Haraway, la littérature relève les contradictions et les fait coexister sans rêver d'une paix définitive : « On est bien loin d'une conception de l'écriture thérapeutique (ou de l'authenticité) qui serait la version "salvatrice", voire "rédemptrice" de l'acte d'écrire. Façonner, par l'écriture, une vie plus pleine n'a rien à voir avec la plénitude d'une existence dont on aurait apaisé les conflits, elle requiert justement de se coltiner les contradictions » (Despret 2017, 33). Aujourd'hui, face à la crise environnementale, la nature ne peut être réparée sans que l'humain ne soit

---

10 [Le fiabe possono essere contraddittorie. Non obbediscono alla pretesa filosofica della ragione separata da tutto il resto e del suo astratto teorema di non-contraddizione.]

réparé aussi ; mais le programme de recréation d'un lien entre les humains et la nature n'est pas le même qu'à l'époque romantique. Il ne s'agit pas d'aspirer à une fusion réparatrice, mais de façonner de nouvelles histoires qui nous apprennent à échanger entre partenaires égaux. Dans cette perspective, quitter l'anthropocentrisme ne signifie pas mettre en valeur la nature aux dépens de l'humain, mais expérimenter de nouveaux modes de coexistence. Par ses hésitations entre le monologue et le dialogue, entre l'observation d'une nature marâtre et l'immersion végétale, entre l'absence de vie et la présence spectrale de l'enfant, *La lucina* est l'histoire d'échecs et de compromis aboutissant à un épanouissement commun.

Références

Adorno, Theodor W. *Notes sur la littérature*. Trad. Sibylle Muller. Paris : Flammarion, 2009 [1981].
Auerbach, Erich. *Mimesis : la représentation de la réalité dans la littérature occidentale*. Trad. Cornélius Heim. Paris : Gallimard, 1968 [1964].
Benedetti, Carla. *La letteratura ci salverà dall'estinzione*. Turin : Einaudi, 2021.
Benjamin, Walter. *Expérience et pauvreté*, suivi de *Le conteur* et *La tâche du traducteur*. Trad. Cédric Cohen Skalli. Paris : Payot & Rivages, 2011 [1936].
Calvino, Italo. *Sulla fiaba*. Turin : Einaudi, 1988.
Campo, Cristina. *Gli imperdonabili*. Milan : Adelphi, 1987.
Debaise, Didier et Isabelle Stengers. *Gestes spéculatifs : colloque de Cerisy*. Dijon : Les Presses du réel, 2015.
_____. « L'insistance des possible, Pour un pragmatisme spéculatif ». *Multitudes* 65 (2016) : 82–89.
Despret, Vinciane. « En finir avec l'innocence : dialogue avec Isabelle Stengers et Donna Haraway ». *Penser avec Donna Haraway*. Éd. Elsa Dorlin et Eva Rodriguez. Paris : Presses universitaires de France, 2012. 23–46.
Eliot, Thomas Stearns. *The Waste Land*. New York : Northon & Company, 2001 [1922].
Gefen, Alexandre. *Réparer le monde : la littérature française face au XXIe siècle*. Paris : Éditions Corti, 2018.
_____. « De l'écologie à l'écocritique ». *Esprit* (mars 2021) https://esprit.presse.fr/article/alexandre-gefen/de-l-ecologie-a-l-ecocritique (13 mars 2022).
Gefen, Alexandre et Claude Perez. « Extension du domaine de la littérature ». *Elfe XX–XXI* (août 2019) : https://doi-org.janus.bis-sorbonne.fr/10.4000/elfe.736 (21 avril 2022).
Ghosh, Amitav. *The Great Derangement : ClimateCchange and the Unthinkable*. Chicago : The University of Chicago Press, 2017.
Greimas, Algirdas Julien. *Sémantique structurale, recherche et méthode*. Paris : Larousse, 1966.
Haraway, Donna. *Simians, Cyborgs and Women : The Reinvention of Nature*. New York : Routledge, 1991a.
_____. « Situated Knowledges: The Science Question in Feminism and the Privilege of Partial Perspective ». *Simians, Cyborgs and Women: The Reinvention of Nature*. New York : Routledge, 1991b. 183–202.

_____. « The promises of monsters, A Regenerative Politics for Inappropriate/d Others. » *The Monster Theory Reader*. Éd. Jeffrey Andrew Weinstock. Minneapolis : University of Minnesota Press, 2020. 459-521.

_____. *Staying with the Trouble : Making Kin in the Chthulucene*. Durham : Duke University Press, 2016.

Latour, Bruno. *Face à Gaïa, huit conférences sur le nouveau régime climatique*. Paris : La Découverte, 2015.

Leopardi, Giacomo. *Zibaldone*. Trad. Bertrand Schefer. Paris : Allia, 2003 [1898].

Moresco, Antonio. *Clandestinità*. Turin : Bollati Boringhieri, 1993.

_____. *Gli esordi*. Milan : Feltrinelli, 1998.

_____. *Le favole della Maria*. Turin : Einaudi, 2007.

_____. *Gli incendiati*. Milan : Mondadori, 2010.

_____. *La lucina*. Milan : Mondadori, 2013.

_____. *La petite lumière*. Trad. Laurent Lombard. Lagrasse : Verdier, 2014.

_____. *Fiaba d'amore*. Milan : Mondadori, 2014.

_____. *Fiabe*. Milan : Società Editrice Milanese, 2017.

_____. *Fiaba bianca*. Milan : Rizzoli, 2018.

_____. *Il grido*. Milan : Società Editrice Milanese, 2018.

_____. *Lettere a nessuno*, Milan : Mondadori, 2018 [1997].

Plumwood, Val. « Journey to the heart of stone ». *Culture, Creativity and Environment : New Environmentalist Criticism*. Éd. Fiona Becket et Terry Gifford. New York : Rodopi, 2007. 17-36.

Propp, Vladimir. *Les racines historiques du conte merveilleux*. Trad. Lise Gruel-Apert. Paris : Gallimard, 1983 [1946].

_____. *Morphologie du conte*. Trad. Marguerite Derrida, Tzvetan Todorov et Claude Kahn. Paris : Seuil, 1965 [1929].

Tsing, Anna Lowenhaupt. *The Mushroom at the End of the World: On the Possibility of Life in Capitalist Ruins*. Princeton : Princeton University Press, 2015.

Fabiola Obame
De l'imagination environnementale à la restauration des liens écouméniques

Résumé : À la croisée des théories écocritiques et des théories postcoloniales, l'écocritique postcoloniale contribue à poser une réflexion sur les questions d'un vivre en commun. Bien que les deux théories échappent à toute tentative de définition et soient différentes dans leurs méthodes d'interprétation, elles se rejoignent par leur volonté d'élargir les frontières identitaires en rhizomes et en posant une réflexion sur la nature en tant qu'archive. Elles dépersonnalisent le récit historique et redistribuent la parole aux actants non anthropomorphes. Ce travail a en cela pour ambition de montrer que la fiction littéraire participe à une prise de conscience écocentrée. C'est notamment le cas dans les espaces narratifs sur lesquels notre analyse se porte : le Gabon, l'Australie et l'Afrique du Sud, la Martinique. Les thématiques abordées dans les œuvres du corpus donnent une vue panoptique de la fracture environnementale. Elles ont en commun de représenter les incidences induites par le rejet de l'étrangeté, car cela a constitué un problème dans l'habitation de la terre et la relation aux autres. La rencontre avec l'autre devient alors un moment primordial qui détermine la relation.

Mots clés : écocritique postcoloniale et littéraire, imagination environnementale, histoire environnementale, crise écologique, reterritorialisation

Avec le déclin de la pensée moderniste, de nouvelles réalités sont apparues reconfigurant considérablement les modes de pensée. C'est dans un climat d'instabilité qu'une crise du monde s'est installée, devenant rapidement un état constitutif d'une société de surconsommation. Dans la sphère écologique, cette crise est visible par la remise en question de présupposés qui semblaient aller de soi et par la prise en compte de l'action de l'homme sur l'environnement. Le fait que les régimes de connaissance soient marqués par l'opacité restreint la saisie optimale du réel. C'est que la crise contemporaine plonge dans une série de questionnements incessants visant à déterminer l'origine d'un malaise. On prend peu à peu conscience du fait que l'on ne contrôle plus rien et que toutes nos certitudes étaient des illusions qui se trouvent aujourd'hui ébranlées. La crise écologique étant une crise de nos valeurs, la littérature intervient à ce niveau, car elle participe à une prise de conscience écologique véhiculant une vision environnementale grâce à l'imaginaire environnemental.

La parole littéraire permet d'éveiller les consciences à un imaginaire environnemental. Elle fait entendre à l'humain les voix des choses qui jusqu'alors étaient des entités sans vie et apparaître les êtres qui étaient invisibles pour remettre sur la scène du visible, ce dont on ne faisait plus attention. « L'imagination environnementale » de Lawrence Buell s'avère ainsi importante par le principe de responsabilité mimétique qu'elle pose et qui suppose que c'est dans la « facticité » des « images » qu'on peut susciter le désir du monde extérieur. Il affirme de fait que l'imagination et l'art sont essentiels : « the only or even the best way of restoring the natural world for art and imagination » (Buell 1995, 92). Il s'agirait alors de montrer que le texte détient les moyens de faire renaître un désir de sortie vers le « Grand dehors » et de reconnecter l'homme à la nature.

Dans cette anthropologie d'un nouveau vivre ensemble multiculturalisé, la littérature est à percevoir comme ce qui pourrait permettre d'éveiller les consciences à un imaginaire environnemental en montrant que l'homme et l'écosystème sont interdépendants. En effet, la poétique apparaît comme un intermède qui recrée un contact salvateur à l'environnement, et pose les termes d'un nouveau vivre-ensemble. Elle est ce qui approfondit en nous une existence en manque d'extase et de valeurs transcendantes : c'est une façon d'être au monde qui vient justement mettre sur le devant de la scène les publics marginalisés ou oubliés. Et, en retranscrivant la musicalité du langage naturel, la littérature fournit les moyens à la nature de communiquer avec les hommes et des pistes pour habiter poétiquement et écologiquement le monde.

Dès lors, cette étude ambitionne de montrer, à partir d'une approche écocritique postcoloniale, les pièces par lesquelles la réconciliation devient une nécessité et l'esthétique littéraire qui la rend envisageable dans les œuvres de Nadine Gordimer (*The Conservationist*, 1974), Kate Grenville (*The Secret River*, 2005) et Bessora (*Petroleum*, 2004). Les thématiques abordées dans les œuvres du corpus donnent une vue panoptique de la fracture environnementale. Elles ont en commun de représenter les incidences induites par le rejet de l'étrangeté, car cela a constitué un problème dans l'habitation de la terre et la relation aux autres. Les autrices, issues d'aires géographiques et d'époques différentes, donnent aussi une vue de ce qu'a été la colonisation pour les colonisés, les conséquences qui s'en sont suivies pour la planète et posent enfin une réflexion sur les différents moyens de réparer ce qui se présente comme étant irréparable. La rencontre avec l'être différent devient alors un moment primordial qui détermine la relation.

Si la réparation vient de la volonté de construire un vivre-ensemble plus juste en tentant de repenser la relation qui affecte l'asymétrie entre les êtres vivants, elle engage pourtant une responsabilité commune qui souligne l'importance de réorienter les enjeux de nos sociétés actuelles. À ce titre, on peut se demander : de quelle façon la littérature fait-elle retrouver une capacité *agissante* aux victimes dont la voix peine à émerger ? Dans quelle mesure un travail sur la mémoire et sur le passé est-il nécessaire pour comprendre la crise environnementale ? Comment l'imagination environnementale met-elle en place un rituel de pénitence du *nous* pouvant se traduire par une tentative de réparation ?

1 La place des marginalisés

La thématique de la marge est apparente dans les œuvres que nous étudions au travers du rapport de l'exclu à la terre. Les personnages hors normes sont confinés dans des espaces clos qui se situent dans les zones d'ombre de l'espace géographique. Si ce modèle semble à première vue reproduire le binarisme colonial centre et périphérie, on peut aussi lire là une forme d'interrogation sur la relation existante entre l'espace d'habitation et le vivant.

Nadine Gordimer écrit la frontière pour décrire l'exclusion à laquelle les peuples de couleur sont confrontés en Afrique du Sud. Cette écriture de la frontière se déploie comme une image dans l'œuvre pour venir figurer les barrières géographiques, raciales et humaines. Établir des frontières, revient indirectement à exclure dans *The Conservationist*. La présence des termes « kraal », « compound », « township », « bantoustans » est représentative de deux rapports de société distincts où le faible se trouve relégué dans les marges, placé à l'écart. Ces mots désignent dans l'ensemble les divisions territoriales. Ils matérialisent l'idée de frontière et lui confèrent une signification très poussée, car ce sont des habitations dont l'usage est destiné aux non-blancs. Que cette césure soit géographique ou identitaire, elle divise l'espace en deux parties, entérinant de la sorte un partage discriminatoire de l'espace. La répartition des espaces sur le territoire sud-africain place les individus de « couleur » et les Noirs hors d'une société à laquelle ils ne sauraient appartenir. La frontière est justement là pour mettre à distance les différences et pour causer l'exclusion. Cette coexistence manichéenne montre l'espace des uns comme un lieu privilégié et celui des autres comme un lieu de lutte, comme le soulignent les propos d'un vieillard lorsqu'il explique au vacher Jacobus la réticence de l'Indien à embaucher un serviteur noir : « You know they're not supposed to stay there, this place is for white people » (Gordimer 1974, 36). Les Indiens ne sont pas autorisés à résider sur cet emplacement. Ils sont, comme les autres peuples de couleurs, soumis à une répartition géographique qui se base sur la couleur de la peau, en vertu des lois de l'Apartheid.

Les descriptions qui sont faites de l'espace mettent de ce fait en évidence la précarité dans laquelle les populations vivent. Le compound est décrit comme un espace insalubre, situé à proximité de l'enclos spécialement réservé aux veaux pour la nuit que Mehring perçoit de la sorte : « In that enormous location these things happen every day, or rather every weekend, everyone knows it, they are murdered for their Friday pay-packets or they stab each other after drinking. A hundred and fifty thousand of them living there » (Gordimer 1974, 28).

Mehring, le maître fermier blanc et personnage principal, en parle avec beaucoup de détachement, comme si cela ne l'émouvait guère et que c'était là l'ordre naturel des choses comme l'atteste la présence de « tout le monde le sait ». Mehring apparaît détaché, il brosse cyniquement le tableau de leurs vies, car leur *monde* est ainsi fait, la violence y est omniprésente. C'est un univers où des assassinats et des beuveries se produisent « tous les jours », « tous les week-ends » sans que cela interpelle parce que c'est devenu une habitude. Personne ne peut contrôler le danger encouru. Mehring précise que la « location » est « énorme » et qu'on peut compter jusqu'à « cent cinquante mille » habitations, comme s'il expliquait le fait qu'on ne puisse avoir aucun contrôle sur la forte indigénisation de la « location ». Ces détails montrent aussi la présence d'une grande insécurité et d'une population délaissée sans qu'aucune intervention extérieure ne vienne réguler l'ordre des choses.

Le système ségrégationniste engendré par l'Apartheid a fait naître une frontière qui influe à bien des égards sur la vie sociale et les répartitions géographiques dans *The Conservationist*. Cette ligne de démarcation, matérielle et symbolique, place la population à distance en se basant sur la race et la couleur de la peau. Néanmoins, en dépit de cette volonté de séparer, la frontière n'a pas toujours produit le résultat escompté et a fini par devenir un espace de résistance pour les personnages marginalisés. Bien que dans *The Secret River*, l'espace n'a pas officiellement été délimité, nous verrons que cela n'a pas empêché le même processus de division.

Depuis que William Thornhill et sa famille ont pris possession de « son doigt de terre », inspirés par Blackwood et suivis dans ce projet par d'autres bannis, des frontières tacites ont fini par se tracer. Celles-ci laissent d'un côté les indigènes dans la forêt et de l'autre part se trouvent les bannis en manque de reconnaissance sur les espaces visibles : « In Thornhill's world, a person might own some sticks of furniture, a few clothes, perhaps a lighter. That was wealth. But no one that Thornhill knew personally had bought so much as a yard of land » (Grenville 2006, 109). La situation en Nouvelle-Galles du Sud est propice pour y remédier. L'acte de possession offre une seconde vie à chacun de ces hommes, car la possession de la terre est un symbole de renaissance. Nombreux sont ceux qui désirent posséder leur lopin de terre et lui attribuer un nom, signe ultime de possession dans cette colonie naissante. C'est la raison pour laquelle William s'empresse de mettre son talon à terre et de tracer les quatre carrés qui forment sa future maison. Or, malgré toutes ces précautions, la présence silencieuse des sauvages cachés dans l'ombre demeure une peur constante qui fait planer la menace de la perte du territoire. Le comportement des Noirs les rend davantage suspicieux : entre les flèches volantes qui transpercent les peaux en prenant soin de les déchiqueter et les réunions secrètes que

Thornhill les soupçonne de tenir, la tension est palpable. La famille et les deux employés savent que l'attaque est imminente. À chacune de leur réunion, la peur s'empare d'eux :

> Out there, between the cracks in the walls, the night was as black as the inside of an ear. The huge air stirred, full of hostile life. He imagines it: the blacks creeping up to the hut, silent as lizards on their wide quiet feet. They might at this very moment be peering in at them. The noises were getting louder, the sort of sound it would take an army to make. The words not said were like a creature pacing up and down between them (Grenville 2006, 250).

La peur du couple se transforme en une « créature » les épiant. Ils s'imaginaient que là-bas, dans la forêt, les Noirs profiteraient de la « nuit hostile » pour lancer un assaut contre eux. L'écriture que l'auteure emploie s'appuie fortement sur des images qui tantôt animalisent les aborigènes, tantôt transforment la nature environnante en un lieu de vie monstrueux. En effet, la couleur des parois est comparée à celle de « l'intérieur d'une oreille », la nuit est un monstre « plein[e] de vie », les Noirs sont comparés au « lézard ». De la personnification à l'animalisation, ils semblent se dissoudre pour former les deux images d'une même pièce de telle sorte que les époux font de la nature l'alliée des Noirs. L'indigène australien est assimilé à un animal. Il est aidé dans sa tâche par cette nature-alliée qui joue en sa faveur et exerce une pression sur le couple. Cette perception déshumanisante a pour effet, en premier lieu, de faire du Noir une créature silencieuse, mais dangereuse qui s'insinue partout et de montrer qu'il représente une menace constante. Et en deuxième lieu, elle a pour fonction de légitimer l'exclusion qui devient une stratégie nécessaire pour conserver l'équilibre de la frontière. La peur grandissante du couple a atteint son point culminant. L'impossibilité de vivre sereinement sur ce territoire conduit à cet ultime acte que représente le traçage des frontières comme l'indique l'intitulé dudit segment narratif « L'heure de tracer des limites ».

L'espace est en cela un personnage acteur de l'énonciation. Les personnages sont relégués en arrière, décrits comme des « strangers », tandis que l'attention est accentuée sur les espaces parcourus, comme si c'était eux les véritables actants du livre. Et cette hypothèse se trouve accentuée par le fait que la guerre qui traverse le récit est surtout une guerre de territoires. C'est l'espace que les uns et les autres discutent pour un motif légitime ou non qui conduit aux luttes que le récit raconte. C'est pour cette raison que l'auteure, plutôt que de mettre l'accent sur les personnages, fait de l'environnement l'actant principal à parcourir pour lire l'histoire de son livre. Le « river » du titre de l'œuvre *The Secret River* ferait donc référence à toutes ces histoires que le cours d'eau embrasse tout au long de son parcours. Face à cette géographie parlante, l'homme est invité à déployer ses sens pour lire le discours inscrit derrière la chromatique, les odeurs, les sons pour que sortent de l'ombre ces impensés qui concourent pourtant à construire une histoire environnementale.

Dans *Les mots et les choses* (1966), Michel Foucault relève au sujet du langage qu'il « est à la fois révélation enfouie et révélation qui peu à peu se restitue dans une clarté montante » (Foucault 1966, 50–51). Les choses, dit-il, se manifestent sous forme de mots, dans un langage qui rend efficient le savoir parce qu'il révèle les « figures visibles de la nature » (Foucault 1966, 50). Ainsi, la vérité se donne à voir et s'énonce au travers d'un langage qui se « mêle aux figures du monde et s'enchevêtre à elles » (Foucault 1966, 49). L'espace discursif devient le lieu où se déchiffrent les choses par lesquelles la vie prend forme et éveille à un langage écocentré.

2 Blessures du vivant

Daniel-Henri Pageaux explique que la poétique joue de stratégies narratives pour créer un réseau de mots qui produit des espaces. Le texte s'organise comme un espace où tout le mécanisme narratologique prend sens pour construire une littérature spatialisée. Le sens de cet appareillage discursif étant de mettre en place « une possible médiation entre les mots et le réel où il nous est donné de vivre » (Pageaux 2003, 20), ces médiations nous intéressent en ceci qu'elles rendent visible ce que Glissant a nommé la Trace pour faire allusion à tous ces discours omis qui seraient restés dans la spatialité et qui peuvent être des pistes pour remplir les blancs de cette mémoire historique dont certaines parties manquent La pensée de la Trace de Glissant pourrait être pertinente dans cette analyse dans le sens où elle permet d'investir ce qui reste des pratiques colonisatrices dans l'espace. La trace a son importance, car elle est une forme de langage pour les déportés. Ils trouvent dans les chants, les contes, les croyances, des éléments qui leur permettent de recomposer ce qui a pu disparaître dans les cales du bateau négrier. La mémoire de l'esclave ou du colonisé ne pouvait survivre que sous forme de traces étant donné qu'il leur a été imposé d'oublier tout ce qui leur était intrinsèque comme les éléments culturels. En ce sens, la trace est un élément essentiel du processus de créolisation, puisqu'elle devient une marque de l'Histoire. C'est avec elle que se compose le savoir absent de l'espace caribéen si bien qu'elle donne lieu à un nouveau langage qui reconstruit l'histoire. Pour Glissant, les lieux historiques deviennent des témoins de l'horreur : ce sont des signes du passé pouvant se mettre en relation par le biais des traces qui représentent les vestiges de ce qui a été. Il institue donc l'espace comme une trace qui permettrait de pister la mémoire. Cet exercice suppose de mobiliser la mémoire de la collectivité car cette pensée mnésique est en quête de l'histoire. La Trace contourne ce que Ricœur appelle les « manipulations de la mémoire », tous ces éléments institutionnels qui oblitèrent le passé, et « s'intercale[nt] entre revendication d'identité et les expressions publiques de la mémoire » (Ricœur 2003, 99). Reconnaître l'absence d'une partie du passé, suppose donc de partir récupérer le discours oblitéré, ces bribes de paroles disséminées qui constituent la racine d'un savoir.

Dans les œuvres de Gordimer par exemple, ces traces reviennent par le biais des éléments naturels qui participent à donner voix au passé. Ainsi, la sécheresse qui s'abat sur la ferme, les hippopotames qui avortent, la poussière brune qui encercle le compound, l'équinoxe, l'incendie, l'inondation ne sont pas que des éléments qui bouleversent la vie de Mehring dans la ferme. Ils participent aussi à rendre compte de la violence historique de la société sud-africaine, violence qui se retrouve dans la nature et décrite dans d'autres œuvres de Gordimer (c'est notamment le cas dans *A World of Strangers* dans lequel l'histoire tourne autour des raisons qui ont conduit Max à la mort). À ce titre, quand le narrateur parle de la présence du cyanure dans la campagne, il conduit le lecteur à observer la trace d'un bouleversement de l'écosystème dû à l'action coloniale lorsqu'il parle du poids du cyanure sur la campagne.

Le cyanure qui a été utilisé pour extraire l'or fut la cause de plusieurs maux. Mehring explique que l'usage du composé chimique lors des extractions aurifères a une importance dans le développement économique du pays : « It is what saved the industry in the early 1900s. It is what makes yellow the waste that is piled up in giant sandcastles and crenellated geometrically-stepped bills where the road first leaves the city » (Gordimer 1974, 195–196). Le produit, fortement utilisé dans l'industrie minière, connut une croissance démesurée en Afrique du Sud. Depuis que les prospecteurs amateurs George Walker et Georges Harrison ont fait la découverte d'un filon d'or en 1985, le pays a la réputation d'être le plus grand producteur d'or au monde. Des scientifiques établirent que le bassin du Witwatersrand contient à lui seul une quantité d'or qui dépasse celle des autres pays du monde. Le minerai est la principale ressource économique du pays. Et la cyanuration est essentielle ; elle « permettrait de quadrupler le taux de progression mensuel de l'extraction, tout en réduisant d'un tiers les effectifs » et en élevant la production qui passe alors d'un « taux d'extraction moyen de 60 à 97 % » (Lageat 1997, 114). Cependant son impact à long terme sur les nappes souterraines est irréversible puisque le cyanure pollue les eaux et les sols. Ce produit inflammable et asphyxiant constitue une menace pour l'homme et la biodiversité. En 2015, la Chine en fit la cruelle expérience avec l'explosion dans la ville portuaire et industrielle de Tainjin, d'un entrepôt contenant 700 tonnes de cyanure qui tua 114 personnes et contamina l'eau et l'air. À ce désagrément causé par les extractions aurifères, s'ajoute la problématique d'une ville qui se métamorphose avec des déchets qui forment des « châteaux de sable géants » et des « collines crénelées ». L'action du narrateur, ou plutôt la perspective à partir de laquelle il choisit d'orienter son récit, participe à faire de l'environnement naturel un espace où peuvent se lire les traces de la crise écologique.

Dans *Petroleum* de Bessora, la focalisation est également révélatrice de la place de la nature dans la trame narrative. On constate par exemple que les histoires d'amour des personnages principaux sont reléguées au second plan. Le narrateur livre très peu ce type de détails mais se montre pourtant très démonstratif quand il s'agit de décrire les élans émotionnels de la nature qui occupent plusieurs pages dans le roman. Par effet de personnification, l'écriture s'anime pour décrire les effets de présence d'une nature qui ressent tout le poids du colonialisme. Mise en avant dès l'incipit et l'excipit, le roman résonne tout le long des bruits d'une nature qui se veut insoumise à l'humain. Dans « Espace et bruit », Hélène Ussac dit au sujet de la tonalité textuelle que :

> La langue sonne car elle est désormais émise par un sujet sentant et non plus exclusivement pensant. En-deçà de la représentation elle-même, il est frappant en effet de voir comment la langue, dans sa strate linguistique et non pas seulement lexicale, se charge de son. Le sens passe par le son. C'est comme si la phrase n'était plus seulement lue, mais qu'elle était faite pour être entendue (Ussac 2006, 49).

Le bruit dans le texte a effectivement pour fonction de matérialiser la violence. C'est le cas dans *Petroleum* où l'anthropomorphisation et les effets de bruitage permettent de percevoir la nature comme un être vivant doté de caractéristiques humaines, capable d'agentivité et de conserver les traces des exploitations coloniales. S'agissant de cette capacité à s'humaniser, Bessora la met à jour en animant les descriptions environnementales d'attitudes anthropomorphes. Dans le roman, quand les premiers géologues abattent la forêt, le texte décrit les cris de la forêt : au premier coup de hache, le mot « …BAM… » sonorise la puissance du coup qui s'abat sur l'arbre suivi de près par d'autres cris « …Han !… », « HAAAA !!! », « CRRrrrrîîîîîîîîîhhhhshshshhs…BOUM » (Bessora 2004, 62-63). Ce bruit prend sens parce qu'il désigne un dysfonctionnement. Il donne à la narration un caractère vraisemblable, comme si ce qu'il y avait à dire ne pouvait s'énoncer que dans le bruit pour faire percevoir au lecteur la violence. Le bruit narratif acquiert en effet une fonction inclusive en immergeant géologues et pisteurs dans l'action qui se déroule devant eux. Ces sons rendent aussi la scène vraisemblable pour le lecteur parce qu'ils suspendent le récit pour donner une information : la douleur ressentie par les arbres sous les coups de hache. Cette vocalité de la souffrance sert par ailleurs à faire découvrir les blessures de la forêt et à présenter l'homme comme son bourreau.

Le recours aux processus humanisants démontre que le langage de la nature est plurivoque. Il se place à contre-courant de la rationalité pour faire entendre d'autres voix : celles qui crient parce qu'elles sont profanées, victimes de multiples manipulations scientifiques et vidées de leurs substances. Ce langage nous porte au seuil de la morale. Il nous conduit, sans pour autant le signifier, à prendre position et acte de ces réalités dérangeantes que l'on côtoie sans signifier ce qu'elles supposent. Or, pour l'environnement, le pétrole est une plaie parce qu'il conduit à des formes de manipulation qui le désacralisent et le vident de sa vitalité. C'est par conséquent un échange à sens unique entre l'humain et le non-humain qui s'instaure car la nature porte la trace de toutes ces pratiques destructrices contre lesquelles elle tente de lutter.

Finalement, à la manière d'une photographie de la colonisation, l'espace témoigne d'une vision du réel. Il livre un point de vue environnemental qui vient défaire les discours institutionnels. Lambert Barthélémy avance de ce fait que « si l'histoire humaine est au cœur des récits, elle est aussi histoire des usages [...] de l'espace et elle peut, en tant que telle, être éclairée à partir de l'histoire environnementale » (Barthélémy 2017, 269). Cette mémoire du vivant se déploie sous la forme d'un plaidoyer contre les différentes formes de l'emprise spatiale. L'environnement devient certes le lieu où le récit se cristallise mais aussi le lieu où se donne à lire une *autre* histoire de la colonisation : celle qui révèle les traces qui permettent de témoigner d'une géopathologie coloniale et de modifications morphologiques. La nature devient alors un artefact qu'il est nécessaire de questionner en le considérant comme un espace mémoriel, car c'est là qu'émerge une histoire environnementale parallèle à celle qui échappe aux humains. L'espace devient par cette évidence inséparable de la mémoire. Il est donc riche des nombreuses histoires que recèle chacune de ses transformations et s'impose comme sujet énonciatif puisqu'étant détentrice d'un imaginaire (social, narratif, mythologique et postcolonial) qui pourrait ouvrir la voie à une tentative de réparation.

3 Habiter le monde autrement

Le corpus met en scène des situations qui soulignent l'importance d'habiter l'espace différemment : la fuite, les intempéries, les conflits, le besoin de se reterritorialiser, la crise généralisée... sont des signes, parmi tant d'autres, qui montrent que quelque chose de distinct doit germer. Les lignes de faille sont plurielles ; certaines d'entre elles ont un caractère irrévocable qui rend impossible un retour à un monde différent. Par des moyens distincts, chacun d'entre eux essaie d'instaurer des attitudes qui rendent envisageable une forme d'habitation communautaire : dans *Petroleum*, Louise la prêtresse tente de changer les choses en adoptant la posture de jardinière qui prend soin d'un jardin communautaire.

Le jardin se pense sous le signe de l'hétéroclite. Espace indiscipliné, c'est le lieu où le désordre émerge, comme s'il était façonné à l'image d'un monde pluriel en constantes interactions. Et en effet, à l'inverse du jardin édénique, le jardin auquel nous faisons ici référence est une construction humaine qui reproduit la société tout en essayant de s'affranchir de sa logique binaire. Halte de la modernité, le jardin symbolise le commencement, en ceci qu'il est le début d'une nouvelle manière d'habiter mettant en avant la beauté du diversel. Cette ouverture à l'autre, Glissant la conçoit comme un moyen de décoloniser les imaginaires en ouvrant le modèle occidental à d'autres possibilités que celles qui reposent sur l'atavisme des racines. Son œuvre est traversée par une pensée archipélique qui place la vérité dans le diversel car il envisage le comme un cercle dans lequel se croisent et se confrontent des identités plurielles.

Cet espace hétérotopique vert crée ainsi un nouvel équilibre fondé sur l'idée de ressourcement et de mélange car il met le monde en branchement. Il organise le monde de façon à lui donner une forme et à panser ses blessures. C'est notamment le cas pour Louise dans *Petroleum*, dont l'engagement à la nature la fait passer pour une protectrice des espaces verts. L'investissement acharné dont elle fait preuve est tel qu'elle se met elle-même en danger dans des tâches souvent périlleuses. En effet, dans le village de Louise, tout le monde, humains et non-humains, craint les divinités de la nature : « Avaleur d'âmes...tu es craint de tous ceux qui ne te voient pas. À ton passage, les oiseaux arrêtent de chanter » (Bessora 2004, 192). Ils sont nombreux à ne pas oser s'aventurer dans le cœur de la forêt par peur d'éventuelles représailles. Isanya, le vieux sorcier du village a autrefois prédit les conséquences pour tous ceux qui seraient tentés de toucher l'arbre sans respecter les rituels. La mort frapperait : « l'arbre tuerait encore et demanderait du sang » (Bessora 2004, 227). De même, la réputation de la déesse des eaux est tristement célèbre auprès des hommes pour sa maléfique beauté : « Quiconque la laisse s'accoupler à lui est promis au trépas. Tous, ils le savent... Mais tous, ils succombent aux charmes de Mamiwata » (Bessora 2004, 227). Tous, hormis Louise qui circule librement en continuant de se mettre au service des dieux des eaux et de la forêt parce qu'elle est animée par le désir de prendre soin de la nature. Elle sait pourtant ce dont ils sont capables puisqu'elle a perdu certains proches qui lui étaient chers comme son oncle Zéphyrin dévoré par un crocodile, son père Zbiniew avalé par un serpent et Paulin le charpentier mort dans des sables mouvants. Louise accomplit cependant sa mission avec dévouement. La protection de la nature passe avant toute considération personnelle, quand bien même elle court de grands dangers. Si la peur l'anime, elle ne le montre pas, au contraire ; elle va volontairement se mêler au cœur de la crise, allant même jusqu'à se mettre en danger alors que les autres personnages la considèrent comme un être faible : tant parce que c'est une femme qu'en raison de sa vieillesse précoce. Pour Nathalie Blanc, cette façon que certains habitants ont d'investir l'espace et de se tendre vers autre chose est spécifique à l'habitant jardinier qui « se caractérise par sa conscience des interfaces [les espaces de transition] et sa gestion des liens dehors/dedans à différentes échelles [. . .] Il jardine, considère ces végétaux comme des êtres vivants et apprend par expérience à adapter ses soins » (Blanc 2009, 93). Louise la prêtresse procède avec la même logique : elle met en avant l'importance du décentrement du regard dans la saisie du réel. C'est par lui qu'elle parvient à s'extraire des verticalités et à regarder le monde dans un versant diversel. Il est en cela significatif qu'elle connait des métamorphoses progressives qui, indirectement, participent à faire d'elle un être relationnel.

Dès lors que ses cheveux ont commencé à blanchir et que son dos s'est voûté, Louise a été assimilée à une vieille sorcière parce que « la bosse de Louise, disait-on, enfermait les souvenirs du monde » (Bessora 2004, 190). La prêtresse représente également la mémoire du récit étant donné que c'est elle qui retrace le passé des lieux géographiques. La conteuse rend compte d'une série d'événements réels et mythiques selon une logique qui fait d'elle le pont entre les villageois et l'espace parce qu'elle raconte l'origine de la crise. Elle est la médiatrice, celle dont les souvenirs véhiculent un nouveau moyen de recréer ou d'élaborer les jardins communautaires surtout parce qu'elle insuffle par ces contes un désir. Sa métamorphose est en cela essentielle : elle la fait devenir artisan d'un jardin qui incarne la survivance et qui s'ouvre sur la diversité. Et en effet, Louise grâce à tous les récits qu'elle relate à Jason devient une prêtresse conteuse. Cette transformation peut signifier que rien n'est figé mais tout est mouvant et en redéfinition perpétuelle. Elle indique aussi la pluralité de la vie que le jardinier doit sauvegarder parce qu'il a le devoir de se connecter à la globalité du monde et de rappeler à tous les citoyens qu'ils sont de potentiels jardiniers, donc des écocitoyens en devenir tel que l'affirme Gilles Clément : « Le jardin planétaire postule que nous sommes tous dans un enclos dont la limite est celle de la biosphère, dont le jardinier représente l'ensemble de l'humanité » (Clément 2001, 86).

On peut alors avancer qu'être jardinier, c'est façonner un environnement habitable et veiller à ce que la nature soit protégée. Il s'agit d'utiliser les ressources nécessaires pour créer un écotone, c'est-à-dire une bordure riche où chaque chose est évolutive que Florence Krall décrit en ces termes : « the concept of ecotone, then, to represent that place of meeting and tension between diverse and sometimes conflicting aspect of our lives [. . .] that place of crossing over, provides sanctuary solitude and peace, growth and transformation, as well as isolation and inner or outer conflict » (Krall 1994, 6). Dans cet entre-deux à mi-chemin entre des écosystèmes différents, toutes les espèces se trouveraient mises en contact. Le jardinier pour cela doit regarder au-delà du microcosme de son jardin, il doit relier la matière vivante dans un état d'esprit qui promeut la vie.

Finalement, le jardinier est un élément essentiel du jardin, c'est un habitant dont la présence au monde prend sens dans la relation vis-à-vis de l'altérité et par la protection du jardin. Le jardinier assure la fonction de gardien, tel qu'on le voit dans *Petroleum* à travers la figure de Louise qui prend des décisions importantes pour la protection de la nature. Un deuxième rôle, premier en réalité, se dessine, c'est celui du jardinier qui cherche à rendre simplement la nature belle. Cette charge est celle de Mehring puisque, tel qu'on le voit, il tente d'organiser la nature de la manière à la rendre belle et productive. Il souhaite aménager l'espace dans lequel il vit comme un territoire rentable et reflétant sa capacité à asseoir son autorité de maître. Mehring représente le jardinier moderne dont la complexité de la tâche repose sur la difficulté à prendre soin de la nature tout en veillant à la préservation de la diversité d'éléments qui s'y trouvent : l'humain, l'animal, le végétal, les sols, l'air, etc. Si Louise parvient plus ou moins à comprendre la complexité de cette tâche, ce n'est pas toujours le cas pour Mehring. Quoi qu'il en soit, pour chacun de ces jardiniers, il s'agit davantage de prendre les bonnes décisions afin de créer un milieu propice à la vie, car le jardinier doit veiller sur le jardin et lui apporter les soins dont il a besoin pour faire proliférer le vivant dans sa diversité.

A contrario, dans *The Secret River*, Kate Grenville montre que la fiction littéraire permet des juxtapositions qui viennent éclairer l'importance d'habiter le monde poétiquement. Pour elle, la restauration ne peut être effective que si elle passe par une décolonisation du savoir. Elle en fait un élément primordial sans lequel toute cohabitation avec les formes de vie humaines devient impossible, comme si pour tisser une relation au vivant, il est au préalable nécessaire de repenser le lien au monde. Deuxième fils de la famille Thornhill, Dick naît lors d'une escale au Cap, durant la grande traversée maritime conduisant les prisonniers en Australie et grandit, comme le reste de la fratrie, à Sydney (en dehors de Willie, l'aîné né à Londres). Très peu mis en avant, il passe pour être un personnage excentrique, en raison de ses idées et de son mode de vie décalé de celui des autres personnages. Le narrateur le présente d'ailleurs comme un personnage insouciant, « Dick was willing enough but useless » (Grenville 2006, 146–147). Toujours à rêvasser durant les tâches quotidiennes, son temps libre, il le passe à jouer avec les enfants noirs de la clairière auprès de qui il s'initie et adopte un mode de vie indigène qui repose sur des valeurs et des coutumes qui s'opposent à l'éducation que lui inculquent ses parents. Dick aime en effet à passer du temps avec les enfants noirs qui habitent à proximité de chez eux :

> At other times Dick went down to the river. Thornhill had seen him there more than once, around on the other side of the point. The black's side was what they called it. He had seen Dick there on a spit of sand, playing with the native children, all bony legs and skinny arms shiny like insects, running in and out of the water. Dick was stripped off as they were, to nothing but skin. His was white and theirs was black, but shining in the sun and glittering with river-water it was hard to tell the difference. He ran and called and laughed with them, and he could have been their pale cousin (Grenville 2006, 218).

L'enfant n'hésite effectivement pas à braver l'autorité parentale et à délaisser ses frères pour rejoindre les Noirs. Dick se fond dans la masse et prend plaisir, plus que tous les autres, à expérimenter cette nouvelle forme de vie grâce à laquelle il apprend qu'il est possible de récolter sans semer, de manger sans fournir trop d'efforts, d'allumer du feu avec peu : « Then he stood in that way they did, without any of the cumbersome procedure of getting up » (Grenville 2006, 220). Auprès d'eux, il redécouvre une nouvelle façon d'habiter le monde, portée sur l'écoute et la confiance en cette entité naturelle. Progressivement, il s'écarte du mode de vie de ses parents qui s'épuisent à longueur de journée dans des tâches interminables qui, pourtant, ne parviennent pas à améliorer leur labeur quotidien. Il finit donc par se fondre dans la communauté noire et à leur ressembler, si bien, tel que le constate son père, qu'il est difficile de le différencier d'eux. Son rapprochement avec eux n'est pas que corporel, car même sur le plan idéologique, l'enfant a désormais en partage avec les Noirs une façon de concevoir les choses qui le conduit à s'opposer à sa mère, lorsque celle-ci tente de lui faire comprendre qu'il doit maintenir une frontière avec eux : « *They's savages, Dick. We're civilised folk, we don't go round naked*. Thornhill watched the boy's face go blank and tight, although her tone was mild enough. Among his own family he was a watchful and wary boy » (Grenville 2006, 222–223). Inconscient de ce qui se joue et des craintes de ses parents, il fait remarquer que : « *They don't need no flint or nothing, like you do, he sulked. And no damned weeding the corn all day* » (Grenville 2006, 223). Il place face à face les deux ordres d'habitation que sa mère lui présente en faisant remarquer à cette dernière que ceux qu'elle tient pour sauvages ont su développer des compétences qui rendent la vie des Aborigènes enviable. Il arrive, comme à ce moment-là, que William trouve son fils buté.

D'ordinaire, il s'abstient d'intervenir et le regarde faire de loin, l'air soucieux. Mais, cette fois-ci, le père ne peut s'empêcher d'infliger une correction à son fils. Lui qui ne frappe jamais ses enfants estime que l'affront contenu dans ses mots est de trop grande ampleur pour rester passif parce que, une fois de plus, son fils vient relever une vérité qu'il refuse de voir, ainsi qu'il l'avait déjà fait en soulignant que la clairière n'est pas une terra nullius. Dick est celui qui vient poser des questions sur les savoirs et les cultures non légitimés. Il pousse son père à prendre en compte des connaissances occultées, en démantelant des conceptions figées qui s'opposent à la modernité. De façon plus approfondie, ce qui est en jeu, c'est la capacité à vivre-ensemble, et la mise en dialogue de rationalités, de cultures, de visions différentes. Ce mode de pensée suppose la fin de la supériorité de l'épistémè occidentale placée comme étant plus légitime que les autres. Il s'agirait dans un premier mouvement de sortir des modes de pensée acquis pour, dans un deuxième mouvement, établir de nouveaux paradigmes de savoirs non occidentalisés. Le concept de *colonialité du savoir* repose sur l'élévation des seules valeurs européennes tenues pour valides. Elle permet de rendre compte de la dimension géopolitique du savoir hégémonique et de comprendre les processus par lesquels d'autres conceptions du savoir sont tenues pour « non-existants ». Depuis le XVIe siècle, les humanités et les sciences, à travers leurs postulats et leurs pratiques, n'ont cessé de reproduire un savoir essentiellement colonial et eurocentré. Elles s'inscrivent dans un modèle de progrès et de croissance, caractérisé par un dualisme réducteur. La croyance aveugle en la prétendue universalité de nos dispositifs de connaissance nous empêche de comprendre que les crises climatiques, alimentaires ou politiques qui frappent le globe sont avant tout les symptômes d'une crise civilisationnelle, celle de l'homme occidental. La colonialité du savoir, en mettant à nu le « projet de mort » qui constitue la trame sous-jacente de la modernité, nous permet d'envisager la possibilité d'alternatives cognitives au paradigme rationalité moderne/coloniale.

La colonialité du savoir révèle une asymétrie de l'épistémologie. L'universalisation de ce savoir établit, à l'échelle des connaissances, une place de choix à la science européenne. C'est au nom de cette suprématie du pouvoir et du savoir sur laquelle reposent les convictions de William qu'il est outré par les propos de son fils, puisqu'ils révoquent une tradition idéologique et philosophique qu'il tenait pour incontestable. Thornhill est hors de lui parce que son fils relève là un point précis qu'il n'arrive pas à supporter : malgré la nonchalance et la paresse qui les caractérisent, les Aborigènes ne vivent pas dans la précarité et semblent vivre dans l'autosuffisance. La punition que Thornhill inflige à Dick, quand elle tombe, vise à le punir davantage pour ses paroles et sa réflexion que pour ses escapades, parce que les mots qu'il profère bouleversent une façon de concevoir l'ordre du monde plaçant la science aborigène au-dessus de celle des Occidentaux. Cette difficulté à penser la diversalité est ce qui causerait la ruine du monde, car elle conduit à un rejet qui brise la chaine relationnelle. L'enfant n'hésite pourtant pas, dans un autre passage du livre, à braver l'autorité parentale et à délaisser ses frères pour rejoindre les Noirs. Dick se fond dans la masse et prend plaisir, plus que tous les autres, à expérimenter une nouvelle forme de vie grâce à laquelle il apprend qu'il est possible de récolter sans semer, de manger sans fournir trop d'efforts, d'allumer du feu avec peu : « Then he stood in that way they did, without any of the cumbersome procedure of getting up » (Grenville 2006, 220). Auprès d'eux, il redécouvre une nouvelle façon d'habiter le monde, portée sur l'écoute et la confiance en cette entité naturelle. Progressivement, il s'écarte du mode de vie de ses parents qui s'épuisent à longueur de journée dans des tâches interminables qui, pourtant, ne parviennent pas à améliorer leur labeur quotidien. : c'est la conséquence d'une vision universelle de ce qui est considéré en tant que norme.

Dans cette optique, la prise en compte des cultures des sociétés non occidentales est importante, car celles-ci ouvrent une perspective vers un autre point de vue, à savoir, celui du regard que portent ces cultures sur la nature. Les sortir de l'ombre de l'Occident revient concrètement à décoloniser l'écologie pour prendre en compte d'autres réalités. Pour M. Ferdinand, penser l'écologie décoloniale suppose de la porter sur une échelle globale et de la sortir de la domination coloniale. Il avance qu'une véritable écologie est celle qui ne reste pas figée dans une vision dualiste de la nature et qui sait se hisser hors d'une fracture coloniale qui rend invisible certaines réalités/pratiques écologiques. C'est à cet égard qu'il fait remarquer la nécessité d'aborder autrement l'écologie puisque la colonialité du savoir écologique inférioise l'existence d'une écologie du marginal :

> Les effondrements environnementaux ne touchent pas tout le monde de la même façon et n'effacent aucunement les effondrements sociaux et politiques en cours. Une double fracture persiste entre ceux qui craignent la tempête écologique à l'horizon et ceux à qui le pont de la justice fut refusé bien avant les premières rafales (Ferdinand 2019, 13).

L'idée qui est d'insérer des pratiques permettant d'habiter le monde de façon écocentrée ne peut être effective qu'en bâtissant une « écologie-du monde » (Ferdinand 2019, 27) sachant intégrer des visions différentes de la nature.

4 Conclusion

Finalement, le récit littéraire, en instruisant sur l'urgence écologique, donne des tentatives d'explication à cette crise. Il relie à la fois la géographie (la littérature, perçue dans son versant spatialisant est la scène sur laquelle s'inscrivent des lieux réels ou inventés, c'est le cadre géographique des récits) et l'histoire (l'histoire humaine et l'histoire terrestre se croisent dans le même flux temporel) pour s'inscrire comme la source d'un imaginaire environnemental, capable de susciter une éthique et une conscience écologiques. L'interculturalité est, de ce fait, souhaitée, dans le sens où elle invite à mettre en discussion la diversité des éléments existant dans une société. La scène littéraire présente ce contact interculturel en plaçant le lecteur au carrefour de plusieurs éléments culturels parce que l'hégémonisme culturel, dans les œuvres étudiées, a été un frein à la découverte de l'autre. Dans son essai *Habiter le monde* (2017), le poète Felwine Sarr explique que l'absence de relationnalité est au cœur de la crise actuelle étant donné que les liens à l'étranger et à l'environnement sont traversés par la violence. Il fait de la relation autant la cause de l'exclusion que le motif par lequel peut s'envisager une pratique nouvelle du monde. Aussi explique-t-il que les problèmes environnementaux prennent autant d'ampleur en raison d'une difficulté à penser le vivant :

[. . .] il est nécessaire de renouveler les imaginaires de la relation que nous établissons avec les êtres et les choses qui nous environnent. Cohabiter avec le vivant en respectant ses cycles. Considérer la nature non pas comme une ressource que nous exploitons, mais comme un lieu qui nous abrite et nous offre la vie, comme une bibliothèque vivante et inépuisable de laquelle nous apprenons (Sarr 2017, 12).

Ainsi, c'est un décentrement de la pensée qui doit se produire, lequel soulignerait que ce dont il est question, c'est en réalité de poser les termes d'une éthique fondée sur la conservation et la protection du vivant. C'est peut-être la raison pour laquelle les personnages sont présentés comme des jardiniers qui, à leur manière, tentent de prendre soin et de préserver l'espace des agressions qu'il peut subir. Finalement, le jardinier est un élément essentiel du jardin, c'est un habitant dont la présence au monde prend sens dans la relation vis-à-vis de l'altérité et par la protection du jardin. Il peut assurer la fonction de gardien, tel qu'on le voit dans *Petroleum* à travers la figure de Louise qui prend des décisions importantes pour la protection de la nature. Un troisième rôle, premier en réalité, se dessine, c'est celui du jardinier qui cherche à rendre simplement la nature belle. Cette charge est celle de Mehring puisque, tel qu'on le voit, il tente d'organiser la nature de la manière à la rendre belle et productive. Mehring représente le jardinier moderne dont la complexité de la tâche repose sur la difficulté à prendre soin de la nature tout en veillant à la préservation de la diversité d'éléments qui s'y trouvent : l'humain, l'animal, le végétal, les sols, l'air, etc. Si Louise parvient plus ou moins à comprendre la complexité de cette tâche, ce n'est pas toujours le cas pour Mehring. Quoi qu'il en soit, pour chacun de ces jardiniers, il s'agit davantage de prendre les bonnes décisions afin de créer un milieu propice à la vie, car le jardinier doit veiller sur le jardin et lui apporter les soins dont il a besoin pour faire proliférer le vivant dans sa diversité.

Références

Barthélemy, Lambert. « Communauté et environnement dans la fiction océanienne contemporaine (pêle-mêle sur quelques récits d'Albert Wendt, Alexis Wright, Patricia Grace, Chantal Spitz et Déwé Gorodé) ». *Revue Canadienne de Littérature Comparée* 44.2 (2017) : 268–281.
Buell, Lawrence. *The Environemental Imagination, Thoreau, Nature Writing, and the Formation of American Culture*. London : Harvard University Press, 1995.
Bessora. *Petroleum*. Paris : Denoël, 2004.
Blanc, Nathalie. *Vers une esthétique environnementale*. Versailles : Éditions Quae, 2008.
Clément, Gilles. « Paysage, environnement et jardin : réflexions sur la notion de jardin planétaire ». *Horizons Maghrébins – Le droit à la mémoire* 45 (2001) : 83–86.
Ferdinand, Malcom. *Une écologie décoloniale. Penser l'écologie depuis le monde caribéen*. Paris : Seuil, 2019.

Foucault, Michel. *Les mots et les choses*. Paris : Gallimard, 1966.
Grenville, Kate. *The Secret River*. Edinburgh : Canongate Books Ltd, 2006.
Gordimer, Nadine. *The Conservationist*. London : Jonathan Cape Ltd, 1974.
Krall, Florence R. *Ecotone. Wayfaring on the Margins*. Albany : State University of New York Press, 1994.
Lageat, Yannick. « L'or en République sud-africaine ». *Cahiers d'outre-mer* 122.31 (1997) : 105–151.
Pageaux, Daniel-Henri. « Ouverture ». *Littérature et espaces*. Éd. Juliette Vion-Dury, Jean-Marie Grassin et Bertrand Westphal. Limoges : Presses Universitaires de Limoges, 2003.
Sarr, Felwine. *Habiter le monde. Essai de politique relationnelle*. Montréal : Mémoire d'encrier, 2017.
Ricœur, Paul. *La Mémoire, l'Histoire, l'oubli*. Paris : Seuil, 2003 [2000].
Ussac, Hélène. « Espace et bruit. Le monde sonore dans la littérature française du XVIIIe siècle ». *Les Belles lettres* (« L'information littéraire ») 58.2 (2006) : 46–50.

Contributors / Contributeurs

Kader Attia is an artist exploring the wide-ranging effects of western cultural hegemony and colonialism. Central to his inquiry are the concepts of injury and repair which he uses to connect diverse bodies of knowledge, including architecture, music, psychoanalysis, medical science, and traditional healing and spiritual beliefs. Attia's approach is informed by his experience of growing up between Algeria and the Paris banlieues. (kaderattiaberlin@gmail.com)

Ibou Coulibaly Diop is a university teacher and researcher. Since his studies in romance philology and German as a foreign language at Technische Universität Berlin and Potsdam University, he has been focusing his research on contemporary literature, and especially on questions of globalization. (iboucdiop@googlemail.com)

Lucia della Fontana is a doctoral researcher in Italian Studies at Sorbonne University. She is also a lecturer at the Italian Studies Department of Sorbonne University. (lucia.della_fontana@sorbonne-universite.fr)

Alexandre Gefen, director of the CNRS research group "Theory and History of Modern Art and Literatures," is an historian of ideas and literature. He is the author of numerous articles and essays dealing in particular with questions of culture, contemporary literature, and literary theory. (alexandre.gefen@cnrs.fr)

Hannah K. Grimmer is a PhD student, research assistant, and lecturer at the Chair for Art and Society at both Kassel University and documenta-Institute. She works on the connection between memories, social movements, and visual art in South America. (hannah.grimmer@uni-kassel.de)

Mario Laarmann is a doctoral researcher at the Chair for Romance Literatures and Comparative Literary and Cultural Studies and lecturer at the Department for Romance Languages, Literatures, and Cultures at Saarland University. He is part of the collective barazani.berlin and member of the executive board of the Society for Caribbean Research (SoCaRe). (mario.laarmann@uni-saarland.de)

Markus Messling is full professor of Romance Literatures and Comparative Literary and Cultural Studies at Saarland University, and principal investigator of the project "Minor Universality. Narrative World Productions After Western Universalism," funded by the European Research Council. (markus.messling@uni-saarland.de)

Clément Ndé Fongang is a doctoral researcher, employed with the project "Minor Universality" at Saarland University. He is preparing a dissertation in media analysis and sociology of art / literature at Saarland University. (clement.ndefongang@uni-saarland.de)

Open Access. © 2023 the author(s), published by De Gruyter. This work is licensed under the Creative Commons Attribution-NonCommercial-NoDerivatives 4.0 International License.
https://doi.org/10.1515/9783110799514-017

Fabiola Obame holds a doctorate degree from Université de Bretagne Occidentale and is an associated researcher at the laboratory "Heritage and Construction in Text and Image" (HCTI). She is the author of several articles, all of which are accessible at https://univ-brest.academia.edu/FObame. (obamefabilola@gmail.com)

hn. Iyonga is a multi-genre writer, MA student in American Studies at Humboldt University Berlin, co-founder of the Black Student Union at Humboldt, member of the AK Museen und Sammlungen of Decolonize Berlin e.V., and of the Kuratorium of barazani.berlin – Forum Kolonialismus und Widerstand. (hnlyonga@gmail.com)

Patricia Oster is full professor of French Literature at Saarland University, member of the research group "European Dream Cultures" (founded by the German Research Foundation), and member of the Académie de Berlin. (p.oster-stierle@mx.uni-saarland.de)

Angelica Pesarini is an assistant professor in Race and Cultural Studies / Race, Diaspora, and Italian Studies at the University of Toronto. Her work seeks to expand the field of Black Italia focusing on dynamics of race, gender, identity, and citizenship. Interested in the racialization of the political discourse on immigration, she is among the co-founders of *The Black Mediterranean Collective*. (drangelicapesarini@gmail.com)

Sahra Rausch is a research assistant for the coordination office "Thuringia's Colonial Legacy" at Friedrich-Schiller-University Jena. In 2022, she completed her binational doctoral studies in sociology and history at Justus-Liebig University in Giessen and Paris 1 Panthéon-Sorbonne with a thesis on emotions in postcolonial memory politics in France and Germany since the 1990s. (sahra.rausch@uni-jena.de)

Olivier Remaud is full professor of philosophy at the Ecole des Hautes Etudes en Sciences Sociales in Paris, France (EHESS). (remaud@ehess.fr)

Igiaba Scego is a Somali-Italian writer holding a doctorate degree in pedagogy from University Roma Tre. She is the author of award-winning short stories and novels, writes for newspapers and magazines such as "L'Unità" and "Internazionale," and is the editor of several anthologies.

Carla Seemann is a doctoral researcher at the Chair for Romance Literatures and Comparative Literary and Cultural Studies and lecturer at the Department for Romance Languages, Literatures, and Cultures at Saarland University. (carla.seemann@uni-saarland.de)

Ibrahima Sene is a PhD candidate candidate in German Studies at Cheikh Anta Diop University (Dakar) and DAAD doctoral scholarship holder (June 2019–September 2021) with Univ.-Prof. Dr. Hans-Jürgen Lüsebrink at Saarland University (Saarbrücken). (sene.ibrahima@yahoo.fr)

Christiane Solte-Gresser is full professor of General and Comparative Literature at Saarland University and the spokeswoman of the Research Training Group "European Dream-Cultures" funded by the German Research Foundation (DFG). (solte@mx.uni-saarland.de)

Jonas Tinius is a socio-cultural anthropologist, scientific coordinator and postdoctoral researcher in cultural anthropology in the ERC project *Minor Universality. Narrative World Constructions After Western Universalism* at Saarland University. (jonas.tinius@uni-saarland.de)

Laura Vordermayer is research assistant at the Chair for General and Comparative Literature at Saarland University. In 2021, she completed her doctoral studies with a thesis on literary dream reports in the writings of Georges Perec, William S. Burroughs, Ingeborg Bachmann, and Michel Butor. (laura.vordermayer@uni-saarland.de)

Index

1er Congrès des Écrivains et Artistes Noirs 210
3rd UNESCO World Conference against
    Racism 3

A68A 245–247
Abungu
– Georges-Okello 124, 127
Achebe
– Chinua 15, 209, 211, 213–214
Addis Abeba 26
Adenauer
– Konrad 7, 113
Adichie
– Chimamanda Ngozi 110–111, 211
Adoua 25, 30–31, 49
aesthetic / esthétique 1, 15–16, 46, 52–53, 124,
    166, 207–208, 217–218, 220–222, 226,
    257, 272
Afghanistan 34
Africa / Afrique 25–27, 29–31, 34, 38, 56, 70, 79,
    98–99, 101, 109–110, 115, 119–121, 123–130,
    136, 177–179, 182, 184, 186, 193, 208–209,
    213, 226–228, 236–237, 271, 273, 277
African Union 119
afro-diasporique 212
Ahidjo
– Ahmadou 116, 123–124
Ahmed
– Sara 96–97, 182, 189
Ajayi
– Ade 109–111, 118–119, 121
Alaska 250
Alliances françaises 118
America / Amérique 70, 87, 136, 208
anthropocene / anthropocène 36, 252
antisemitism 2
apartheid 98, 226, 231–232
Appiah
– Kwame 8
Archer
– Michael 168
Arendt
– Hannah 2

Argentinian(s), Argentina 155–157, 159, 161, 163,
    166, 169
Aristide
– Jean-Bertrand 4
Assmann
– Aleida 159–160, 168, 171, 229,
    232, 236
Atangana
– Engelbert 113
Attia
– Kader V, 1–2, 4, 9, 11–12, 14, 37, 46, 65, 91,
    94–95, 98–100, 105, 289
Auschwitz 145
Australie 271, 282
Axoum 25–28
– stèle de; obélisque de 33–34, 39–41, 43–44,
    47–48, 50, 53, 57
Azoulay
– Ariella 2, 11

Baer
– Alejandro 170
Bakweri 202
Bal
– Mieke 166
Bamoun/Bamum 122
Barazani.berlin V, 11, 199, 289–290
Barbéris
– Isabelle 219
Barkan
– Elazar 178, 180–181, 186
Barthes
– Roland 57
basilique Saint Marc 141–142
Bayena
– Ngitir Victor 110, 120, 123, 125, 127
Benjamin
– Walter 259
Berlin V, 1–2, 3, 11–12, 15, 82, 94, 99, 110, 116,
    135, 140, 142–148, 166, 188, 190–191, 225,
    227–230, 237, 289–290
Berlin Biennale 1–2, 94
Bessora 16, 272, 278, 280–281

Bianchi
- Rino 40–41, 43
Biederman
- Karl 149
Biennale de Dak'Art 211
Biya
- Paul 116–117
Bolte
- Rike 156, 158–160, 163–164
Bonaparte
- Napoléon 80, 140–144, 148
Braque
- Georges 149
British Council 114
Brown
- Bill 56
Bugul
- Ken 209, 213–214
Buti
- Carlo 28
Butler
- Judith 96–97, 180–181

Calvino
- Italo 261
Cameroon 11, 109, 111–113, 115–119, 121–126, 128–129, 202, 237
Caraïbe 213
Casamance 73, 86
Casiroli
- Nino 28
Cassin
- Barbara 38, 98
Centre culturel Blaise Cendras 114
Centre culturel François Villon 114
Césaire
- Aimé 2, 9, 14, 109, 111, 212, 214
Chakrabarty
- Dipesh 36
Chamoiseau
- Patrick 14
Chebli
- Sawsan 187
climate change / changement climatique 16, 246, 259
Coats
- Ta-Nihisi 38

Cold War / guerre froide 4, 144, 160, 178
collective ideals 177, 181, 189, 194
collective memory 159, 166, 170
colonial crimes 3, 5, 192, 227, 236–237
colonial power 3, 112, 185
colonialism / colonialisme 2–3, 8–9, 34, 39–40, 46, 51–53, 56–57, 65, 86, 91, 95–96, 102, 137, 177, 187, 193, 207–208, 214, 218, 220, 225–227, 235–236, 240, 278, 289
colonialité 207–208, 283–285
colonization / colonisation 16, 67–68, 76, 83, 100, 114, 121, 127, 207, 209, 214, 228, 231, 272, 279
Commission Vérité et Réconciliation 38
compensation 6–9, 12, 37, 87, 110, 182, 186–187, 189–192, 194, 233–234, 237–238, 240
conférence de Kinshasa 39
Constantinople 141–142
cosmologie(s) 70, 74, 76–77
Craps
- Stef 164, 181
créoles 90, 213
crime against humanity 3, 102, 156, 190
critical heritage 91
cultural relativism 228
cultural studies 2, 157, 220

DAAD 119, 290
Dahomey 67
De Bono
- Emilio 30
de Gaulle
- Charles 113–114
de Lusignan
- Guy 114
de Toledo
- Camille 1, 17
decolonization / décolonisation V, 11, 13–14, 17, 91, 102, 109, 111
Deltombe
- Thomas 115
Demanou
- René 226, 230–231, 237
Demanze
- Laurent 15, 45–46
democracy / démocratie 2, 116, 120, 219

démocratisation culturelle 219
demusealisation 109, 127
Derrida
– Jacques 38, 218
destruction 7, 16, 37, 53, 95, 99, 105, 122, 136, 147–148, 207–208, 259, 262
detenidos desaparecidos 155–156, 158, 161, 164, 166–167, 171–172
Diagne
– Souleymane Bachir 1, 9, 34, 36–38, 53, 102, 227, 233
Die LINKE 182, 186–187
Diola 86–87
Diome
– Fatou 209, 212
Diop
– Cheikh Anta 211, 290
Diouf
– Awa Cheikh 12
Djebar
– Assia 15, 213–214
Djimassé
– Gabin 120
Dodds
– Alfred Amédée 67–68, 89
Dogon 87
Durkheim
– Emile 181

Earth 17, 248–249, 252
ecocriticism / écocritique 16, 258, 271–272
ecological crisis / crise écologique 16, 258, 271, 277
ecology 17, 247
Ela
– Jean-Marc 109, 121, 127–128
empowerment 220
Entschädigungen 186
environmental humanities 255
Erll
– Astrid 156–157, 159–160, 170–171, 226
Eshetu
– Théo 40
Espagne 208
Eurocentrism 3, 128

Europe 7, 10, 70, 79, 91, 96, 101–102, 109, 111–112, 115, 119, 121–122, 128–129, 135–137, 139, 144, 150, 208, 219, 232, 238, 260
exploitation 2, 16, 36, 101, 111, 130, 207–208, 210, 235, 256

Fanon
– Frantz 36, 94, 97, 208
FAO 25
Farnesina 24
Fanso
– Verkijika 121
Federal Compensation Act 7
Feuer
– Guy 113–114, 228
Fischer
– Eugen 229–230, 235–236, 238
Fischer
– Urs 12, 135, 137, 139
Florence 137, 140, 218, 281
Fon 82, 125
Fontes
– Claudia 13, 155–156, 159, 165–166, 168–172
Forced disappearance / desaparición forzada 156–157, 164
Foucault
– Michel 44, 276
fracture environnementale 271–272
frame of memory 159
Françafrique 115
France 3, 5, 68, 79, 82, 89, 101, 111–118, 120, 122–123, 126, 140, 143, 147, 149, 208, 220, 290
Franco
– Bridget 169
Fraser
– Nancy 10, 180, 250
Frédéric II 141
French Development Fund 117
French National Research Institute for Sustainable Development 117
Fünf Kontinente Museum 120

Gabon 271
Garoua 114
Gatti
– Gabriel 156, 158, 163–165
Gefen
– Alexandre V, 15, 46, 56–57, 217, 257–258, 289
genocide / Völkermord 3, 5, 115, 122, 177–191, 193, 225, 227–228, 230, 235–237, 240
geopolitics / géopolitique 11, 284
German colonialism 236
German Lost Art Foundation 3
Germany / Allemagne 3, 5–6, 80, 82, 92, 95–96, 103, 111, 113, 144, 116–117, 120, 122, 147, 149, 177–180, 182, 184–186, 189–193, 203–204, 208, 225, 227–231, 235–239, 290
Giambologna 137, 139–140, 144
Gilgamesh 222, 251
Gilroy
– Paul 208
Ginzburg
– Carlo 45, 47
Glissant
– Edouard 213, 276, 280
Goethe
– Johann Wolfgang von 118, 217, 260
Gordimer
– Nadine 16, 272–274, 277
Göttsche
– Dirk 226, 228
Gouaffo
– Albert 117, 119, 129–130
Grand Corps Malade 222
Grenville
– Kate 16, 272, 274–275, 282–284
Guèye
– Massamba 73, 76, 85, 87
Guézo
– Khéglabé 67
Guézo
– Serge 67

Halbwachs, Maurice 159, 229
Hamidou Kane
– Cheikh 209, 213–214
Hampathé Ba
– Amadou 214

Haoussa 87
Haraway
– Donna 247, 252, 255–258, 261, 268
Harrison
– Georges 277
Hegba
– Meinrad 210–211
Heidegger
– Martin 142
Héra 145
Heumen Tchana
– Hugues 121, 125–126, 128
histoire environnementale 271, 275, 279
historical narratives 225, 228
historiography / historiographie 15, 47, 51, 53, 56, 229, 240
Hoffmann
– Ida 188
Holocaust 2–3, 13, 96, 178, 184, 186
Huffschmid
– Anne 158, 167
Humboldt Forum 3, 11, 110
Huyssen
– Andreas 156, 160–161, 166, 168, 170–172

identity / identité 33, 41, 46, 96, 118, 122, 125–126, 146, 158, 163, 168, 180, 213, 232–233, 259, 276, 290
Igbos 209
implicit observer 169
indemnity / indemnisation 5, 220
Institut Français d'Afrique Noire 123
interconnectedness 3, 12
irreparability / irréparabilité 65, 91, 94, 100, 103
irreparable / irréparable 1, 9, 17, 33, 37, 53, 85, 100, 255, 265, 272

Jaumann
– Bernhard 5, 225–231, 236–237, 239–240
Jawaharla Nehru University in New Delhi 8
Jelloun
– Tahar Ben 213
Jewsiewicki
– Bogumil 109, 120–121
Jouy
– Etienne 143

Kaboul 34
Kalibani
– Mèhèza 119–120
Kansteiner
– Wulf 158, 160, 164
Kemp
– Wolfgang 169
Kérékou
– Mathieu 82
Kohl
– Helmut 82
Konaté
– Yacouba 211
K'omoks 250–253

Laely
– Thomas 128
Lammert
– Norbert 183–185
Latin America 155–156, 158, 164
Latour
– Bruno 56, 260, 262
Lazali
– Karima 86
Levi
– Giovanni 45, 47
littérature africaine 207, 209, 213
Loi Taubira 3
Louis XVIII 142–143
Loumpet
– Germain 122–123, 125–127
Louvre 68, 77, 101, 142–143, 147, 149

Maas
– Heiko 179, 189–190, 192
Macron
– Emmanuel 3, 11, 39, 101, 234
Mandela
– Nelson 38, 98
Marcks
– Gerhard 145–146
Marseille 101–102
Martinique 4, 271
Marxism 35

Mataga
– Jesmael 119
Mbembe
– Achille 3, 10, 102, 111, 213
Medici
– Ferdinando de 140
Médicis
– Marie de 140
Mefe
– Tony 118
Memorial Park Cemetery 185
memory / mémoire 2–3, 12–13, 94, 100, 33, 41, 43, 45–46, 49, 51, 85–86, 135, 147, 153, 157–160, 162, 164–165, 168, 170–172, 177–183, 186–187, 189–191, 193, 199, 202, 207, 209, 211–214, 226, 229, 231, 235, 240, 248, 252, 290, 272, 276, 279, 281
memory artist(s) 171
memory studies 2, 155–157, 159–160, 181
métis 67–68, 89–90
Miano
– Léonora 209, 214
Micheli
– Guiseppe 28
micro-histoire 34, 45–46
Míguez
– Pablo 155–156, 163, 165, 169, 172
Milan 30
Mitterrand 82, 117
– François 82, 117
mnemonic function 171
mnemonic restitution 155, 163
modernity / modernité 1–3, 14, 16, 17, 35–36, 42, 45, 65, 98, 99, 102, 209, 213, 280, 283–284
monde 17, 24–25, 27–28, 34, 45–46, 52–53, 56–57, 79–80, 85–86, 89, 121, 135–137, 139, 145, 150, 207–214, 218–221, 255–258, 261, 263, 265–268, 271–272, 274, 276–277, 279–286
mondialisation 217, 219
Monumento a las Víctimas del Terrorismo de Estado 161, 166
moral collective 177, 180–181, 184, 189, 191, 193–194
Moro
– Aldo 24–26, 28, 39, 47, 49, 54

Mpegna
– Belmond 111, 113–114, 116–117, 119, 126
museum / musée 63, 70, 73, 77, 83, 85, 91, 98, 99, 100, 104, 103, 105, 109, 124, 136–137, 139, 122–123, 141, 147–148, 166
Mutengene 202
Mveng
– Engelbert 123–124

Namibia 5, 179, 182, 184–191, 193, 225–232, 236–239
Nantes 68, 102, 126
narration 15, 33–34, 57–58, 256, 261–262, 266, 278
National Archive in Windhoek 185
National Socialism 8
Nazi 5, 7, 92, 186
NDiaye
– Malik 12
Ndobo
– Madeleine 124–125
Neiman
– Susan 6
neo-colonialization 115
New Zealand 248
Newman 29
– Paul 29
Ngavirue
– Zedekia 187
Nkrumah
– Kwame 109, 111
non-representable 155
Nunca más, Never again 161, 170

Obama
– Barack 1, 9
Occident 34, 42, 102, 139, 208, 210, 213–214, 285
Ogoun 67
Okello
– Christina 115, 124, 127
Operación Condor 160–161
Oswald
– Magareta von 110, 119
Ousman
– Mahamat Abba 122, 123, 125

Pageaux
– Daniel-Henri 276
Paris 39, 101, 135–136, 140–150, 218, 264, 289–290
Parque de la Memoria 156–157, 161, 171
Patnaik
– Utsa 8
patrimoine africain 80
Paul Ango Ela Linear Report 118
percepticide 155, 163, 166, 172
Pertini
– Sandro 27
Pétrarque
– Francesco 141, 146
Peuhl 214
Picasso
– Pablo 149
place de Porta Capena 25, 27, 33
Place Vendôme 143
Plumwood
– Val 259
poétique du savoir 34, 47–48
Poirrier
– Philippe 121
Polenz
– Ruprecht 186–187
Pont Neuf 12, 135, 140, 142, 144
postcolonial 4, 11, 14, 16–17, 35, 38, 51, 94, 109–111, 121, 177, 179, 187, 192, 226, 279, 290
postcolonial present 4, 17
postcoloniality 35
Potsdam Agreement 6
Priority Solidarity Fund 117
Propp
– Vladimir 260–261
Pulau Galang 1

Quadriga / Quadrige 12, 135, 140
Quadrige de la Porte de Brandebourg 140
Quai Branly 68, 100
Queneau
– Raymond 217
Queneesh 250–252

racism / racisme 2, 15, 28, 52, 96, 98, 207–208, 232–233
Ravenhill
– Philipp 109
recognise 180, 184, 189–191, 193
recognition 3, 5, 10–11, 95, 109, 127, 177–185, 187, 189–194, 225, 227–228, 233–234, 236, 238–239
Reconstrucción 155–157, 159, 161, 165–166, 168–169, 171–172
Renan
– Ernest 2
repair 1–2, 4, 9, 12, 14–17, 91–92, 94–95, 99–100, 102–105, 109, 111, 120, 191, 233, 240, 289
repairing 109, 177, 185
reparation / réparation III, V, 1, 6, 8–9, 10, 12, 14, 16–17, 21, 33–34, 36–38, 40, 44, 45–47, 49, 51, 53–54, 56–58, 65, 85–87, 91–92, 99–100, 109–112, 117–120, 122, 197, 207–208, 210–211, 213, 217, 220–222, 225, 227, 233–234, 243, 255–257, 261, 263, 266, 272, 279
réparation écologique 255, 257
Reparations Agreement 6
resocialization 12
Restitution III, V, 1–2, 3, 10–12, 14–15, 17, 21, 28, 33, 38–40, 43–44, 47, 49–50, 53, 56, 58, 65, 80, 82–83, 85, 87, 91–92, 94, 101–102, 104, 109–111, 120, 129–130, 135–136, 141, 143, 145, 148–150, 155, 207, 220–221, 225, 228–231, 234–235
Restoration 126
reterritorialisation 271
Revel
– Jacques 45
revolution / révolution 80, 116, 82, 217, 221–222, 228
Ricœur
– Paul 57, 276
Río de la Plata 159, 161, 162, 167, 171
Robel
– Yvonne 178–179, 181–182, 194
Rome 15, 25–26, 28–29, 33, 39, 41, 44, 48–49, 51, 56, 141–142, 156
Rückenfigur, back figure 168, 172
Rukoro
– Vekuii Reinhard 185, 188, 190

Ryan
– Marie Laure 51

Salvago
– Acellino 148
Salzborn
– Samuel 7
Sankale
– Sylvain 67–68, 70, 83, 89
Santi
– Massimiliano 41, 44
Sarr
– Felwine 11–12, 17, 38–39, 102, 104, 109–110, 119–120, 124, 129, 213–214, 234, 285–286
Sartre
– Jean-Paul 36
Savoy
– Bénédicte 11–12, 38–39, 102, 104, 109–110, 119–120, 124, 142–143, 234
Schadow 141, 144
Schäfer
– Martin 183
Schindel
– Estela 164–165, 167–168
Schinkel
– Karl Friedrich 144
Scilingo
– Adolfo 161
Scott
– David 4, 17, 34–36
Sélassié
– Haïlé 23–31, 54
Senghor
– Léopold Sedar 79, 111, 211–212, 214
Simaga
– Leonie 120
Sitoe
– Aline 86
slavery / esclavage 2–3, 30, 38, 67, 87, 100, 110, 225
Sloterdijk
– Peter 137, 139
Smolenski
– Sonja 7
Solbiac
– Rodolphe 14

Sow Fall
– Aminata 209, 214
Sparing
– Frank 8
SPD 179, 182, 187, 189–190
Steinmeier
– Frank-Walter 34, 189, 193
Stoler
– Ann Laura 181
Swakopmund 185

Tadao
– Ando 136
Táíwò
– Olúfẹ́mi 227
Tamagnino
– Antonio 148
Taylor
– Charles 180
Taylor
– Diana 155, 163
Tharoor
– Shashi 9, 37–38, 94
Tigray 39
Tin
– Louis-Georges 3, 5
Torre
– Susanna 169
trauma / traumatisme 47, 50, 55, 57, 86, 95, 119, 122, 207
travelling memory 160, 170
Turin 29

ubuntu 38
UNESCO 3, 28, 44, 115, 119, 125–126, 234
universalism / universalisme 34–35, 42, 91, 217, 219–220, 222, 289, 291

universel 35–36, 42, 45, 217–220, 222, 265
Ussac
– Hélène 278

vallée du Tembien 31, 49, 53
Venise 23–26, 30, 46, 49, 51, 55, 141–142
Versailles
– Treaty of 6
Videla
– Jorge Raphael 157
Villa Vigoni 12, 91–93, 95, 98, 103–105, 135
vuelos de la muerte 161

Wajsbrot
– Cécile 135, 144–150
Wallerstein
– Immanuel 2, 34
Weltliteratur / world literature / littérature mondiale 15, 217–218
Wieczorek-Zeul
– Heidemarie 182–183, 190
Wiedergutmachung 7–8, 186
World War I 1, 6, 95
World War II 3, 6, 46, 50, 92, 94–96

Young
– Robert 14
Young
– James Edward 14, 170

Zerbini
– Laurence-Anick 123–124, 127
Zimmerer
– Jürgen 178, 184

www.ingramcontent.com/pod-product-compliance
Lightning Source LLC
Chambersburg PA
CBHW050516170426
43201CB00013B/1975